Thomas Wentworth Higginson, Thomas B. Stockwell

A History of Public Education in Rhode Island

Thomas Wentworth Higginson, Thomas B. Stockwell

A History of Public Education in Rhode Island

ISBN/EAN: 9783337379322

Printed in Europe, USA, Canada, Australia, Japan

Cover: Foto ©ninafisch / pixelio.de

More available books at **www.hansebooks.com**

A

HISTORY

OF

PUBLIC EDUCATION

IN

RHODE ISLAND,

FROM

1636 TO 1876:

EMBRACING

AN ACCOUNT OF THE RISE AND PROGRESS OF THE PRESENT SCHOOL SYSTEM OF THE STATE; THE VARIOUS CITY AND TOWN SYSTEMS; TOGETHER WITH SKETCHES OF BROWN UNIVERSITY AND MANY OF THE ACADEMIES, LIBRARIES AND LITERARY ASSOCIATIONS OF RHODE ISLAND.

COMPILED BY AUTHORITY OF THE BOARD OF EDUCATION,

AND EDITED BY

THOMAS B. STOCKWELL,

COMMISSIONER OF PUBLIC SCHOOLS.

PROVIDENCE:
PROVIDENCE PRESS COMPANY, PRINTERS TO THE CITY AND STATE.
1876.

CONTENTS.

	Page.
State of Rhode Island	1
Rhode Island State Normal School	118
Rhode Island Institute of Instruction	123
City of Providence	129
University Grammar School	211
Brown University	217
Dr. Stockbridge's School for Young Ladies	225
Scholfield's Commercial College	227
English and Classical School	228
Mount Pleasant Academy	232
Providence Association of Mechanics and Manufacturers	234
Providence Franklin Society	246
Franklin Lyceum	247
City of Newport	251
Redwood Library and Athenæum	267
The Peoples' Library	277
Town of Barrington	281
" " Bristol	285
" " Burrillville	310
" " Charlestown	340
" " Coven	346
" " East ... wich	352
" " East Providence	362
" " Glocester	364
" " Jamestown	367
" " Hopkinton	368
" " Johnston	375
" " Middletown	383
" " North Kingstown	389
" " Richmond	404
...pham Institute	412
...wn of Smithfield	415
" " Warwick	436
" " Woonsocket	439
...ex	440

A

HISTORY

OF THE

PUBLIC SCHOOL SYSTEM

OF

RHODE ISLAND,

BY

THOMAS WENTWORTH HIGGINSON.

I. COLONIAL SCHOOLS.

(1636 – 1776.)

Roger Williams, after returning in 1654 from a two years' visit in England, wrote thus of some of his employments while in that country: "It pleased the Lord to call me for some time, and with some persons, to practice the Hebrew, the Greek, Latin, French and Dutch. The secretary of the council (Mr. Milton) for my Dutch I read him, read me many more languages. * * * I taught two young gentlemen, a parliament man's sons, as we teach our children English, by words, phrases and constant talk."

In these brief sentences we see the founder of Rhode Island as a scholar, a teacher, and the friend of Milton. It will always seem a surprising thing that the colony founded by such a man should not have established for itself, like the adjoining colonies of Massachusetts and Connecticut, a system of common schools. Yet nothing is plainer than the reasons which led to this; and they cannot be more clearly stated than they were given a quarter of a century ago by Hon. E. R. Potter, a man who has rendered this State almost equal service in law and in education:—

"One of the first things which strikes an observer in considering the early history of Rhode Island, is, that the population was not homogeneous. Massachusetts was settled by colonies from one people, and all actuated by the same notions of religious and civil government, and of a similar religious creed. Connecticut was an offshoot from Massachusetts, and the same principles and ideas had a controlling influence in its settlement.

"Rhode Island, on the contrary, was settled by men of all religious views and opinions. As the first settlers fled from persecution in Massachusetts, it naturally became an asylum for all who like them were persecuted for conscience' sake. The predecessors of our Baptists were all fugitives from persecution. The Quakers nearly all came here from the same cause and to avoid the severe laws which were made against them in other colonies. And the friends and followers of Mrs. Hutchinson constituted a respectable portion of the new community. Here, too, half a century after the first settlement, came a colony of French Huguenots, driven from their country by the same spirit which had expelled Roger Williams from our sister colony.

"For the very reason that in this colony no religion was established, nor the observance of any religious forms compelled by law, it was natural that many should resort here who had no religion at all; and that the settlement should include many wild spirits, who came here because in the then thinly peopled country on the borders of our beautiful bay, they could obtain an easy subsistence, free from the restraints of all law whatever.

"Rhode Island thus differed entirely from the neighboring states in its mode of settlement. Its population resembled more the population of one of our western states at the present day; a collection of people coming from different nations and at different times, some actuated by the desire of religious freedom, some by desire of freedom from all law; some by the spirit of speculation, (for even that then prevailed); and some from that wild love of adventure which has always exercised such a sway in the breast of man.

"Driven from Massachusetts under such circumstances, the original settlers viewed everything which they had left behind them with hostility. In Massachusetts, as in most early settlements, the clergy being the only class of leisure, were the depositories of the learning of the infant commonwealth. The clergy also always exercised an active control in their government; and wars, leagues and important government measures, were seldom undertaken without their sanction.

"Hence, in a great measure, has arisen the feeling against a settled and salaried clergy, which has always been a characteristic of our people, and which prejudice remains in some parts of the State to the present day in undiminished strength. Hence, we have lost the influence which such a body of men would always have exerted in favor of education. * * *

"Another circumstance, and a very important one to be considered, in accounting for the want of a system of public education among our forefathers was, that for nearly one hundred years, Rhode Island could not be said to have any settled government.

"On the East, Plymouth claimed to Narragansett Bay, and for the first hundred years Rhode Island had no jurisdiction east of it. On the west, Connecticut claimed to Narragansett Bay, under her charter, which she claimed to be prior to that of Rhode Island. The first settlers of the Narragansett country were obliged to defend themselves by force, from the attempts of Connecticut to assert her jurisdiction. She incorporated towns with boundaries extending into Rhode Island, appointed officers at Wickford and other places, and made grants of land which were the origin of some of the existing titles. Some portion of the inhabitants, probably from a desire to have the protection of a stronger government, acknowledged her jurisdiction, and thus there was a sort of civil war constantly going on within our own limits. Citizens of Rhode Island were repeatedly seized, carried off and imprisoned for refusing to obey the Connecticut authorities. Land titles were disputed, and there seemed little security for person or property except in the strength of the possessor.

"After the Pequod War, Massachusetts and Connecticut claimed the south western portion of the State by right of conquest, and in the division it fell to Massachusetts, who erected the country about Westerly into a township, by the name of Southertown. Here was another claimant for jurisdiction. But Connecticut seems afterwards to have again asserted her jurisdiction, and Massachusetts at last gave up the contest.

"The settlement at Warwick had also similar difficulties to contend with. A part of their inhabitants had submitted themselves to Massachusetts, who asserted her claims to that country, and imprisoned its people for resisting her authority.

"Again, in the great Indian war of 1676, the western portion of our State was made the battle ground on which Massachusetts and Connecticut contended for victory over the Indians. The settlers of Rhode Island had always maintained a friendly intercourse with the Indians, and had no cause to complain of them. The war arose from causes growing out of the policy and past wars of the neighboring colonies. Yet next to the Indians, Rhode Island was the principal sufferer. The armies of the united colonies desolated the country, and what they left, the Indians, exasperated and driven to desperation, burnt and destroyed. Almost all the inhabitants on the west side of the Bay were obliged to retreat to Newport, for shelter and protection.

"After the war, the settlers returned to their ruined homes. But Connecticut, powerful from her recent victory, continued the contest for jurisdiction. Rhode Island, weak and exhausted by a war she had not provoked, was subjected to the burden and expense of almost continued negotiations in England; and it was not until 1728, nearly one hundred years from the date of the arrival of Roger Williams, that the boundary was settled, and Rhode Island acquired undisputed control of Narragansett.

"It was not until 1709, that Rhode Island felt strong enough and sure enough of the success of her cause, to grant land titles in Narragansett. Before that time, the country along the shore of the Bay had been settled, and the rights of the settlers undisturbed, but all the central and western portions of the Narragansett country, were occupied as our public lands in the West now are, by squatters, as they are called. Their claims were acknowledged, their conflicting boundaries settled by surveys, and deeds given them from the State, about 1709.

"As may be supposed, during these troubles, the population of the western part of the State, then colony, was small in number, scattered and feeble. When, in 1661, a company was formed at Newport, for the purpose of settling Misquamicuck, there was a powerful nation of Indians between them and their destined western abode. In leaving their old homes they had the same difficulties to encounter, the same anxieties for the future, which the emigrants of the present day meet with in our western wilderness. And when afterwards they were incorporated as a township, it received the name of Westerly.

"It would be unreasonable to expect of a people so situated much progress in the comforts and elegancies of life. Occupied with keeping up a friendly intercourse with the natives on the one side, and defending their lives and property from the attacks and machinations of rival colonies, who regarded and treated them as heretics, rebels or intruders, on the other; it required all their energies to gain a bare subsistence. No wonder, therefore, that they did not establish schools and colleges, and that we do not find among them the arts, and the refinement of manners, which we could only expect in an older and more settled state of society.

"There is another fact in the social history of Rhode Island which ought not lightly to be passed over, because its influence is still to be traced among us. The institution of domestic slavery for a long time existed here. * * * *

"But slave labor was nearly confined to the towns along the Narragansett Bay,—Newport, Portsmouth, South Kingstown, North Kingstown, Exeter, Warwick, Bristol and Jamestown. South Kingstown had the greatest number next to Newport.

"All along the belt of land adjoining the west side of the Bay, the country, generally productive, was owned in large plantations by wealthy proprietors, who resided on and cultivated their land. They had the cultivation which would naturally result from a life of leisure, from intercourse with each other, and with the best informed men of the colony, and from the possession of private libraries, for that day, large and extensive. But any *common* system of education they could not have, from their very situation and distance from each other.

"In the interior and westernmost portions of the State the population was scattered, the roads and means of communication poor, and the people themselves enjoying but few of the comforts and luxuries of life. There were no towns, and but few villages, to serve as centres of communication and information, and to set an example to the rest of the community; for nearly all the villages in the western part of the State are of recent growth, and the result of manufacturing industry. Their only opportunities of adding to their knowledge were their religious meetings, their town meetings, and the county courts."*

It must be also remembered that the population of Rhode Island, exclusive of Indians, did not exceed 7,000 in 1680, and was only 10,000 at the end of the century. A census taken in 1730 gave but 17,935. Except in a few of the larger settlements, therefore, there was no great opportunity for the organization of a public school system; and the school history of a few of these settlements is the early history of education in Rhode Island.

Among these settlements Newport clearly took the lead in respect to schools. The early town records are in very imperfect condition, having been carried off by a Tory Sheriff when the British entered the island; having been sunk at Hurlgate, been kept in New York a year without drying, and been returned in a mutilated state by the British commander. But it is known from other authority that, in two years from the foundation of the town, a school was established under the following circumstances:

---

* Address delivered before the Rhode Island Historical Society, on the evening of February 19th, 1851, by Elisha R. Potter, member of the society. Providence, 1851. (Reprinted, 1875.) Compare the similar views expressed in an article in Barnard's Journal of R. I. Institute, &c., II, 33. It was attributed to Judge Staples.

Rev. Robert Lenthal, a clergyman of the church of England, was called by the people of Weymouth, Massachusetts, to be their pastor; but left Massachusetts from some ecclesiastical trouble, and came to Newport, where he assisted Rev. Dr. Clarke in the ministry. According to Callender's Historical Discourse, which was for many years the only history of Rhode Island, Mr. Lenthal was admitted as freeman, August 6, 1640.

"And August 20, Mr. Lenthal was, by vote, called to keep a public school for the learning of youth, and for his encouragement there was granted to him and his heirs, one hundred acres of land, and four more for an house lot; it was also voted 'that one hundred acres should be laid forth and appropriated for a school, for encouragement of the poorer sort, to train up their youth in learning, and Mr. Robert Lenthal, while he continues to teach school, is to have the benefit thereof.' But this gentleman did not tarry very long; I find him gone to England the next year but one." *

It is not clearly established that any community in New England can claim an earlier school record than this. The first public teacher in Salem, Massachusetts, was apparently elected in 1640, for it is not clear that the school taught in that city by Rev. John Fisk, in 1637, was established by any public vote. The first petition for a free school in Boston, Massachusetts, is dated in 1636; but the first record concerning such schools in Boston was made in 1642,† as was the first record in Hartford, Ct.

This school tract of one hundred acres was allotted in what is now the town of Middletown, but in 1661 was exchanged for a tract afterwards known as Newtown, or school land. In 1663, this tract was ordered to be divided into lots, "and to be sold or loaned on condition that the purchasers should pay to the town treasurer an annual rent to constitute a fund for the schooling and educating of poor children, according to the direction of the town council for the time being, who are hereby empowered to direct, regulate and manage the said charity in behalf of the town, to the best advantage, according to the true intent and meaning thereof." ‡

It is plain from the records, that the original school-house existed in 1685, and that it was decaying in 1700, when, at a quarter meeting, there appears an entry "that Ebenezer Mann may have some of the lumber that has fallen down about the old school-house, to help build his house." A new school-house was ordered to be built, January 31, 1704–5, but the order was revoked in April, and land was granted to Samuel

---
* Callender's Discourse; Elton's edition. p. 116.
† Annual Report of School Committee of Salem, Mass., (1876) p. 33.
‡ Barnard's Journal of R. I. Institute of Instruction, III, 145.

Cranston and others, for the purpose of building a school-house there. In October, 1706, additional land was granted and ordered to be sold " for finishing the school house in or near the market place in Newport."

It appears, however, that in a few years the subscribers to the school-house had become weary of their undertaking, and surrendered the building to the ownership of the town. The vote receiving it was as follows:

"At an adjourned quarter meeting, August 18th, 1708.—Voated, That the town council of Newport are empowered to take ye school-house into their hands, to manage all ye prudential affairs belonging to said house, always reserving to ye quarter meeting in said town ye power of choosing ye school masters for said house, always provided that ye freemen of said town assembled in their quarter meeting have power further to alter or order ye above premises and the * * power always be invested therein."

But the building does not seem to have been finally completed, belfry and all, until April, 1739.

Thus Robert Lenthal, and after him John Jethro and Thomas Fox, schoolmasters, had buildings in which to teach, and had, moreover, an allotted salary from the income of the school lands. Thomas Fox at one time had the salary of £2, which would now hardly procure the services of a first class teacher; but as the whole school lands were let for £8, it is evident that a little money, in those days, bought a good deal. Farther details of these negotiations sometimes occur as follows:

"Quarter meeting, April 17, 1709.—Mr. William Gilbert being chosen schoolmaster for ye town of Newport, and proposing that upon conditions, the quarter meeting grant him of the benefit of the school land, viz., the chamber and sellar and the profit arising from ye school land in this part of the town, and some conveniency for keeping of fire in the winter season, he is willing to teach school for the year ensuing, and to begin the second Monday in May next, voated and allowed an act of the quarter meeting."

Eighteen months later (October 4, 1710) came this step toward "the higher education."

"The petition of Mr. Gallaway, for the liberty of teaching of a latin school in the two little rooms in the school-house of this town, is hereby granted."

In 1729, it seems, besides the central school of Newport, there were two schoolmasters, paid £10 each, " in the woods part of the town." This part was set off as Middletown, in 1743, after which there was apparently but the central school again. The first schoolmaster chosen in annual town meeting was John Callender, June 3, 1746. This gentleman was also pastor of the First Baptist Church, and was the author of the historical discourse already quoted. It was a centennial address delivered in 1738, in commemoration of the first settlement of the island. Mr. Callender was again chosen schoolmaster in 1747, and died during the January following, being succeeded by "Terrence Donally," whose name indicates his origin.

In 1763, the town voted to sell a portion of the school lands, and the purchase money was assigned to be used as follows:

"Voted, That ye monies, arising by the sale of said lots and also ye annual quit rents forever, shall be paid to ye town treasurer, for ye time being, and yt ye same shall be a fund for ye schooling and educating of poor children, according to ye discretion of ye town council, for ye time being, who are hereby empowered to direct, regulate and manage ye said charity in behalf of said town to ye best advantage, according to ye true intent and meaning thereof."

But it appears that the town school-house was destroyed by fire, in 1774, and that for the next half century, no school was supported from the income of the school land. Thus ended the first experiment at public education in the leading settlement of Rhode Island.*

The first public action in behalf of education in Providence took place in May, 1663, when the proprietors passed the following order: "It is agreed by this present Assembly that one hundred acres of upland and six acres of meadow (or lowland to the quantity of eight acres, in lieu of meadow) shall be laid out within the bounds of this town of Providence; the which land shall be reserved for the maintenance of a school in this town; and that after the said land is laid out, and the bounds thereof set, it shall be recorded in our town records, according to the bounds fixed, and shall be called by the name of the school lands of Providence."

Judge Staples, in his Annals of Providence, states that "this is the earliest grant now to be found in the records, and the earliest reference to a school or any means of education. From a petition of John Whipple, Jr., in the files of the city clerk's office, presented to the town, January 28, 1684, it appears that a whole purchase right of land had long before that time been set apart for the use and benefit of a school."†
In 1696, again, a piece of land was assigned to certain persons for the erection of a school-house. The same thing took place in 1751; and earlier than this, (in 1725,) Mr. George Taylor had the use of a room in the State House to keep a school in. The first reference to a town

---

*The passages in the early town records bearing on education have been carefully transcribed by the Probate Clerk of Newport, Mr. Benjamin B. Howland, and were printed in the *Newport Mercury* of Dec. 4, 18, 1875; Jan. 15, 29, 1876. Compare Barnard's Journal, III., 145.

† Staples' Annals of Providence, p. 492.

school-house is found in the records of 1752, and it is probable that the town simply allowed the schoolmaster the use of it, at a fixed rent, the pupils paying him for his services. At a town-meeting held December 2, 1767, the citizens went so far as to vote to build " three school-houses for small children and one for youth, to provide instructions, and pay the expense from the treasury, and these schools to be under the supervision of the school committee." A plan for the organization of these schools was reported by the committee, through Governor Jabez Bowen, and may be found in the pages of Staples' Annals of Providence. It is an admirable report, and is based upon this wide provision : " That every inhabitant of this town, whether they be free of the town or not, shall have and enjoy an equal right and privilege of sending their own children, and the children of others that may be under their care, for instruction and bringing up, to any or all of the said schools."

It appears, however, that this beneficent project was defeated, and the grounds of defeat are thus quaintly given by Moses Brown, another member of the committee reporting the plan :

" 1768. Laid before the town by the committee, but a number of the inhabitants (and what is most surprising and remarkable the plan of a Free School, supported by a tax, was rejected by the POORER sort of the people,) being strangely led away not to see their own as well as the public interest therein, (by a few objectors at first,) either because they were not the projectors, or had not public spirit to execute so laudable a design, and which was first voted by the town with great freedom. M. B."

Rejecting this liberal plan, the town, after several abortive efforts, built a school-house jointly with private proprietors, the town owning only the lower story, and appointing masters to teach what was apparently a free school. The town passed rules for both schools and appointed a committee to visit both public and private schools. This was the condition of affairs in Providence until after the American Revolution.*

The first schoolmaster in Providence, of whom any definite memorial remains, was William Turpin, whose earliest record is on June 11th, 1684, when he executed an indenture with William Hawkins and Lydia his wife, " to furnish Peregrine Gardner with board and schooling one year for six pounds ; forty shillings of which in beef and pork ; pork at two-pence, and beef at three pence half-penny, per lb. ; twenty shillings in corn, at two shillings per bushel ; and the balance in silver money." This instrument is in the handwriting of Mr. Turpin, and according to Judge Staples, does him credit in point of chirography. During the following January, he presented this petition to the town :

* Staples' Annals of Providence, pp. 492-502.

"The humble request of William Turpin, now schoolmaster of the said town, is, that whereas there was a parcel of land formerly granted by the ancestors of said town, and was to be to the use and benefit of a schoolmaster, as by the records of the town book will more at large appear, which said order or grant was read to me in the presence of several gentlemen, that were the occasion of my settling at this town, who promised to be instrumental in the performance thereof. Gentlemen, my desire is that the aforesaid land may be forthwith laid out, according to the said order or grant, and that the said master or his heirs may be invested in the said land, so long as he or any of them shall maintain the worthy art of learning. Thus leaving it to you, gentlemen, to give a speedy answer, according as you shall think meet, I rest yours to command.

WILLIAM TURPIN."*

There is no record as to the answer given to this petition, nor does it appear how long the petitioner could "maintain that worthy art of learning." He must have been a man of some weight and influence as he was afterwards, successively, town representative, town clerk and town treasurer.

Thus much for Newport and Providence. In Barrington, then a part of Swansea, Mass., a school was established in 1673, "three years after old Plymouth had voted a free school within her borders," "for the teaching of grammar, rhetoric and arithmetic, and the tongues of Latin, Greek and Hebrew, also to teach English and to write." Of this school Rev. John Myles was appointed teacher " at a salary of £40 per annum in current country pay." It is probable that this included his clerical services also, as one of his successors had but £18 per year, " one quarter in money and the other three quarters in provisions at money price," and another had "£12 current money of New England, to be paid quarterly, and the town to 'pay for his diet'," besides 20s. " toward the keeping of his horse." Each of these teachers was expected " to teach in the several places of the town by course," so that the horse was quite essential.†

In Bristol it appears that the original proprietors, in 1680, granted land " for the common improvement, for the encouragement and use of an able orthodox minister, and for the use and encouragement of an able schoolmaster in the town." The first recorded act of the citizens of Bristol in regard to schools is dated in September, 1682, when it was voted :

"That each person that hath children in town ready to go to school, shall pay three pence the week for each child's schooling to the schoolmaster, and the town by rate according to each ratable estate shall make the wages to amount

---

* Staples' Annals of Providence, p. 494.
† Stone's Hist. R. I. Inst. p. 9.

to £24 the year. The selectment to look out a grammar schoolmaster and use their endeavor to obtain £5 of the cape money granted for such an end." "September, 1684, voted £24 the year for Mr. Cobbitt, he officiating in the place of a schoolmaster in this town."*

These seem to have been the main attempts made, before the Revolution, to establish popular education in the Rhode Island towns. There were also some local efforts for the instruction of the Indians, of whom there were, in 1730, nearly a thousand (985), in the colony. These efforts began with a gift of land made by Judge Sewall, for that purpose, to Harvard College, in 1696. The colored population was still more numerous and the Newport *Mercury*, of March 29, 1773, contained the following advertisement:

"Whereas a school was established, several years past, in the town of Newport, by a society of benevolent clergymen of the church of England, in London, with a handsome fund for a mistress to instruct thirty negro children in reading, sewing, &c. And whereas it hath hitherto been found difficult to supply the said school with the number of children required; notice is hereby given, that the said school is now kept by Mrs. MARY BRETT, in High Street, nearly opposite to judge Johnston's, and is open to all societies in the town, to send their young blacks, to the number of thirty; And, provided, that the number cannot be nearly kept up for the future, the gentlemen to whose care and direction the said school has been entrusted will be obliged to give it up entirely at the expiration of six months."

As the colored population of Newport must at this time have comprised seven or eight hundred, (having numbered 649 in 1730,) it certainly seemed discouraging that "all societies" could not furnish thirty pupils. But the appeal seems to have been successful, and Mrs. Brett, at any rate, renewed the advertisement of her school, still addressed to "all societies," in the *Mercury* for March 14, 1774.

Furnishing an unconscious link between these slave-children and the more favored class, the same newspaper, on April 19, 1773, shows us Peleg Barker, Jr., advertising his "morning and afternoon school for young misses," adding in the same advertisement that "he has for sale a likely, well-limbed negro lad, eleven years old." Rising to a higher flight of culture, Francis Vandeleur advertises (October 17, 1774,) that he is ready to teach French and Italian to young ladies at their dwellings. It was to Francis Vandeleur, perhaps, that the lovely Hunters and Champlins, of that day, owed the French accent, be it better or worse, with which they charmed the hearts of Lauzun and Deux-Ponts.

*Barnard's Journal, R. I. Inst., III, 137.

It is rare to find in the school advertisements of that period, any distinct recognition of young girls as pupils; and even when this appears, it is sometimes evident from the hours announced, that they were admitted only at times not devoted to boys. Thus in May, 1767, a school was advertised in Providence for the instruction of young ladies in writing and arithmetic; and the hours were from 6 to 7.30 A. M., and from 4.30 to 6 P. M.—the price of tuition being $2 per quarter. There was a teacher of French at Providence in 1773. The demand for ornamental accomplishments seems to have made itself manifest earlier than this, for in 1763, the want of a teacher of dancing had been found an evil so serious that a correspondent of the Providence *Gazette* expressed the opinion that "a competent teacher who could play his own fiddle," would meet with encouragement in Providence. This suggestion led to a long controversy, in that newspaper, as to the comparative merits of dancing-master and spinning-wheel; but the dancing-master arrived soon after, and has certainly held his own against the spinning-wheel, down to the present day.

In the reminiscences of an aged citizen of Providence, Samuel Thurber, as recorded by himself for Judge Staples, there are the following facts in regard to education before the Revolution:

"As respects schools, previous to about the year 1770, they were but little thought of; there were in my neighborhood three small schools, perhaps about a dozen scholars in each. Their books were the Bible, spelling-book, and primer. One kept by John Foster, Esq., in his office; one by Dr. Benjamin West. Their fees were seven shillings and sixpence per quarter. One kept by George Taylor, Esq., for the church scholars. He, it was said, received a small compensation from England. Besides these, there were two or three women schools. When one had learned to read, write and do a sum in the rule of three, he was fit for business. * * * The Rev. James Manning did great things in the way of enlightening and informing the people. Schools revived by means of his advice and assistance. Previous to him it was not uncommon to meet with those who could not write their names." *

This important testimony links Brown University with the history of public education in Rhode Island. This Dr. Manning was President of Rhode Island College at the time of its removal to Providence in 1770, and the impulse given by him might have made itself felt throughout the State, but for the absorbing excitements of the Revolution. A colony which saw one of its chief towns in actual possession of the enemy could hardly give much attention to school-books or school-houses. The conflict left the young State terribly depleted and impoverished, and it had scarcely recovered itself when it was urged on to the adoption of a school system, by the far-seeing public spirit of one man.

* Staples' Annals of Providence, pp. 515, 533, 601-2.

II. JOHN HOWLAND AND HIS ENTERPRISE.

(1776 – 1803.)

The public school system of Rhode Island dates back, as distinctly as can be the case with any institution, to the labors of one man; and that man neither highly educated, nor wealthy, nor occupying what was, or is held as a peculiarly elevated social position. John Howland was born in Newport in 1757, and was sent to Providence at thirteen to be a hairdresser's apprentice. At eighteen, he enlisted in the Revolutionary army, where he remained eighteen months, and among other experiences fought under Washington at Trenton. After his return to Providence he seems still to have served as barber to high military functionaries, recording in his diary his professional attendance on General Prescott, General Arnold and General Gates. Later he had a shop of his own, which was a favorite resort of the leading people of the town, so that Judge Thacher, of Massachusetts, records in his diary that he was recommended to go and be shaved by Mr. Howland as the best preliminary to any important information on subjects of local history. In later life he was treasurer of the first savings bank in Providence, was President of the Rhode Island Historical Society, and atoned to his conscience for his early share in war by assisting in the formation of a Peace Society, of which he was also President. He was also, happily for the community, a member of the Mechanics' Association; and it was through this body that he began to work for a system of public schools. We fortunately have his record of the events of that time, and the history of the agitation may be given in his own graphic language:

"In 1789, the Mechanics' Association was formed, and in this body begun the agitation that led to the establishment of public schools. When we came together in our association, we made the discovery of our deficiencies. There were papers to be drawn, and various kinds of writing to be done, that few of us were competent to execute. Then we began to talk. The question was asked, ought not our children to have better advantages of education than we have enjoyed? And the answer was, yes. Then it was asked, how shall those advantages be secured? The reply was, we must have better schools. So when we had talked the matter over pretty thoroughly among ourselves, we began to agitate. As I was something of a talker, and had practiced writing more than most of my associates, a good deal of this work fell to my lot. And I was very willing to do it, because I felt and saw its importance. So I wrote a number of pieces for the newspaper, and tried to induce others to do the same. I prevailed, however, with only one, Grindall Reynolds. He felt as I did about the the matter, and wrote a piece for the Gazette in favor of schools. We had, indeed, the good will of many educated men. There were Thomas P. Ives, Thomas L. Halsey, David L. Barnes, and others, who had been educated in the public schools in Massachusetts, all of whom understood our wants and favored our movement. Governor Bowen and the Bowen family were also friendly. So was Governor William Jones. We met no opposition from the wealthy, but they having the advantages for their sons and daughters that wealth can always procure, did not feel as we poor mechanics did. They were not active. In this beginning of the movement, they seemed willing to follow, but were unwilling to lead the way. It is a curious fact, that throughout the whole work, it was the most unpopular with the common people, and met with the most opposition from the class it was designed to benefit. I suppose this was one reason why the most influential citizens did not take hold of it heartily in the beginning. They thought its success doubtful, and did not wish, in a public way, to commit themselves to an enterprise that would curtail their popularity and influence. This was not the case with all, but it was so with many.

"The more we discussed the subject, the greater became its importance in our eyes. After a good deal of consultation and discussion, we got the Mechanics' Association to move in the matter. This was an important point gained, and an encouragement to persevere. A committee was chosen to take up the subject. Of this committee I was a member. They met at my house, and after due deliberation, it was resolved to address the General Assembly. I told them, that as neither of us were qualified to draw up a paper in a manner suited to go before that body, we had each better write a petition embodying our individual views, and bring it to our next meeting. Out of these mutual contributions we could prepare a petition that would do. This was agreed to, and the committee separated. When we next met, it was found that but two had been written according to previous recommendation. Those were by William Richmond and myself. Richmond then read his. It was in the usual *petition* style, ending, 'as in duty bound will ever pray.' I told the committee I did not like the doctrine of that paper. It was too humble in tone. I did not believe in *petitioning* legislators to do their duty. We ought, on the contrary, in addressing that body, to assume a tone of confidence that with the case fairly stated, they would decide wisely and justly for the rising generation. I then took out my memorial and read it. It was not in the shape of an 'humble petition.' It expressed briefly our destitution, and the great importance of establishing free schools to supply it. It received the approbation of the committee, and was adopted.

"This memorial was presented to the General Assembly in the name of our association. It was there warmly debated, and after pretty severe opposition, the Assembly referred the whole subject to a committee, with directions to report by bill. This bill, embodying a general school system, was drawn up by James Burrill, jr., Attorney General of Rhode Island. I was with him all the while, and he readily complied with my suggestions.

"When the bill was reported, the Assembly was afraid to pass it, until the sense of the towns could be obtained. So it was printed, and sent out to the freemen for instructions. The great object now was to get the towns to vote right. When the subject came before the town meeting in Providence, I moved that a committee be appointed to prepare instructions to our representatives, and report at the present meeting. This was carried, and William Richmond, Samuel W. Bridgham, afterwards our first mayor, George R. Burrill, Wm. Larned, and myself, were constituted the committee. It was now late in the afternoon, and Bridgham, said, 'Mr. moderator, this is an important matter. It will require some time to draft instructions, and as it is now almost night, I think the subject had better be postponed until the next town meeting.' 'Never fear,' replied Richard Jackson, the moderator, 'I guess Howland has them already written in his pocket.' 'O,' rejoined Bridgham, 'I didn't think of that —then we can go on." The committee accordingly retired to the office of George R. Burrill for consultation. The questions then came up, what shape shall the instructions take? Who shall write them? Various opinions were expressed, but I kept silent. Bridgham then turned to me and said, 'what do *you* think, Mr. Howland?' I had anticipated the course of events, and was prepared to answer the question. I had set up, the night before, till 11 o'clock, to prepare a document I intended to submit to the town meeting. I therefore said to the committee, 'I have got *my* opinion in my pocket. If you wish to hear, I will read it.' 'Let us hear, by all means,' was the reply. So I took out my document, and read it. When I got through, Burrill said, 'well, that is just what we want. All we need do is to sign our names.' They accordingly signed it, without suggesting any alteration, and we returned and reported it to the meeting. The paper was adopted by the town, as its instructions to its representatives.

"But though Providence was thus committed to the good work, the country towns generally were not so safe. In many, the movement was decidedly unpopular, and there was ground for apprehension that it might fail. One of the most influential men in the State councils was then a resident of Newport. I felt very anxious to secure the favorable expression of that town. I therefore wrote to the town clerk, urging him to get an article inserted in the warrant for the town meeting, to instruct their representatives to vote for the bill before the Assembly. And so fearful was I that this precaution would be neglected, that I made a special journey to Newport to secure the measure. Much to my gratification, Newport voted for the instructions, and valuable services were rendered by Mr. George Champlin, the principal representative from that town. Essential aid was also rendered by a member from Smithfield.

"At the autumn session, (1799,) the bill passed the House of Representatives, and was sent up to the Senate. That body was afraid to pass it, and did not dare reject it. So with other unfinished business, they laid it over until the next session. The Assembly met in February in this town. I resolved to persevere in my efforts to get the school bill passed. I saw the secretary, and at my suggestion, he placed the deferred bill among the papers first to be called up.

"One day, in the early part of the session, I met Joel Metcalf, a man of strong good sense, who had interested himself in the matter of public schools. 'Come,' said I, 'you and I must go up to the Senate to-day and get them to call up the school bill.' 'Well,' he replied, 'I don't know as we can influence that honorable body.' 'We can try,' I responded. And so we went. We saw John Innis Clarke, a senator, and told him our errand. 'Well,' said he, 'the governor and senate are to dine with me to-day, and I will do what I can to secure favorable action.' We left, and went up to the senate chamber in the afternoon. As soon as I opened the door, Clarke rose and came to me, and said, 'the school bill has just passed.' 'Was it opposed?' I inquired. 'No,' he replied. 'I called it up, and it was passed without a word in opposition.' Thus we achieved our great State triumph—not of long duration indeed, as the act was repealed in 1803,—but long enough to secure a permanent blessing to Providence.

"I shall not confine my narrative to the strict order of dates, as I have no minutes of the events I am relating by me. My object is to give a brief view of the part I took in this work. The town resolved to establish four schools, three on the east, and one on the west side of the river. I was on a committee to carry out the design. Having made a motion in town meeting, June 3, 1799, that a committee be appointed to purchase the shares held by the proprietors of 'Whipple Hall,' and the brick school-house, standing near the State house, I was made chairman, and entered at once upon my duties. The other members of the committee were Richard Jackson, jr., and John Carlile. Afternoon after afternoon, accompanied by Paul Allen, I traversed the north end in search of the proprietors. Sometimes we found one at home, and another in the street. In this way, we picked up forty-five shares, at $10 each—I making the contract, and Allen, as justice of the peace, legalizing it. Five of the old proprietors we never could find, nor could we ascertain who were their heirs. To this day, they have not been purchased. One of the proprietors, a sturdy, self-willed man, at first refused to sell. He 'was'nt going to educate other people's children.' But after being made to see that the system would go on, and his refusal would injure no body but himself, (the town then owning over forty shares, and thus able to control the house,) he relented, and acceded to our terms. We next bought the brick school-house. This was more easily done, as the principal number of shares was in the hands of Moses Brown, and the town already owned the land on which the building stood. These shares were purchased at $10.50 each. It was not so easy, however, to obtain the lot wanted for a school house site at the south end. This land belonged to a gentleman who was unwilling to have a school of two hundred scholars so near his house and garden. I was not on the committee to make this purchase, but when I heard he had refused to sell, I went to see him. I asked the ground of his objections. He said if a school was established there, the neighborhood would be a perfect bedlam every time it was dismissed. Besides, his garden would be robbed of all its fruit. These were very natural fears. But I assured him they were groundless. Under our rules, the school would be dismissed by classes, and not permitted to loiter about the premises, and as to his garden, so strict a watch would be kept over the scholars, that his fruit would be safer than ever. I cannot repeat all my arguments on the occasion. It is sufficient to say, that before I left him, he consented to sell.

"Some time after, when the schools had gone fairly into operation, the town council, accompanied by the school committee, made their first visit to this school. When opposite his residence, I requested the company to pause till I went in and invited him to go with us. They did so. I went in and said, 'I have been deputed by the honorable town council and the school committee, to invite you to accompany them in their first visit of examination to the Transit street school. He appeared gratified with the attention, and readily complied with our invitation. I will not say there was not a little policy in this. At all events, it had a good effect. Our skeptical friend was delighted with all he saw and heard, and was ever after a firm supporter of the public schools.

"Among the exercises of this occasion, was a poetic address made to the gentlemen of the honorable council and committee. It was written by Paul Allen, and spoken by a lad nine years of age.

"It was clear, that to carry out our system successfully, a larger sum of money than hitherto appropriated for schools must be secured. Here we experienced the strongest opposition, and were in greatest danger of defeat. I moved, in town meeting, for an appropriation of $4,000. Some said it was too much, and others, hoping to defeat the motion, opposed it on the ground that the sum was insufficient. After listening some time to the discussion, I rose and said, that as there appeared to be a difference of opinion in the meeting, with a view to obviate the last objection, I would move the insertion of $6,000 in the place of $4,000, first proposed. This was seconded by one of the opponents, thinking thereby to give the motion its quietus. Much to his surprise, however, the motion was adopted. When the result was announced, great excitement prevailed. Two of the strongest opponents came up to me and said, 'you have taken us in—you have taken us in—we did'nt intend to vote you so much money.' 'You have taken yourselves in, and I am glad of it,' I replied. This agitation of the school matter induced many of the mechanics to attend town meeting, and take an active part in town affairs, who never went before.

"April 16, 1800, the town appointed James Burrill, Jr., John Corliss, Richard Jackson, Jr., John Carlile, Joel Metcalf, William Richmond and myself, a committee to devise and report a plan for carrying the school act into effect. This plan I drew up. It was reported to an adjourned town meeting, April 26th, and adopted.

"The first school committee under the act of the General Assembly, was chosen in August, 1800. It consisted of President Maxcy, Rev. Dr. Gano, Rev. Dr. Hitchcock, David L. Barnes, Jabez Bowen, Amos M. Atwell, James Burrill, Jr., William Jones, John Carlile, and myself. The town council, in conjunction with this body, appointed a sub-committee to draw up rules and regulations for the government of the schools. On this committee were President Maxcy, Rev. Dr. Hitchcock, and Rev. Dr. Gano. When nominated, Dr. Gano said the schools had his warmest wishes for success, but as he was not much acquainted with the matter, and as Mr. Howland had done so much, and understood the wants so well, he would decline in his favor. His wish was complied with, and I was placed on this important committee.

"When the work of drawing up the rules came to be done, to my surprise, the burden of the labor was assigned to me. President Maxcy was pressed with the cares of the college, and could not conveniently attend to the duty. Dr. Hitchcock's health was declining, and though warmly devoted to the cause of education, was unable to give the subject the attention it deserved. So it was left for me to go on with it. This was rather a formidable undertaking, but as I had the approbation of the literary gentlemen, I boldly put my hand to the work. To aid me in the matter, I sent to Boston, and procured the rules established there, and also a list of the books used in school. After my rules and regulations were prepared, I submitted them to the committee and town council. They were accepted, and adopted October 16th, less than two months after my appointment.

"Up to this time I had never seen a grammar—a sorry confession for a school committee man, some may think—but observing that 'The Young Ladies' Accidence' was used in the Boston schools, I sent to the principal bookseller in that town, and purchased one hundred copies for the use of ours. For whatever accuracy I have obtained in writing, I am indebted to observation and practice.

"The introduction of grammar was quite an advance in the system of education, as it was not taught at all except in the better class of private schools. The same was true of geography, which had never been taught before. Geographies could not be bought in this town, so I sent to Boston and purchased as many as were wanted for our schools. Dr. Morse, of Charlestown, had published the first volume of his geography, and that was the work we adopted. Many thought it an unnecessary study, and some in private objected to it because it would take off their attention from arithmetic. But it met with no public opposition.

"To some this recital may seem egotistical. But I have no such feeling. I was so constantly connected with the school movement, that I cannot speak of it without speaking of myself. I take no improper pride in the part I acted. If better educated and more influential men had seen fit to take the lead, I should have been contented to follow. But I felt that somebody must do the work, and as others would not, I resolved that I would. I thank a kind Providence that I have been able, in my humble way, to be of service to my fellow-men; and I wish to occupy no other place in their memories, or on the page of history, than that which truth shall assign me."*

The memorial mentioned by Mr. Howland in the previous paper, was in the following form:

" To the Honorable General Assembly of the State of Rhode Island and Providence Plantations, to be holden at Greenwich, on the last Monday of February, A. D. 1799:

"The Memorial and Petition of the Providence Association of Mechanics and Manufacturers, respectfully represents:—

* Life and Recollections of John Howland, late President of the Rhode Island Historical Society, by Edwin M. Stone, Providence, 1857, pp. 138-148.

"That the means of Education which are enjoyed in this State, are very inadequate to a purpose so highly important:

"That numbers of the rising generation, whom nature has liberally endowed, are suffered to grow up in ignorance, when a common education would qualify them to act their parts in life with advantage to the public, and reputation to themselves;

"That in consequence of there being no legal provision for the establishment of schools, and for want of public attention and encouragement, this so essential a part of our social duty is left to the partial patronage of individuals, whose cares do not extend beyond the limits of their own families, while numbers in every part of the State are deprived of a privilege which it is the common right of every child to enjoy;

"That when to that respect, which, as individuals we feel ourselves bound to render to the representatives of the people, we add our public declaration of gratitude for the privileges we enjoy as a corporate body, we at the same time solicit this Honorable Assembly to make legal provision for the establishment of Free Schools, sufficient to educate all the children in the several towns throughout the State; with great confidence, we bring this our earnest solicitation before this Honorable Assembly, from the interest we feel in the public welfare, and from the consideration that our society is composed of members not originally of any one particular town, but assembled mostly in our early years from almost every town in the State.

"That we feel as individuals, the want of that education which we now ask to be bestowed on those who are to succeed us in life, and which is so essential in directing its common concerns. That we feel a still greater degree of confidence from the consideration that while we pray this Honorable Assembly to establish Free Schools, we are at the same time, advocating the cause of the great majority of children throughout the State, and in particular, of those who are poor and destitute—the son of the widow, and the child of distress.

"Trusting that our occupation as mechanics and manufacturers ought not to prevent us from adding to these reasons an argument which cannot fail to operate on those to whom is committed the guardianship of the public welfare, and that is, that liberty and security, under a republican form of government, depend on a general diffusion of knowledge among the people.

"In confiding this petition and the reasons which have dictated it, to the wisdom of the Legislature, we assure ourselves that their decision will be such, as will reflect on this Honorable Assembly the praise and the gratitude, not only of the youth of the present generation, but of thousands, the date of whose existence has not commenced.

Respectfully submitted by

John Howland,
Joel Metcalf,
William Richmond,
Peter Grinnell, } *Committee.*
Richard Anthony,
Grindall Reynolds,
Samuel Thurber, Jr.,
Nathan Fisher,

The First School Law.

The subject was referred by the General Assembly to a committee which reported, in June, 1799, a bill that was ordered to be printed, and to be distributed to the several towns for instructions. In the following October, a bill was passed by the House of Representatives, but it was postponed by the Senate to the session held in February, 1800, when it became a law. The bill was as follows:—

"AN ACT TO ESTABLISH FREE SCHOOLS.

"*Whereas*, the unexampled prosperity, unanimity and liberty, for the enjoyment of which, this nation is eminently distinguished among the nations of the earth, are to be ascribed, next to the blessing of God, to the general diffusion of knowledge and information among the people, whereby they have been enabled to discern their true interests, to distinguish truth from error, to place their confidence in the true friends of the country, and to detect the falsehoods and misrepresentations of factions and crafty pretenders to patriotism; and this General Assembly being desirous to secure the continuance of the blessings aforesaid, and moreover to contribute to the greater equality of the people, by the common and joint instruction and education of the whole :—

"SECTION 1. *Be it enacted by the General Assembly, and the authorities thereof, and it is hereby enacted;*—That each and every town in the State shall annually cause to be established and kept, at the expense of such town, one or more free schools, for the instruction of all the white inhabitants of said town, between the ages of six and twenty years, in reading, writing and common arithmetic, who may stand in need of such instruction, and apply therefor.

"SEC. 2. *And be it further enacted,* That it shall be the duty of the Town Council of every town, to divide said town into so many school districts as they shall judge necessary and convenient.

"SEC. 3. *And be it further enacted,* That each of the towns of Newport and Providence shall cause to be established and kept every year, so many free schools, and for such terms of time, as shall be equivalent to keeping three such schools eight months each; that each of the towns of South Kingstown, Glocester and Smithfield shall cause to be established and kept every year, so many free schools as shall be equivalent to keeping three such schools six months each; That each of the towns of Portsmouth, Tiverton, Little Compton, Scituate, Cumberland, Cranston, Johnston, Foster, Westerly, North Kingstown, Charlestown, Exeter, Richmond, Hopkinton, Bristol, Warwick, East Greenwich, West Greenwich and Coventry, shall cause to be established and kept, in every year, so many free schools as shall be equivalent to keeping three such schools four months each; and that the towns of Middletown, Jamestown, New Shoreham, North Providence, Warren and Barrington, shall cause to be established and kept, in every year, so many free schools as shall be equivalent to keeping one such school four months.

"SEC. 4. *And be it further enacted,* That for the encouragement of institutions so useful, there shall be allowed and paid to the Town Treasurer of each town, or his order, out of the general treasury, at the end of every year, computing from the first Wednesday in May next, twenty per centum of the amount of the State taxes of the preceding year paid into the general treasury by said town; provided the said sum or allowance of twenty per cent. shall not exceed, in the whole, the sum of six thousand dollars in any one year.

"And the town making application to the general treasurer for said allowance, shall exhibit and deliver to him a certificate, signed by the town council, town treasurer, and school master or school masters of such town, that a school or schools have been established and kept in said town, according to the provisions of this act, and specifying the number of schools and the term of time for which each school shall have been kept.

"SEC. 5. *And be it further enacted*, That the allowances aforesaid, when paid to the town treasurers, shall be, and remain exclusively appropriated to the establishment and support of free schools, and shall be paid out, under the orders of the several town councils, for the benefit of the school or schools which shall be kept in the districts established by them, as aforesaid, in proportion to the number of persons in the several districts entitled to instruction in the said schools, by virtue of this act.

"SEC. 6. *And be it further enacted*, That if any town shall neglect, or refuse to establish and keep free schools, in the manner prescribed in this act, such town shall forfeit all right or claim to the allowance aforesaid for the year in which such neglect or refusal shall happen, and the said forfeited allowances shall make and constitute a part of the unappropriated moneys in the general treasury; and that all certificates for obtaining said allowances, shall be presented to the general treasurer within six months after the expiration of the year, within which the said allowances shall have become due, or the same shall be forfeited as last aforesaid.

"SEC. 7. *And be it further enacted*, That the general treasurer shall annually make a report to the General Assembly of the operation and execution of this act, accompanied with copies of the certificates aforesaid, and an account of the allowances paid thereon.

"SEC. 8. *And be it further enacted*, That if any school district in any town shall think fit to keep a school in said district for a longer time than the town shall provide for the same, or to erect a school-house, or to enlarge, ornament or repair any already erected, it shall and may be lawful for any seven freemen of such school district, to make application to any justice of the peace in the town, for a warrant for calling a meeting of the freemen of such district, and the said justice shall thereupon grant such warrant, directed to the town sergeant and constables of said town to warn the freemen of said district to assemble at a proper time and place, to be prescribed in said warrant, to take into consideration the subjects therein mentioned; and the said warrant being first served, in the manner in which warrants for calling town meetings are served in said town, the freemen of said district (any seven of whom shall be a quorum) shall and may assemble and appoint a clerk, treasurer, collector, and such other officers and committees as occasion may require, and order and assess such taxes on the inhabitants of said district, to be assessed in the proportions of the last town tax, as they may think necessary for the purposes aforesaid, which taxes shall be collected by warrant from the clerk of said school district, directed to the district collector, and shall be levied and collected in the same manner and under the same laws and regulations as town taxes, and shall be appropriated to the uses aforesaid, according to the votes and orders of the said school district meetings; and the freemen of said district, assembled as aforesaid, shall and may make such other lawful orders and regulations, relative to the continuance and support of their district schools, as to them may appear useful, and may be called by their clerk by warrant, on request of any seven of said freemen, and the meeting so called shall and may have and exercise the powers and privileges aforesaid.

"SEC. 9. *And be it further enacted,* That no person shall establish or direct as master or preceptor, any school or academy of instruction established by virtue of this act, unless he shall be a native or naturalized citizen of the United States, and be approved of by a certificate in writing from the town council of the town in which he shall teach.

"SEC. 10. *And be it further enacted,* That the town councils of the several towns shall have the government of the town and district schools in their respective towns.

"SEC. 11. *And be it further enacted,* That this act shall take effect and be in force from and after the first Wednesday of May next, and shall be published in all the newspapers in this State."

The law met with great opposition and was repealed in a few years. I can find in the Providence *Gazette* and in the *U. S. Chronicle* of that period no hint of the special influences which brought about the repeal. It appears from the Newport *Mercury* of November 4, 1800, that a motion was made (October 31,) by Mr. J. Davis, seconded by Mr. A. Taylor, in pursuance of instructions from the town of Little Compton, to repeal the whole bill, and that, "after considerable debate," the motion was defeated, 32 to 25. Again it appears from the same authority that on June 17, 1801, "instructions from several towns were read against the school-bill, which occasioned a motion for its repeal. It was finally referred to a committee, who are to report an amended bill at the next session."* No such bill appears to have passed; the whole measure was virtually defeated by simple non-enforcement, and the law was repealed at the February session, 1803.

Providence was the only town which had ever carried it into effect. But as the Providence schools have been sustained ever since under the organization then begun, and as the whole State was afterwards brought under a system essentially identical with that proposed by Mr. Howland, he may justly be called the founder of the school system of the State. Indeed it was the opinion of that high authority, Henry Barnard, when he took charge of the public schools forty years later, that if a competent officer had been at once appointed, at the time of the passage of the act of 1800, to explain its provisions, meet objections, urge ad-

* Newport *Mercury,* June 23, 1801.

vantages, and suggest modifications, it would not have been repealed, and Rhode Island would have had the best school system in New England

The "freemen" of Providence at once proceeded to organize schools under the new law; four school-houses were bought or built and four "masters" appointed, each with an usher. Two gentlemen, Dr. Enos Hitchcock and Tristam Burges, Esq., "being about to visit Boston, were requested by the town council to visit the public schools of that city and obtain, if possible, a copy of the rules and regulations of its public schools." It appears that Mr. Burges obtained a copy of these rules, for which the town council voted to pay him one dollar, and gave him a vote of thanks. On October 16, 1800, a committee of which Dr. Hitchcock was chairman, read this excellent report to the town council:

"The public schools being established for the general benefit of the community, all children of both sexes admissible by law, shall be received therein and faithfully instructed without preference or partiality.

"The system of instruction shall be uniform in the several schools, and the pronunciation as near alike as possible, and to this end, it shall be the duty of the several instructors to have frequent intercourse with each other, and agree upon some measures for carrying this important article into effect.

"The good morals of the youth, being a matter of the highest consequence, both to their own comfort, and to their progress in useful knowledge, they are strictly enjoined to avoid idleness and profaneness, falshood and deceitfulness, and every other wicked and disgraceful practice, and to conduct themselves in a sober, orderly and decent manner, both in and out of school.

"The principal part of the instruction will consist in teaching spelling, accenting and reading both prose and verse with propriety and accuracy, and a general knowledge of English grammar and composition; also writing a good hand, according to the most approved rules, and vulgar and decimal fractions, including tare and tret, fellowship, exchange, interest, &c.

"The books to be used in carrying on the above instruction, are Alden's Spelling Book, 1st and 2nd parts, the young Ladies' Accidence, by Caleb Bingham, the American Preceptor, Morse's Geography abridged, the Holy Bible in select portions, and such other books as shall hereafter be adopted and appointed by the committee. The book for teaching arithmetic shall be agreed on by the masters. As discipline and good government are absolutely necessary to improvement, it is indispensable that the scholars pay a particular attention to the laws and regulations of the school.

"If any scholar should prove disobedient and refractory, after all reasonable means have been used by the master to bring him or her to order and a just sense of duty, such offender shall be suspended from any further attendance or instruction in any school in the town, until the next visitation of the committee.

"That each scholar shall, after having entered a school, be punctual in his attendance at the appointed hour, and be as constant as possible in his daily attendance.

"That excuse for absence shall be by a note from the parents or guardians of such scholar.

"That monitors be appointed by the masters of each school, to notice the absence or tardiness of the delinquent scholars, the list of whose names shall be preserved and exhibited to the committee at their next visitation. Submitted by Enos Hitchcock, John Howland, Jonathan Maxcy, Joseph Jencks, committee."

The above report having been accepted, it was voted and resolved, that the rules therein recommended, be adopted for the regulation of the schools, viz.:

"That as far as possible they exclude corporeal punishment from the schools: and in particular, that they never inflict it on females.

"That they inculcate upon the scholars the proprieties of good behavior during their absence from the school. That they consider themselves in the place of parents to the children under their care, and endeavour to convince them by their treatment, that they feel a parental affection for them.

"That they never make dismission from school at an earlier hour than usual, a reward for attention or diligence, but endeavour to lead the children to consider being at school as a privilege, and dismission from it as a punishment.

"That they never authorize one scholar to inflict any corporeal punishment on another.

"That they endeavour to impress the minds of their pupils with a sense of the Being and Providence of God, and the obligation they are under to love and reverence Him; their duty to their parents and masters; the beauty and excellence of truth, justice and mutual love; tenderness to brute creatures; the happy tendency of self-government and obedience to the dictates of reason and religion; the observance of the Sabbath as a sacred institution; the duty which they owe their country, and the necessity of a strict obedience to its laws; and that they caution them against the prevailing vices."*

Four public schools were thus opened in Providence on the last Monday in October, 1800. The number of scholars was beyond anticipation, and a fifth school was soon required. For twelve years, however, the whole attendance rarely exceeded eight hundred. The four original schools had each a master with a salary of $500, and an usher who was paid $200. After a time the rules were revised and new regulations established, from which the following is an extract:

"The public schools are established for the general good of the community; and all children of both sexes, having attained the age of six years, shall be received therein, and faithfully instructed without preference or partiality. The instruction shall be uniform, in all the schools, and shall consist of spelling, reading, the use of capital letters, and punctuation, writing, English grammar and arithmetic.

* Barnard's Journal of R. I. School Inst., III. p. 41.

"The pronunciation shall be uniform in all the schools, and the standard shall be the Critical Pronouncing Dictionary of John Walker.

"The following books, and none other, shall be used in the several schools, viz.: Alden's Spelling Book, first and second parts; New Testament, American Preceptor, Murray's Sequel to the English Reader, Murray's Abridgement of English Grammar, and Daboll's Arithmetic.

"Each scholar shall be punctual in attendance at the appointed hour, and as regular as possible in daily attendance, and all excuses for absence shall be by note from the parent or guardian of the scholar.

"It shall be the duty of the Preceptor to report at each quarterly visitation, the names of those scholars who have been grossly negligent in attending school or inattentive to their studies."*

These were the provisions made for public schools in Providence, at the beginning of the present century. The system has never been abandoned, in that city, but only expanded; and as it ultimately spread from Providence through the State, it is clear that the whole State must trace its school system to these early efforts. But for many years the children of the State were mainly left to the instruction given in private schools; and I must next endeavor to give, so far as it is possible, some indication of what those private schools were.

* Barnard's Journal, R. I. School Inst., III. 42.

III. PRIVATE SCHOOL INSTRUCTION AT THE BEGINNING OF THIS CENTURY.

The longevity often attributed to Rhode Islanders has this great advantage, that tradition preserves much which has found no other record. It is to Rev. George G. Channing, now approaching his ninetieth-year, that we owe the most graphic picture of the private schools of this State, from 1794 to 1804. No apology is therefore needed for some citations from his " Early Recollections of Newport, R. I."

" Accompany me, if you will, to the primary school where I first commenced ' the art of spelling and reading the English language with propriety.'

" The room occupied by the matron-teacher, Mrs. Sayre, and her daughter ('Miss Betsy,' as she was called), situated near the corner of Mary and Clarke streets, was a low, square chamber, on the second floor, having no furniture, no desks, nor chairs, excepting a few for teachers or visitors. The children, boys and girls (the former dressed the same as girls), were furnished by their parents with seats made of round blocks of wood of various heights. These movable *seats*, at least thirty in number, would constitute as great a curiosity at this day of school accommodations and luxury, as would the old 'ten-footer' district school-houses, were they set up for public gaze in one of our streets. Mrs. Sayre was a model teacher in her day. It was at the time of reading from Noah Webster's spelling and reading book, when an urchin, *alias* brat, sometimes softened into varlet, being pinned to the mistress's apron, was hammering or stuttering over a monosyllable, turning red and pale by turns as she jostled the poplar rod at her side,—it was just at that moment, when her eyes were bent on the sewing she was preparing for the girls, and on the garter-knitting for the boys, and she listening to and correcting the poor boy's mistakes,—it was just then that the block gyrations commenced, not exactly on a pivot, but in sweeps, forming larger or smaller circles according to the whim of the block-mover,—it was just at that moment of astounding commotion, when the old lady, taking notice of the tumult, raised the wand, viz., the poplar pole, and with distinct, nay fearful articulation, cried out, in regular, syllabic order. 'Mi-rab-i-le-dictu,' which Latin word sounded in my right ear very much like 'My rabble dick you.' Of course, this, to us, meaningless word excited as much open-eyed and open-mouthed admiration as is produced by a grandiloquent orator, * * *

"To return to Mrs. Sayre's primary school: I recollect very well the disagreeable sensations connected with the "dark closet," the prison of the disobedient. It was not resorted to, save in extreme cases. I remember what a fright was caused by one of the boys swallowing a marble (he is still alive), which led to a sudden dismission of the school. At the close of the school on Friday afternoons, we were sent to a vacant room below stairs, where we recited the 'commandments,' repeated the 'Lord's Prayer,' and received commendation or censure according to our good or bad conduct during the week. I remember most gratefully the happy influence of Mrs. Sayre's discipline and instruction. She was firm but gentle in manner and speech, governing by signs rather than by words. My preparation was excellent for the higher school I was soon to enter, especially in reading and spelling. The junior teacher (Miss Betsy) had under her care children of advanced standing. She was an excellent teacher, and was affectionately remembered for her assiduity in behalf of her scholars. During the recess twice a week, Mrs. Sayre taught colored children spelling and reading, gratis. This good lady and her daughter were greatly respected and beloved. The latter married Joseph Rogers, Esq., of Philadelphia.

"The first school-house of any note in the town was owned and managed by a gentleman of acknowledged ability for those days. Compared with buildings used for similar purposes now, it was a mere shanty, a 'ten-footer.' It was scant in length, breadth, and height, and poorly ventilated. The furniture, viz., the desks and benches, was of the most ordinary stamp. The former, used for the writing exercises, had leaden inkstands in the centre; and their surface was more or less disfigured with rude indentures, so as to render straight or curved strokes with the pen next to impossible; and the latter, the benches without backs, were so tall and shaky as to be very uncomfortable, especially to the shortest boys, whose legs had to be suspended, causing often extreme pain, and consequent disturbance; bringing on them undeserved punishment from the monitors, unless warded off by a bribe, in the shape of a top or a knife, or a handful of marbles. On the *rostrum* were two or three chairs for distinguished visitors, and a small desk for the master, on which *reposed*, not often, a punctured ferule, surmounted by an unpleasant-looking cowskin. So exceedingly disagreeable were the daily ministrations of these instruments of *instruction*, that every method was adopted for their destruction. But the master was more than a match for our organ of destructiveness. Such was school No. 1 in the State of Rhode Island and Providence Plantations. It certainly was not the prototype of the school at Rugby, where Dr. Arnold ruled successfully, without making any of the distinguishing *marks* which characterized my pupilage. As the school grew, assistants were employed. Mr. Maxy was an excellent teacher of the languages. Mr. Taylor (a most worthy citizen) taught the lower branches. The tree is known by its fruit; whilst, therefore, it must be granted that the greater number of the scholars were of the genus Booby, there were some of rare brightness of mind, whose intellectual culture did credit to those efficient and faithful teachers.

"Our school-room had to be swept and dusted twice or thrice a week, and the classes were obliged to do this in turn. As this was a disagreeable task, those boys who had money (and these were generally of Southern parentage) could easily buy substitutes from among the poorer boys. During my nonage, the Puritan spirit did not die out. It was an age of force. Punishment was deemed necessary. Exhibitions of authority constituted, day by day, a series of domestic *tableaux*. The discipline of the school was in accordance with the government of the home. It was arbitrary, with rare exceptions, in the extreme. Children were required to bow or kiss the hand, when entering or leaving either home or school. The school to which I was sent differed in no respect from inferior ones in the matter of corporal punishment. The ferule and cowskin were almost deified. Apologies increased, rather than abated, the swellings of the hand, and the wales upon the back. An appeal to parents was of no more avail than beating the air. This severe discipline was not interfered with by the clergy; for, in their day, *they* had to run the gauntlet; and as the men, and even the boys, of that age were notoriously addicted to swearing, drinking, gambling, and other vices, it was deemed necessary to subdue these evils by blows. No faith existed then in behalf of moral suasion. It is delightful to remember that none of my name, as boys, at least, were guilty of uttering an oath.

"The only classical school in Newport, strictly speaking, during my pupilage, was kept in New Church Lane, by Mr. John Frazer, a Scotchman. He was a good teacher, especially in Greek, Latin, and mathematics. * * *

"Mr. Clarke Rodman (*a Friend*) had, in his own house in Mary street, quite a large school, devoted to the education of a class of boys and young men living at the South End, who were styled the 'roughs.' It was thought singular, that a man belonging to the 'Society of Friends,' a non-resistant by profession, should have attracted to his school so many disorderly youths. But, though avowedly a non-resistant, he never suffered any act of disobedience to go unpunished. His manner of conducting the spelling was original. The word being given out, followed by a blow from a strap on his desk, the whole class, simultaneously, would bellow out the word, — say the word 'multiplication,'—properly divided. His ear was so true, that he easily detected any misspelling. When this happened, he would demand the name of the scholar who had failed: if there was any hesitancy in giving the name, the whole class, instead of being dismissed,—spelling being the last exercise,—was detained, until, by repeated trials, accuracy was obtained. So many voices upon a single word, in so many keys, produced an amusing jingle, which invariably attracted to the spot all passers-by. A Mr. Knox, with remarkably long feet and an ungainly appearance, devoted most of his time to teaching very poor children their A B C, in a small building in the rear of Trinity Church.

"Having given the reader a brief but accurate statement of the schools in Newport during my boyhood, I will give, in the next place, my recollections of some of the school-books then used. The advanced scholars in our school studied the Greek and Latin text-books of the day. The principal English books were Murray's Grammar, Noah Webster's Spelling-book, the Columbian Orator, Woodbridge's Dictionary, Daboll's, Pike's and Walsh's Arithmetics, and Morse's small Geography."*

* Early Recollections of Newport, R. I., from 1793 to 1811, by George G. Channing. (Newport, R. I., 1868,) pp. 43-54.

Most of the schools mentioned by Mr. Channing appear to have been open to boys only. In 1794,* however, the Newport *Mercury* announces that " Miss Vinal, lately from Boston," will open a school at the house of Mr. William Coggeshall, " and will be obliged to those ladies and gentlemen that will favor her with their custom." In 1797,† James Wallace offers a " morning school for young ladies in reading, writing and arithmetic," he also teaching navigation and book-keeping as usual, doubtless to young men. In 1805,‡ William Bridges offers to " teach young ladies and gentlemen. Private rooms for young ladies and board if required." In 1807,§ Mrs. LaSalle and daughter advertise a school, probably for girls, at their home ; and the Misses Smith announce a Female Academy at Bristol.|| In 1808,¶ Mrs. Eliza C. Brenton announces instruction for girls at Washington Academy, South Kingstown ; her list of studies including " Epistolary Style," as well as " Temple Work, Paper Work, Fringing and Tufting." And in 1811,** Mr. J. Rodman offers to young ladies " the elegant art of writing," and also arithmetic.

One of the most characteristic of these school advertisements, especially in the order assigned to the studies, is the following in the *United States Chronicle*,†† of Providence :

" Mrs. Hurley, from London, offers to instruct young ladies in all kinds of Needlework, Tambour and Embroidery, with Drawing, Painting, and Music on the Piano Forte.
Likewise,
In Reading, Writing, Arithmetic, French and English, Grammar, Geography, and History—which will be explained by Rev. Mr. Hurley."

We are, finally, indebted to Mr. Channing for this tribute to one teacher of young ladies during this period :

" Eloise Payne, the daughter of Schoolmaster Payne (a teacher of great celebrity in his day, in Boston, Mass.,) and sister of John Howard Payne (the renowned dramatist and poet), came to Newport about the year 1807-8, and opened one of the most noticeable schools in America; and, until her health failed, she exerted a great influence for good in the moral and intellectual culture of girls,—not only the residents of Newport, but also of many from New York and Boston, who boarded in Miss Payne's family. Perhaps no young lady-teacher ever enjoyed more deserved repute than Miss Payne. Her voice was delightfully sweet and winning. Her face was the index of unusual intellectual power. Her eye, lustrous and penetrating when she spoke, awakened confidence and love when she was silent. Her skill in penmanship was admirable. She attracted many, and held them spell-bound by her grace in conversation.

* April 22.   † April 18.   ‡ July 20.   § April 4. || Aug. 29.   ¶ April 16.   ** Feb. 23.
†† Dec. 18, 1800.

Her religious faith yielded the fruit of holy living; so that, though her life was short, her death was deeply lamented. I have frequently been gratified by the expression of affectionate remembrance of this faithful teacher by the few pupils who still survive to call her blessed."*

Other advertisements of private schools, usually without mention of sex, appear in plenty during this period, and are subjects of never-failing curiosity to the reader in the singular selection of hours for instruction. Thus Mr. Wallace, already mentioned, taught young ladies "from 6 to 8 A. M.," and Mr. Jastram, in Providence, from 6 to 8 A. M., and from 10 to "12 at noon." A morning and evening school, advertised in the *Mercury*, March 29, 1806, was taught from 5½ to 8 A. M., and from 5 to 7 P. M., for "both sexes." Mr. Hall had a "Morning School," from 6 to 8 A. M., and Mr. Fraser an evening school, from 5½ to 8 P. M. Mr. Colburn teaches penmanship to ladies from 11 A. M. to 1 P. M., and to gentlemen from 3 to 5 and from 7 to 9 P. M.: then his successor, Mr. Dillingham, has the ladies at 3 and the gentlemen at 7 P. M., and a year later reaches the modern hours and has both classes at 9 A. M. in two separate rooms.† These morning schools were probably arranged in order not to interfere with the regular instruction of the teacher, or with the daily occupations of the pupils. Our "evening schools" are the only vestige now remaining of this system.

For the more ornamental branches, schools were re-opened soon after the Revolution. Thomas Berkenhead, lately from Liverpool, offers, through the Newport *Mercury*, in 1796, to teach "the Organ, Harpsichord, and Forte-Piano;" another offers "a grand Kirckman's Harpsichord for sale;" another teaches "Vocal Music in the evening;" and a nameless person proposes to "teach the violin."‡ French and Dancing were taught by Frenchmen, and commonly combined. M. Francisquy offered lessons in dancing "to children and persons more advanced in life," and stated that "the principles of his mode of instruction are founded upon reflection and long professional experience." M. Nugent, announcing a school for the two arts, says of himself, "As a French teacher, besides his having been bred to Letters in France, he has the advantage of possessing the English language: and as a dancing-master he presents it as a sufficient Proof of his Abilities that he has been principal Dancer in the Theatres of Philadelphia and Boston." It is to be observed that a lower price was charged for the language than for the other accomplishment. Later, the newspapers begin to contain adver-

---

* Channing's Early Recollections, p. 63.
† Newport *Mercury*, July 29, 1815; June 14, Oct. 18, Nov. 22, 1817; Dec. 19, 1818.
‡ Aug. 16, 1796; Feb. 4, March 14, 1797.

tisements from "a unfortunate gentleman," or "a sufferer by the unfortunate circumstances of the war," still teaching French and sometimes dancing.* On January 14, 1794, we may read of "The young married gentleman from Cape François who lately announced in the Newport *Mercury* his deplorable situation and his desire of teaching the young ladies and gentlemen of Newport the art of dancing;" and this striking appeal is continued, with undiminished pathos, for several successive weeks.

The early academies of this State, especially the Washington Academy, of South Kingstown, are advertised freely in the newspapers from 1800 onwards. The "Frenchtown Catholic Seminary" appears in 1804, and the "Pawcatuck Academy" at Westerly in 1807. To these must be added a few attempts in the direction of gratuitous teaching, apart from the public school system of Providence. A school had existed in Newport before the Revolution, having been established by the will of Nathaniel Kay, Esq., collector of the King's customs, in order "to teach ten poor boys their grammar and the mathematics gratis." It was in charge of the minister, church wardens and vestry of Trinity Church, and the master must be "Episcopally ordained." This school existed from 1741 till the Revolution; and was revived in 1799 and continued for many years, though in a somewhat modified form.†

The Newport *Mercury* of August 8th, 1807, announces that Mr. E. Trevett—a well-known teacher—will "gratuitously teach as many poor children as he can attend to in the State House, a few hours in the morning," and that a subscription is in circulation to purchase stationery. The editor adds, "the want of free schools is a serious evil to society." On October 31, 1807, the same announcement is renewed, with the statement that more than seventy had attended in the summer, more than forty in the winter; and an appeal was made for clothes to cover them. About the same time the "Female Benevolent Society" informs those who wish to put children under their care that a few can be admitted into their school.‡ In the following year the "African Benevolent Society" opens a school kept by Newport Gardner, "the object of which is the free instruction of all the colored people of this town who are inclined to attend." § Eight years after, this school seems still to have been in existence; and the school of the "Female Benevolent Society" was described, in 1817, as having been established for twelve years, and as having habitually taught and partially clothed twenty-five or thirty children.

* *Mercury*, Sept. 6, Oct. 11, 1796; June 20, Oct. 3, 1797.
† Updike's Narragansett Church, pp. 397-407.
‡ *Mercury*, Oct. 24, 1807; Sept. 13, 1817.
§ *Mercury*, March 26, 1808.

To these should be added the Sunday schools, just introduced from Europe, and applied at first mainly to secular instruction. These schools were first established by Robert Raikes in England, in 1781; but the first organized in America is believed to have been in 1796, by Samuel Slater—the father of cotton manufactures in the United States—for the children employed in his cotton mill at North Providence. They were introduced into Providence itself in 1816, but only in their present form, for religious instruction.* But in Newport, during the following year, they were established in their original form, for secular teaching. In the *Mercury* of August 2d, 1817, appears the announcement of the " First Sabbath School Society " for the instruction of indigent children " in the first principles of education." The school was to be held at " Mr. Hitchcock's Meeting-House," at 8½ A. M. and 1 P. M. Among the signers of the notice were prominent day-school teachers, such as Messrs. Hall and Trevett. It appears from later issues of the *Mercury*† that these schools were gradually established by several other societies, and reference is made to their becoming general throughout the country.

There were thus in Newport alone, five different avenues for the gratuitous instruction of poor children—the Kay school, Mr. Trevett's school, the Female Benevolent Society, the African Benevolent Society and the Sunday schools. To these was presently added a sixth, as we shall see, and these all contributed, together with the constant example of the town of Providence, to swell the growing public sentiment in favor of a State system of public schools.

* Staples' Annals of Providence, p. 533.
† Oct. 17, Nov. 7, 1818.

IV. LOTTERIES AND THEIR RESULTS.

For twenty-five years after the final defeat of John Howland's enterprise, Rhode Island had no public school system, even on paper. The Providence schools held on their course, under local authority, but under no other. There existed, however, a means, familiar in those days, now wholly discarded hereabouts, by which the means of civilization were to be freely obtained. It is almost impossible to open a Rhode Island newspaper, printed in the first quarter of this century, without finding the advertisement of a lottery; and the only difference in this respect between New England and other parts of America was, that the avowed aim of the enterprise was here usually a church, a school-house, a charity, or some municipal improvement. It was employed with as little compunction as young ladies feel in these days in organizing a raffle. In my limited investigation I have come upon advertisements of lotteries for paving streets, for the Redwood Library, and for relieving the maritime losses of Gideon Almy; for churches in Providence, Newport, Bristol, Warren, Warwick, Coventry, Little Compton and East Greenwich; for churches of the Baptist, Methodist, Congregational and Presbyterian faiths; for "Catholic" and Episcopal academies; for the Washington Academy at East Greenwich, and the academy at Hopkinton, Mass.; for the universities of Brown, Harvard, Union, and William and Mary.* All these are advertised in Rhode Island newspapers, between 1773 and 1825; and they are sometimes reinforced by mixed appeals like

---

* *Newport Mercury* for March 29, 1773; August 8, 22, September 12, 1774; April 3, 17, June 19, 26, August 14, December 18, 1781; January 27, February 17, 21, June 30, September 15, 1795; May 10, 17, 6; May 8, 1798; April 1, December, 2, 24, 1800; September 6, December 17, 1803; February 18, 1801; April 13, May 11, July 29, 1805; June 6, 1807; February 17, March 3, 1810; March 2, 9, November 9, 1811; May 16, July 18, 1812, etc., etc.

this, which is offered in connection with the Newport Methodist chapel lottery of 1807 : " Now is the time to make your fortune. * * * It is presumed that those who wish to encourage religion, laying aside the prospect of a fortune, will call and purchase liberally."*

Such were the lotteries of that day, and among these came one which had so definite a relation with the public schools of Rhode Island, that it deserves to be specially chronicled. In the newspapers of 1795 appears an advertisement of the "Newport Long Wharf and Public School Lottery," of which George Gibbs and George Champlin, then among the foremost citizens of the town, were the managers. The history of this enterprise was as follows : The plan of the lottery had originated in 1769, though then, it would seem, for Long Wharf purposes alone ; but it was revived in 1795, when an act passed the legislature, at the January session, as thus stated in a legal report officially rendered by Hon. W. R. Staples :

"Without petition or complaint from any one, on motion, the Assembly authorized thirty-six persons, citizens of Newport, who are named in the act, to set forth a scheme to raise by lottery twenty-five thousand dollars.

"They were to appoint managers of the lottery, who were to give bonds to the general treasurer for the faithful performance of their trust as managers. The powers conferred on them were very broad. How the wharf should be rebuilt, after a title to it had been procured, what kind of a hotel and where to be located, are left to the discretion of these trustees, who are to act without bond or oath, in discharge of their part of the trust.

"After the wharf and hotel were completed, the trustees were to apply the rents and profits arising from them to such a public school for the children of Newport, and in such way and manner, and under such regulations as the trustees should impose. And the trust to last through all time, the right of filling vacancies in the number being specially conferred on the survivors. The board of trustees originated with the Assembly ; the funds which they were to raise and appropriate, were provided by the Assembly. No person was compelled to contribute toward the fund, and no person was compelled to be benefited by it."

The original call for a meeting of the trustees of this enterprise appears in the Newport *Mercury* for February 10th, 1795, and the first announcement of the lottery itself on March 24th. There were to be 2,000 shares, at $125 each. There were 12,000 prizes, varying from $10 to $30,000 ; so that each share was sure to draw six prizes, amounting at least to $60, nearly half the purchase money ; while the maximum of prizes

* Newport *Mercury*, June 6, July 15, 1807.

attainable by any share was $72,000. For convenience, many of the shares were divided into twenty-seven tickets, at $5 each. The total amount actually drawn at last appears to have been $30,000.*

The accounts of the managers of the lottery do not appear to have been settled until March 22nd, 1798, when the committee reported the cash in their hands as being $6,576.17, and the amount of accounts and notes to be collected as being $5,973.39. What was the total amount of profits cannot now be ascertained, but the committee reports that the lottery, on the part of the managers, has been conducted with the most perfect regularity and fairness, and they have generously relinquished their commissions for the management. The proceeds of the venture went to the rebuilding of Long Wharf; the projected hotel was never built, and it is doubtful whether a school-house would have been obtained, had not a private citizen made sure of it, by offering a building for the purpose. The following letter was received by the trustees of the lottery, soon after its first announcement:

"SWANSEA, May 16, 1795.

"*Messrs. George Gibbs and George Champlin:*

"GENTLEMEN:—I saw in the Boston *Centinel*, a scheme of a lottery, for the laudable intention of rebuilding the Long Wharf in Newport, the building a hotel, and more especially establishing a free school, which has determined me to make a free gift of my estate on the point called Easton's Point, which came to me by way of mortgage, for a debt due from Hays and Pollock; if you will accept of it in trust to support a free school forever, for the advantage of the poor children of every denomination, and to be under the same regulations as you desired the free school should be that you design to erect. If you, gentlemen, will please to get a deed wrote agreeably to the intentions here manifested, I will sign and acknowledge the same, and send it to you for recording. I would only mention that if the situation is agreeable to you, the house and garden would do for a schoolmaster, and the oil house, which is large, might be fitted up for the school-house. This as you may think proper. There is no person here that understands writing such a deed, or I would have sent it to you completely executed.

"I am, gentlemen, with respect,

"Your very humble servant,

"SIMEON POTTER."

On receipt of this letter, it was at once

"*Voted and Resolved*, That G. Gibbs and G. Champlin be requested to present the thanks of the trustees to Simeon Potter, Esq., for his liberal donation, and

* Newport *Mercury*, May 31, 1796.

to assure him that it shall be inviolably appropriated to the establishment and support of public schools, he has so generously patronized.

"*Voted*, That Thomas Dennis and John L. Boss, be requested to take charge of the house, store and land, presented by Simeon Potter, to rent the same, and appropriate the rents to the repairs, in such manner as they may deem most advantageous."

On April 28, 1800, it was

"*Resolved*, That the use of the building presented by Simeon Potter, Esq , be tendered to the town for a school-house, on condition of the town repairing the same, and paying such rent as may be agreed upon, provided it is appropriated for a school, conformably to the act of the Assembly for establishing free schools, and that it be called the Public School."

This was in anticipation of the town's compliance with the law carried through by John Howland, but nothing seems to have come of the proposition. During the war of 1812 the trustees of the Long Wharf did not meet; but on August 19th, 1814, they had got into working order again, and " a committee was authorized to devise a plan for the commencement of a school, taking into consideration the present limited funds." This plan, reported August 25th, 1814, was as follows:—

"*August* 25.—The school committee reported a plan for the commencement of a school for poor children as follows : five trustees to be appointed a school committee to rent the Potter House to a suitable person to keep a school, for such a number of boys belonging to families in the town who are unable to educate them; that they be instructed in reading, writing and arithmetic, necessary for ordinary business and navigation; the committee to superintend and adopt a code of rules for the government thereof, to be rigidly observed. As many boys admitted as the funds will support.

"The committee report that they have visited the Potter House, and find a room fifteen by forty feet, with two fire-places, which, at small expense, can be converted into a good school-room, sufficiently large for fifty or sixty scholars, and the tenants, Joseph Finch and wife, who occupy the chambers keeping a school, who will undertake to instruct twenty or thirty children in reading, and find the necessary fire wood at $1.80 each, per quarter, a plan which the committee recommend to be adopted for the ensuing winter, preparatory to enlarging the plan at the annual meeting, should the funds then admit. Job Gibbs, a carpenter who occupies the first floor, and is largely in arrears for rent, can be employed for making the necessary repairs for the accommodation of the pupils, on enlarging the establishment under the direction of an instructor in the higher branches.

" J. L. Boss and four others were appointed a committee to carry the same into effect, and they are to have the sole charge of the Potter House, renting the same to the best advantage, to receive the rents either in tuition, labor, materials requisite for repairs, or money. The room for the school to be fitted up in such manner as they think proper. The committee to make up quarterly accounts of expenses, and receipts for the house, tuition, books, and stationery; are authorized to draw on the treasury for the balance, and to make a report of the same to the annual meeting, or any other meeting of trustees; to keep a record of the pupils admitted, time of admission and dismission, books and stationery furnished. They are also authorized to call a meeting of the trustees."

It appears from a later report that it was really "with Elizabeth Finch" that the contract was made, and that "on the 16th October, 1814, school commenced, consisting of twenty-five small boys, who, on examination by the school committee from time to time, and more particularly at the expiration of the second quarter, were found to have made much greater progress in their learning than was anticipated, and that Mrs. Finch, with the assistance of her husband, had done ample justice to the pupils." It would appear from this that it was really an old-fashioned "dame's school," the husband of the "dame" rendering incidental assistance. On April 10th, 1815, the school was increased to forty, nominally; but the actual number in 1820 was only about twenty;* and it was finally abandoned in 1832. The house which it had occupied was ordered to be sold, and the proceeds were deposited in the savings bank, where they remained until 1863, when they were appropriated, with other funds, in the hands of the Long Wharf trustees, to building what is now the Willow street public school-house.

As a companion picture to the school-boy reminiscences of Mr. Channing, it may be well to quote a reminiscence of the worthy Captain Finch, as given by Hon. W. C. Cozzens, in his public address on the dedication of the Willow street building:

"I well remember this school from 1820 to its close, and shall never forget the novel and most peculiar method adopted to give notice of school-time. The teacher, having been an old sea captain, was more accustomed to use his lungs than hand-bells, and as there was no bell belonging to the school, the teacher with great punctuality would go first to the west window on Washington street (second story), and call out at the top of his voice—and that voice was not weak or delicate—three times, 'Boys! Boys! Boys!' Then he would appear at another window on the east side of the house, and repeat the same call. 'Boys! Boys! Boys!' This being on the side of the cove, with buildings on all four sides, forming a hollow square at least a thousand feet across, over the water, it would at times produce a most prodigious noise, heard as far almost as a steam whistle in these days. I have often heard it, in my boyhood days, while sailing about the cove in a boat, echo in every direction, east, north, south and west. Sometimes the second and third call

---

* Barnard's Journal of R. I. Inst., III, 145.

would catch the echo of the first, and with the roguish boys in their boat joining in the general chorus, shouting at the top of their voices, ' Boys,' too. Thus on many a bright morning, with a calm, clear atmosphere, has there been a confusion of sounds over that, at times, crystal sheet of water, far surpassing the efforts of the most gifted ventriloquist. What effect these interferences of the boys, or the echoes, had upon the old schoolmaster's disposition and temper, I never heard." *

* Address at the dedication of the school-house erected by the trustees of Long Wharf, at Newport, R. I., p. 18.

V. REVIVAL OF PUBLIC SCHOOLS.

(1820 – 1828.)

THE second movement for a State system of public schools seems to have begun in a resolution passed by the General Assembly, early in 1820, " calling on the several towns for information on the subject of public schools."* The call could not have been very efficacious, for scarcely a town in the State had any information to give. Providence could honestly reply that she had five public school-houses and eight hundred and forty-six pupils under instruction. A committee of the town of Newport could only report as follows :

"Their duty obliges them reluctantly to state, that except about twenty children educated at the Newport Long Wharf Public School, the children of indigent persons in this town rely on individual bounty, or the limited provision made by benevolent institutions for the small portion of instruction they obtain : the consequence is that a large number are totally neglected, or perhaps through the medium of Sunday schools are taught to spell and read very indifferently. After stating these facts, the committee cannot but recommend that the town instruct their representatives in General Assembly to unite in their best endeavors to procure an act of the legislature for such general system of Public Schools as their wisdom may devise, and so framed as to secure to this town its fair proportion of the sum appropriated to the object." †

No immediate result followed, but at the Newport town-meeting a report was read, showing plainly that the original school fund of the town had been diverted from its proper use, and that the town was bound " in justice to itself" as well as to posterity, to provide for the support and

* Barnard's Journal of R. I. Institute of Instruction, III, 145.
† Barnard's Journal, III, 145.

maintenance of public schools for the education of all the children of the town at the public expense."* A vote to establish such schools had been passed at a previous meeting, but was reconsidered at a subsequent one; and it all ended in a vote to petition the General Assembly for authority to carry out the above plan. Permission was accordingly obtained to levy a local tax for the purpose, and to apply to the same end the proceeds of the school lands; and before proceeding farther the Newport committee called John Howland to the front again, and obtained from him a letter which gives us another vivid glimpse at the gradual progress of the only public schools, properly so called, in the State.†

"PROVIDENCE, September 20, 1824.
" To Richard K. Randolph and Dutee J. Pearce, Esqs.:

"GENTLEMEN:—Your communication dated 16th instant was duly received, and the intelligence it affords that the good people of my native town have set themselves seriously to work to establish public schools will render a compliance with your request the greatest pleasure.

"The preparatory measures establishing the system in this town resulted from the provisions of an act of the General Assembly, passed in 1800, for the encouragement of public schools throughout the State. This act placed the power of commencing and carrying the system into effect, principally in the several town councils; and although the act of the State was repealed in less than two years after it had passed, yet the town never withdrew the powers confided by the town to the town council in the first instance, in conformity to the State law, being satisfied they could devise no better method. Before the system was completed, the town, on the request of the town council, appointed a school committee (at first consisting of twelve) to attend with them in any consultation on measures to be adopted relative to the schools.

"The town was at first divided into four, at present into five school districts; two old school-houses were purchased of proprietors, and three new ones have been built, two of brick and one of stone. During the time the new houses were building and the old ones repairing, a sub-committee devised and reported the rules for the government of the schools, and designating the books to be used. The rules as first established are continued with little variation, but changes have been made in the books as new ones have appeared, better adapted.

"The appointment and removal of the masters and ushers, remain solely with the town council, though in the appointment of a master to fill a vacancy, (as there are generally several applicants,) the school committee are convened with the council, and the qualifications of the candidates discussed.

"Presuming these preliminary observations may come within the scope of your enquiries, I now proceed to answer as correctly as possible, the special interrogations.

"1st. Of how many pupils do the schools consist? The average number in the winter season is about nine hundred, in summer eight hundred; the school-houses are calculated to accommodate two hundred each.

* Barnard's Journal, III, 145.   † Barnard's Journal, III. 44.

"2d. Are there one or more masters to a school? One master and one usher to a school.

"3d. At what age are pupils admitted, or at what age discharged? The children are admitted at the age of six years, the time of continuance not limited. Before the establishment of the public schools the means of education were very limited, and on their being opened, the scholars were of all ages between six years and twenty, there are now but few over fourteen years, mostly from six to twelve. Although the age for admission as a general rule, is six years, yet the preceptors receive some under that age, when they belong to a family from which older children attend; but when the number in a school is two hundred or more, which has frequently been the case, then all under six are excluded.

"4th. Are females admitted? Females are admitted. The school-rooms have an aisle lengthwise through the middle, the boys occupy one side, the girls the other; the floors rise from the side of the broad alley to the walls, and there is a desk and a seat for every two scholars; the size of the room fifty feet by thirty.

"5th. Does the method of instruction differ from that practised in ordinary schools? The method of government and instruction differ materially from that practised in schools before, or at the time the public schools were established. The old pedagogue system of the cow-skin and the ferule is laid aside. The government partakes more of the paternal character; the boys have the appellation of masters and the girls of misses; emulation is excited by promotion to a higher class, and by public commendation by the preceptor, of particular instances of attention to order or improvement. The upper class of boys are supposed to be in the character of young gentlemen, and the misses are addressed as young ladies. After all, the application of the general system of government depends much on the peculiar qualifications and address of the preceptor; he is not addressed by the term master, that is exclusively applied to the boys. The number of males exceeds the number of females, probably about one-fifth through winter, but in the summer season they are nearly equal.

"6th. What are the branches taught? This may be answered generally, by an extract from the first regulation, viz.: 'The principal part of the instruction will consist in learning spelling, accenting, and reading, both prose and verse, with propriety and accuracy, and a general knowledge of English grammar, and composition; also writing a good hand, according to the most approved rules, and arithmetic,' &c.

"7th. What is the expense of each and all the free schools in Providence?

Five masters, $500 per year, each, - - - $2,500
Five ushers, at 250 dollars each, - - - 1,200
                                         $3,750

To this may be added necessary repairs of school-houses, stove pipes, etc., and a few books furnished occasionally to poor children by the town council.

"8th. What are the results of the system? As to the effect which the public schools have had on the state of society, the evidence must be circumstantial, as it is impossible to tell what would have been the case had they not been established; but the circumstances are so numerous and co-incident, that they appear to establish the fact beyond a doubt, that they have been highly beneficial. Many of our citizens who pay through the tax collector for their support, and who, having no children of their own to instruct, care but little about the education of others: but from their observation of the good effect of the schools in their own neighborhood, or in the town at large, are now among the most zealous for their support. You, gentlemen, were probably well acquainted with the late Marshal E. K. Dexter, Esq., and his testimony with you will be important. At the time the public schools were first established, Mr. Dexter and his father, who paid a large tax, were two of our strongest opposers. Their principal argument was, that it was wrong to compel those who had been at the expense of their own education, and now have no children of their own to be benefited, to pay for the schooling of other people's children; but before the death of the father, he was well satisfied with the result, and the Marshal, for ten or twelve years past, has been one of the firmest friends of the schools, and frequently declared that he owed the safety of his gardens and orchards to the public schools.

"There are now many among our most active and valuable citizens, merchants, mechanics, manufacturers, and masters of ships, who were poor boys, without other means of instruction, and who owe their present standing, and in some instances large property, entirely to the education and manners acquired in these public schools.

"Two schools, on the Lancasterian plan, are now in operation in this town, by individuals from abroad, without any support from the town. This is matter of experiment; they are well spoken of, and I think will be useful for children who have been altogether without instruction. In these they can commence the first rudiments, and be prepared to take their places in the other schools to more advantage. A committee appointed by the town at April meeting, made a report (highly favorable to the plan) in June. They were continued, and probably will, at a future meeting, recommend one school on the plan of Lancaster, for the support of the town.

"I have not at present a moment's time to review what I have written, or to add any further details or remarks. With the best and most ardent wishes that the gentlemen who have begun the good work in Newport, may persevere in the good cause to the great benefit and everlasting honor of the place of my birth, I remain,
"Your obedient servant,
"JOHN HOWLAND."*

During the year 1820, the Providence newspapers, echoed in some degree by the Newport *Mercury*, urged upon the community the importance of public education, and at the February session, 1821, the General Assembly appointed a committee " to prepare and report a bill establishing Free Schools." The Providence *American*, in October, urges action and says, " A decided majority of the people have already expressed their sentiments in favor of free schools." But if so, the majority exerted their influence but slowly; at the October session the committee explained that they were not yet ready to report. They had addressed circulars to the town clerks, and many had answered, but not all. As a

* Stone's Life of Howland, p. 151.

matter of fact, the report never came, and the impulse died away for a year or two.

It was helped to revive by the action of Newport, where a certain uneasiness of mind had always existed in regard to the school lands, so long diverted from their original purpose. Town meetings were held from September 14, 1824, onwards, many legal points were discussed, and full educational plans devised. It is a curious indication of these times that there seems to have been much the same hesitation about the necessity of common school education for girls that is now felt by many in regard to their collegiate education. In a report printed in the Newport *Mercury* of March 12, 1825, for instance, it is stated that "in the present situation of the town, your committee have thought it advisable that the education of males only should be provided for." This committee's estimate for the annual education of four hundred boys was $850, for eight hundred boys and girls $1,360; this being on the Lancasterian or monitorial plan, the elder pupils assisting in the instruction. On the ordinary plan the cost would rise to $1,768. The highest estimated cost for eight hundred pupils was thus about half the salary now paid to the High School Principal in Newport.

These plans were duly considered, and there were votes and reconsiderations, petitions to the legislature and counter-petitions. As usual, a lottery was thought of, and a bill was read once in the Assembly, allowing Newport to raise $10,000 for a school fund by that means. Finally, however, at the June session, 1825, the town of Newport was authorized by the legislature to raise a tax of $800 "for educating the white children of the town who are not otherwise provided with the means of education." This $800 was devoted for the first year to building a school house on Mill street, in which a public school for boys was opened May 9, 1827; a school on the Lancasterian plan, in which children who could afford it were expected to pay from twenty-five cents to a dollar per quarter, according to the instruction they received. This was followed by a school for girls opened June 16, 1828. All the present school system of Newport is the expansion of this modest provision.*

It was, to be sure, a local movement, but it was undertaken under permission from the State, and Governor Fenner had given it a sort of official recognition, by offering to the school fund of Newport the sum of $100 which it was usual for the governor in those days to contribute towards the rather jovial festivities of Election Day. In his letter, dated May

---

* Newport *Mercury*, Sept. 18, 1824; Feb. 26, March 12, May 21, June 11, 25, July 2, 9, Sept. 10, 1825; April 1, June 10, 1826; March 31, May 5, 12, June 7, 1827.

2, 1827, the Governor seems rather to apologize for this interference with a "good old custom," but the trustees of the school fund reassure him in their letter of acceptance ; and Lieutenant-Governor Collins, it seems, reinforced the donation by fifty dollars more.*

All this indicated or promoted an increase of sympathy for the public school system, and this finally took form in January, 1828. There was, indeed, one final effort to revert to the lottery system, on a large scale, for at the May session, in 1825, it appears, "An act for the establishment of lotteries, for the purpose of raising a fund for the support of free schools, by which, it is believed, from $3,000 to $5,000 may be raised annually, without risk or expense to the State, was received and referred to the next session."† But the next session had, apparently, the wisdom to suppress it.

In 1827, Mr. Joseph L. Tillinghast, of Providence, was the leader in urging free schools upon the Assembly. The subject was first introduced by memorials from Smithfield, Cumberland, Johnston, East Greenwich and other towns. The East Greenwich memorial, which is an excellent one, may be found in full in Barnard's Journal of the Rhode Island Institute of Instruction,‡ together with reports of the more important speeches. These reports are taken from a pamphlet entitled, "Debate on the Bill establishing Free Schools at the January session of the Rhode Island Legislature, A. D. 1828, reported for the Rhode Island American, by B. F. Hallett." The bill finally passed through both houses, by a vote of fifty-seven to two in the House, and unanimously, after a few amendments, in the Senate. The bill itself is as follows :

"SCHOOL ACT OF 1828.

"SECTION 1. *Be it enacted by the General Assembly, and by authority thereof it is enacted,* That from and after the passing of this act, all money that shall be paid into the general treasury, by managers of lotteries or their agents; also all money that shall be paid into said treasury by auctioneers, for duties accruing to the State, shall be set apart and paid over to the several towns in this State in manner hereinafter mentioned, in proportion to their respective population under the age of sixteen years, as exhibited in the census provided by law to be taken from time to time, under the authority of the United States, always adopting for said ratio the census next preceding the time of paying out each annual appropriation of said money as herein provided, to be by said towns appropriated to and for the exclusive purpose of keeping public schools, and paying expenses thereof; the sum, however, hereby appropriated to be paid over in any one year, not to exceed ten thousand dollars.

*Newport *Mercury*, May 5, 1827. † Newport *Mercury*, May 14, 1825. ‡ Vol. II. p. 41.

"Sec. 2. That each town shall be and is hereby empowered to raise so much money, by tax in each year, as a majority of the freemen in town-meeting shall judge proper to be appropriated to the purposes of public schools, not exceeding, in any one year, double the amount to be in that year received by such town out of the general treasury, by the provisions of this act; provided that notice be inserted in the warrant, issued for calling the town meeting at which such tax shall be laid, that such tax will be acted upon at such town meeting.

"Sec. 3. That at the annual town meetings, holden for the choice of town officers, each and every town in the State shall, after passing of this act, appoint a committee, which shall be called the school committee, and shall consist of not less than five, nor more than twenty-one persons, resident inhabitants of each of said towns, to act without compensation; which committee, after acceptance of their appointment, shall be duly engaged to the faithful performance of their trust; and shall appoint a secretary and treasurer from their number, and the secretary shall keep a record of their proceedings; and said committee, after being duly organized, shall meet as often as once in every three months, and oftener, if occasion require, for the transaction of all such business as may come before them, relative to the performance of their duties, and a majority shall be necessary for this purpose.

"Sec. 4. That the school committee of each town shall have power to make all necessary rules and regulations, which they may deem expedient, for the good government of the public schools in their respective towns; shall appoint all the school masters or school mistresses, to be employed in teaching the schools, taking care that such masters and mistresses are qualified for the task; shall have power to dismiss a school master or school mistress, in case of inability or mismanagement, shall determine upon the places where the school houses in the respective school districts in the town, shall be located; and it shall be the duty of said committee to visit all the schools in their respective towns as often as once in every three months during their continuance; and generally to superintend, watch over and provide for the good order and well governing of the same; and in case of death, resignation, or removal from the town, of any one of said committee, they shall have power to fill the vacancy so occasioned, until their annual election aforesaid; and, moreover, said committee, at any quarterly meeting thereof, for the better and more convenient performance of their duties, may pass such by-laws and regulations as they may deem expedient; provided such laws and regulations are not repugnant to the provisions of this act, nor in violation of any law in this State; and shall audit, and cause to be certified, all bills for the compensation of masters and mistresses, and all other expenses incurred in the support and maintenance of such schools, before the same shall be paid by the town treasurer; and shall also, at said annual town meeting, (and oftener, if required by their town,) render an account of all their proceedings for the preceding year.

"Sec. 5. That the general treasurer shall keep a separate account of all sums of money paid into the general treasury, by lottery managers or their agents, and by auctioneers for duties accruing to the State; and shall make a report thereof to the General Assembly once a year, to wit, at the May session, particularly setting forth the sums arising from each of said sources during the preceding year.

"Sec. 6. That the town council of each town shall, each year after the first distribution, certify to the general treasurer that the money received the previous year has been faithfully applied to the objects contemplated by this act· the certificate whereof shall be left with the general treasurer, before such town shall receive its proportion of the next distribution.

"Sec. 7. That the said sum of ten thousand dollars, annually to be paid over and distributed according to the provisions of this act, be payable to the order of the town treasurer of each town as aforesaid, on and after the first day of June in each year, commencing with the first day of June next.

"Sec. 8. That of the sum now in the treasury, there be appropriated and set apart the sum of five thousand dollars for the commencement and formation of a permanent fund, for the support of public schools; and for that purpose, the said sum of five thousand dollars shall be immediately, or as soon as may be, invested by the general treasurer, with advice of the governor, by purchase or subscription, in the stock of some safe and responsible bank; to which sum shall be added, and in like manner invested from year to year, all the money that shall accrue as aforesaid, from lotteries and auctioneers, over and above said yearly sum of ten thousand dollars, mentioned in the first section hereof; and all donations that may be made to said fund for the purposes thereof, and the dividends and interest that shall from time to time accrue on said fund, shall in like manner be added thereto and invested; but whenever in any year, the amount received as aforesaid, from lotteries and auctioneers, shall fall short of said sum of ten thousand dollars, annually to be distributed, the dividends and interest only of said fund then accrued, or so much thereof as may be necessary to supply such deficiency, shall be added to said last named sum, and paid over and distributed according to the provisions of this act.

"Sec. 9. That whenever, in any year, the money paid into the treasury, from the sources provided in this act, shall fall short of said sum of ten thousand dollars, the deficiency for said year shall be made good from any money in the treasury not otherwise appropriated."

This act is the foundation of the present school system of the State.

VI. THE CONDITION OF AFFAIRS ON THE INTRODUCTION OF THE PUBLIC SCHOOL SYSTEM.

(1828—1839.)

The school law of 1828 was an honest effort to do a very difficult thing, namely: to unite in one school system a city like Providence, which had long since established schools of its own, and various country towns to which the whole enterprise was a wholly new one. To the country towns, the law seemed to attempt too much; while the experienced friends of education in Providence thought it attempted too little. John Howland, always clear and graphic in his statements, wrote of it with some dissatisfaction, in a letter to Captain George Howland, of Newport:

"By the new State law, for the encouragement, or rather for the *discouragement* of schools, each town is to receive a small sum, annually, from the State treasury, and are allowed to assess a small sum, I don't recollect how much, in a town tax for the same purpose. This limitation, beyond which the towns are prohibited from assessing, was passed in the General Assembly by the influence of members who were opposed to the general instruction of the children throughout the State, and wished to confine it to paupers. But the town of Providence insisted on their right to assess as much as they pleased, or thought necessary for the support of their schools, and sufficient for the education of all the children in town, and this privilege was reserved to us in the State law, but it is allowed to no other town in the State. The rich men of Providence are and always have been in favor of all the children being educated at the town's expense, and if a representative of this town, in the General Assembly, should oppose this system, he would never be sent to the Assembly again. But it does not altogether depend on rich men in this town. The Mechanics' Association consists of three hundred members, most of whom are voters, and all in favor of the schools. The number of children at the last quarterly visitation in our public schools, was twelve hundred and seventy-seven." *

---

* Stone's Life of Howland, p. 156.

But inasmuch as the law endured and did its work, the main point of interest is now to ascertain in what condition it found the schools of Rhode Island. Here again we have from John Howland, in the same letter, some glimpses. He says of Providence:

"Twenty-eight or twenty-nine years ago, the town established public schools sufficient for the instruction of all the children, of both sexes. The school-houses were built, or purchased at the expense of the town, and the salaries of the instructors are paid out of the town treasury. The town is divided into five school districts, in each of which there is a school-house, with a master, or principal instructor, and an usher. The salary of each master is $500, and of the usher $250. About two years since, there was, in addition to the above, five primary or women's schools established, one in each district, for the small children to be taught the alphabet, and to be able to read and spell properly. The salary of the mistresses in each of these schools is a hundred and seventy-five dollars per year. In two of these primary schools, the teacher has an assistant, at a less salary. Agreeably to the report of the school committee, at the late June town meeting, the amount of all the salaries is - $4,596 46
Estimated contingent expenses for repairs of school-houses, stove pipes, premiums of rewards to children, etc., etc., - - $160 00

Total, - - - - - - - - $4,756 46*

We fortunately have also a full and careful exhibition of the condition as to schools of every town in the State, in the year 1828. It was prepared for the Rhode Island *American and Gazette* of January 16, 1828; and is preserved in Barnard's Journal of the Rhode Island Institute,† as follows:

RHODE ISLAND SCHOOLS IN 1828.

"Schools are now kept up in our country towns at a very considerable expense to the people; an expense much greater than would be required of them should they raise an equal amount with the sum they would be entitled to receive from the treasury, under the proposed act for establishing free schools. To show this, we refer to the following statements gathered from the representatives of the towns named, the general correctness of which may be relied on, though the statement is not as full as could be wished. In 1821, a committee, appointed on the state of education, collected from most of the towns the exact account of the number of school-houses, schools, etc., in each town. Their report was never made to the legislature, and the information is not to be found on file. In order to supply this defect, as far as possible, we have applied to the several representatives, and now give the result, with the exception of Providence, which is abundantly provided with schools.

"NEWPORT.—One free school with about two hundred scholars. Forty-two

---

* Stone's life of Howland, p. 155.   † Barnard's Journal, II. 38.

private schools, having about one thousand one hundred scholars. These schools are supported winter and summer. Inhabitants, 7,319.

"WEST GREENWICH. Two school-houses, built by subscription. Eleven schools are regularly kept about three months in the winter; three of which are continued nearly the year round. Inhabitants, 1,927.

"RICHMOND.—Two school-houses, in which schools are kept a part of each season; also a well attended Sunday school. Inhabitants, 1,423.

"HOPKINTON.—Nine school-houses, in three of which—in the vicinity of factories—schools are kept through the year, the others in winter. Inhabitants, 1,821.

"NORTH KINGSTOWN,—The Elam Academy, and one private school in Wickford. There is but one school-house in the town, near William Reynold's factory—in all six schools, three of which are kept winter and summer. Inhabitants, 3,007.

"EXETER.—Three school-houses, in which winter schools are kept—no other schools in the town. Inhabitants, 2,581.

"EAST GREENWICH.—Academy and one private school in the village, kept year round; four in other parts of the town— in all six school-houses. Seven schools are kept in the winter and three or four women's schools in the summer. Inhabitants, 1,519.

"JOHNSTON.—Five school-houses; six or seven schools are kept in the winter and two or three in the summer. Inhabitants, 1,542.

"CHARLESTOWN.—One school-house—from five to seven schools in the winter, and three in the summer. Inhabitants, 1,160.

"COVENTRY.—Ten school-houses, fourteen schools in winter, and seven in summer. Inhabitants, 3,139.

"PORTSMOUTH.—Four school-houses, in which schools are kept pretty regularly in winter, and in one or two in summer. Inhabitants, 1,645.

"FOSTER.—Fifteen school-houses—all open in the winter season, and most of them in summer. Inhabitants, 2,000.

"NORTH PROVIDENCE.—Seven school-houses—an academy, and four other schools in Pawtucket, two men's and three women's, kept most of the year; in all eleven schools in the town, most of them kept open but a part of the year. Inhabitants, 2,420.

"CRANSTON.—Is divided into eleven districts, and has eleven school-houses, though schools not regularly kept in all. There are five other schools—in all sixteen schools, but a small part kept through the year. Inhabitants, 2,274.

"MIDDLETOWN.—Five school-houses, in which are schools regularly in winter, and irregularly in summer. Inhabitants, 949.

"WARWICK.—Seven school-houses, in which are kept men's schools, besides two or three others; six women's schools in winter and summer—in all sixteen schools. Inhabitants, 3,643.

"SMITHFIELD.—Has thirteen school-houses. Two of these are well conducted academies, kept the year round, at Woonsocket and Slatersville, two flourishing manufacturing villages. There is also a private school at Woonsocket. Two school-houses on the east road, four on the Worcester road; one Sayles' hill; one in Angell's neighborhood; one Louisquisset turnpike, of brick, and one near R. Mowry. Besides schools regularly kept in these places, there are five others, in all nineteen schools. Inhabitants, 4,678.

"CUMBERLAND.—Is divided into districts and has thirteen school-houses, schools regularly kept and well attended in all. Inhabitants, 2,653.

"BURRILLVILLE.—Eleven school houses; schools in all in the winter, averaging forty scholars each; one kept the year round. There are four or five private schools in summer. Inhabitants, 2,164.

"SCITUATE.—Five school-houses. There are probably some other schools in the town, but a correct statement could not be obtained. Inhabitants, 2,834.

"GLOCESTER.—Eleven school-houses, and about fifteen schools in the winter. Inhabitants, 2,504.

"JAMESTOWN.—Three school-houses, schools kept in but two in winter. Inhabitants, 448.

"BARRINGTON.—Three school-houses; schools kept winter and summer. Inhabitants, 634.

"LITTLE COMPTON.—Eight school-houses open in winter, and most all in summer. Inhabitants, 1,580.

"WESTERLY.—Six school-houses open the year round; limited to thirty scholars each. There are two academies, one at Pawcatuck, a manufacturing village, kept the year round; in all eight schools. Inhabitants, 1,972.

"BRISTOL.—Four school-houses, one of which is an academy, with two schools in it. There are five men's schools in winter, and seven women's schools through the year. The town appropriates about $350 annually for support of schools, arising from the rent of market, licences, and some land given for that purpose. Inhabitants, 3,197.

"WARREN.—One academy and four school-houses; three built by the town and one by an individual. There are five men's schools in winter (including the academy), and an average of twelve female schools through the year; in addition to the above, sometimes as many as twenty female schools. Inhabitants, 1,806.

"NEW SHOREHAM.—One school-house. There are four schools, averaging thirty scholars each; kept four months in winter, and about six months in summer. Inhabitants, 955.

"SOUTH KINGSTOWN.—One academy, in which a school is kept the year round, and seven school-houses, in which schools are kept winter and summer. There are a number of schools kept irregularly in private houses. Inhabitants, 3,723.

"TIVERTON.—Ten school-houses, in which schools are kept pretty regularly. There are a few other small schools. Inhabitants, 2,875.

"PROVIDENCE.—There are eight public schools in this town, at which about nine hundred children are taught. Six or seven academies where the higher branches are taught, including the Friends' Seminary, and probably eighty or ninety private schools. In 1821, a regular return was made of all the schools in town. Exclusive of the public schools, there were then ten men's schools, and forty-four kept by females. Since then this number has greatly increased. The expense of the public schools paid by tax on the inhabitants, is not much short of $5,000. The amount paid by parents for private tuition is doubtless double that sum, making at the lowest estimate $15,000, annually paid for the tuition of the children of Providence. It is obvious, therefore, that in a pecuniary point of view, Providence will gain nothing by the system of free schools becoming general, as she would pay much more into the treasury towards the support of schools in other towns than she would be entitled to draw out, besides making up the deficiency in the support of her own schools. Inhabitants in 1820, 11,767; since increased to upwards of 17,000.

"Population of the counties in 1820,—Providence, 35,736; Newport, 15,771; Washington, 15,687; Kent, 10,228; Bristol, 5,637.

"Supposed number of children to be educated, viz.: Providence county, 15,815; Newport, 6,527; Washington, 7,093; Kent, 4,547; Bristol, 2,361. In the State, 35,843 children.

"From an examination of the above statement, it will be seen that there is a much larger number of school-houses erected than has been generally supposed, and but few additional ones will be required. It is obvious, too, that the expense to all the towns of keeping up the schools they now maintain, is a much greater sum than they will be required to assess in order to entitle them to their proportion of any money that may be appropriated out of the treasury, thus giving them at a less expense than the inhabitants of those towns now voluntarily incur, nearly double the advantages of education they are now receiving.

"The total number of school-houses erected in all the towns in the State (excluding Providence and Newport), are 181, and ten academies. The number of winter schools, averaging at least three months in a year, maintained by the inhabitants of these towns is 262. A winter school for three months must cost at least $100, which gives $26,200, the sum now annually paid by the inhabitants of the towns above alluded to, for the education of their children, besides the expense of keeping female schools in summer. If the blank in the bill now before the General Assembly is filled with $10,000, the proportion which those towns will receive from that sum will so much diminish their expense of education; or if they add it to what they now pay within themselves, will greatly extend the means of instruction among their children, without one cent additional burden, the only effect being to equalize the payment of the sums now voluntarily raised in the several towns.

"Taking the estimate for the criterion of apportionment, the several towns would be entitled to receive the following sums out of an annual allowance from the treasury of $10,000, viz.: Newport, $609.40; Portsmouth, $245.08; New Shoreham. $37.32; Jamestown. $107.22; Middletown, $137.86; Tiverton, $175.36; Little Compton, $153.18; Providence, $2,910.54; Smithfield, $551.46; Scituate, $291.04; Glocester, $208.32; Cumberland, $266 48; Cranston, $306.38; Johnston, $196.08; North Providence, $382.96; Foster, $193; Burrillville, $199.80; Westerly, $143.98; North Kingstown, $266.54; South Kingstown. $336.71; Charlestown, $107.22; Exeter, $183.86; Richmond. $91.90; Hopkinton, $143.98; Bristol, $459.49; Warren, $189.94; Barrington, $58.60; Warwick, $398 28; East Greenwich, $140.74; West Greenwich, $190 74; Coventry, $175.22."

Such was the condition of the Rhode Island schools when the school law went into operation. These schools had been heretofore detached and isolated, dependent wholly on the degree of enlightenment or energy which prevailed in a particular town. Henceforward they were to be a part of a State system, such as it was, and were to be brought under the general influence which revived all the schools of New England from 1826 to 1830.

Some modifications of the school law took place during the next fifteen years; the most important being the temporary adoption of a rule by which the school-money was distributed—not, as at first, according to the number of inhabitants below the age of sixteen, but according to the number of the white population under the age of fifteen years, and the number of the colored population under the age of ten years, together with five-fourteenths of the said population between the ages of ten and twenty-four years. This complicated method remained in force from 1832 to 1845. There were also some additional provisions as to the sources of the school fund and as to the forms of school returns, besides various local enactments as to school-houses and school districts. In 1837-8 the schools of Providence underwent a great revolution for the better; and in 1839 the school laws of the State were codified as follows:

School Law of 1839.

"An act to revise and amend the several Acts relating to Public Schools.

Be it enacted by the General Assembly as follows:—

"Section 1. The annual income of the money deposited or that may be deposited with this State by the United States in pursuance of 'an act to regulate the deposit of the public money,' passed by the Congress of the United States, and approved June 23, 1836, shall annually be paid over to the several towns in this State; to be appropriated for the purpose of maintaining public schools, in manner hereinafter provided.

"Sec. 2. To the money derived from said source, shall annually be added enough from any money in the general treasury not otherwise specially appropriated, to make up the sum of twenty-five thousand dollars, to be annually paid out for the purpose aforesaid. The money received by the State from the managers of lotteries or their agents, or from auctioneers for auction duties accruing to the State, shall be hereafter annually appropriated, to pay the debt now due from the general treasury to the permanent school fund, until said debt is paid; after which time the revenue derived from those sources shall be applied to the increase of said fund. The money paid out by virtue of this act, shall be divided among the several towns in proportion to the respective white population of each town under the age of fifteen years; the colored population of such town under the age of ten years, and five-fourteenths of the colored population between the ages of ten and twenty-four years; computing the same according to the United States census next preceding such annual payments, and excepting Narragansett Indians in all cases.

"SEC. 3. Each town may raise by tax every year so much money as a majority of the freemen may deem proper, to be appropriated to the purpose of keeping public schools, not exceeding in any one year double the amount received by such town from the general treasury: provided that notice be inserted in the warrant issued for calling the town meeting, that such business will then be acted upon.

"SEC. 4. The money received by each town from the general treasury, shall be applied to pay for instruction, and not for room rent, fuel or any other purpose whatever.

"SEC. 5. The general treasurer shall keep a separate account of all moneys paid to the State by lottery managers, or their agents, or auctioneers as aforesaid, and shall report the same to the General Assembly annually, at the May session thereof: particularizing the sums received from each of said sources.

"SEC. 6. The school committee of each town shall every year certify to the general treasurer, that the money received the previous year has been faithfully applied according to this act. No town shall receive its proportion of the next distribution until such certificate be made.

"SEC. 7. The money payable by virtue of this act, shall be paid to the order of the town treasurers of the several towns which shall comply with the terms of this act, on or after the first day of June in every year; and the said town treasurers shall apply for and receive said money from the general treasurer, as soon after it is payable, as it may be required for school purposes in their respective towns: and shall charge and receive no compensation for their services in collecting the same.

"SEC. 8. Each town shall, at its annual town meeting for the choice of town officers, appoint a school committee, to consist of not less than five, nor more than thirty persons resident in such town, to act without compensation; and to be engaged to the faithful discharge of their duties before entering upon the same.

"SEC. 9. The school committees shall appoint a president or chairman and secretary from their number, and shall keep a record of all their proceedings: they shall meet at least as often as once in every three months, and a majority of the whole number chosen shall constitute a quorum; but any less number may adjourn a meeting, giving reasonable notice of the time and place of the adjourned meeting.

"SEC. 10. The school committee of each town may direct the books to be used, and make all necessary rules and regulations for the good government of the public schools therein; they may suspend or expel any scholar for misconduct; they shall determine the places where the school-houses shall be located, or the school kept, in the different districts, having regard to the accommodation of the greatest number of inhabitants; and for satisfactory reasons may alter the location of any school-house; and in case of the death, resignation, or removal of a member of the committee, they may fill the vacancy for the remainder of the year: - and at any regular meeting they may make, alter and repeal such by-laws and regulations for the delegating or more conveniently discharging any or all of the duties assigned to them as they shall deem proper: *Provided*, they are not repugnant to the provisions of this act, nor in violation of any law in this State.

"SEC. 11. The school committee shall appoint all instructors and instructresses, taking care that they be of good moral character, temperate and otherwise well qualified for the office; and may dismiss said instructors or instructresses in case of inability, or misconduct; said committee shall visit all the schools in their respective towns, at least as often as once in three months during their continuance, and shall generally superintend, watch over and provide for the well ordering and governing the same.

"SEC. 12. The school committee shall allow and certify all bills for compensation for instruction and all other expenses before the same shall be paid by the town treasurer; they shall also at the annual town meeting for choosing town officers, (and oftener if required) render an account of all their doings for the preceding year.

"SEC. 13. All divisions of any town into school districts, and all alterations of such divisions, whether made by a town or school committee, shall be recorded in the town clerk's office of such town.

"SEC. 14. The school committee of every town shall hold quarterly meetings on the second Mondays of January, April, July and October in every year.

"SEC. 15. There shall but one school be kept in any school district, unless the school committee shall otherwise order.

"SEC. 16. The school committee of any town, with the assent of the school committee of an adjacent town, may permit such children as will be better accommodated thereby, to attend the school in such adjacent town, and may pay such portion of the expense thereof, as considering the number of children and other circumstances, may be just and proper.

"SEC. 17. The money which each town shall receive by virtue of this act, shall be expended among the different schools and school districts, in such proportions as the school committee shall deem most advisable.

"SEC. 18. The freemen of any town may, at any legal town meeting, divide their town into suitable school districts, and may from time to time alter the number and limits thereof. All divisions heretofore made by any town or school committee, shall remain in force until legally changed.

"SEC. 19. Every school district shall be a body corporate, by such name or designation as the school committee shall select, so far as to prosecute and defend in all actions relating to the property or affairs of the district, and to take and hold such real estate as may be given to or purchased by them for the purpose of supporting schools in the district.

"SEC. 20. The school committee of the several towns and of the city of Providence, shall on or before the first Wednesday of May, annually, make official returns to the secretary of state, of all the public schools in such towns and the city respectively, for the year preceding the date of the returns; the amount of school money received from the general treasury; the amount of money raised by the town or city for supporting public schools; the number of districts; the number of schools in each district; the amount of money expended in each school, designating the portion paid for furniture, fuel and incidental expenses, and the portion paid for instruction only; the number of children, male and female, attending each school, and their average attendance; the time and season of keeping each school; the number, names and salary of instructors; the branches taught and books used. They shall also the next and subsequent years, report the number of academies and private schools in their respective towns; the length of time and season of the year they are kept; the names of the instructors; prices of tuition; and the average number of scholars attending each of them: *Provided, however,* that the returns aforesaid to be made by the school committee on or before the first Wednesday in May next, shall be conformable to the blank returns already furnished the several towns under the act of June last.

"Sec. 21. The secretary shall annually furnish every town and the city of Providence, with the blank forms of the returns required by the last section, which forms shall contain a copy of this and said last section; and the secretary shall annually at the session of the General Assembly first holden after the annual session in May, report an abstract of said returns. No town or city shall be entitled to any part of the money appropriated to be paid out of the general treasury, to the support of public schools, which shall have failed to make such returns for the year next preceding the time of the appropriation; and the names of all such delinquent towns or city shall be by the secretary returned to the general treasurer, on or before the first Monday in June annually.

"Sec. 22. There shall annually be paid out of the general treasury to the town treasurer of the town of Charlestown, the sum of one hundred dollars, to be expended under the direction of some suitable person to be annually appointed by the governor, in the support of a school for the use of the members of the Narragansett tribe of Indians and the incidental expenses thereof, and in purchasing school books for the use of said school: and an annual account of the appropriation of all said money shall be rendered to the general treasurer, on or before the first Wednesday of May.

"Sec. 23. Two or more contiguous districts in adjoining towns, the majority of the taxable inhabitants of each district, at a duly notified meeting agreeing thereto, may unite together for the purpose of keeping one school, if they may deem it more advantageous to do so; and in such cases the committee men of the districts so uniting, may examine and appoint the instructor.

"Sec. 24. Whenever any persons to the number of five or more, have associated or shall hereafter associate together for the purpose of building and maintaining a school-house, they shall be entitled to all the privileges of a body corporate, by such name and style as they may select, and upon such terms and subject to such regulations as they may have adopted upon the formation of their association; and may hold, control and convey, by their corporate name, the school-house so erected, and the lot of land upon which it may stand; and the shares or ownership therein, may be transferred in the same manner as personal estate.

"Sec. 25. Whenever any persons to the number of five or more, have associated or shall hereafter associate together, for the purpose of procuring and maintaining a library, they shall be entitled to all the privileges of a body corporate, by such name as they may designate, and upon such terms and subject to such constitution and rules as they may have adopted upon the formation of their association; and may hold, control and convey by their corporate name, real and personal, to an amount not exceeding two thousand dollars, exclusive of their books, maps and library furniture. *Provided*, that in all such cases, the constitution or articles of association, and all alterations thereof, shall be recorded in the town clerk's office in the town where such library shall be established.

"SEC. 26. All general acts heretofore passed relating to public schools, excepting so much of the eighth section of 'an act to establish public schools,' passed January session, A. D. 1828, which relates to the permanent school fund, as is not inconsistent with this act, are hereby repealed. *Provided*, that every thing done under said acts shall be valid, and all things omitted or neglected to be done, shall be punished by the same penalties and forfeitures as if this act had not been passed.

"SEC. 27. The secretary shall immediately cause to be printed a sufficient number of copies of this act and of all laws and acts in force relating to public schools, or the building of school-houses in the several towns, and shall send a suitable number to the town clerk of each town, for the purpose of distribution."

VII. FIRST RESULTS.

(1839 – 1843.)

WE have accurate means of knowing, by statistics, the results produced, within a few years, by the school law. The first report, prepared by any officer or committee, so far as I know, giving any precise school statistics for the State, was presented to the public, May 17, 1832, and published in a pamphlet form. It was prepared by Oliver Angell, a veteran Rhode Island teacher, in behalf of a committee appointed at a public meeting held in the Providence Town House, during the previous year. The report recognizes progress already made, mentions a great deficiency of school-houses, and a great want of some medium of intercourse between persons interested in education in the different towns. It closes as follows:

"Upon a review of the subject, your committee find much cause for congratulation in the increase and increasing means of education in the State. There is not a town in which *all* the children may not have the means of acquiring a common school education, and when we consider the nature of our institutions and how much their preservation depends on the general spread of information and on the correct morals of our youth, we have much cause to rejoice at the present favorable prospects, and we look forward to the period when Rhode Island shall be as celebrated for the facilities afforded to education, as she now is for her industry and manufactures." *

The most important part of the report, however, is to be found in the following table, for the year 1832:

* Barnard's Journal of R. I. School Inst., II. 49.

First Results.

TOWNS.	Public Schools.	Number Scholars.	MaleTeachers employed. Months.	Female Teachers employed. Months.	Appropriated by the Town.	Private Schools.	Number Scholars.	Male Teachers. Months.	Female Teachers. Months.
Providence.....	11	1,150	6s 12	5s 12	$5,000	56	1,682	14s 12	42s 12
N. Providence..	8	400	3	3	574	10	300	12	12
Smithfield.....	24	2,049	3	3	600				
Cumberland....	17	1,200	2	2	500	17	1,000	2	2
Burrillville.....	16	800	2½	4	300	16	500		2
Glocester	17	510	3	4	550	17	400		4
Scituate........	16	680	3½		300	20	550		4
Foster..........	19	1,197	3	3					
Johnston.......	11	400	3	3	366				
Cranston.......	11	550	3½		500				
Bristol.........	3	275	4 & 12	6	500	11	240	12	12
Warren.........	4	230	3 & 12	3 & 12	350	9	200	1 for 12	8 for 3 m
Barrington.....	3	113	3	3					
Warwick.......	13	1,040	4		500				
Coventry.......	18	900	4		300				
East Greenwich	5	250	3		100	3	80	1 for 12	12
West Greenwich	11	300	3			5	100		3
Newport........	2	400	12	12	800	32	900	12	12
Tiverton........	12	600	2	2		20	400	1	2
Portsmouth.....	8	360	2			3	60		2
Little Compton.	7	245	1			7	175	2	4
New Shoreham.	3	100	2						
Middletown....	5	210	4			3	155	3	3
Jamestown.....	2	100	3						
No. Kingstown.	12	550	2¾	3		8	250		4
So. Kingstown.	12	360	2			4	200	12	
Exeter.........	13	390	2¾						
Westerly.......	11	400	3½		150	8	250		4
Hopkinton.....	12	350	3½		100	9	225		4
Richmond	9	225	3			5	100		3
Charlestown....	8	500	3			4	80		3
Total	323	17,034	Teachers 318	Teachers 147	$11,490	269	7,847	Teachers 83	Teachers 186

Whole number of public schools in the State, - - - 323
Whole number of scholars taught in them, - - - 17,034
Number of male teachers employed, - - - - 318
Number of female teachers employed, - - - 147
Number of schools continued through the year, - - 20
Average time of the others, - - - - - 3 months.
Whole amount appropriated by the towns for the support of schools, $11,490
Amount drawn from school fund, - - - - $10,000
Whole amount expended for support of public schools, - - $21,490
Number of private schools continued through the year,* { Male teachers, 30
{ Female " 88

*In nearly all the country towns, the private schools may be considered as the public schools continued by individual subscription, from three to six months.

Whole number of scholars taught in them, (exclusive of the Friends'
  Boarding School, Providence,*) - - - - 3,403
Estimated expense of the private schools which continue through
  the year, at twenty dollars per scholar, - - - $68,040
Estimated expense of other private schools, at three dollars per scholar, $13,335
Total estimated expense of private schools, - - - $81,375
Sum total expended for support of schools for one year, - $102,865

The first abstract of school returns was presented in 1839 and gives ground for comparison with the table just cited. Other tables are added, which show the gradual progress down to 1844.

ABSTRACT OF RETURNS OF PUBLIC SCHOOLS, MAY, 1839.

TOWNS.	Proportion of $25,000 which each town will receive, June, 1839.	Amount raised by Towns.	No. Districts.	No. of Schools.	No. Instructors.	Expended fuel, furniture, rent, repairs &c.	Expended for Instruction.	No. of Scholars. Agg.	No. of Scholars. Aver.
Newport	1,739 52	800 00	1	2	2	295 20	1,025 00	265	215
Providence	3,818 20	7,000 00	5	15	34	535 51	8,426 90	1,753	1,753
Portsmouth	440 53	....	8	8	8	....	487 69	245	225
Westerly	499 45	....	11	12	12	....	598 68	473	385
Warwick	1,454 50	400 00	14	14	12	178 67	1,082 42	746	746
N. Shoreham	359 00	84 00	4	4	4	21 00	394 43	190	200
N. Kingstown	827 62	....	14	16	16	124 17	792 05	479	421
S. Kingstown	1,042 75	....	18	18	18	94 67	1,059 71	645	645
E. Greenwich	389 15	....	5	5	5	44 50	386 30	209	189
Jamestown	80 15	....	1	3	3	14 00	159 00	53	53
Smithfield	1,738 85	1,000 00	25	30	30	....	2,511 56	1,206	960
Scituate	1,048 92	300 00	16	16	16	....	1,472 00	734	577
Glocester	690 60	627 34	18	16	20	87 54	858 95	384	384
Charlestown	359 00	....	8	8	8	....	379 85	246	246
W. Greenwich	530 28	....	12	15	16	15 00	572 00	253	227
Coventry	1,059 20	....	19	19	19	....	1,172 30	470	470
Exeter	685 80	....	13	13	13	28 40	479 65	284	284
Middletown	252 80	....	1	5	5	50 00	490 88	200	200
Bristol	790 62	....	3	5	10	297 52	1,367 50	320	320
Tiverton	787 90	....	15	17	21	135 12	637 11	349	310
L. Compton	359 00	....	7	7	13	7 43	390 00	530	227
Warren	403 52	360 00	3	3	3	127 87	445 09	132	109
Cumberland	970 83	500 00	19	19	22	....	1,594 42	412	432
Richmond	413 80	....	12	10	10	....	458 00	219	182
Cranston	680 33	500 00	9	13	13	501 03	606 82	407	407
Hopkinton	481 65	....	12	12	12	....	689 26	478	337
Johnston	604 95	350 00	11	12	15	113 47	718 47	333	333
N. Providence	864 62	260 00	8	10	13	124 08	1,091 30	463	388
Barrington	160 31	93 75	3	3	3	100 70	170 10	194	143
Foster	821 45	....	19	19	19	....	938 22	619	431
Burrillville	644 70	300 00	16	16	32	75 62	927 70	446	447
	25,000 00	12,575 09	330	365	427	2,971 50	32,383 36	13,748	12,246

*This flourishing institution contains, on an average, 160 scholars.

First Results.

Abstract of the Returns of Public Schools, made May, 1844.

TOWNS.	Received from State.	Received from Town.	No. District.	No. Schools.	Instructors. Males.	Instructors. Females.	Expended for Fuel, Rent.	Expended for Instruction.	No. of Scholars. Agg.	No. of Scholars. Aver.
Newport.......	176659	1600	2	11	5	8	600	3095	690	600
Providence.....	505742	1648920	6	26	11	49	257162	18975	4118	3159
Portsmouth....	37442	......	8	8	6	4	120	1020	282	192
Westerly.......	45395	8654	11	14	12	2	......	53852	531	344
Warwick.......	155636	500 00	15	22	18	9	31583	191891	1491	1087
N. Shoreham...	29982	......	5	9	8	......	150	29982	232	171
N. Kingstown..	66681	26287	15	20	19	2	......	92938	514	400
S. Kingstown..	96432	378	21	21	21	......	......	113835	822	521
E. Greenwich..	33044	75	5	5	5	......	1202	39416	283	200
Jamestown.....	6633	1632	1	5	7	2	......	156	94	72
Smithfield.....	217523	137093	35	38	20	10	50	3496	2790	1200
Scituate.......	96310	51658	17	18	13	5	......	147968	880	570
Glocester......	55118	400	19	17	13	14	1731	109196	483	332
Charlestown ..	25094	......	8	8	7	1	......	26504	218	140
W. Greenwich..	33635	......	12	12	10	2	......	......	232	148
Coventry......	81781	18608	18	18	17	1	912	98142	716	427
Exeter	44673	5007	13	13	12	1	......	49680	374	225
Middletown....	19839	41	2	5	4	1	35	23939	93	93
Bristol	81857	1000	3	6	4	3	200 09	153425	444	352
Tiverton	80443	63937	16	19	14	5	......	109577	698	434
Little Compton.	32321	4129	9	9	9	9	......	36450	285	200
Warren........	45789	39675	3	4	3	4	12522	78625	263	134
Cumberland....	116809	98356	20	20	15	14	20080	202575	1090	774
Richmond......	34076	6156	13	12	12	......	......	32532	49732	218	200
Cranston	68126	744	9	12	12	......	24887	81080	407	332
Hopkinton.....	42242	......	12	12	12	......	......	38960	407	251
Johnston	58995	400	14	14	13	3	13030	85965	592	428
N. Providence..	98282	115921	9	13	5	8	24730	1750	1752	750
Barrington	12656	100	3	3	3	3	3562	236	128	102
Foster.........	62453	......	19	18	18	3	......	62453	495	304
Burrillville.....	46906	42050	16	16	18	10	1117	89591	503	386
Total	2509574	279183	359	428	342	173	540547	4833576	22156	14528

Yet in spite of all the progress shown by these tables, Rhode Island was far from keeping pace with the progress made elsewhere. It must be remembered that it was just at this time—from 1837 to 1848—that Horace Mann was revolutionizing the common schools of Massachusetts, and through them, stimulating those of all the eastern States. Accordingly there seems to have been a latent demand for some more vigorous organization in Rhode Island, and this found expression at last, in a bill introduced into the Assembly by Wilkins Updike, Esq., of South

Kingstown, in Oct., 1843. Introducing this bill, Mr. Updike made the bold statement that

"The free school system as it then existed, was not a blessing to the State, except in the city of Providence, and possibly in a few other towns, where a similar course was pursued. This was not owing to the want of liberal appropriation from the general treasury. This was large enough, or at least, was larger than was made by any other State to the several towns. But the difficulty lay with the towns, and with the want of any thorough system for the examination of teachers, the regulation of books, and supervision of schools, by officers qualified to discharge these duties. Our teachers come from abroad, are employed without producing evidence either of moral character, or their fitness to teach, remain in the schools two or three months, and within twenty-four hours of the close of the term are gone to parts unknown. The books for our schools are selected by authors and publishers, or itinerant venders, and all that parents have to do about the matter is to get new books every year, and pay the bills. As to visiting the schools, who ever heard of committees going about into the different districts, or of parents being seen in the school-room? These things should be looked into. The legislature should know what becomes of the sum of $25,000, which is drawn annually from the general treasury. The people should have their attention called to the actual state of education among us. Our self-respect should be roused by a knowledge of the fact brought out by the last census of the United States, from which it appears that Rhode Island is behind the other New England States in this matter. With a population of 108,830, we have over 1,600 adults who cannot read or write, while Connecticut with a population of 309,978, has only 526. The other New England States not only educate their own teachers, lawyers, doctors and clergymen, but help to supply our demand for these classes of men. It is time to bestir ourselves in this matter. We need not act with precipitation. All that this bill provides for, is information as to the real state of things, and upon such information the legislature and the people can act understandingly. Pass this bill—sustain the agent who may be appointed—act upon his recommendations when they are sustained by facts and sound arguments—engraft upon our system the tried improvements of other States—enlist the people, the whole people, in this great work of elevating the schools where all the children of the State may be well educated, and this little bill of three sections will be the beginning of a new era in our legislation on the subject of education."*

The bill introduced by Mr. Updike—which passed unanimously—was as follows:

"An Act to provide for ascertaining the condition of the Public Schools in this State, and for the improvement and better management thereof.

"Be it enacted by the General Assembly as follows:

"Section 1. The Governor of this State shall employ some suitable person

---

* Barnard's Report for 1845, p. 109.

as agent, for the purposes hereaftermentioned, at a reasonable compensation for his services.

"SEC. 2. The said agent shall visit and examine the respective public schools in this State; ascertain the length of time each district school is kept, and at what season of the year; the qualifications of the respective teachers of said schools—the mode of instruction therein—collect information of the actual condition and efficiency of our public schools and other means of popular education; and diffuse as widely as possible among the people, a knowledge of the most approved and successful methods of arranging the studies and conducting the education of the young, to the end that the children of this State who depend upon common schools for instruction, may have the best education that those schools may be made to impart; and shall make a report to the legislature, with such observations and reflections as experience may suggest, upon the condition and efficiency of our system of popular education, and the most practicable means of improving the same.

"SEC. 3. It shall be the duty of the preceptors of the public schools in the respective districts in this State, from time to time, to furnish said agent with all the information he may require, in order to enable him to carry out the provisions of this act.

"Passed October Session, 1843.

"HENRY BOWEN, *Secretary.*"

This act was promptly promulgated by the Governor of the State, with the following circular:

"TO THE PEOPLE OF RHODE ISLAND.

"In pursuance of An Act 'to provide for ascertaining the condition of the public schools of this State, and for the improvement and better management thereof,' I have secured the services of Henry Barnard, who has had several years experience in the discharge of similar duties in a neighboring State, and has observed the working of various systems of public instruction in this country and in Europe.

Mr. Barnard will enter immediately on the duties of his office. His great object will be to collect and disseminate in every practicable way information respecting existing defects and desirable improvements in the organization and administration of our school system, and to awaken, enlighten, and elevate public sentiment, in relation to the whole subject of popular education. With this view, he will visit all parts of the State, and ascertain, by personal inspection, and inquiries of teachers, school committees, and others, the actual condition of the schools, with their various and deeply interesting statistical details. He will meet, in every town, if practicable, such persons as are disposed to assemble together, for the purpose of stating facts, views and opinions, on the condition and improvement of the schools, and the more complete and thorough education of the people. He will invite oral and written communications from teachers, school committees, and all others interested in the subject, respecting their plans and suggestions for advancing the intellectual and moral improvement of the rising, and all future generations, in the State. The results of his labors and inquiries will be communicated in a report to the General Assembly.

"In the prosecution of labors so delicate, difficult and extensive, Mr. Barnard will need the sympathy and coöperation of every citizen of the State. With the most cordial approval of the object of the legislature, and entire confidence in the ability, experience and zeal of the gentleman whom I have selected to carry it out, I commend both to the encouragement and aid of all who love the State, and would promote her true and durable good, however discordant their opinions may be on other subjects.

"JAMES FENNER.

"PROVIDENCE, December 6, 1843."

The appointment thus announced was the most important step yet taken in the school history of Rhode Island. So great was the confidence felt in Mr. Barnard, that the school legislation of the State was virtually placed in his hands—a few temporary acts concerning schoolhouses being excepted—and he was instructed by the General Assembly to prepare and present the draft of a school law which should cover the whole ground of existing statutes.

VIII. HENRY BARNARD'S SCHOOL LAW.

(1843 - 1845.)

At the session of the Assembly in May, 1844, the new school agent made his report of a school law, which was considered and printed. At the June session it was passed by the House, and the Senate ordered it to be printed—together with the remarks of the agent, explaining each section—and voted that it should be circulated among the school committees of the several towns. The year after, 1845, it was again considered by the Senate, carefully revised by a committee and passed by a large majority. It was also passed by the House, but with the condition that the law should not go into operation until after the rising of the General Assembly in October, in order that its provisions should be thoroughly understood.

The chief advocate of the bill in the Assembly, during the debate, appears to have been Mr. Updike, whose pictures of the need of education were very vivid. In the course of his remarks, he said:

"There is a wide-spread dissatisfaction with the schools as they are; with the inefficient manner in which the system is administered; with the shortness of time for which the schools are kept,—although they are quite long enough, unless they can be kept by better teachers; with the amount of money which is now appropriated by the State without calling forth any corresponding efforts and appropriations from the towns and districts; with the want of any suitable regulation as to books and studies; with the defective methods of instruction, and the harsh, unnecessarily harsh, discipline pursued by many of the schools; in fine, with the entire organization and administration of the system, as far, at least, as the great mass of the towns are concerned. True, there are good schools in Providence, Bristol, Warren and Newport, and in some of the eastern towns of Providence county, but the returns to the secretary of state, and the report of your school commissioner, will show that the public schools are not kept in the country districts, on an average, three months in the year; that there are a great variety of text-books in every school, and that this variety is made greater every year through the activity of book agents, authors and publishers. * * Let us have a law by which the enormous evil and expense, arising out of a constant change of school books shall be remedied; and all new school-houses erected after judicious plans and directions. Let us have a law by which the public interest shall be kept alive and vigilant, to look after the expenditures of the public money, and see that the results correspond with the outlay. Let us have an officer whose intelligence, experience, and constant oversight, shall give efficiency and uniformity to the administration of the system—who shall go round among the schools, hold meetings of teachers, parents, and the friends of education, break up the apathy which prevails in some parts of the State, enlighten the ignorant, and direct the efforts of all to one great and glorious end, the training of all the children, the rich and the poor, in all sound knowledge and worthy practice. Let us have a State pride on the subject.

"Let us aim to be, what I am sure we can become from our compact population, and the comparative wealth of all our people, the educated and educating State of this Union. Instead of being set down in the census of the United States as the seventh State in the scale of ignorance and neglect of public education—instead of having one in forty of our population who cannot read and write—instead of giving occasion for geographers and travellers to say, that Rhode Island is behind every other New England State in the means and results of common school education—instead of all this, let us make an immediate and vigorous effort to reverse the picture. Let us stand at the head of the list, for a wisely organized and efficiently administered system of public instruction."† * *

The act finally passed was as follows:

"AN ACT RELATING TO PUBLIC SCHOOLS.

"Passed June 27, 1845.

"It is enacted by the General Assembly as follows:

"I. STATE APPROPRIATION AND SUPERVISION. Sections I.—III.

"SECTION I. For the uniform and efficient administration of this act, and the supervision and improvement of such schools as may be supported in any manner out of appropriations from the general treasury, the governor shall appoint an officer, to be called the commissioner of public schools, who shall hold his office one year, and until his successor shall be appointed, with such compensation for his services, and allowance for his expenses, as the General Assembly shall determine.

"SEC. II. For the encouragement and maintenance of public schools in the several towns and cities of the State in the manner hereinafter prescribed, the sum of twenty-five thousand dollars is hereby annually appropriated, payable out of the annual avails of the school fund, and of the money deposited with this State by the United States, and other moneys not otherwise specially ap-

† Barnard's Journal R. I. School Inst., II. pp. 54-6

School Law of 1845.

propriated; and the general treasurer is authorized and directed to pay all orders drawn by the commissioner of public schools in pursuance of the provisions of this act, or of resolutions of the General Assembly: *Provided*, the aggregate amount of such orders in any one year shall not exceed the sum of twenty-five thousand dollars.

"Sec III. The commissioner of public schools is authorized and it is made his duty—

"1. To apportion annually, in the month of May, the money appropriated to public schools, among the several towns of the State, in proportion to the number of children under the age of fifteen years, according to the census taken under the authority of the United States, next preceding the time of making such apportionment.

"2. To draw all orders on the general treasurer, for the payment of such apportionment in favor of the treasurers of such towns as shall comply with the terms of this act, on or before the 1st of July annually.

"3. To prepare suitable forms and regulations for making all reports, and conducting all necessary proceedings under this act, and to transmit the same, with such instructions as he shall deem necessary and proper for the uniform and thorough administration of the school system, to the town clerk of each town, for distribution among the officers required to execute them.

"4. To adjust and decide, without appeal and without cost to the parties, all controversies and disputes arising under this act, which may be submitted to him for settlement and decision; the facts of which cases shall be stated in writing, verified by oath or affirmation if required, and accompanied by certified copies of all necessary minutes, contracts, orders and other documents.

"5. To visit as often and as far as practicable, every school district in the State, for the purpose of inspecting the schools, and diffusing as widely as possible by public addresses, and personal communication with school officers, teachers and parents, a knowledge of existing defects, and desirable improvements in the administration of the system, and the government and instruction of the schools.

"6. To recommend the best text-books, and secure, as far as practicable, a uniformity in the schools of at least every town, and to assist, when called upon, in the establishment of, and the selection of books for school libraries.

"7. To establish teachers' institutes, and one thoroughly organized normal school in the State, where teachers, and such as propose to teach, may become acquainted with the most approved and successful methods of arranging the studies, and conducting the discipline and instruction of public schools.

"8. To appoint such and so many inspectors in each county, as he shall, from time to time, deem necessary, to examine all persons offering themselves as candidates for teaching public schools, and to visit, inspect, and report, concerning the public schools, under such instructions as said commissioner may prescribe; *Provided*, that as far as practicable such inspectors shall be experienced teachers, and shall serve without any allowance or compensation from the general treasury.

"9. To grant certificates of qualification to such teachers as have been approved by one or more county inspectors, and shall give satisfactory evidence of their moral character, attainments, and ability to govern and instruct children.

"10. To enter, or cause to be entered, in proper books to be provided for the purpose in his office, all decisions, letters, orders on the treasurer, and other acts as commissioner of public schools; and to submit to the General Assembly at the October session, an annual printed report, containing, together with an account of his own doings,—

"First,—A statement of the condition of the public schools, and the means of popular education generally in the State;

"Second,—Plans and suggestions for their improvement;

"Third,—Such other matters relating to the duties of his office, as he may deem useful and proper to communicate.

"II. POWERS AND DUTIES OF TOWNS. Sections IV—IX.

"SEC. IV. To provide for the education of all the children residing within their respective limits, the several towns and cities of the State are empowered and it shall be their duty—

"1. To lay off their respective territory into primary school districts, and to alter or abolish the same when necessary; *Provided*, that unless with the approbation of the commissioner of public schools, no new district shall be formed with less than forty children, over four and under sixteen years of age; and that no existing district, by the formation of a new one, shall be reduced below the same number of like persons; And that no village or populous district shall be subdivided into two or more districts for the purpose of maintaining a school in each under one teacher, when two or more schools of different grades for the younger and older children, can be conveniently established in said district; or

"2. To establish and maintain, (without forming, or recognizing when formed, districts as above,) a sufficient number of public schools of different grades, at convenient locations, under the entire management and regulation of the school committee hereinafter provided.

"3. To raise by tax at the annual meeting, or at any regular meeting called for the purpose, such sums of money for the support of public schools, as they shall judge necessary, which tax shall be voted, assessed and collected as other town taxes; *Provided*, that a sum equal to one-third of the amount received from the general treasury for the support of public schools for the year next preceding, shall be raised, before any town shall be entitled to receive its proportion of the annual State appropriation.

"4. To elect by ballot, or otherwise, at the annual town meeting, or at a meeting of the town previously designated for this purpose, a school committee, to consist of three, six, nine, or twelve persons resident in such town, as the town shall determine at the first meeting held for the choice of said committee after the passage of this act.

"SEC. V. The school committees of the several towns, when qualified by oath or affirmation, to the faithful discharge of their duties, are authorized and it shall be their duty—

"1. To elect a chairman, and in his absence or inability to serve, a chairman *pro tem.*, who shall preside in all meetings, and sign all orders and official papers of the committee; and a clerk, who shall keep minutes of their votes and proceedings, in a book provided for that purpose, and have the custody of all papers

School Law of 1845.   67

and documents belonging to the committee; and either chairman or clerk when qualified may administer the oath or affirmation required of said other members of the school committee, and of trustees of school districts.

"2. To hold at least four stated meetings, viz.: on the second Monday of January, April, July, and October, in each year, and as often as the circumstances of the schools require; and a majority of the whole number chosen, shall constitute a quorum for the transaction of business, but any less number may adjourn to any time and place.

"3. To form, alter, and discontinue school districts, and to settle the boundaries between them when undefined or in dispute, subject to the direction or concurrence of the town, or the commissioner of public schools.

"4. To locate all school-houses, and not to abandon or change the site of any without good cause.

"5. To examine by the whole board, or a sub-committee appointed for that purpose, all candidates as teachers in the public schools of the town, and give to such as may be found qualified, in respect to moral character, literary attainments, and ability to govern and instruct children, a certificate signed by the chairman, which shall be valid for one year, or until annulled.

"6. To annul the certificates of such teachers as shall prove, on trial, unqualified, or who will not conform to the regulations adopted by the committee.

"7. To visit, by one or more of their number, every public school in town, at least twice during each term of schooling, once within two weeks after the opening, and again within two weeks preceding the close of the school, at which visits they shall examine the register of the teacher, and other matters touching the school-house, library, studies, discipline, modes of teaching, and the improvement of the schools.

"8. To suspend during pleasure, or expel during the current school year, all pupils found guilty, on full hearing, of incorrigibly bad conduct, and re-admit the same, on satisfactory evidence of amendment.

"9. To prescribe, and cause to be put up in each school-house, or furnished to each teacher, a general system of rules and regulations, for the admission and attendance of pupils, the classification, studies, books, discipline and methods of instruction in the public schools.

"10. To fill any vacancy in their own committee, or in the trustees of school districts, occasioned by death, resignation, or otherwise, by an appointment, to continue till the next succeeding annual election, and no longer, at which time such vacancies shall be filled by the town or district respectively.

"11. To apportion as early as practicable in each year among the several school districts, in case the public schools are maintained through their organization, the money received from the State, one-half equally, and the other half according to the average daily attendance in the public schools of each district, during the year next preceding, which money shall be designated as 'teachers' money,' and shall be applied to the wages of teachers, and for no other purpose whatever; and further to apportion any other money, either raised by tax over the sum received from the State, or derived from the registry tax or funds, grants, or other sources of revenue appropriated to public schools, in such manner as the town may determine.

"12. To draw an order on the treasurer of the town in favor of such districts, and such districts only, as shall have made a return to them in matter and form required by said committee, or by the commissioner of public schools, from which it shall appear, among other things, that for the year ending the first of May previous, one or more public schools had been kept for at least four months by a teacher properly qualified, and in a school-house approved by the committee, and that the money designated 'teachers' money,' received from the treasurer of the town for the year previous, had been applied to the wages of teachers, and for no other purpose whatever.

"13. To prepare and submit annually, *First*, a return to the commissioner of public schools, on or before the first of July, in matter and form as shall be prescribed by him; and *Second*, a written or printed report to the town, at the annual town meeting when the school committee is chosen, setting forth the doings of the committee, and the condition and plans for the improvement of the public schools of their respective towns; which report, unless printed, shall be read in open town meeting.

"Sec. VI. Whenever a town is not divided into school districts, or shall vote in a meeting duly warned for that purpose, to provide public schools of different grades without reference to such division, the school committee of said town shall perform all the duties devolved by this act on the trustees of school districts, and pay all necessary expenses of the system, by drafts on the treasurer of the town.

"Sec. VII. Any town may establish and maintain a public school library for the use of the inhabitants generally of the town, and such library may be kept together at some convenient place, or be distributed into several parts, and transferred from time to time for the convenience of different districts or neighborhoods, under such rules and regulations as the town may adopt.

"Sec. VIII. The town clerk of every town shall keep a record of all votes and proceedings of the town relating to public schools, in a book provided for that purpose; shall receive and keep all school reports and documents addressed to the town, and receive such communications as may be forwarded by the commissioner of public schools, and dispose of the same in the manner directed by him.

"Sec. IX. The treasurer of each town respectively shall apply to the general treasurer, and receive all moneys to which the town may be entitled under the apportionment and order of the commissioner of public schools; shall keep a separate account of all moneys thus received, or appropriated by the town; shall give notice to the school committee, within one week after the regular annual town meeting, of the amount of moneys remaining in his hand, at the time, or subject to the order of said committee, specifying the sources from whence derived; and shall pay out said money from time to time, to the orders of the school committee, signed by the chairman.

"III. School Districts. Sections X—XIX.

"Sec. X. Every regularly constituted school district shall be numbered, and its limits defined by the town, or the school committee of the town, which number and limits, and any alteration thereof, shall be entered on the records of the clerk of the town, and the records of the district.

"Sec. XI. When any two or more districts shall be consolidated into one, the new district shall own all the corporate property of the several districts;

School Law of 1845.

and when a district shall be divided, or a portion set off to another district, the funds, property, or the income and proceeds thereof, belonging to such district, shall be distributed or adjusted among the several parts, by the school committee of the town or towns to which such district belongs, in a just and equitable manner.

"Sec. XII. 1. Notice of the time, place, and object of holding the first meeting of any district, shall be given by the committee of the town to which such district belongs.

"2. Every school district shall hold an annual meeting in the month of May in each year, for the choice of officers, and the transaction of any other business relating to schools in said district, and shall also hold a special meeting whenever the same shall be duly called.

"3. The trustees may call a special meeting whenever they shall think it necessary or proper, and shall call a special meeting on the written request of five residents in the district qualified to vote, which request shall state the object of calling the same.

"4. District meetings shall be held at the district school-house. If there be no school-house, the trustees shall determine the place of meeting. If there be no trustees, the committee of the town to which such district belongs, shall determine the place of meeting, which shall, in all cases, be within the limits of the district.

"5. Notice of the time and place of every annual meeting. and of the time, place, and object of every special meeting of the district, shall be given at least five days inclusive, previous to holding the same.

"6. The trustees, or if there be no trustees, then the committee of the town, shall give the notice of a district meeting, either by publishing the same in a newspaper printed in the district, or by putting the notice on the district schoolhouse, or on a sign-post within the district, or in some other mode previously designated by the district; but if there be no such newspaper, school-house, or sign-post, or other mode so designated, then the committee of the town to which such district belongs, shall determine how and where the notice shall be given.

"7. Every person residing in the district may vote in district meetings, to the same extent, and with the same restrictions, as he may at the time be qualified to vote in town meeting.

"8. Every district meeting may appoint a moderator, and adjourn from time to time.

"Sec. XIII. Every school district shall be a body corporate, and shall have power—

"1. To prosecute and defend in all actions relating to the property and affairs of the district.

"2. To purchase, receive, hold and convey any real or personal property for school purposes.

"3. To build, purchase, hire and repair school-houses, and supply the same with black-boards, maps, furniture, and other necessary and useful appendages; *Provided*, that the erection and repairs of the district school-house shall be made according to plans and specifications approved by the school committee of the town, or the commissioner of public schools.

"4. To establish and maintain a school library.

RHODE ISLAND.

"5. To employ one or more teachers.

"6. To raise money by tax on the ratable estates of the district, for school purposes; and to fix a rate of tuition to be paid by the parents, employer or guardian of each child attending school, towards the expense of fuel, books, and other estimated expenses of the school, over and above the sum accruing to the district from the State and town appropriations; *Provided,* that the rate of tuition, for any one term of three months, shall not exceed one dollar per scholar; *and provided further,* that the amount of such tax and the rate of tuition, shall be approved and authorized by the school committee of the town.

"7. To elect at the annual meeting, by ballot or otherwise, one person, resident in the district, to serve as trustee for the district, and to hold his office for three years; *Provided,* that the first election after the passage of this act, three persons shall be thus elected, one of whom shall serve one, a second, two, and the third, three years, to be determined by lot among themselves; *and provided further,* that any new district may choose three trustees as above, at the first meeting called after its formation, and the term of office of the one designated by lot to serve one year, shall expire at the next annual meeting of the school districts.

"8. To appoint a clerk, collector and treasurer of the district, who shall exercise the same powers and duties in their respective districts, as the clerk, treasurer and collector of the town, in their respective towns.

"Sec. XIV. The trustees of every school district, when qualified to the faithful discharge of the duties of their office, are authorized, and it shall be their duty—

"1. To have the custody of the school-houses and other property of the district.

"2. To give notice of all meetings of the districts in the manner provided.

"3. To employ at their discretion, one or more qualified teachers, for every fifty scholars in average daily attendance, provide school-rooms, and furnish the same with fuel, properly prepared.

"4. To visit the schools by one or more of their number, twice at least during each term of schooling.

"5. To see that the scholars are properly supplied with books, and in case they are not, and the parents, guardians or masters, have been notified thereof by the teacher, to provide the same at the expense of the district, and add the price thereof to the next school tax or rate bill of said parents.

"6. To make out the tax and rate bills for tuition, against the persons liable to pay the same, as shall be voted by the district.

"7. To make such returns to the school committee in matter and form, as shall be prescribed by them, or the commissioner of public schools, and perform all other lawful acts that may be required of them by the district, or which may be necessary to carry into full effect the powers and duties of school districts.

"Sec. XV. 1. Whenever a tax shall be voted by any district, the same shall be levied on the ratable estate in said district, according to the estimate and apportionment in the tax bill of the town to which such district belongs, last completed, or next to be completed, as said district may direct.

"2. Whenever any real estate situated within the district is so assessed and entered in the tax bill of the town, in common with other estate situated out of said district, that there is no distinct or separate value upon it, the trustees of the district may call upon one or more of the assessors of the town, not residing in said district; and it shall be the duty of said assessors on such application, to assess the value of said real estate so situated, and in making such assessment, to proceed as in making the tax bill of the town.

"Sec. XVI. If any school district shall neglect or refuse to establish a school and employ a teacher for the same for nine months, the school committee of the town may establish such school, and employ a teacher, as the trustees of the district might have done; and any school district may, with the consent of the school committee, devolve all the powers and duties relating to public schools in said district, on said committee.

"Sec. XVII. Any town, at any legal meeting, may vote to provide schoolhouses, furnish the same with fixtures and necessary and useful appendages, in all the districts, from time to time, at the common expense of the town.

"Sec. XVIII. 1. Any two or more adjoining primary school districts in the same or adjoining towns, may by a concurrent vote, agree to establish a secondary or grammar school, for the older and more advanced children of such districts, under the management of a committee, composed of one member from each of said districts, to be appointed annually for each district, by the school committee of the town, or towns to which such districts belong respectively; and said secondary school committee shall locate the school, provide schoolhouse, fuel and furniture, employ teachers, regulate the studies, the terms of admission, the number of pupils to be admitted, the rate of tuition, and have the general control of the school; *Provided*, that no teacher shall be employed in any secondary school, without exhibiting a certificate of qualification, signed by a school inspector for the county, or the commissioner of public schools.

"2. The school committee of the town or towns in which such secondary school shall be established, shall draw an order in favor of the committee of said school, to be paid out of the public money appropriated to each district interested in said secondary school, in proportion to the number of scholars from each.

"Sec. XIX. 1. Whenever it shall be found convenient to form a school district of two or more contiguous districts, or parts of two or more contiguous districts in adjoining towns, such towns respectively concurring therein, may form such district, and alter and discontinue the same.

"2. The first meeting of any district composed of parts of two or more towns, shall be called by a notice signed by the school committees of the several towns to which such parts belong, and set up in one or more public places, in each town within the limits of the joint district; and said district may, from time to time thereafter, prescribe the mode of calling and warning the meetings, in like manner as other school districts may do.

"3. Every district established by two or more towns, shall have all the powers, and perform all the duties allowed or prescribed in regard to school districts, and shall be subject to the supervision and general management of the school committee of the town in which the school of the joint district may be kept, or the school-house, when erected, may stand.

"4. Whenever a joint district shall vote to build or repair a school-house by tax, the amount of such tax, and the plan and specification of such building or repairs shall be approved by the school committee of the towns out of which said district is formed.

"IV. TEACHERS. Sections XX—I.

"SEC. XX. No person shall be employed to teach as principal or assistant, in any school supported in part, or entirely, by public money, unless such person shall exhibit a certificate of qualification, signed either—

"1. By the chairman of the school committee of any town, or the sub-committee appointed for this purpose, which shall be valid for one year from the date thereof, in any public school or district in said town, unless annulled; or

"2. By an inspector for the county, which shall be valid for two years from the date thereof, in every town and district of the county for which such inspector shall be appointed, which last certificate, when signed by the commissioner of public schools, shall be valid in any public school of the State, for three years, unless the same is annulled.

"*Provided*, That neither of the above authorities shall sign any certificate of qualification, unless the person named in the same shall produce evidence of good moral character, and be found on examination, or by experience, qualified to teach the English language, arithmetic, penmanship, and the rudiments of geography and history, and to govern a school.

"SEC. XXI. Every teacher in any public school, shall keep a register of all the scholars attending said school, their ages, their parents or guardians, the date when each scholar entered and left said school, and their daily attendance, together with the day of the month on which said school was visited by any of the authorities named in this act, with the names of the visitors.

MISCELLANEOUS PROVISIONS.

"SEC. XXIII. No child shall be excluded from any public school in the district to which such child belongs, if the town is divided into districts; and if not so divided, from the nearest public school, except by force of some general regulation, applicable to all children under the same circumstances; and in no case, on account of the inability of the parent, guardian, or employer of the same, to pay his or her tax, rate, or assessment, for any school purpose whatever.

"SEC. XXIV The school committee of any town, or the trustees of any school district, are authorized to make arrangements with the committee of any adjacent town, or the trustees of any adjacent district, for the attendance of such children, as will be better accommodated in the public schools of such adjacent town or district, as the case may be, and to pay such a portion of the expense of said schools, as may have been agreed upon, or as may be just and proper.

"SEC XXV. Any money appropriated to the use of public schools, which shall be applied by a town, school district, or any officer thereof, to any other purpose than that specified by the law, shall be forfeited to the State; and any officer or person who shall fraudulently make a false certificate or order, by which any money appropriated to public schools shall be drawn from the treasury of the State, or the town, shall forfeit the sum of fifty dollars to the State; and it shall be the duty of the commissioner of public schools to bring a suit to recover said forfeitures in behalf of the State.

"Sec. XXVI. In the construction of this act, the word 'town' shall include the city of Providence, so far only as to entitle the same to a distributive share of the money appropriated to the support of public schools, on making the annual report required of the several school committees, in matter and form as prescribed by the commissioner of public schools.

"Sec. XXVII. Any person conceiving himself aggrieved in consequence of any decision made by any school district meeting, or by the trustees of any district, or the committee of any town, or by a county inspector, or concerning any other matter arising under this act, may appeal to the commissioner of public schools, who is hereby authorized and required to examine and decide the same; and the decision of said commissioner, when approved by any judge of the supreme court, shall be final and conclusive.

"Sec. XXVIII. All general acts and resolutions heretofore passed relating to public schools, and all acts authorizing particular towns and districts to build school-houses, and perform other duties now provided for in the preceding sections, are hereby repealed.

"*Provided*, That all acts and resolutions relating to the public schools in the city of Providence, and the town of Newport, are hereby continued in force.

"*Provided further*, That all rights vested in any person or persons by virtue of any of the acts hereby repealed, shall remain unimpaired and unaltered by this act; and that all matters commenced by virtue of any of the laws aforesaid, now depending or unfinished, may be prosecuted and pursued to final effect, in the same manner as they might have been, if this act had not been passed.

"Sec. XXIX. This act shall not take effect till after the next session of the General Assembly, and in the meantime the existing law relative to public schools shall continue in force.

"Passed June Session, 1845.

"HENRY BOWEN, *Secretary.*"

"NARRAGANSETT INDIANS.

"Sec. XXII. The general treasurer shall pay to the treasurer of the town of Charlestown, the sum of one hundred dollars annually, to be expended under the direction of some suitable person or persons to be appointed annually by the governor, in support of a school for the use of the members of the Narragansett tribe of Indians, and for the purchase of books and other incidental expenses of said school; and an account of the expenditure of said money shall be rendered annually to the General Assembly, and a report of the condition of the school be transmitted to the commissioner of public schools, on or before the first Monday of May; *Provided*, that in the apportionment of the public money, by the said commissioner, and by the school committee of the town of Charlestown, the number of the Narragansett Indians in such town shall not be included.

"AN ACT to provide for the education of the indigent blind, and the indigent deaf mutes in this State.
["Passed January 25, 1845.]

"*It is enacted by the General Assembly as follows:*

"SECTION 1. The sum of fifteen hundred dollars is hereby annually appropriated for the education, at ' the American Asylum of Hartford, for the instruction of the deaf and dumb,' of the indigent deaf mutes of this State; and for the education of the indigent blind of this State, at the institution for education of the blind located at South Boston.

"SEC. 2. Said sum shall be paid out of the general treasury to the orders of Byron Diman, of Bristol, who is hereby appointed commissioner for the distribution of said appropriation, with full authority to determine which of said persons in this State shall be admitted to the benefit thereof, and the portion which such shall receive; *Provided*, that no one person shall receive any portion thereof for more than five years, nor a greater sum in any one year than one hundred dollars."

IX. SCHOOLS UNDER MESSRS. BARNARD AND POTTER.

(1845-1854.)

From the time of Mr. Barnard's appointment, the course of the Rhode Island school system was not only more honorable, but became far easier to trace. A series of State reports, at first irregular, then regular, together with local reports of a more fragmentary nature, make the career of development comparatively easy to follow. Of these reports, that first submitted by Mr. Barnard—in 1845—was naturally the fullest and most valuable, because it marked the era of transition. In it he spoke with extreme frankness as to the existing defects of the public schools. Thus, of the actual number taught, he said:

"With these views as to the desirable standard of school attendance, let us see how far the State fell below it in 1844, and what are some of the means by which a nearer approach can be made in future years.

"The whole number of persons over four and under sixteen years of age, the ordinary but not exclusive subjects of school education, in the different towns of the State, including the city of Providence, was about 30,000.

"The whole number of persons of all ages who attended any school, public or private, any portion of the year, was 24,000. Of this number 21,000 were enrolled as attending the public schools, and 3,000 as receiving instruction at home, or in private schools of different grades, at periods of the year when the public schools were open. At other periods of the year the number attending private schools, taught by teachers of public schools, was much larger.

"Of the 21,000 connected with the public schools during the year, 18,000 only were between the ages of four and sixteen years. One-third of the whole number enrolled, attended school so irregularly, that the average attendance of children of all ages in the public schools, did not exceed 13,500, or less than one-half of all the children of a proper school age. The number who attended school during the whole year, allowing for vacations of ordinary length, did not exceed 5,000, including scholars in primary schools, while more than 6,000 on an average did not attend a public school three months in the year. Less than half of the whole number of scholars were girls. Of the scholars over sixteen years of age, the proportion of boys to the girls was as five to one. Of the scholars over ten years of age, the number of boys were to the girls as four to one."

Of the condition of school-houses he said:

"With these general views of school-architecture, let us contrast the condition of the places where most of the public schools of the State were kept in the winter of 1843-44, as presented in an abstract of the returns of teachers and committees, corrected from notes taken during my first circuit through the several towns.

"As the schools were then organized, four hundred and five school-houses were required, whereas but three hundred and twelve were provided. Of these, twenty-nine were owned by towns in their corporate capacity; one hundred and forty-seven by proprietors; and one hundred and forty-five by school districts. Of two hundred and eighty school-houses from which full returns were received, including those in Providence, twenty-five were in very good repair; sixty-two were in ordinary repair; and eighty-six were pronounced totally unfit for school purposes; sixty-five were located in the public highway, and one hundred and eighty directly on the line of the road, without any yard, or out-buildings attached; and but twenty-one had a play-ground enclosed. In over two hundred school-rooms, the average height was less than eight feet, without any opening in the ceiling, or other effectual means for ventilation; the seats and desks were calculated for more than two pupils, arranged on two or three sides of the room, and in most instances, where the results of actual measurement was given, the highest seats were over eighteen inches from the floor, and the lowest, except in twenty-five schools, were over fourteen inches for the youngest pupils, and these seats were unprovided with backs. Two hundred and seventy schools were unfurnished with a clock, blackboard, or thermometer, and only five were provided with a scraper and mat for the feet. In view of these facts, the following summary of the condition of the school-houses was given in my report on school-houses, which is repeated here, as still applicable to many places where public schools are now taught.

"They are, almost universally, badly located, exposed to the noise, dust and danger of the highway, unattractive, if not positively repulsive in their external and internal appearance, and built at the least possible expense of material and labor.

"They are too small. There was no separate entry for boys and girls appropriately fitted up; no sufficient space for the convenient seating and necessary movements of the scholars; no platform, desk, or recitation-room for the teacher.

"They are badly lighted. The windows were inserted on three or four sides of the room, without blinds or curtains to prevent the inconvenience and danger from cross-lights, and the excess of light falling directly on the eyes or reflected from the book, and the distracting influence of passing objects and events out of doors.

"They are not properly ventilated. The purity of the atmosphere is not preserved by providing for the escape of such portions of the air as had become offensive and poisonous by the process of breathing, and by the matter which is constantly escaping from the lungs in vapor, and from the surface of the body in insensible perspiration.

"They are imperfectly warmed. The rush of cold air through cracks and defects in the doors, windows, floor and plastering is not guarded against. The air which is heated is already impure from having been breathed, and made more so by noxious gases arising from the burning of floating particles of vegetable and animal matter coming in contact with the hot iron. The heat is not equally diffused, so that one portion of a school-room is frequently overheated, while another portion, especially the floor, is too cold.

"They are not furnished with seats and desks, properly made and adjusted to each other, and arranged in such a manner as to promote the comfort and convenience of the scholars, and the easy supervision on the part of the teacher. The seats are too high and too long, with no suitable support for the back, especially for the younger children. The desks are too high for the seats, and are either attached to the wall on three sides of the room, so that the faces of the scholars are turned from the teacher, and a portion of them at least are tempted constantly to look out at the windows,—or the seats are attached to the wall on opposite sides, and the scholars sit facing each other. The aisles are not so arranged that each scholar can go to and from his seat, change his position, have access to his books, attend to his own business, be seen and approached by the teacher, without incommoding any other.

"They are not provided with black-boards, maps, clock, thermometer, and other apparatus and fixtures which are indispensable to a well regulated and instructed school.

"They are deficient in all of those in and out-door arrangements which help to promote habits of order, and neatness, and cultivate delicacy of manners and refinement of feeling. There are no verdure, trees, shrubbery and flowers for the eye; no scrapers and mats for the feet; no hooks and shelves for cloaks and hats; no well, sink, basin and towels to secure cleanliness; and no places of retirement for children of either sex.

"Such was the condition of most of the places where the public schools were kept in the winter of 1843–44, in the counties of Kent, Washington and Newport, and in not a few districts in the counties of Providence and Bristol. In some districts, an apartment in an old shop or dwelling-house was fitted up as a school-room; and in eleven towns, the school-houses, such as they were, were owned by proprietors, to whom in many instances, the districts paid in rent a larger amount than would have been the interest on the cost of a new and commodious school-house. Since the passage of the Act of January, 1844, empowering school districts to purchase, repair, build and furnish school-houses, and since public attention was called to the evils and inconvenience of the old structures, and to better plans of construction and internal arrangement, by public addresses, and the circulation of documents, the work of renovation in this department of school improvement has gone on rapidly. If the same progress can be made for three years more, Rhode Island can show, in proportion to the number of schools districts, more specimens of good houses, and fewer dilapidated, inconvenient and unhealthy structures of this kind, than any other State. To bring about thus early this great and desirable result, I can suggest nothing beyond the vigorous prosecution of the same measures which have proved so successful during the past two years."

"In all the schools visited the first winter, or from which returns were received, out of Providence, and the primary departments of a few large central districts, I found but six female teachers; and including the whole State, and excepting the districts referred to, there cannot have been more than twice that number employed. This is one evidence of the want of prudence in applying the school funds of the districts, and of the low appreciation of the peculiar talents of females, when properly educated as teachers—their more gentle and refined manners, purer morals, stronger interest and greater tact and contentment in managing and instructing young children, and of their power when properly developed, of governing even the most wild and stubborn minds by moral influences. Two-thirds at least of all the schools which I visited, would have been better taught by female teachers, who could have been employed at half the compensation actually paid to the male teachers, and thus the length of the winter school prolonged on an average of two months. Convinced as I am from many years observation in public schools, that these institutions will never exert the influence they should on the manners and morals of the children educated in them, till a larger number of well trained and accomplished females are employed permanently as teachers, either as principals or assistants, I have every where and on all occasions urged their peculiar fitness for the office. I have reason to believe that at least fifty female teachers, in addition to the number employed last year, are now engaged in the public schools of the State. But before the superior efficiency of woman in the holy ministry of education, can be felt in its largest measure, her education must be more amply and universally provided for, and an opportunity afforded for some special training in the duties of a teacher; and a modification of the present practice and arrangement of districts be effected." *

In pointing out what has been already done during his brief administration, Mr. Barnard claims that more than fifty additional female teachers have been employed, during his influence, within the past year, and that, within two years, more than fifty school-houses have been built, or have been so thoroughly repaired as to be substantially new, and most of them after plans furnished by himself. His first report is a perfect encyclopaedia of popular education, and perhaps covers more ground than any single report by Horace Mann. Mr Barnard's activity also equalled that of Mr. Mann; and the obstacles that he encountered were of essentially the same kind. It would be possible to cull from Mr. Mann's early lectures and reports a series of extracts almost as dis-

* Barnard's Report for 1845, pp. 11, 30, 35.

couraging as the above; * and the two brave combatants fought, each on the same ground, with the same exhaustless ammunition of lectures, documents and newspapers. In this Mr. Barnard elicited as hearty coöperation as Mr. Mann, and perhaps, from his temperament as well as his smaller sphere, excited less antagonism. He found a powerful ally in the "Rhode Island Institute of Instruction," formed January 24, 1845, and in the Washington County Teachers' Institute. In these and in all his work, he had the valuable aid of Mr. Updike, with whom his appointment had originated, and of Hon. E. R. Potter, who was to be his successor in office. Mr. William S. Baker, also, who was for two years the official agent of the Rhode Island Institute, rendered important aid to the school agent.

Mr. Barnard remained five years in office, retiring in 1849, because of failing health. On retiring, he was presented with a testimonial by the teachers of the State, and the committee presenting it thus testified to his services:

"Of the extent of your labors in preparing the way for a thorough re-organization of our system of public schools, and in encountering successfully the many difficulties incident to the working of a new system, few of us can probably be aware. But we can speak from a personal knowledge of the value of the Teachers' Institutes which have from time to time been held by your appointment, and provided (too often, we fear, at your expense) with skillful and experienced instructors, and practical lecturers; and of the many books and pamphlets on education and teaching, which you have scattered broadcast over the State.

"We can speak, too, of what the teachers of the State know from daily observation,—many of them from happy experience,—of the great change,—nay, revolution,—which you have wrought in our school architecture; by which old, dilapidated, and unsightly district school-houses have given way for the many new, attractive, commodious and healthy edifices which now adorn our hills and valleys. We have seen, too, and felt the benefits of the more numerous and regular attendance of scholars, of the uniformity of text-books, the more vigilant supervision of school committees, and the more lively and intelligent interest and co-operation of parents in our labors, which have been brought about mainly by your efforts.

* "In 1837, not one-third part of the public school-houses in Massachusetts would have been considered tenantable by any decent family, out of the poor-house or in it."—HORACE MANN'S REPORT (FOR MASSACHUSETTS) IN 1846.
"One-third only of the whole number (of school-houses) visited were found in good repair; another third in ordinary and comfortable condition only. In this respect—in other words, barely sufficient for the convenience and accommodation of the teachers and pupils; while the remainder, consisting of 3,319, were to all intents and purposes unfit for the reception of man or beast."—HON. SAMUEL YOUNG'S REPORT (FOR NEW YORK) IN 1844.

"The fruits of your labors may also be seen in the courses of popular lectures which are now being held, and in the well-selected town, village and district libraries, which you have assisted in establishing, and which are already scattering their life-giving influence through our beloved State. In the consciousness of having been the main instrumentality in effecting these changes, for which the generations yet unborn will bless your memory, you have your own best reward. * * * * May your future course be as honorable to yourself, as the past has been useful to the children and youth of Rhode Island."

Rev. Edwin M. Stone, the historian of the Rhode Island Institute of Instruction, thus sums up the labors of Mr. Barnard:

"During the five years of service by Mr. Barnard, more than eleven hundred meetings were held, expressly to discuss topics connected with the public schools, at which upwards of fifteen hundred addresses were delivered. One hundred and fifty of these meetings continued through the day and evening; upwards of one hundred through two evenings and a day; fifty through two days and three evenings; and twelve, including Teachers' Institutes, through the entire week. In addition to this class of meetings and addresses, upwards of two hundred meetings of teachers and parents were held for lectures and discussions on improved methods of teaching and for public exhibitions or examinations of schools. Besides these various meetings, experienced teachers were employed to visit particular towns and sections of the State, and converse freely with parents, on the condition and improvement of the public schools. By these agencies a meeting was held within three miles of every home in Rhode Island. In addition to all this, more than sixteen thousand educational pamphlets and tracts were distributed gratuitously through the State; 'and one year not an almanac was sold in Rhode Island without at least sixteen pages of educational reading attached.' This statement does not include the official documents published by the State, nor the Journal of the Institute, nor upwards of twelve hundred bound volumes on teaching purchased by teachers or added to public or private libraries. * * * * Before Mr. Barnard left the State a library of at least five hundred volumes had been secured for twenty-nine out of the thirty-two towns." *

The successor of Mr. Barnard was Hon. Elisha R. Potter, who ranks second to his predecessor only in the quantity of his labors, not in their quality. His reports from 1851 to 1854 show services of the greatest value. The work of Mr. Barnard was after all only the preliminary work. He created the system, but it was in a community so unequally prepared, and in many regions so unprepared, that he could not carry the organization beyond a certain point. It was not till 1852 that the towns had even supplied themselves with school-houses. In his report for that

* Stone's Hist. R. I. Inst., p. 32.

year, Mr. Potter announces with satisfaction that "nearly all the districts have school-houses belonging to the districts as their corporate property. Very few of the districts now depend on the old proprietors' school-houses. In many cases they have been purchased by the district and repaired." Again, it appears, that after all Mr. Barnard's efforts, no free-school system, in the thorough sense, had yet been established throughout the State. In the report for 1850, Mr. Potter says: "In several of the larger towns the schools are now made entirely free by town taxation; but in most of the towns, the State and town appropriations are insufficient, and the remainder of the expense is assessed upon the scholars. And although the law provides that no child shall be excluded from school on account of poverty, and that the trustees shall exempt the poor from the assessment, yet many of the poor refuse to avail themselves of it." He also points out that, in the State of New York, the rate-bill system had lately been abolished by an immense popular majority. In the Rhode Island reports for January, 1852, and January, 1853, it appears that about ten per cent. of the amounts expended were obtained by assessment on scholars; but the report of January, 1854, shows only five per cent., and the rate-bill system has now wholly disappeared. This result is largely due, no doubt, to the remonstrances of Mr. Potter.

This gentleman's legal experience was also of the greatest value in codifying the school-laws of the State; laws which he, on the bench, was afterwards able to expound and apply with authority. Other important services rendered by him were the recommendation (in 1850) of a Board of Education, and the persistent advocacy of a Normal School. Under his efforts a Normal Department was first established (in 1850) in Brown University, and was placed under the charge of Prof. S. S. Greene, then Superintendent of the Providence Schools, but whose title in the University was that of "Professor of Didactics." To this arrangement succeeded (in 1852) a private Normal School in Providence, taught by Messrs. Greene, Russell, Colburn and Guyot; and finally (in 1854) a State Normal School took its place, under charge of Mr. Dana P. Colburn. This school, it will be remembered, was afterwards removed to Bristol, and was placed, after Mr. Colburn's death, under Mr. Joshua Kendall's charge. It was, however, abolished in 1865, but was reëstablished at Providence in 1871, under charge of Mr. J. C. Greenough, who still remains its principal.

Still another great service rendered by Judge Potter was the thorough discussion and elucidation of the religious question in public schools. It shows the recurrence of the same public questions that we find, so far back as 1840, the same demand as now, from certain quarters, for the substitution of church schools in place of common schools; and the treasury of argument and illustration accumulated on this subject in Mr. Potter's reports has really done the work permanently, and left little for his successors to do. Fortunately the State had, in its school commissioner, a man thoroughly trained in its constitutional principles, and the wise cautions inserted by him in the decisions of the "School Manual," have saved the State from much of the contest which has prevailed elsewhere. In this Manual, which is the authoritative statute-book for every school-committee in the State, these principles are distinctly laid down:

"The constitution and laws of the State give no power to a school committee, nor is there any authority in the State by which the reading of the Bible, or praying in school, either at the opening or the close, can be commanded or enforced. On the other hand, the spirit of the constitution, and the neglect of the law, to specify any penalty for so opening and closing a school, or to appoint or allow any officer to take notice of such an act, do as clearly show that there can be no compulsory exclusion of such reading and praying from our public schools. The whole matter must be regulated by the consciences of the teachers and inhabitants of the district and by the general consent of the community. Statute law and school committee's regulations can enforce neither the use nor disuse of such devotional exercises. School committees may recommend, but they can go no further."*

Judge Potter was chairman of the commission which framed this volume, and the germ of this passage may be found in his report for October, 1854, where he stated his views as follows:

"The school committees have indeed the power by law to regulate the literary exercises of a school, but not to prescribe religious exercises for a school. They have indeed the power to prescribe the books to be used in a school, but this power, and all their powers, must be construed subject to the provisions of the constitution relating to religious freedom. The constitution is the supreme law, and overrides all other laws.

"It has been said also, that if one objector can drive the Bible out of school, he can drive all other books out of school on the same ground, and so may render necessary an expurgation of our whole school literature to suit every individual conscience. This objection can only be made by those who misunderstand the principles I have laid down and endeavored to defend. As no one by objecting can drive the Bible out of school, but will only be taken out of the class which uses it, and allowed to pursue his other studies; so if he objects to any other book, he could not effect its expulsion from school, but merely would not be compelled to read in it or hear it read himself. And knowing that he could not prevent others from using the book, objections would seldom be made from ill-will or obstinacy, but only from real scruples of conscience.

* R. I. School Manual, (1873,) pp. 198, 258.

"And it seems to me that the ground I have taken with regard to the use of the Bible in public schools, is the only one upon which the consciences of all, majority and minority, can be properly regarded. The teacher cannot make it a public school exercise, and require the attention of the whole school to it, if any one objects. But if any one does object, the majority can still use it in a class by themselves, leaving the objector out of the class; and he has then no more right to object to their reading in it, than he has to their using any other book, which he does not wish, or is not required to use himself. * * * *

"Although it is a repetition of what has already been said, I will again state, in conclusion, the principles upon which I consider that all these cases should be decided, viz.: that all public religious exercises, by which I mean prayer and the reading of the Bible, or any religious book by the teacher and the whole school, the school being required to listen to it, can only be had by general consent. And it does not remove the difficulty to authorize a scholar who has conscientious objections, to leave the school-room while the exercises are proceeding. For school purposes, the house is his house, as much as his private dwelling-house, and he has a right to be there.

"But if objection be made, which would seldom be the case if a teacher manages properly, then the Bible, or any religious book may be used in classes, like any other book, by those whose parents do not object to it.

"If any other grounds than these can be supported at the present day, it would imply a most wonderful change in the feelings of the people of this State. We should need to reprint and restudy the noble words of John Milton, Jeremy Taylor and John Locke in defence of religious freedom, to bring us back again to the doctrines avowed by our ancestors when they first settled this colony. The total separation of religious and civil affairs was with them their cardinal principle."†

† School Report for October, 1854, pp. 27-9.

X. LATER HISTORY OF THE SCHOOLS.

(1854—1876.)

From this time forth, the schools of Rhode Island have had a career of quiet development; yet their condition in some of the smaller towns has lingered far behind what could be desired. The district system has never been abolished, in spite of the efforts of about every successive commissioner; and the district system can rarely be made to produce schools of high order.

Mr. Potter's successor was Rev. Robert Allyn, of East Greenwich, who remained in office from 1854 to 1857. He edited the *Rhode Island Schoolmaster*, which took the place of the *Educational Magazine*, and carried on the same work of popular enlightenment. Mr. Allyn, in his report for 1856, points out that less than half the children of school age throughout the State, are to be found at any given time within the school-house doors, the percentage of attendance being but .48$\frac{3}{3}$, while the percentage of enrolled membership is but .69. In the next year's report (1857) he returns again to the charge, and shows the number of enrolled pupils in the State to have actually diminished within five years, having been more by 761 in 1852 than in 1857. While the increase of taxation has been nearly forty-two per cent., he declares that "the decrease in scholars actually enrolled is, since 1852, three per cent., and the decrease in the average attendance is two per cent. The growth of population during that time must have been, at least, seven per cent. About twenty-two per cent. of the children in our State between the ages of six and fifteen, are not attending school." * Yet, he declares the school system of the State to be a model one, and finds the chief source of trouble in the immense increase of manufacturing industry and of a foreign born population.

* Report for 1857, p. 13.

Mr. Allyn's successor, John Kingsbury, Esq., who held the commissionership from 1857 to 1859, points out in his first report another source of difficulty in the lingering indifference of the towns to their schools. He points out that some of the towns fail to print their annual reports, and that the schools are very insufficiently visited. In one town the committee give these two reasons for making no report: "1st, The freemen at the annual town-meeting pay no attention to the reading of it; and second, the secretary was unable to draw up one."* Even from Providence, the commissioner complains that he can obtain only the most meagre returns, although he claims that the Providence school system is unsurpassed in the nation.

Mr. Kingsbury seems to have entered on his work in an unusual spirit of thoroughness. Considering, as he says in his report for 1859, the school law of the State to have been brought to a high degree of perfection, he devoted himself mainly to a thorough inspection of the actual working of the system. With the exception of three or four districts, he visited every school-house in the State, and a large proportion of the schools. His testimony as to the condition of the buildings is therefore peculiarly valuable. It is as follows:

"After the passage of the school act in 1844, which authorized districts to purchase, repair, build and furnish school-houses, the progress of improvement was so rapid that Mr. Barnard predicted, that if the same progress could be made for three years more, Rhode Island could show, in proportion to the number of school districts, more specimens of good houses, and fewer dilapidated, inconvenient and unhealthy structures of this kind, than any other State. This prediction, was without doubt, fulfilled, yet there are some school-houses in the State now, to which Mr. Barnard's unfavorable description applies as well to-day as it did fifteen years ago. It may be that the prediction itself, uttered with the praiseworthy desire of encouraging and stimulating the people of the State, together with the numerous compliments bestowed upon us by persons from abroad for what was really accomplished in that period, may have, instead of producing the intended effect, lulled into inactivity and self-complacency those very districts which it ought to have aroused. The credit which is due to those districts and those towns which did improve their schools, has been assumed as belonging to the whole State. Those districts which have not kept pace with the current improvements of the age, so far from indulging feelings of satisfaction in what others have done, and making it a reason for their own inactivity, ought to be aroused to action by the simple fact alone, that they are in painful contrast with the general progress. Rhode Island has done well. She takes a high rank among her sister States in furnishing the inestimable privileges of a good common school education to every child in the State. This credit, however, is not due equally to all the towns and districts. It is due in spite of those towns and districts which as yet remain comparatively indifferent.

*Report for 1858, p. 31.

"A large number of our school-houses are creditable specimens of school architecture. They are commodious, well arranged, well adapted to school purposes, furnished with maps, black-boards and other conveniences, and some of them are beautifully located, with good grounds adorned with shade trees. Many of them have been erected at a cost quite as great as the means of the districts will justify. Two or three, perhaps, have exceeded the ability of the districts, so that they are a standing bugbear to all further improvements in their neighborhoods. They are like expensive dwelling-houses, whose owners have so crippled themselves in building that they cannot afford to live in their houses after they have been built. In respect to such school-houses, the standing argument is, we have expended so much money in building our house, that we cannot afford to tax ourselves for a good school. Happily, the number is very small where there is the least ground of complaint on this point. A considerable number of the school-houses which have recently been built or repaired, have cost less than what is absolute economy in expenditure. This is true in regard to the size of the structures, their location, play-grounds, out-houses, fences, and especially their interior arrangements. In some of the new houses there are no maps, except one of Rhode Island, furnished at the expense of the State, and not a single work of reference, even a dictionary of the English language. Notwithstanding all that has been done to improve our school-houses, there are many which are entirely unfit places for the education of children, since in them these children are to spend so many of the precious hours of their lives. They are old, needing repairs even for a temporary occupancy; cramped in size, with uneven floors which allow a large ventilation; having desks arranged on the sides of the room, or even in the still more ancient method, on the outside of the room, with the old-fasioned slab seats. Some of them are located in the highway, where land is not worth ten dollars an acre, in the most desolate place in the district, and are destitute of all attraction both without and within. It is gratifying to be able to report that the progress of improvement has, within the past year, reached some of these districts. Several of them have repaired their houses or built new ones, and two or three districts which have never owned a school-house before, are now the fortunate owners of such a structure. There is reason to believe that there are others which are taking measures that will prove successful in securing the same blessing, so that shortly it may be said that there is not a district in the State, which does not possess a creditable school-house.

"The most remarkable circumstance to be noticed in this connection, is the great contrast, not so much between the structure and condition of the school-houses of the different towns—though there is here enough to challenge attention as between the structure and condition of the school-houses of the same towns, and sometimes between those of adjacent districts. Why is it so? Here is the same school-law operating equally for the good of both, the same school committee to whom the supervision of each is committed. In the one district you will find the school-house beautiful, commodious, everything without and within being so arranged as to attract and win the hearts of the young. In the very next district everything is reversed. Instead of attraction, the prevailing principle, as seen in the school-house and its surroundings, is repulsion. Again it may be asked, why is it so? It is found on inquiry, that there is an equal amount of wealth in both districts, an equal number of children to be educated, and that these children are equally dependent upon their education for the stations in life which they are to occupy. It may be found that all this difference may be traced to the activity, energy and liberality of a single individual. May such individuals be multiplied till not a discreditable school-house can be found in Rhode Island.

"It is also worthy of notice that in some of the towns there is a great contrast between the school-houses and dwelling-houses. As you enter these towns the impression made on your mind by so many excellent, commodious and elegant dwelling-houses, is that there must be not only competence but abundance, and even great wealth. You draw the very natural conclusion that here, at least, you will find good if not beautiful school-houses. In this you are quite liable to labor under a mistake; for there are towns where the dwelling-houses and out-houses are indicative of wealth, and yet the school-houses are among the very poorest in the State. Whenever this contrast is found, it is not owing to want of wealth, but of something better—a knowledge of the true manner of using wealth."

The next commissioner was Dr. Joshua B. Chapin, who held the office from 1859 to 1861, and again from 1863 to 1869, his place being filled during that two years' interval by Henry Rousmaniere, Esq. In Dr. Chapin's report for 1861, he again points out the evils of the district system, at least so far as it leads to the appointment of teachers by the district trustees acting singly. He points to a diminution of absenteeism in some districts, from thirty-eight per cent. to ten or eight per cent. He boasts that the improvements in school architecture are so great that "at the present rate of progress, the next generation will look in vain for an absolutely poor school-house within the borders of our State,"—a hope not yet fulfilled. He thus refers, also, to the increasing employment of women as teachers :—

"Experience has proved that for the larger part of our common district schools, females are much better instructors than males. Profiting by this experience, their number, especially in our winter schools, has largely increased. When Mr. Barnard first assumed the office of commissioner, he says that, 'out of Providence and the primary department of a few central districts, I found but six female teachers, and with the exceptions referred to, there cannot have been more than twice that number employed.' Had he visited the same schools during the past year, he would have found more than two hundred. Without intending to underrate males, as teachers, I am free to say that two-thirds of all the schools which I have visited, taught by males, would be better taught, and better disciplined, too, by females. Females have peculiar talent, and when properly educated, have greater power over the manners, morals and minds of children. They have a stronger interest, more skill, patience, tact. They have a facility for placing themselves in sympathy with young hearts. In matters of government and discipline they often succeed best, when it was predicted they would uniformly fail. * * *

"They should also be better paid. I have yet to learn a good reason why a female teacher, doing the same service as a male teacher, and doing it better. should not have at least equal pay. The most of our teachers are miserably compensated for the amount and character of the labor which they perform. The pay for farm labor and kitchen service is, in many cases, in advance of teachers' wages; though we are every year getting the better of this evil. Wages are each year advancing, and, within the past five years, have increased from one-third to one-half. Especially is this true in our cities and larger towns; and yet with all this increase they have hardly kept pace with the increased expense of living. * * *

"There is far less occasion for a resort to the severer forms of discipline in our schools of the present day than formerly. Wholly insubordinate spirits are seldom found. Twenty years ago it was no uncommon occurrence for a dozen schools to be utterly broken up in the course of the winter, and many more were rendered wholly useless by the presence of vicious, incorrigible boys. During the past year, only one instance of serious disturbance has come to my knowledge, and this was due quite as much to the incompetency and inefficiency of the teacher as to anything else."

Dr. Chapin was succeeded in June, 1869, by T. W. Bicknell, Esq., in whose reports we begin at once to see that greater thoroughness and method which we are now accustomed to expect in such documents. For the first time, in connection with his first report, every town in the State published its school report in full. The various points of school discipline, absenteeism, truancy, normal instruction and school supervision were not only discussed in the main document, but illustrated from the local experience of different towns. Mr. Bicknell at once urged the creation of a State board of education, and the re-establishment of the normal school. Both these measures were almost immediately carried; the former in 1870, and the latter, as has already been said, in 1871. From this time forth, the annual reports of the board of education have accompanied those of the school commissioner.

By his annual reports and personal efforts, Mr. Bicknell also did much as to procuring liberal legislation on public libraries, as to the extension of the term of school committees from one to three years, and as to the legal authorization of a school superintendent for every town. As Providence was the first city in New England to appoint (in 1838) a city superintendent, it was appropriate that the State should also be prominent in wise legislation on this point. Mr. Bicknell also urged the appointment on school committees of a reasonable proportion of experienced and intelligent women, mentioning one town in the State where the committee had even consisted of women only, with favorable results.* He collected valuable data as to evening schools from dif-

* Report, January, 1872, p. 69; January, 1874, p. 90.

ferent towns in the State.* He fearlessly presented the facts as to illiteracy in Rhode Island, as follows:

"It may occasion surprise in many minds to learn that more than one in eight, of all the people of this State over ten years of age, cannot read nor write, and that more than one in nine of all the population of the State will remain for life unable to read a page of the simplest reading, or to sign a document, except with their mark.

"In order that the growth of illiteracy may be apparent, the following figures from the censuses of 1850, 1860, 1865 and 1870 are presented:

"In 1850, the number of persons in Rhode Island, over twenty years of age, who could not read and write, was given as 3,607, of whom 1,248 were native, and 2,359 were foreign by birth; 3,340 were whites, and 267 were colored.

"In 1860, the number, over 20 years of age, who could not read and write, was 6,112. Of these, 1,202 were of native, and 4,910 were of foreign birth; 5,582 were white, and 260 colored.

"The whole number of persons upwards of 20 years of age, in 1865, who could not read and write, was 10,181; of American birth, 1,552; of foreign birth, 8,629.

"According to the census of 1870, the illiterate population of Rhode Island, over 10 years of age, is 21,901; of whom 8,681 are males, and 13,220 are females; 4,444 are of native birth, and 17,477 are foreign born; 21,011 are white, and 890 are colored.

"The minor illiterate population, from 10 to 21 years old, is 5,115, and the adult illiterate population, 21 years old and over, is 16,786.

"Notice the rapid increase of illiterates in twenty years:

"1850,	Illiterates (over 20 years),	American born.	1,248;	Foreign,	2,359;	Total,	3,607;
1860,	"	"	1,202;	"	4,910;	"	6,112;
1865,	"	"	1,552;	"	8,629;	"	10,181;
1870,	(over 21 years),	"	......;	"	......;	"	16,786;
1870,	(over 10 years),	"	4,444;	"	17,477;	"	21,901.

"A glance at the above figures shows the extent and the source of this mass of ignorance in our State. 16,786 of our citizens have passed the age for obtaining the rudiments of knowledge in our public schools, and they will probably never acquire the ability to read and write, unless by the agency of the evening school, or by private instruction; and beyond the age referred to, ignorance is too liable to perpetuate itself, and to bind its shackles upon its own victim.

"There is still opportunity, if there is but little hope, for those between the ages of ten and twenty-one, that they will yet learn to read and write. In a large degree, they either belong to our truant and vagrant population, which is now in preparation by idleness, petty offences and public crimes, to become inmates of the Reform School, the State Farm and the State Prison; or to another class, which by the cupidity of parents or employers, is obliged to pass the tender and formative period of childhood and youth in the factory, where nimble fingers are made to enrich the capitalist, or to aid in the support of the

* Report, January, 1872, p. 34.

family, at the expense of that necessary intelligence which fits boys and girls for the ranks of society and citizenship. Add to these, a class of children whose only birthright is poverty, neglect and misfortune, who must keep the wolf and the sheriff from the door, by early toil, trial and sorrow, and we have before us the unpromising minor illiterates of our State."*

Mr. Bicknell's proposed remedies for this illiteracy are the following:

"1. Excellent common schools.

"2. An intelligent and interested public sentiment, strongly positive in favor of universal education.

"3. The enforcement of a law which shall not allow a child to be employed in a manufacturing establishment under twelve years of age.

"4. The enforcement of a law requiring the children employed in the manufacturing establishments of our State to attend school at least five months in each year.

"5. A truant and vagrant law, by which every child between the ages of six and sixteen years, not attending any school, or without any regular and lawful occupation, or growing up in ignorance, may be committed to some suitable institution, or bound as an apprentice at some good home, for the purpose of gaining the rudiments of an education, and of learning some useful trade.

"6. The establishment of evening schools in every town, for the benefit of all persons over sixteen years of age, who may desire to attend.

"7. A constitutional enactment, which shall require of every person who shall possess a franchise in the State, a certificate of his ability to read and write."

As to this last provision I must venture to differ from Mr. Bicknell. The experience of Massachusetts shows that such a law, if made, is not likely to be strictly enforced; and it seems to me plain that if enforced, it would defeat its own end. Enfranchise all, and it is for the obvious interest of every man of wealth that all should be educated. Disfranchise the ignorant, and every rich man is tempted to leave the common people in ignorance, lest they should acquire votes.

At the session of the General Assembly in 1873, a committee was appointed, consisting of Hon. Elisha R. Potter, Associate Justice of the Supreme Court; Hon. T. W. Bicknell, School Commissioner; and Hon. J. M. Addeman, Secretary of State, to print a manual of the school laws, which had just been revised, and to include therewith such forms and decisions as might be needful. Two thousand copies of this work were distributed among the school districts; and it still furnishes a sufficient manual of the school legislation of Rhode Island.

* Report, January, 1872, p. 61.

In Mr. Bicknell's last report, he devotes especial attention to the subject of drawing in schools, and urges reasons why it has peculiar importance for the Rhode Island school system. Some of these reasons are as follows:

"Attention is called to a single branch of instruction which demands an important place in the course of studies in our common schools, not only for the reason that it is a subject of great practical value to the various State industries, but on account of its influence in educating the mental faculties. Like mathematics or language, the acquisition of the several departments of drawing has an influence upon the easier reception of all knowledge, and in that sense has a relation to every sphere of labor, and every field of thought. Not only do the best educators of the State and country so regard it, in its influence as an intellectual stimulus, but the business men of the community so regard it, as practical in a double sense for its utility and its discipline.

"The population of no State is so generally engaged in manufactures as that of Rhode Island. Her manufactures are varied in kind and in quality, they demand all grades of skill not only in those who take the general charge, but in the workmen. Every one who has studied the subject knows that it is not enough to have intelligent, skillful, reliable supervision of labor; the best, and therefore the cheapest results can be secured only when the laborers are also intelligent, skillful and reliable. Ignorant labor is always costly labor. It is generally conceded, and all Europe is acting upon the belief, that a knowledge of drawing, since it deals with the representation of form, which all objects possess, is the most essential element of skilled labor. This explains the action which Massachusetts has recently taken for the art-education of her whole people. Rhode Island must not hesitate to follow the example of Massachusetts, unless she is content to see herself out-stripped in all the more skilled and profitable manufactures.

"To enumerate the industries of Rhode Island is to enumerate nearly all the industries of the whole country. There are her manufactures of cotton and wool, of machinery, locomotives, fire-arms, stoves and iron castings generally, her manufactures of wood, cloth and leather, her silver-ware, jewelry, and a hundred other things in metal. Then there is her building-construction and her quarrying. To give details would be to make a lengthy catalogue indeed.

"Now, into the products of all these industries enters the element of design, usually in its relation both to form and to decoration. Of all the things that Rhode Island manufactures, there is scarcely one that will not command a better price for being beautiful. Many of her products, as machinery, locomotives, involve also a knowledge of working-drawings in their construction. When we consider that nearly everything is now made from a drawing, that a beautiful object cannot be made by a person lacking in taste, that one cannot work from a working-drawing without previous instruction, unless he works under the direct supervision of a second person, it is evident that there is good reason for the declaration that a knowledge of drawing will add, on an average, one-third to the daily wages of the workmen, and increase the profits of him who employs.

"According to the census of 1870, the total population of Rhode Island was

217,853. The number of persons engaged in all occupations was 88,574. Of this number, 11,780 were engaged in agriculture; 19,679 in professional and personal services; 10,108 in trade and transportation; 47,007 in mechanical and mining industries. As every teacher would be directly helped by knowing how to draw, and as good taste is a thing of direct commercial value to all engaged in trade as well as to all engaged in manufactures, it is clear that nearly the whole occupied population of Rhode Island, and so all dependent on them, can be directly benefited by drawing, while there is no one whose interests will not be indirectly subserved. Indeed, of all the States, Rhode Island is the last which should neglect the art-education of her people." *

These remarks deserve especial prominence, inasmuch as the introduction of drawing into the schools is a reform still to be effected throughout the State as a whole, Newport being the only place where it is yet taught systematically. The experiment has been tried there for a year, under a teacher trained in the Massachusetts Normal Art School, and the results have been so wholly satisfactory that it may indeed be said no longer to be an experiment.

After nearly six years of eminently useful service, Mr. Bicknell retired from office in January, 1875, in order to assume the editorship of the *New England Journal of Education*. The best verdict on his labors was that pronounced by the Board of Education in saying that he had labored for the schools " with a diligence, a wisdom, and a contagious enthusiasm, which, it is believed, have resulted in lasting benefit to the cause with which his name is identified." His successor, Hon. T. B. Stockwell, has been in office one year only ; and his first report shows him to be a worthy successor of the efficient men who have preceded him.

* Report, Jan., 1875, p. 57.

XI. CONCLUSION.

The Commissioner's Report for January, 1875, gives this simple summary of what the Rhode Island schools now attempt:

"An examination of our schools shows that reading, spelling, penmanship, arithmetic (mental and written) and geography are taught in all the schools of the State of an intermediate and grammar grade. United States history and English grammar are taught in most of our grammar schools. Vocal music is practised in many of our schools, and taught in a few, particularly in those of all grades in Providence and Newport. Drawing is taught in the intermediate and grammar grades of Providence and Newport. Sewing is taught in a few of the schools in Providence.

"In the high schools we find the pupils pursuing the studies of natural philosophy, chemistry, astronomy, botany, algebra, geometry, trigonometry, book-keeping, general history, mental and moral philosophy, English literature, Latin and Greek." *

To comprehend the full bearing of this brief schedule, we must look back to the time (1800) when a leading school-committee man in Providence had never even seen a grammar, and could find no geography for sale in the town.†

In regard to the number attending public school, the transformation is quite as wonderful. It seems now hardly credible that forty-four years ago there were but twenty public schools in the State which were kept through the year, and that the average term of the rest was but three months. It seems hardly credible that in 1832 even Providence had but eleven public schools and fifty-six private schools, while Newport had but two of the former class and thirty-two of the latter.‡ By the first

* Report, Jan., 1875, p. 55.
† See statement of John Howland, *ante*, p. 17.
‡ See *ante*, p. 57.

official report (1839) Newport exhibited an aggregate of 265 scholars ; whereas it has now 1,769 ; and Providence had 1,753 against its present 12,507.* In the whole State there were, in 1839, but 13,748 public school pupils, an amount now nearly equalled by Providence alone, while the whole State has now 38,669.† The whole amount spent for public schools in 1839, was but $35,354.86 ; whereas, in 1875, it was $764,-643.74. The detailed comparison will be found in the following tables :

TOWNS.	School Expenditures 1839.	School Expenditures 1875.
PROVIDENCE COUNTY.		
Burrillville..	$1,003 32	$11,466 05
Cranston..	1,107 82	10,840 30
Cumberland..	1,594 42	9,773 40
East Providence......................................	....	9,015 92
Foster...	938 22	3,644 89
Glocester...	946 49	4,082 64
Johnston...	831 94	9,203 08
Lincoln...	....	15,382 84
North Providence.....................................	1,215 38	2,365 15
North Smithfield......................................	....	4,682 48
Pawtucket..	....	45,949 95
Providence...	8,962 41	428,260 86
Scituate...	1,472 00	5,880 54
Smithfield..	2,511 56	5,070 56
Woonsocket...	....	42,664 99
NEWPORT COUNTY.		
Jamestown...	173 00	581 53
Little Compton.......................................	397 43	2,544 95
Middletown...	540 88	2,465 00
Newport..	1,320 20	40,355 32
New Shoreham.......................................	415 43	1,112 50
Portsmouth..	487 69	4,249 71
Tiverton..	772 23	3,750 24
WASHINGTON COUNTY.		
Charlestown...	379 85	3,574 63
Exeter...	508 05	3,922 16
Hopkinton..	689 26	7,069 01
North Kingstown.....................................	916 22	5,700 74
Richmond..	458 00	4,323 97
South Kingstown.....................................	1,154 38	7,205 12
Westerly..	598 68	18,667 69

* See *ante*, p. 58.
† Report, Jan., 1876, p. 195.

Conclusion.

TOWNS.	School Expenditures 1839.	School Expenditures 1875.
Kent County.		
Coventry...	$1,172 30	$6,587 00
East Greenwich..	430 80	3,499 41
Warwick..	1,261 09	12,136 03
West Greenwich.......................................	587 00	2,663 98
Bristol County.		
Barrington...	270 80	7,084 03
Bristol...	1,665 02	11,124 57
Warren...	572 96	8,102 50
Totals...	$35,354 86	$764,643 74

Analysis of the Above.

	1839.	1875.
For permanent expenditures; sites, buildings and furniture, libraries and apparatus...............	$2,971 50	$275,835 02
For current expenses.................................	32,383 36	488,808 72
Totals...	$35,354 86	$764,643 74

The following table exhibits the changes in the aggregate number of pupils actually attending public schools in the different towns of the State. In a few cases, apparent diminution has occurred from a sub-division of the town; in other cases there has been a real diminution through the diminished population of certain places, usually small farming towns.

The total increase is, however, large, though bearing but a small proportion to the increase of appropriation, the number of pupils having increased about three-fold, and the amount of appropriation more than twenty-fold.

Aggregate Number of Pupils Attending Schools.

TOWNS.	Aggregate of pupils, 1830.	Aggregate of pupils, 1875.
Providence County.		
Burrillville	446	995
Cranston	407	757
Cumberland	412	801
East Providence		697
Foster	619	438
Glocester	384	405
Johnston	333	1,001
Lincoln		1,895
North Providence	463	201
North Smithfield		462
Pawtucket		3,090
Providence	1,753	12,507
Scituate	734	719
Smithfield	1,206	539
Woonsocket		1,996
Newport County.		
Jamestown	53	55
Little Compton	530	269
Middletown	200	175
Newport	265	1,769
New Shoreham	190	233
Portsmouth	245	383
Tiverton	349	418
Washington County.		
Charlestown	246	236
Exeter	284	263
Hopkinton	478	716
North Kingstown	479	578
Richmond	219	461
South Kingstown	645	970
Westerly	473	1,026
Kent County.		
Coventry	470	730
East Greenwich	209	473
Warwick	746	1,628
West Greenwich	253	249
Bristol County.		
Barrington	194	155
Bristol	320	796
Warren	132	583
Totals	13,748	38,669

Conclusion.

The following table, for which I am indebted to Hon. T. B. Stockwell, gives, more in detail, the steps in progress within the last thirty years:

Public Day Schools.

Schools.	1845.	1855.	1865.	1875.
Number of Schools	428	447	512	737
Average length of Schools	*4 m. 1 d.	*7 m. 18 d		8 m. 18 d.
Teachers and Teachers' Wages.				
Number of different teachers	554	679	*792	1,056
Male	362	275	*219	195
Female	192	404	*573	861
Average number of teachers	515	*560	*630	822
Average wages of male teachers per month		$33 65		$85 18
" " " female " " "		$17 96		$46 17
Total amount paid teachers	*48,335 76	*$121,675 15		$383,284 14
Attendance.				
School population, 5 to 15 years, inclusive	*25,580	*32,217	*36,903	53,316
Number of different pupils	22,156	26,883	*29,500	38,554
Average number belonging				30,102
Average attendance	14,528	18,998	*21,300	26,163
Expenditures.				
Permanent		$16,001 56	$17,578 29	$275,835 02
Current	$53,741 23	$131,675 15	$143,613 66	$472,024 39
Appropriations.				
State	$25,000 00	$50,000 00	$50,000 00	$90,000 00
Town	$25,434 83	$62,564 89	$105,595 54	*340,506 14
School Property.				
Number of school-houses		378	*388	426
Estimated value of sites, buildings, etc.			*$850,000 00	$2,360,017 00

The detailed history of the other educational institutions of the State—its academies, its university, its teachers' institutes, its public libraries, its learned societies,—will be found elsewhere; as will the present system of school laws. The task assigned me was simply to give a continuous sketch of the history of public school education in the State, this necessarily including some reference to the private school instruction in the early days, when public schools were to be found only here and there.

In most respects, the results of this system have gone far beyond the predictions of those who organized it. John Howland's imagination would hardly have pictured to him the costly buildings, the elaborate

* Estimated when what appears to be reliable data for estimates can be obtained.

appliances, the high salaries now to be found in Rhode Island. He would also find the standard of instruction far higher, with a greater range of studies, better text-books and a better system of teaching. He would be forced to admit, however, that much still remains to be done, and that in some of our most ambitious schools, the instruction is still formal and technical, while the text books are too often addressed to the memory only, without recognizing that the memory itself can be best reached through the reason and the imagination, in accordance with Horace Mann's pithy axiom, "That which interests is remembered." He would also find that while the normal school benefits the common schools, the latter may do much to restrict and hamper the normal school, by furnishing it with material very imperfectly prepared.

In one respect there has been, it must be allowed, some disappointment. It is true that the public schools have effected—at least since the abolition of the separate schools for colored children, in 1866—something of that actual mingling of all classes which was predicted as a desirable result. But Henry Barnard's theory,—that a manufacturing community, "from its necessary concentration in villages,"* must be favorably situated for a public school system,—has not stood the test of time. Or rather, however true it might have been for a race of manufacturing operatives, drawn originally, as he says, "from the country homes of New England," the case was greatly changed when the factory population came to be mainly of Irish or French Canadian parentage. The average poverty has been greater than was expected, and this has brought with it an unexpected indifference of parents to the education of their children. It has proved, in the long run, that although the compactness of a factory village is favorable, as Mr. Barnard pointed out, to a system of graded schools, yet such a village offers greater obstacles to a full attendance than the more thinly-settled farming towns. To overcome this evil of irregular attendance; to resist the pecuniary necessities of parents and the pressure on the part of manufacturing corporations to keep children at work instead of at school; this still remains the hardest problem of Rhode Island education. In Woonsocket, for instance, it appears by the report for 1874 that "the number of truants and absentees is four times as large as in many, if not in most towns and villages in Massachusetts."† It is well known that by the joint influence of parents and manufacturing corporations the laws are openly violated in many of our manufacturing villages; the laws, namely, which

---

* Report for 1845, p. 71.
† State School Report, January, 1875, p. 30.

prohibit the employment, in manufacturing establishments, of children under twelve, and permit no minor under fifteen to be so employed unless after attending school three months in the previous year.* Until so simple a law can be enforced, it is almost useless to talk of uniform compulsory education. The prosperity of a community must depend at last on the training of its children. Disfranchised ignorance is as dangerous as enfranchised ignorance; the evil is still there, without the degree of self respect and the stimulus to mental action given by the ballot. The only safety is in bringing to bear upon the children of the ignorant all the knowledge of the wise.

* General Statutes, chapter 153.

PRESENT SCHOOL LAW.

1876.

The last revision of the school law of the State was made in 1872, in connection with a general revision of the statute law. Since that time a few amendments have been made, but it remains very nearly as then established, and as it is to be found in the Common School Manual, already mentioned. As given below, it has been so altered as to include every amendment or addition up to the present time.

I.—OF THE BOARD OF EDUCATION.

SECTION 1. The general supervision and control of the public schools of this State, with such high schools, normal schools and normal institutes, as are or may be established and maintained wholly or in part by the State, shall be vested in a State board of education, which shall consist of the governor and the lieutenant-governor, as members by virtue of their office, and of one other member from each of the counties of the State, with the exception of Providence county, which shall have two other members. The board of education shall elect the commissioner of public schools.

SEC. 2. The members of the board of education shall continue to be divided into three classes, and to hold their offices until the terms for which they were respectively elected shall have expired.

SEC. 3. Two members of the board of education shall be elected annually at the May session of the General Assembly, in grand committee, from the counties in which vacancies shall occur in said board, who shall hold their office for three years, and until their successors shall have been elected and qualified; vacancies in said board shall be filled for any unexpired term by an election from the county for which the member whose office is vacant was elected, in the same manner, at any session of the General Assembly.

Sec. 4. The governor shall be president, and the commissioner of public schools shall be secretary, of the board of education.

Sec. 5. The board of education shall hold quarterly meetings in the first week of March, June, September and December of each year, at the office of the commissioner of public schools, and may hold special meetings at the call of the president or secretary. They shall prescribe, and cause to be enforced, all rules and regulations necessary for carrying into effect the laws in relation to public schools.

Sec. 6. The board of education may cause to be paid annually to and for the use of each free public library established and maintained in this State, and to be expended in the purchase of books therefor, a sum not exceeding fifty dollars for the first five hundred volumes included in such library, and twenty-five dollars for every additional five hundred volumes therein: *Provided*, that the annual payment for the benefit of any one such library shall not exceed the sum of five hundred dollars.

Sec. 7. The board of education shall from time to time establish rules prescribing the character of the books which shall constitute such a library as will be entitled to the benefits conferred by the foregoing section, regulating the management of such library so as to secure the free use of the same to the people of the town or city and neighborhood in which it shall be established, and directing the mode in which the sums paid in pursuance of this act shall be expended. No library shall receive any benefit under the foregoing provisions, unless such rules shall have been complied with by those in charge thereof, nor until they have furnished to said board satisfactory evidence of the number and character of the books contained in said library.

Sec. 8. Any payment herein authorized shall be made by the general treasurer upon the order of the commissioner of public schools, approved by the board of education, and payable to the librarian, or other person having charge of such library, or of the funds applied to its support designated by said board.

Sec. 9. The board of education shall make an annual report to the General Assembly, at the adjourned session at Providence.

Sec. 10. The members of the board shall receive no compensation for their services, but the State treasurer may pay, upon the order of the State auditor, the necessary expenses of the members, when attending the meetings of the board, or when travelling upon official business for and within this State, after the bills have been approved by the General Assembly.

II.—Of the Commissioner of Public Schools.

Section 1. There shall be annually elected a commissioner of public schools in the manner prescribed in the next preceding chapter, who shall devote his time exclusively to the duties of his office. In case of sickness, temporary absence, or other disability, the governor may appoint a person to act as commissioner during such absence, sickness, or disability.

Sec. 2. The commissioner of public schools shall visit, as often as practicable, every school district in the State, for the purpose of inspecting the schools, and diffusing as widely as possible, by public addresses and personal communications with school officers, teachers and parents, a knowledge of the defects, and of any desirable improvements in the administration of the system, and the government and instruction of the schools.

SEC. 3. He shall, under the direction of the board of education, recommend and secure, as far as is practicable, a uniformity of text-books in the schools of all the towns; and shall assist in the establishment of, and selection of books, for school libraries.

SEC. 4. He shall annually, on the last Monday in December, make a report to the board of education, upon the state and condition of the schools and of education, with plans and suggestions for their improvement.

III.—OF THE APPROPRIATION FOR PUBLIC SCHOOLS.

SECTION 1. The sum of ninety thousand dollars shall be annually paid out of the income of the permanent school fund, and from other money in the State treasury, for the support of public schools in the several towns, upon the order of the commissioner of public schools.

SEC. 2. The sum of sixty-three thousand dollars of the amount aforesaid shall be apportioned annually, in May, by the commissioner, among the several towns, in proportion to the number of children therein under the age of fifteen years, according to the census of the United States, or of this State, then last preceding; and the sum of twenty-seven thousand dollars shall be apportioned among the several towns in proportion to the number of school districts in each town.

SEC. 3. The money appropriated from the State as aforesaid shall be denominated "teachers' money," and shall be applied to the wages of teachers, and to no other purpose.

SEC. 4. No town shall receive any part of such State appropriation, unless it shall raise by tax for the support of public schools, a sum equal to the amount it may receive from the State treasury for the support of public schools.

SEC. 5. If any town shall neglect or refuse to raise or appropriate the sum required in the section next preceding, on or before the first day of July in any year, its proportion of the public money shall be forfeited, and the general treasurer, on being officially informed thereof by the commissioner of public schools, shall add it to the permanent school fund.

SEC. 6. The commissioner of public schools shall draw orders on the general treasurer, in favor of all such towns, for their proportion of the appropriation for public schools, as shall, on or before the first day of July, annually, comply with the conditions of the fourth section of this chapter.

IV.—OF THE POWERS AND DUTIES OF TOWNS, AND OF THE DUTIES OF THE TOWN TREASURER AND TOWN CLERK RELATIVE TO PUBLIC SCHOOLS.

SECTION 1. Any town may establish and maintain, with or without forming districts, a sufficient number of public schools, of different grades, at convenient locations, under the management of the school committee, subject to the supervision of the commissioner of public schools as provided by this title.

SEC. 2. Any town may be divided by a vote thereof, into school districts.

SEC. 3. Any town may vote, in a meeting notified for that purpose, to provide school-houses, together with the necessary fixtures and appendages thereto, in all the districts, if there be districts, at the common expense of the town: *Provided*, if any district shall provide, at its own expense, a school-house approved by the school committee, such district shall not be liable to be taxed by the town to furnish or repair school-houses for the other districts.

SEC. 4. Any town may, at its first annual town meeting after this act shall go into effect, for the choice of State or town officers, elect a school committee to consist of not less than three residents of the town, who shall serve without compensation unless voted by the town, and shall hold their offices as follows, to wit: immediately after being assembled in consequence of such election, they shall be divided by lot as equally as may be into three classes. The term of office of the first class shall expire at the end of one year, that of the second class at the end of two years, and that of the third class at the end of three years. As the office of each class becomes vacant as aforesaid, or the office of any member of either class by resignation, or otherwise, such vacancy or vacancies may be annually filled by the town at its annual town meeting, for the election of State or town officers, or at any time by the town council, until the annual town meeting for the election of State or town officers.

SEC. 5. Any town may elect, or failing to do so, its school committe shall appoint, a superintendent of the schools of the town, to perform, under the advice and direction of the committee, such duties, and to exercise such powers, as the committee may assign to him, and to receive such compensation out of the town treasury as the town may vote.

SEC. 6. The town treasurer shall receive the money due the town from the State treasury for public schools, and shall keep a separate account of all money appropriated by the State or town, or otherwise for public schools in the town, and shall pay the same to the order of the school committee.

SEC. 7. The town treasurer shall, within one week after the school committee is elected, submit to them a statement of all moneys in his hands belonging to schools, specifying the sources whence derived.

SEC. 8. The town treasurer shall, on or before the first day of July, annually, transmit to the commissioner of public schools a certificate of the amount which the town has voted to raise by tax for the support of public schools for the current year; and also a statement of the amount paid out to the order of the school committee, for the year ending with the thirtieth of April next preceding, and until such return is made to the commissioner, he may, in his discretion, withhold the order for the money in the State treasury belonging to such town.

SEC. 9. The town clerk shall record the boundaries of school districts and all alterations thereof, in a book to be kept for that purpose, and shall distribute such school documents and blanks as may be sent to him, to the persons for whom they are intended.

V.—OF THE POWERS OF SCHOOL DISTRICTS.

SECTION 1. Every school district shall be a body corporate, and shall be known by its number, or other suitable or ordinary designation.

SEC. 2. Every school may prosecute and defend in all actions in which said district or its officers are parties, may purchase, receive, hold and convey real or personal property for school purposes, and may establish and maintain a school library.

SEC. 3. Every such district may build, purchase, hire and repair school-houses, and supply the same with black-boards, maps, furniture and other necessary and useful appendages, and may insure the house and appendages against damage by fire: *Provided*, that the erection and repairs of the school-house shall be made according to the plans approved by the school committee, or, on appeal, by the commissioner of public schools.

SEC. 4. Every such district may raise money by tax on the ratable property of the district, to support public schools; and to carry out the powers given them by any of the provisions of this title; *Provided*, that the amount of the tax shall be approved by the school committee of the town.

SEC. 5. Every such district shall annually elect a moderator, a clerk, a treasurer, a collector, and either one or three trustees, as the district may decide, and may fill vacancies in either of said offices at any legal meeting. The moderator may administer the oath to all the other officers of the school district.

SEC. 6. The clerk, collector, and treasurer, within their respective school districts, shall have the like power, and shall perform like duties, as the clerk, collector, and treasurer of a town; but the clerk, collector and treasurer need not give bond, unless required by the district.

SEC. 7. All district taxes shall be collected by the district or town collector, in the same manner as town taxes are collected.

SEC. 8. Any district may vote to place the collection of any district tax in the hands of the collector of town taxes, who shall thereupon be fully authorized to proceed and collect the same, upon giving bond therefor satisfactory to the school committee.

SEC. 9. If any school district shall neglect to organize, or if organized, shall for any space of seven months, neglect to establish a school, and employ a teacher, the school committee of the town may, themselves, or by an agent, establish a school in the district school-house, or elsewhere in the district, in their discretion, and employ a teacher.

SEC. 10. Any district may, with the consent of the school committee, devolve all the powers and duties relating to public schools in the district, on the committee.

VI.—OF DISTRICT MEETINGS.

SECTION 1. Notice of the time, place, and object of holding the first meeting of a district for organization, or for a meeting to choose officers or transact other business, in case there be no trustees authorized to call a meeting, shall be given by the school committee of the town, at such time, and in such manner as they may deem proper.

SEC. 2. Every school district when organized shall hold an annual meeting, in the month of March, April, or May, of each year, for choice of officers, and for the transaction of any other business relating to schools.

Sec. 3. The trustees may call a special meeting for election, or other business, at any time, and shall call one to be held within seven days on the written request of any five qualified voters, stating the object for which they wish it called; and if the trustees neglect or refuse to call a special meeting when requested, the school committee may call it and fix the time therefor.

Sec. 4. District meetings shall be held at the school-house, unless otherwise ordered by the district. If there be no school-house or place appointed by the district for district meetings, the trustees, or if there be no trustees, the school committee, shall determine the place, which shall always be within the district.

Sec. 5. Notice of the time and place of every annual meeting, and of the time, place, and object of every special meeting, shall be given, either by publishing the same in a newspaper published in the district, or by posting the same in two or more public places in the district for five days inclusive before holding the same: *Provided*, that the district may, from time to time, prescribe the mode of notifying meetings, and the trustees shall conform thereto.

Sec. 6. Every person residing in the district may vote in district meetings, to the same extent and with the same restrictions as would at the time qualify him to vote in town meeting; but no person shall vote upon any question of taxation of property, or expending money raised thereby, unless he shall have paid, or be liable to pay, a portion of the tax.

Sec. 7. The clerk of the district shall record the number and names of the persons voting, and on which side of the question, at the request of any qualified voter.

VII.—Of Joint School Districts.

Section 1. Any two or more adjoining primary school districts in the same or adjoining towns, may, by a concurrent vote, establish a school, for the older and more advanced children of such districts.

Sec. 2. Such associating districts shall constitute a school district for the purposes of providing a school-house, fuel, furniture, and apparatus, and for the election of a board of trustees, to consist of one member from each district, so associating, and for levying a tax for school purposes, with all the rights and privileges of a school district, so far as such school is concerned.

Sec. 3. The time and place for the meeting for organization of such associate district may be fixed by the school committees, and any one or more of the associating districts may delegate to the trustees of such school, the care and management of its primary school.

Sec. 4. The school committee of the town or towns in which such school shall be established, shall draw an order in favor of the trustees of such school, to be paid out of the public money appropriated to each district interested in such school, in proportion to the number of scholars from each.

Sec. 5. Any two or more adjoining school districts in the same town may, by concurrent vote, with the approbation of the school committee, unite and be consolidated into one district, for the purpose of supporting public schools, and such consolidated district shall have all the powers of a single district.

Sec. 6. Such consolidated district shall be entitled to receive the same proportion of public money as such districts would receive if not united.

Sec. 7. The mode of organizing such consolidated district and calling the first meeting thereof, shall be regulated or prescribed by the school committee, and notice thereof given as prescribed in section five of chapter forty-nine.

Sec. 8. Two or more contiguous districts, or parts of districts in adjoining towns, may be formed into a joint school district by the school committees of such towns concurring therein, and all joint districts which have been, or shall be formed, may by them be altered or discontinued.

Sec. 9. The meeting for organization of such joint district shall be called by the school committees of such towns, and notice thereof shall be given as prescribed in section five of chapter forty-nine.

Sec. 10. Such joint district shall have all the powers of a single school district, and shall be regulated in the same manner, and shall be subject to the supervision and management of the school committee of the town in which the school is located.

Sec. 11. A whole district making a portion of such joint district, shall be entitled to its proportion of public money, in the same manner as if it had remained a single district; and when part of a district is taken to form a portion of such joint district, the school committee of the town of which such district is a part shall assign to it its reasonable proportion.

Sec. 12. Whenever any two or more districts shall be consolidated, the new district shall own all the corporate property of the several districts.

Sec. 13. Whenever a district is divided, and a portion taken from it, the funds and property, or the income and proceeds thereof, shall be divided among the several parts, in such manner as the school committee of the town, or towns, to which the districts belong, may determine.

Sec. 14. Whenever a part of one district is added to another district, or part of a district owning a school-house, or other property, such part shall pay to the district or part of a district to which it is added, if demanded, such sum as the school committee may determine, towards paying for such school-house and other property.

VIII.—Of the Levy of District Taxes.

Section 1. District taxes shall be levied on the ratable property of the district, according to its value in the town assessment then last made, unless the district shall direct such taxes to be levied according to the next town assessment; and no notice thereof shall be required to be given by the trustees.

Sec. 2. The trustees of any school district, if unable to agree with the parties interested, with regard to the valuation of any property in such district, shall call upon one or more of the town assessors not interested, and not residing in the district, to assess the value of such property so situated, in the following cases, namely: When any real estate in the district is assessed in the town tax bill with real estate out of the district, so that there is no distinct or separate value upon it; when any person possessing personal property shall remove into the district after the last town assessment; when a division and apportionment of a tax shall become necessary by reason of the death of any person, or the sale of such property; when a person has invested personal property in real estate, and shall call upon the trustees to place a value thereon; and when property shall have been omitted in the town valuation.

SEC. 3. The assessors shall give notice of such assessment, by posting up notices thereof for ten days next prior to such assessment, in three of the most public places in the district; and after notice is given as aforesaid, no person neglecting to appear before the assessors shall have any remedy for being overtaxed.

SEC. 4. If a district tax shall be voted, assessed, and approved of, and a contract legally entered into under it, or such contract be legally entered into without such vote, assessment, or approval, and said district shall thereafter neglect or refuse to proceed to assess and collect a tax sufficient to fulfil such contract, the commissioner of public schools, after notice to and hearing of the parties, may appoint assessors to assess a tax for that purpose, and may issue a warrant to the collector of the district, or to a collector by him appointed, authorizing and requiring him to proceed and collect such tax.

SEC. 5. Errors in assessing a tax may be corrected, or the tax reassessed, in such manner as may be directed or approved by the commissioner of public schools.

SEC. 6. Whenever any person who has paid a tax for building or repairing a school-house in one district, shall, by alteration of the boundaries thereof, become liable to pay a tax in any other district, if such person cannot agree with the district, such abatement of the tax may be made as the school committee, or, in case of a district composed from different towns, as the commissioner of public schools, may deem just and proper.

SEC. 7. Whenever a joint district shall vote to build or repair a school-house by tax, the amount of the tax and plan and specifications of the building and repairs, shall be approved by the school committees of the several towns, or, in case of their disagreement, by the commissioner of public schools.

SEC. 8. In case of assessing a tax by a joint or associate district, if the town assessments be made upon different principles, or the relative value be not the same, the relative value and proportion shall be ascertained by one or more persons, to be appointed by the commissioner of public schools, and the assessment shall be made accordingly.

IX.—OF THE TRUSTEES OF SCHOOL DISTRICTS.

SECTION 1. The trustees of school districts shall have the custody of the school-house and other district property, and shall employ one or more qualified teachers for every fifty scholars in average daily attendance.

SEC. 2. The trustees shall provide school-rooms and fuel, and shall visit the schools twice at least during each term, and notify the committee or superintendent of the time of opening and closing the school.

SEC 3. The trustees shall see that the scholars are properly supplied with books, and in case they are not, and the parents, guardians, or masters have been notified thereof by the teacher, shall provide the same at the expense of the district.

SEC. 4. The trustees shall make out the tax bill against the person liable to pay the same, and deliver the same to the collector with a warrant by them signed annexed thereto, requiring him to collect and pay over the same to the treasurer of the district.

Sec. 5. The trustees shall make returns to the school committee in manner and form prescribed by them or by the commissioner, or as may be required by law, and perform all other lawful acts required of them by the district, or necessary to carry into full effect the powers and duties of districts.

Sec. 6. The trustees shall receive no compensation for services out of the money received from either the State or town appropriations, nor in any way, unless raised by tax by the district.

Sec. 7. The trustees of any school district may allow scholars from without the district, or without the State, to attend the public schools of such district, upon the payment of such sums for tuition as the trustees may determine, provided that such attendance and tuition shall be approved by the school committee.

Sec. 8. Whenever a town shall not be divided into school districts, or whenever public schools shall be provided without reference to such division, the school committee may exercise the powers provided in the preceding section hereof, to be exercised by trustees.

Sec. 9. All moneys received for tuition as hereinbefore provided, shall be paid into the district or town treasury, as the case may be, and shall be used for school purposes only.

Sec. 10. No attendance upon the public schools authorized by the three preceding sections, shall be reckoned in determining the average attendance for the purpose of regulating the distribution of school money, but such average attendance shall be returned to the district or town where such scholars reside, and be there reckoned with the average attendance of the school of the proper town or district.

X.—OF THE POWERS AND DUTIES OF SCHOOL COMMITTEES.

Section 1. The school committee of each town shall choose a chairman and clerk, either of whom may sign any orders or official papers, and may be removed at the pleasure of said committee.

Sec. 2. The school committee shall hold at least four stated meetings, viz.: on the second Monday of January, April, July and October, in every year, and as much oftener as the state of the schools shall require. A majority of the number elected shall constitute a quorum, unless the committee consist of more than six, when four shall be a quorum, but any number may adjourn.

Sec. 3. The school committee may alter and discontinue school districts, and shall settle their boundaries when undefined or disputed; but no new district shall be formed with less than forty children, between the ages of four and sixteen, unless with the approbation of the commissioner of public schools.

Sec. 4. The school committee shall locate all school-houses, and shall not abandon or change the site of any without good cause.

Sec. 5. In case the school committee shall fix upon a location for a school-house in any district, or shall determine that the school-house lot ought to be enlarged, and the district shall have passed a vote to erect a school-house, or to enlarge the school-house lot, or in case there is no district organization, and the committee shall fix upon a location for a school-house and the proprietor of the land shall refuse to convey the same, or cannot agree with the district for the price thereof, the school committee of their own motion, or upon application of the district, shall be authorized to appoint three disinterested persons, who shall notify the parties and decide upon the valuation of the land; and upon the tender, or payment, of the sum so fixed upon, to the proprietor, the title to the land so fixed upon by the school committee, not exceeding one acre, shall vest in the district, for the purpose of maintaining thereon a school-house and the necessary appendages thereof.

Sec. 6. An appeal in such case shall be allowed to the court of common pleas, in the same manner, and with the same effect, both as to the necessity of taking the particular land condemned, and the valuation thereof, and the like proceedings thereon shall be had, as is provided by law, in case of taking land for public highways.

Sec. 7. The school committee may examine, by themselves, or by some one or more persons by them appointed, every applicant for the situation of teacher in the public schools of the town, and may, after five days' notice in writing, annul the certificate of such as upon examination of the party by them prove unqualified, or will not conform to the regulations of the committee, and in such case shall give immediate notice thereof to the trustee of the district in which such teacher is employed.

Sec. 8. The school committee shall visit, by one or more of their number, every public school in the town, at least twice during each term, once within two weeks of its opening, and once within two weeks of its close, at which visits they shall examine the register, and matters touching the school-house, library, studies, books, discipline, modes of teaching, and improvement of the school.

Sec. 9. The school committee shall make and cause to be put up in each school-house, rules and regulations for the attendance and classification of the pupils, for the introduction and use of text-books, and works of reference, and for the instruction, government, and discipline, of the public schools, and shall prescribe the studies to be pursued therein, under the direction of the school commissioner.

Sec. 10. The school committee may suspend during pleasure all pupils found guilty of incorrigibly bad conduct, or of violation of the school regulations.

Sec. 11. Where a town is not divided into districts, or shall vote in a meeting duly notified for that purpose, to provide schools, without reference to such division, the committee shall manage and regulate said schools, and draw all orders for the payment of their expenses.

Sec. 12. Whenever the public schools are maintained by district organization, the committee shall apportion, as early as practicable in each year, among the districts, the town's proportion of the sum of sixty-three thousand dollars received from the State, one-half equally, and the other half according to the average daily attendance of the schools of the preceding year.

Sec. 13. Whenever the town is divided into school districts having the management of their own concerns, the committee shall apportion equally among all the districts of the town, the town's proportion of the sum of twenty-seven thousand dollars received from the State.

Sec. 14. The school committee shall apportion the money received from the town, from the registry tax, from school funds, or from other sources, either equally or in such proportion as the town may direct, and for want of such direction, then in such manner as they deem best.

SEC. 15. The school committee shall, immediately after making the apportionment among the several districts as provided in the three sections next preceding, give notice to the trustees of the amounts so apportioned to each district.

SEC. 16. The school committee shall draw an order on the town treasurer in favor of such districts only, as shall have made a return to them in manner and form prescribed by them or by the commissioner of public schools, or as may be required by law, from which it shall appear that for the year ending on the first day of May previous, one or more public schools have been kept for at least six months, by a qualified teacher, in a school-house approved by the committee or commissioner, and that the money designated "teacher's money," received the year previous, has been applied to the wages of teachers, and to no other purpose.

SEC. 17. Such orders may be made payable to the trustees or their order, or to the district treasurer, or teacher, and if the treasurer receives the money, he shall pay it out to the order of the trustees.

SEC. 18. The school committee shall not give any such order, until they are satisfied that the services have actually been performed for which the money is to be paid; and the register, properly kept, has been deposited with the committee, or with some person by them appointed to receive the same.

SEC. 19. At the end of the school year, any money appropriated to any district which shall be forfeited, and the forfeiture not remitted, or which shall remain unexpended, shall be divided by the committee among the districts the following year.

SEC. 20. The school committee shall prepare and submit annually to the commissioner of public schools, on or before the first day of July, a report in manner and form by him prescribed, and until such report is made to the commissioner, he may refuse to draw his order for the money in the State treasury belonging to such town, provided, the necessary blank for said report has been furnished by the commissioner on or before the first day of May, next preceding; they shall also prepare and submit annually at the annual town meeting, a report to the town setting forth their doings, the state and condition of the schools, and plans for their improvement, which report, unless printed, shall be read in open town meeting, and if printed, at least two copies shall be transmitted to the commissioner on or before the first day of July in each year.

SEC. 21. The committee may reserve annually, out of the public appropriation, a sum not exceeding forty dollars, to defray the expense of printing their report.

SEC. 22. In any town in this State a change may be made in the school-books in the public schools of such town, by a vote of two-thirds of the whole committee; notice of the proposed change having been given in writing at a previous meeting of said committee: *Provided*, that no change be made in any text-book oftener than once in three years, unless by the consent of the board of education.

XI.—OF TEACHERS.

SECTION 1. No person shall be employed in any town to teach as principal or assistant in any school, supported, entirely or in part, by the public money, unless he shall have a certificate of qualification, signed either by the school committee of the town, or by some person appointed by said committee, or by the trustees of the normal school.

SEC. 2. Such certificate, unless annulled, if signed by the school committee, shall be valid within the town for one year.

SEC. 3. The school committee shall not sign any certificate of qualification unless the person named in the same shall produce evidence of good moral character, and be found on examination qualified to teach the various branches required to be taught in the school.

SEC. 4. The school committee of any town may, on reasonable notice, and a hearing of the party, dismiss any teacher who shall refuse to conform to the regulations by them made, or for other just cause, and in such case shall give immediate notice to the trustees of the district.

SEC. 5. Every teacher in any public school shall keep a register of the names of all the scholars, attending said school, their sex, ages, names of parents or guardians, the time when each scholar enters and leaves the school, the daily attendance; together with the days of the month on which the school is visited by any officer connected with public schools, and shall prepare the district's return to the school committee of the town.

SEC. 6. Every teacher shall aim to implant and cultivate in the minds of all children committed to his care the principles of morality and virtue.

XII.—OF LEGAL PROCEEDINGS RELATING TO PUBLIC SCHOOLS

SECTION 1. Any person aggrieved by any decision or doings of any school committee, district meeting, trustees, or in any other matter arising under this title, may appeal to the commissioner of public schools, who, after notice to the party interested of the time and place of hearing, shall examine and decide the same without cost to the parties: *Provided*, that nothing contained in this section shall be construed to deprive such aggrieved party of any just legal remedy.

SEC. 2. The commissioner of public schools may, and if requested on hearing such appeal by either party shall, lay a statement of the facts of the case before the supreme court whose decision shall be final.

SEC. 3. The commissioner of public schools may prescribe, from time to time, rules regulating the time and manner of making such appeals, and to prevent their being made for trifling and frivolous causes.

SEC. 4. Parties having any matter of dispute between them arising under this title, may agree in writing to submit the same to the adjudication of said commissioner, and his decision therein shall be final.

SEC. 5 If no appeal be taken from a vote of a district relating to the ordering of a tax, or from the proceedings of the officers of the district in assessing the same, or if on appeal, such proceedings are confirmed, the same shall not again be questioned before any court of law or magistrate whatever: *Provided*, that this section shall not be construed to dispense with legal notice of the meeting, or with the votes or proceedings being approved by the school committee or commissioner of public schools, whenever the same is required by law.

SEC. 6. In any civil suit before any court, against any school officer, for any matter which might by this chapter have been heard and decided by the commissioner of public schools, no costs shall be taxed for the plaintiff, if the court are of opinion that such officer acted in good faith.

SEC. 7. Any inhabitant of a district, or person liable to pay taxes therein, may be allowed by any court to answer a suit brought therein against the district, on giving security for costs, in such manner as the court may direct.

SEC. 8. Whenever judgment shall be recovered in any court of record against any school district, the court rendering judgment shall order a warrant to be issued, if no appeal be taken, to the assessors of taxes of the town in which such district is situated, or in case of a joint district, composed of parts of towns, then to one or more of the assessors of each town, with or without designating them, requiring them to assess upon the ratable property in said district a tax sufficient to pay the debts or damages, costs, interest, and a sum in the discretion of the court sufficient to defray the expenses of assessment and collection. Said assessors shall, without a new engagement, proceed to assess the same, giving notice as in case of other district taxes.

SEC. 9. Said warrant shall also contain a direction to the collector of the town, or in case of a joint district, then to the collector of either town, as the court may direct, requiring him to collect said tax; and said warrant, with the assessment annexed thereto, shall be a sufficient authority for the collector, without a special engagement, to proceed and collect the same with the same power as in case of a town tax; and when collected, he shall pay over the same to the parties to whom it may belong, and the surplus, if any, to the district. And the court may require a bond of the collector.

SEC. 10. Whenever any writ, summons, or other process shall issue against any school district, in any civil suit, the same may be served on the treasurer or clerk, and if there are no such officers to be found, the officer charged with the same may post up a certified copy thereof on the door of the school-house, and if there is no school-house, then in some public place in the district, and the same, when proved to the satisfaction of the court, shall constitute a sufficient service thereof.

SEC. 11. The record of the district clerk, that a meeting has been duly, or legally, notified, shall be *primâ facie* evidence that it has been notified as the law requires. The clerk shall procure, at the expense of the district, a suitably bound book for keeping the record therein.

SEC. 12. The commissioner of public schools may, by and with the advice and consent of the board of education, remit all fines, penalties and forfeitures incurred by any town, district, or person under any provisions of this title, except the forfeiture incurred by any town for not raising its proportion of money.

XIII.—OF THE NORMAL SCHOOL, TEACHERS' INSTITUTES AND LECTURES.

SECTION 1. The normal school shall be under the management of the board of education, and the commissioner of public schools, as a board of trustees.

SEC. 2. All applicants from the several towns in the State shall be admitted to free tuition in said school, after having passed such an examination as may be prescribed by the board of trustees, and after having given to such board satisfactory evidence of their intention to teach in the public schools of this State for at least one year after leaving the said school.

SEC. 3. Persons who shall have passed the regular course of studies at the normal school, shall, on the written recommendation of the principal, receive a diploma, signed by the trustees of the school.

Sec. 4. The said trustees shall, by themselves, or by a committee of their board, examine all applicants to teach in the public schools, and shall give certificates to such as are found qualified to teach school.

Sec 5. The trustees of the Normal School may pay to each pupil who shall reside within the State, and not within five miles of said school, who shall have been duly admitted thereto, and who shall have attended the regular sessions of said school, and complied with the regulations thereof, during the term next preceding such payments, not exceeding ten dollars, for each quarter year, for travelling expenses, but such payments in the aggregate for such travelling expenses shall not exceed the sum of fifteen hundred dollars in any one year, and shall be made to the respective pupils entitled to the same, in proportion to the distance they may reside from said school.

Sec. 6. A sum not exceeding five hundred dollars shall be annually paid for defraying the necessary expenses and charges for procuring teachers and lecturers for teachers' institutes, to be holden under the direction of the commissioner of public schools; and a like sum of not exceeding five hundred dollars shall be annually paid for publishing and distributing some journal devoted to educational interests published in this State, among the several school districts.

Sec. 7. The commissioner of public schools shall render an annual account to the state auditor, of his expenditures, under the provisions of this chapter, with his vouchers therefor.

XIV.—OF TRUANT CHILDREN AND ABSENTEES FROM SCHOOL.

Section 1. Town councils shall make needful provisions and arrangements concerning habitual truants, and children not attending school, or without any regular and lawful occupation, or growing up in ignorance, between the ages of six and sixteen years; and also all such ordinances respecting such children as shall be deemed most conducive to their welfare, and to the good order of such town, and may provide penalties for the breach of any such ordinance, not exceeding twenty dollars for any one offence.

Sec. 2. Any such minor convicted under any such ordinance of being an habitual truant, or of not attending school, or of being without any lawful occupation, or of growing up in ignorance, may, at the discretion of the court having jurisdiction of the case, instead of being fined, as aforesaid, be committed to any institution of instruction or suitable situation provided for that purpose.

Sec. 3. Before any ordinances made under the authority of the next two preceding sections hereof shall take effect, they shall be approved by the commissioner of public schools.

Sec. 4. The several towns, availing themselves of the provisions of this chapter, shall appoint, at their annual town meetings, or annually, by their town councils, three or more persons, who alone shall be authorized to make the complaints, in case of violations of said ordinances, to the court which, by said ordinances shall have jurisdiction in the matter; and said persons thus appointed shall alone have authority to carry into execution the judgment of such court.

Sec. 5. The municipal courts of the cities of Providence and Newport, and the justice courts of the several towns of this State, shall have jurisdiction of all cases arising under Chapter 57, Title IX., of General Statutes.

SEC. 6. Any town council or board of aldermen may designate the industrial school in the city of Providence, as the institution of instruction or suitable situation provided for in section 2 of said chapter.

SEC. 7. The general treasurer is hereby directed to pay to the managers of the industrial school of the city of Providence, a sum not exceeding two dollars per week for the board, clothing, and instruction of children committed to said school, in accordance with the provisions of Chapter 57, of the General Statutes, from any town or city in the State.

XV.—GENERAL PROVISIONS RELATING TO PUBLIC SCHOOLS.

SECTION 1. No person shall be excluded from any public school in the district to which such person belongs, if the town is divided into districts, or if not so divided, from the nearest public school, on account of race or color, or for being over fifteen years of age, nor except by force of some general regulation applicable to all persons under the same circumstances.

SEC. 2. Every school officer elected or appointed under the provisions of this title, except the moderator of a district meeting, shall take an engagement before some person authorized to administer oaths, to support the constitution of the United States, the constitution and laws of this State, and faithfully to discharge the duties of his office so long as he shall continue therein.

SEC. 3. The record of the district clerk that any district school officer has been duly engaged, shall be *primâ facie* evidence thereof; and no school district officer shall enter upon the duties of his office, without taking an engagement.

SEC. 4. Every school officer elected or appointed under the provisions of this title shall, without a new engagement, hold his office until the time of the next annual election or appointment for such office, and until his successor is elected or appointed and qualified.

SEC. 5. Every officer who shall make any false certificate, or appropriate any public school money to any purpose not authorized by law, or who shall refuse for a reasonable charge to give certified copies of any official paper, or to account or deliver to his successor, any accounts, papers, or money in his hands, (or shall wilfully or knowingly refuse to perform any duty of his office, or violate any provisions of any law regulating public schools,) except where a particular penalty may be prescribed, shall be fined not exceeding five hundred dollars, or be imprisoned not exceeding six months, and shall be liable to an action on the case for damages, to be brought by any person injured thereby.

SEC. 6. Any school receiving aid from the State, either by direct grant or by exemption from taxation, may be visited and examined by the school committee of the town or city, in which such institution is situated, and by the members of the board of education and the commissioner of public schools, whenever they shall see fit.

SEC. 7. Whenever such school shall refuse to permit such visitation, when requested, its exemption from taxation shall thereafter cease and be determined.

SEC. 8. Every person who shall keep any swine, in any pen or other enclosure, or shall keep, or suffer to be kept, any other nuisance, within one hundred feet of any district school-house, or within one hundred feet of any fence enclosing the yard of any such school-house, shall be fined twenty dollars, one half thereof to and for the use of the school district in which said offence is committed, and the other half thereof to and for the use of the State.

SEC. 9. In the construction of this title, except in the construction of chapter fifty-seven and the sixth and seventh sections of this chapter, the word town shall include the city of Providence only so far as to entitle said city to a distributive share in the public money, upon making a report to the commissioner, in the same manner as the school committees of other towns are required to do.

SEC. 10. The public schools in said city shall continue, as heretofore, to be governed according to such ordinances and regulations as the proper city authorities may from time to time adopt.

SEC. 11. No superintendent or school committee of any town, or any other person officially connected with the government or direction of the public schools, shall receive any private fee, gratuity, donation, or compensation in any manner whatsoever, for promoting the sale or the exchange of any school book, map or chart, in any public school.

SEC. 12. No person shall offer to any public school officer any fee, commission, or compensation whatsoever, as an inducement to effect through such officer any sale, or promotion of sale, or exchange, of any school book, map, chart, or school apparatus; and every person violating any provisions of this chapter, shall be fined not exceeding fifty dollars, or be imprisoned not exceeding thirty days.

SEC. 13. All the public schools in the State, including the State normal school, shall be open to the children of officers and soldiers belonging to the State, mustered into the service of the United States, and of those persons belonging to the State, and serving in the navy of the United States, and who died in said service during the late rebellion against the authority of the United States, or who were discharged from said service, in consequence of wounds or disease contracted in said service, or who were killed in battle, without any cost or expense for taxes, or other charges imposed for purposes of public education.

XVI.—OF FACTORY AND OTHER LABORERS.

SECTION 1. No minor under the age of twelve years shall be employed in or about any manufacturing establishment, in any manufacturing process, or in any labor incident to a manufacturing process.

SEC. 2. No minor under the age of fifteen years, shall be employed in any manufacturing establishment in this State, unless such minor shall have attended school for a term of at least three months in the year next preceding the time when such minor shall be so employed; and no such minor shall be so employed for more than nine months in any one calendar year.

SEC. 3. No minor who has attained the age of twelve years, and is under the age of fifteen years, shall be employed in any manufacturing establishment more than eleven hours in any one day, nor before five o'clock in the morning, nor after half-past seven o'clock in the evening.

SEC. 4. Every owner, employer, or agent of a manufacturing establishment, who shall knowingly and wilfully employ any minor, and every parent or guardian who shall permit or consent to the employment of his or her minor child or ward, contrary to the provisions of the next three preceding sections of this chapter, shall be liable to a penalty of twenty dollars for each offence, to be recovered by complaint and warrant before the justice court in the town in which such child shall reside, or in which the manufacturing establishment in which such child shall have been employed shall be situated, one-half thereof to the use of the complainant, and the other half thereof to the use of the district school of the district in which such manufacturing establishment shall be situated, or, if in the city of Providence, to the use of the public schools of said city.

SEC. 5. Every such complaint shall be commenced within thirty days after the offence complained of shall have been committed, with right of appeal as in other criminal cases.

XVII.—OF THE INDIAN SCHOOL.

SECTION 1. The general treasurer shall annually pay to the treasurer of the town of Charlestown the sum of two hundred dollars, to be expended under the direction of some person or persons to be annually appointed by the governor, in the support of a school, and the purchase of school books for the members of the Indian tribe; *Provided*, that no portion of said appropriation shall be expended, unless the school-house occupied by said tribe shall be put and kept in suitable repair by said Indian tribe.

SEC. 2. The person or persons appointed as aforesaid shall, on or before the first Tuesday of May, annually, transmit to the governor an account of the expenditure of said money together with a statement of the condition of said school.

SEC. 3. No person shall be employed to keep said school, either as principal or assistant, who has not received a certificate of his qualifications to teach a school from the school committee of the town of Charlestown, or other competent authority, in like manner as is required for teachers in other public schools.

SEC. 4. In the apportionment of the public money by the commissioner of public schools and by the school committee of the town of Charlestown, the Indian tribe shall not be included.

RHODE ISLAND STATE NORMAL SCHOOL.

(COMPILED MAINLY FROM STONE'S HIST. R. I. INST. OF INSTRUCTION.)

THE origin of the State Normal School is to be traced, like that of many other of our educational institutions, to the labors of Commissioner Barnard. In the enumeration of the means and agencies employed by him in his work throughout the State and of the purposes he had in view, he says: "I have aimed everywhere to so set forth the nature, necessity and probable results of a Normal School, as to prepare the public mind for some legislative action toward the establishment of one such school." Furthermore, in the first school act drawn up by him, and which was passed by the House in 1844, and also in the amended act of 1845, which became a law in June of that year, he secured the insertion of a clause, among the duties of the commissioner, which read as follows: "To establish Teachers' Institutes, and one thoroughly organized Normal School in the State, where teachers and such as propose to teach, may become acquainted with the most approved and successful methods of arranging the studies and conducting the discipline and instruction of public schools."

However willing the Assembly may have been to pass the law imposing such a duty upon the commissioner, they were not ready to make it operative by the needed appropriation. Repeated efforts were made by Mr. Barnard, seconded by the Rhode Island Institute of Instruction, the school committees of several towns, and others interested in the welfare of the common schools, but all to no purpose, and it seemed almost a "lost cause." The fact, however, that during these years the teachers of the State had been aroused to a sense of their needs, and that a "better way" had been opened before them, created such a demand that, in obedience to the universal law, that a recognized want will always be met with a supply, Brown University, at the time of its reörganization in 1850, incorporated in its course a Normal Department, or Professorship of Didactics.

This department was designed to do the work of a Normal School, and in 1851, Samuel S. Greene, Esq., then recently elected superintendent of public schools in Providence, was permitted by vote of the school committee, to accept the professorship of the same in connection with his duties due to the city. But however gratifying were the fruits of this arrangement, it soon became clear that to secure the best results of a Normal Institution,—to make its work reach further and accomplish more than the Didactic Department of the University was able to do, it must be popularized, and to popularize it, the Institution must stand in close relations with the schools for which its labors were to be performed.

With this conviction, a Normal School was opened in Providence, October 24, 1852, as a private enterprise, by Messrs. Samuel S. Greene, William Russell, Dana P. Colburn and Arnold Guyot; and Mr. Greene having resigned the Professorship of Didactics in the University, was permitted by the school committee to devote a portion of his time to this school. During two sessions of five months each it was attended by a large class of pupils wishing to prepare themselves for teaching, and did much to extend an interest in Normal instruction. But to give it the assurance of permanency, municipal or State sanction and control were necessary.

At this juncture the school committee of Providence took up the subject, looking to the establishing of such a school for its own teachers, and at a special meeting, December 20, 1853, a committee, consisting of Theodore Cook, Edwin M. Stone, William Gammell, Amos D. Smith, and Gamaliel L. Dwight, was appointed to consider the plan, and report at a subsequent meeting. This they did January 13, 1854, and presented the following resolution, which was adopted:

Resolved, That in the opinion of this committee, the time has arrived when a Normal School for the education of teachers should be added to our system of public instruction, and that it be recommended to the City Council to establish such a school, either separately, for the exclusive benefit of the city, or in connection with the government of the State of Rhode Island, for the joint benefit of the city and the State, as in their wisdom they may deem best.

In accordance with this resolution, a code of rules and regulations was drawn up and adopted, and the committee of qualifications was authorized to open the school at such time as it should deem expedient. The city council made the required appropriation, and everything seemed in readiness for continuing the school on a new basis. This movement of the city may have hastened the action of the State, for, at the May session of the General Assembly, an act was passed establishing a State Normal School, and $3,000 were appropriated for its support. Although the city left the field to be occupied exclusively by the State, the school committee showed its cordial approval of what had been done, by authorizing Professor Greene to give a daily lecture to the school on the English language, and on the government and organization of the different grades of schools, for which service he was allowed to receive such compensation as might be agreed upon between himself and the State authorities.

On the 29th of May, 1854, the school was inaugurated with appropriate ceremonies, in the presence of Governor Hoppin and a large assemblage of the friends of the institution. An earnest congratulatory address was made by the governor. The inaugural address was delivered by Commissioner Potter, in which he treated of the province of a Normal School, what might, and what might not be rightly expected of it. He spoke of the difficulties it would have to contend with, and touched upon manners as an essential feature of the school-room, and of moral instruction as a vital element in the system of education.

Thus, after nine years of anxious waiting on the part of the Rhode Island Institute of Instruction for the germination of the seed thought, sown by Mr. Barnard, the Normal School came into being, to fill an unoccupied place, and to elevate the standard of teachers' qualifications. Of this school Mr. Dana P. Colburn was appointed principal, and Mr. Arthur Sumner, assistant, the former at an annual salary of $1,200, and the latter at $750.

The school was continued at Providence with flattering success until the fall of 1858, when it was removed to Bristol, in response to an offer made by the citizens of that town, to provide ample accommodations for its use, free of expense to the State. In December, 1859, the school was suddenly deprived of its able and successful head by an accident which resulted in his instant death. Mr. Colburn's decease was a great blow to the school as well as to the State, which had just begun to feel the effects of his formative work in her schools.

The vacancy thus created was filled by the appointment of Mr. Joshua Kendall, of Meadville, Pa. Mr. Kendall brought to his new and somewhat difficult position a thoroughly trained mind, scholarly attainments, a high ideal of intellectual and moral culture, and an ardent devotion to his work. His services were justly appreciated by the board of trustees, who gave him their hearty coöperation. He continued in the successful discharge of his duties until April, 1864, when he resigned and removed to Cambridge, Mass. The female assistants in the school from 1855 to 1865, were Misses Harriet W. Goodwin, E. T. Brown, A. F. Saunders, Ellen R. Luther, and Ellen G. LeGro. The school was continued upwards of a year after Mr. Kendall's resignation, under the charge of a female principal, but the location having proved unfavorable to its continued prosperity, it was suspended July 3, 1865.

The friends of a Normal School were not discouraged by this event, but were the rather encouraged to persevere in their efforts to secure its reëstablishment in the city of Providence. Several plans were brought forward for a number of years, but no one of them was able to unite a sufficient number of the advocates of the school till 1871, when a bill was introduced into the Assembly at its January session, providing for the establishment of a Normal School, under the control and direction of the Board of Education acting as trustees. This proposition met with general favor, and it was carried through both houses with but very little opposition. A liberal appropriation was made, in order to enable the trustees to inaugurate the school on the most effective basis, and every disposition was manifested to give the system a fair trial and to provide for it a permanent home, so soon as it should demonstrate its worthiness of such an honor. And the same feeling has been displayed up to the present time, there being now an unexpended appropriation providing for the purchase of a site and building, so soon as the present occupants shall be ready to give possession.

The school was opened September 6th, 1871, in Normal Hall, formerly the High Street Congregational Church, in the city of Providence, with impressive services. Governor Padelford delivered the inaugural address, in the presence of an audience that filled the hall to its full capacity. Of the school thus revived, J. C. Greenough, A. B., an instructor of experience from the Normal School at Westfield, Mass., was appointed principal. The school began with a large number of pupils, and has since continued in a highly prosperous condition. From the opening in September, 1871, to January, 1876, 524 have been registered, and 184 have graduated.

As now organized the school is prepared to do the most thorough and effective work. The course of study is comprehensive and carefully adjusted to the capacities and acquirements of the pupils, as well as to the end for which the school has been established, so that the State may be confident that the school furnishes the facilities for imparting as good Normal instruction as any similar institution in the country.

The present corps of instructors is as follows: J. C. Greenough, A. B.,

Principal; Susan C. Bancroft, Mary L. Jewett, Sarah Marble, Ida M. Gardner; Charles H. Gates, teacher of French; E. C. Davis, teacher of Penmanship. Lecturers: Prof. George I. Chace, LL. D., Moral Science; Prof. S. S. Greene, LL. D., Language; Prof. J. Lewis Diman, D. D., Mediæval and English History; Prof. E. W. Blake, A. M., Physiology; Prof. B. F. Clarke, A. M., Mathematics.

RHODE ISLAND INSTITUTE OF INSTRUCTION.

(1845—1876.)

(COMPILED FROM STONE'S HISTORY, R. I. I. OF I)

In the latter part of the year 1844, at the suggestion of Henry Barnard, Commissioner of Public Schools, Mr. Amos Perry, then Principal of the Summer Street Grammar School, in Providence, made arrangements for a meeting of teachers and the friends of education to be held in the City Council chamber, to consider the subject of organizing an association, whose object should be to awaken among the people a broader and deeper interest in public schools, and at the same time lend its support to Mr. Barnard in his work as State Commissioner. The meeting was held according to previous notice, at which Nathan Bishop, Esq., Superintendent of Public Schools in Providence, presided. Twenty-five or thirty teachers, most of them engaged in the public schools, and a few other persons were present. Mr. Barnard being unable to attend in consequense of severe indisposition, Mr. Perry explained the object of the meeting, stating, in substance, Mr. Barnard's views and wishes. After a free interchange of opinions, during which several gentlemen manifested a want of faith in associate action, a committee was appointed to consider the expediency of forming a State Educational Association, and to take such measures for that object as they should deem expedient. This committee consisted of John Kingsbury, Nathan Bishop, Amos Perry, Henry Day, and John J. Stimson.

The representative character of the committee will be noted. All of them were identified with the cause of education. One member was at the head of a private school; one Superintendent of the Public Schools; one at the head of a Grammar school; one the senior teacher in the high school, and one an influential member of the School Committee. The several meetings of this committee were held in the office of the Superintendent of Public Schools. After deliberately considering the question, shall we have an Association? it was agreed that the enterprise should go forward, and the foundation of the Institute was laid.

The Association adopted the name of the eldest educational association of the country, with a view of indicating, on a restricted scale, its general policy and mode of action. The two associations were alike in their general outlines, though different in their sphere of action. One belonged to New England, or the nation, and the other to the little State of Rhode Island. While teachers naturally took a leading part in the deliberations of the Institute, all friends of education without regard to profession or calling, were invited to co-operate for the common cause and to share the honors and responsibilities of membership. Exclusiveness and clannishness were foreign to its spirit and object. A free and cordial intercourse between different classes and professions was invited and encouraged, with a view to breaking down partition walls and introducing life and light to the dark chambers of the mind.

The second meeting was held in the State House in Providence, January 21, 1845, when the committee to whom the whole subject had been committed, made a report. This report, after being discussed, was referred to a committee of which Mr. Barnard was chairman, with instructions to present a constitution at an adjourned meeting. This meeting, at which Hon. Wilkins Updike, of South Kingstown, presided, was held in Westminster Hall on the evening of January 25, 1845, when the constitution, prepared by Mr. Barnard, was reported and adopted. At an adjourned meeting held in the vestry of the First Baptist Church, on the 28th of January, the organization of the Institute was completed by the choice of the following officers: President, John Kingsbury, Providence. Vice Presidents, Wilkins Updike, South Kingstown; Ariel Ballou, Woonsocket. Corresponding Secretary, Nathan Bishop, Providence. Recording Secretary, Joshua D. Giddings, Providence Treasurer, Thomas C. Hartshorn, Providence. Directors, William Gammell, Providence; Amos Perry, Providence; Caleb Farnum, Providence; Joseph T. Sisson, North Providence; J. T. Harkness, Smithfield; J. B. Tallman, Cumberland; L. W. Ballou, Cumberland; J. S. Tourtellott, Glocester; Samuel Greene, Smithfield.

During the first year of the Institute, spirited meetings under its auspices were held in Providence, Newport, Bristol, Warren, Woonsocket, East Greenwich, Valley Falls, Chepachet, Olneyville, Scituate, Fruit Hill, Pawtuxet, Foster and Kingston.

The number and location of these different places reveal the thoroughness with which the Institute entered upon its work. Its aim was to reach every section of the State, and to infuse new life and new principles into the currents of public opinion. In pursuance of this plan it continued its local meetings more or less frequently each year till after the inauguration by the Commissioner of Public Schools in 1870 of local institutes under State patronage. Since that time it has held but one meeting yearly—the annual in January. Of the results of its labors for the first year, the President at the first annual meeting, January 15, 1846, said:

"Through this Association, and county societies of a similar nature, a vast amount of voluntary labor, in this cause, has been performed; and, apparently, a very deep public interest has been created. By these means, united with legislative action, a train of measures has been put in motion which already indicate a great improvement in the public mind—a train, which, if not prematurely interrupted, will ultimately, and at no distant period, raise the public schools of this State to the highest rank among the means of popular education. It is not too much to say, that probably no State in the Union has made greater progress in the same space of time."

In 1845, the Institute appointed Mr. William S. Baker, of South Kingstown, to act as its agent to carry forward the work and promote the objects it had in view. Mr. Baker's experience as a teacher, his singleness of purpose, and his devotion to the cause of popular education, qualified him pre-eminently for the service assigned him. He entered heartily into the work, and became an invaluable coadjutor of the State Commissioner. Under the direction of a committee of the Institute, he traveled from town to town; conversed with the people in their homes, in the field, and in the workshop; visited the schools; held meetings of the parents; and in every other practicable mode endeavored to awaken an interest in educational improvement. The services he rendered were of immense advantage, and his name will ever be held in honor among the friends of public schools.

Another instrumentality employed by the Institute to accomplish the the work of disseminating advanced views on education was that of the press. Arrangements were made for the publication of a serial called the *Journal of the Rhode Island Institute of Instruction*, which should contain full accounts of the proceedings of the various sessions of the Institute, including the papers read and the accompanying discussions so far as it was possible. These volumes were distributed as widely as the society were able to do so with the limited means at their disposal.

In 1856, Mr. Kingsbury declined re-election as President of the Institute, and Prof. Samuel S. Greene, of Brown University, was elected to the office, and held it four years. Professor Greene retired from the presidency of the Institute in 1860. The successive incumbents to January, 1876, have been John J. Ladd, William A. Mowry, Thomas W. Bicknell, Noble W. DeMunn, James T. Edwards, Albert J. Manchester, Merrick Lyon, Isaac F. Cady and David W. Hoyt.

Reference has already been made to the publication of the *Journal of the Institute*. This continued to be published till Mr. Barnard's retirement, when it was given up. Under the administration of Commissioner Potter, a new enterprise was started, called the *Rhode Island Educational Magazine*. This survived for two years, being sustained by gratuitous contributions from various friends of education in the State. In 1855, a third educational magazine was started, and one which, with the exception of one short interim, continued to be published for twenty years. This journal was the *Rhode Island Schoolmaster*, in whose welfare the Institute ever took the deepest interest. At the January meeting in 1856, it was voted to appoint a corresponding committee. In 1860, the *Schoolmaster* was made the official organ of the Institute, and a Board of Editors was appointed. This mutual relation existed till December, 1874, when by vote of the Institute it was decided to unite with the other New England States in the establishment of a *New England Journal of Education*, and to transfer the good will of the *Schoolmaster* to said journal.

At the time of its organization the conditions of membership were signing the constitution and the payment of some fee to the treasurer, the amount being left optional with the individual. In January, 1853, an amendment to the constitution repealed the provision requiring the payment of any fee for membership. This left signing the constitution as the only condition of membership, which soon resulted in a virtual abandonment of any recognized distinction between members and those who were not. This continued till January, 1872, when an amendment to the constitution was voted, making membership dependent upon the payment of an annual tax; one dollar for gentlemen and fifty cents for ladies.

Any sketch of the Institute would be incomplete without a reference to the influence of the annual and subsidiary meetings of the Institute in multiplying friends to the cause of popular education, and in strengthening its hold upon the public mind. This is made evident by the increased attendance upon its meetings, as well as by the high character of the citizens who extended to them their cordial support. This has been a more distinctly marked feature within the last fourteen years. Up to that time, with few exceptions, and those were evenings when a popular speaker from abroad addressed the Institute, the vestry of a church had furnished all needed accommodations. But year by year the circle of interest widened until in 1870 it became necessary to transfer the annual meetings to Roger Williams Hall, capable of seating sixteen hundred people. A single year demonstrated that even this Hall was of too limited dimensions, and in 1872, for this reason, the evening exercises were held in Music Hall, the largest audience room in Providence, if not in the State. The annual meetings of subsequent years, held in this latter hall, have been preëminently distinguished for numbers and enthusiasm. Such gatherings of teachers and the friends of education were never before seen in Rhode Island, if indeed, in any part of the United States. At the evening sessions, each year, not less than three thousand persons have been present.

In reviewing the work of the Institute a glance at the records of more than one hundred meetings, held in various parts of the State shows that the Institute not only commenced its labors with the advocacy of a *Normal School*, but has led public opinion in every movement originated for the improvement of the public school system. It early encouraged the formation of *Town* and *District Libraries*, the introduction of *Music* into the public schools as an important element of culture, the establishing of a *Board of Education*, " by the aid of which the public schools would be safe from the influences of politics and the evils of sectarian prejudices," and the opening of *Evening Schools* in our manufacturing villages, to meet an imperative want of the operative population. The lecturers included many of the ablest educators in our country, while the range of topics considered at these meetings evinced a breadth of view not elsewhere surpassed, and touched upon every point vital to the advancement of our schools.

The officers for the current year are: President, David W. Hoyt, Providence. Recording Secretary, George W. Cole, Pawtucket. Corresponding Secretary, Frederic W. Wing, Olneyville. Treasurer, Benjamin V. Gallup, Providence. Vice Presidents, Rev. Daniel Leach, T. B. Stockwell, J. C. Greenough, Rev. E. M. Stone, L. W. Russell, J. M. Hall, E. H. Howard, J. M. Sawin, J. M. Potter, Ellen M. Haskell, Sarah Dean, B. W. Hood, G. E. Church, Rev. J. M. Brewster, Providence; F. W. Tilton, T. H. Clarke, Miss H. M. Hunt, Newport; J. Eastman, East Greenwich; R. S. Andrews, Bristol; J. M'E. Drake, Westerly; Lysander Flagg, Julia LeFavor, Lincoln; Rev. C. J. White,

Woonsocket; Anna C. Boyd, Portsmouth. Auditing Committee, O. B. Grant, Providence; L. A. Freeman, Watchemoket; D. R. Adams, Centreville. Directors, Merrick Lyon, Wm. A. Mowry, A. J. Manchester, Sarah E. Doyle, Emory Lyon, Alonzo Williams, G. E. Whittemore, Providence; I. F. Cady, Barrington; H. W. Clarke, Newport; A. W. Brown, New Shoreham; Thomas Irons, Glocester; A. C. Robbins, M. H. Way, Miss S. F. Bryant, D. R. Adams, Woonsocket; J. Q. Adams, Natick; W. E. Tolman, J. F. Kent, X. D. Tingley, Pawtucket; Mrs. C. J. Barker, Tiverton; H. A. Wood, Warwick; Rev. F. D. Blakeslee, East Greenwich; J. M. Nye, Crompton.

A CONCISE HISTORY

OF THE

RISE AND PROGRESS

OF THE

PUBLIC SCHOOLS

IN

THE CITY OF PROVIDENCE.

BY EDWIN MARTIN STONE.

PREFACE.

The rise and progress of public free schools in Providence is one of the most interesting and important features in its history, and the centennial year, so replete with patriotic memories, is a period eminently appropriate in which to place its educational story on record. In doing this the author has deemed it proper to bring into view the action of the town as early as 1663, and also the efforts of men on behalf of the common schools, whose enlarged ideas placed them in advance of the popular sentiment of the time. Their disinterested labors, though not immediately successful, prepared the way for the success of others who took up the work where they left it, and have secured for them an honored place among public benefactors.

In preparing this history, free use has been made of the manuscript records and printed reports of the school committee, and of the reports of the superintendent of public schools; of Barnard's reports to the General Assembly of the State of Rhode Island; of Staples' Annals of Providence; and of the author's various publications. To the materials drawn from these sources, has been added whatever could be elsewhere gleaned.

In accordance with the plan of the volume, to which this history is a contribution, the narrative here given is necessarily concise. It is believed, however, that no facts material to a correct exhibit of the past and present condition of the public schools of this city, have been omitted. If what is here written shall in any degree serve to quicken the public mind in a cause with which the highest interests of the State are vitally connected, the author's sole desire will be realized.

Providence, April, 1876.

INTRODUCTION.

(1636—1765.)

The period between 1636, when Roger Williams and five companions crossed the Seekonk river and commenced the settlement of Providence, until 1676, when the town was nearly destroyed by the Indians, was unfavorable for the encouragement of schools. The people were poor, and were constantly harrassed with difficulties. It was only by a mighty effort that they were able to save themselves from being absorbed by neighboring colonies, and secure an independent, chartered existence. The powerful aboriginal tribes in their immediate neighborhood, whose enmity would have been fatal to the young settlement, were to be propitiated, and danger from those quarters warded off. To satisfactorily allot to original proprietors the territory purchased by their leader, and to provide for new-comers, as they were admitted to the rights and privileges of the little commonwealth; to build their homes, clear up the forests, plant their fields, and settle for themselves an efficient form of government; to counteract unpropitious influences acting upon them from without, and to settle perplexing questions constantly rising within; to do all this, filled the years with an activity which left little time to devote to other matters, weighty even as the cause of education. Had the town been settled under circumstances as propitious as those which marked the settlement of Salem, Boston and New Haven; could the little band of Refugees have brought with them the two essential elements of a high civilization, the organized Church and the Schoolmaster, Providence would early, doubtless, have compared favorably in culture with these several towns.

It is not to be assumed, however, that the people here were indifferent to the education of their children. There is reason for the belief that the educational wants of the young were, to a limited extent, provided for by home instruction, or by a Dame school. At the time Providence was burned in 1676, the town comprised, probably, less than sixty families, and such provision would answer the immediate needs of the small number of children then to be cared for. Mr. Williams was a man of liberal education, and as such, could not have been insensib'e to the importance of the school as giving character to his cherished town, but "the pressing demands upon his time and services in adjusting local vexations and in serving the welfare of a neighboring Colony, put it out of his power to give thought to any plan for establishing a system of popular education."

All this being true, it is nevertheless clearly evident that schools had a place in the thoughts and intentions of the people, which only waited a favorable season for expression. Twenty seven years from the settlement of the town, the favorable season came. In May, 1663, the proprietors in public assembly, set apart "one hundred acres of upland, and six acres of meadow, (or lowland to the quantity of eight acres in lieu of meadow,") to be reserved for the maintenance of a school, and to "be called by the name of the School Lands of Providence."

What occurred during the next twenty years in the way of encouraging a school, the town records do not show. It is probable, however, that the children were taught by one or the other of the methods already mentioned. In 1684, a professional schoolmaster first comes to view. This was William Turpin, who wrote an excellent hand, and appears in other respects to have been well qualified for the duties of his office. What year he arrived in Providence, or from whence he came, is not known. There is ground for the belief that he exercised the vocation of a pedagogue previous to the year above named. The first record found of him in this character, is dated June 11th, 1684. It is an agreement drawn up between himself and William Hawkins and his wife Lydia, in which he covenants to instruct Peregrine Gardner, (probably a son of Mrs. Hawkins by a former husband,) in reading and writing for the term of one year. His compensation for this service was to be six pounds; forty shillings of which was to be paid in beef and pork, the former at three-pence-half-penny, and the latter at two-pence per lb.; twenty shillings in corn, at two shillings per bushel, and the balance in silver money. Of such a compensation no one could have complained as being exhorbitant, while the mode of payment must have been entirely satisfactory at a time when to "pay in kind" was more convenient for debtors than to liquidate their obligations in silver and gold.

It appears by a communication addressed to the town in January, following the above named agreement, that Mr. Turpin was induced to select Providence as the field of his usefulness as a teacher, by the encouragement which the grant of land for the maintenance of a school held out. In this communication he styles himself " schoolmaster of the said town," and desires " that the aforesaid land may be forthwith laid out, according to the said order or grant," and that he or his heirs " may be invested in said land so long as he or any of them, shall maintain that worthy art of learning." What action, if any, was taken upon this request by the town, must be left to conjecture. The records are silent.*

The next movement in behalf of schools, we find under date January, 1696, when John Dexter, son of Gregory, William Hopkins and others, petitioned the town for land on Dexter's lane (now Olney street,) or Stampers hill, on which to build a school-house. The petition was granted, but no evidence of the house having been built exists. In 1735 George Taylor had the use of a chamber in the State House to keep a school in; and in 1751, Gideon Comstock, Alexander Frazier, Joseph Potter, Thomas Angell, James Field, Barzillai Richmond and Nehemiah Sprague, had permission to build a school-house on the west side of the river, "on vacant land a little above Joseph Snow, Jr.'s dwelling house, the street being wide enough." They stated that they had subscribed enough to erect a house. The location of this house must have been near the public pump in Broad street.

When the proprietors divided the land lying on the west side, "the Town street," as North and South Main streets were then called, into warehouse lots, they left a lot opposite the west end of "the Court House Parade" for school purposes. The first reference to it is on the plat of the warehouse lots in the proprietors' office, bearing date in 1717. How long before this date the lot was set off for a school-house site or whether it was set off in pursuance to the grant referred to in Mr. Turpin's petition, or in answer to the petition of John Dexter and others, cannot be ascertained. Neither can the year be determined when a school-house was erected there. It must have been, however, previous to 1752, as in that year Nicholas Cooke, Joseph Olney, Esek Hopkins (celebrated as the first Admiral appointed to command the Continental navy,) Elisha Brown and John Mawney, were appointed " to have the

---

* Besides teaching, Mr. Turpin kept an ordinary, or house of public entertainment. His dwelling stood on the west side of North Main street, nearly opposite the Fourth Baptist Meeting House. At one time the General Assembly met there. It was a sightly place, and one of considerable business. He died July 18th, 1709, leaving a widow (Anne, his second wife,) and three children.

care of the town school-house, and to appoint a master to teach in said house." The school committee the following year were Nicholas Cooke, John Mawney, Nicholas Brown, Elijah Tillinghast and Daniel Abbott.

In 1754, a change in the arrangements appears to have been made. The house was leased to Stephen Jackson, schoolmaster, for three months from March 1st. No further action appears until 1763, when the town clerk was directed to lease the house again. The schoolmaster probably received his compensation from his pupils; the town, as a corporation simply furnishing a room at a fixed rent. There were at least two other schools in town as early as 1763. It may be proper here to add, that after the court-house was burned in 1758, the town endeavored to obtain possession of the lot upon which it had stood in lieu of the one on North Main street. There were great difficulties in the way, the court-house lot having been originally granted only for the use of the Colony house, and the school-house lot only for a school-house. The difficulties were, however, overcome, and in February, 1765, a committee of the town transferred the fee simple of the school-house lot, and purchased the other.*

* Staples' Annals of Providence.

SECOND EPOCH.

(1766 – 1791.)

The idea of public free schools was slow in obtaining a strong hold upon the community. Yet there were some who welcomed it with great earnestness, and they set themselves vigorously at work to make it a practical reality. In December, 1767, the subject of education with the apparent design of providing schools for all the children of the inhabitants, was brought before a town meeting, and a resolution passed to purchase or build three school-houses for small children, and one for youth. These schools were to be placed under the supervision of a committee, and the expense of maintaining them was to be defrayed from the town treasury. At this meeting John Brown, John Jenckes, Nathaniel Greene, Charles Keene, and Samuel Thurber were appointed a committee to select locations for the houses, to purchase land and make contracts for their erection. Darius Sessions, Samuel Nightingale, Jabez Bowen, and Moses Brown, all sympathizing warmly with the object, were appointed a committee to prepare an ordinance for the building, supporting and governing the school. These duties were promptly attended to by both committees, and their respective reports were presented to an adjourned town meeting held January 1st, 1768. On testing the sense of the meeting in reference to them, both were rejected. The report of the second committee was written by Hon. Jabez Bowen, Deputy Governor of the State, the substance of which is here preserved as an interesting and honorable memorial of men, who, unfortunately for the children and youth of that day, were too far in advance of a majority of their townsmen to be appreciated in their labors.

It began by affirming the education of youth to be of "first importance to every society." It referred to the vote of the town at a previous meeting, directing the purchase and erection of several school-houses, and recommended how they should be built and where located. To carry out the plan of building, furnishing teachers, firewood, etc., they proposed an assessment or levy of £520, " on the polls and estates of the inhabitants." The house owned by proprietors " on the west side of the great bridge" was to remain under their direction until the new houses were finished and ready for the reception of scholars. The masters were to be furnished " at the expense of the town." A school committee, to be invested with various executive powers, including the appointment of teachers and ushers, and fixing their salaries, was to be chosen annually. The schools were to be free to the children of every inhabitant of the town, and to the children of others under their care. The children of non-resident free-holders were to be admitted into the schools upon the payment of " twelve shillings, lawful money, in the school tax annually." Inhabitants of the town who paid a similar tax annually, having no children or apprentices of their own, were to " have liberty to send the children of any friend or relation of theirs living out of town." Children from other towns were not to be received to the exclusion of those living in Providence. A suitable course of study, including " writing, arithmetic, the various branches of mathematics, and the learned languages," together with necessary rules for the government of the school, were also prescribed. Such, in substance, was this first attempt to embody and organize the free school idea.

Moses Brown, among whose papers this report was many years ago found, made upon it the following endorsement: " laid before the town by the committee, but a number of the inhabitants (and what is most surprising and remarkable, the plan of a free school supported by a tax, was rejected by the poorer sort of the people) being strangely led away not to see their own as well as the public interest therein (by a few objectors at first), either because they were not the projectors, or had not public spirit to execute so laudable a design, and which was first voted by the town with great freedom."

WHIPPLE HALL BUILT.

Notwithstanding this repulse, the friends of education showed a determined purpose to win success. They continued their efforts to organize some plan by which increasing wants could be met. From the town, in its corporate capacity, nothing could be immediately hoped for. At this juncture (1768) a company of public spirited men living in the north part of the town, organized as proprietors, and erected a school house on the site where the Benefit street grammar school-house now stands. The same year, at the October session of the General Assembly, a charter was obtained. The lot was the gift of Captain John Whipple. The house, designed for two schools, was one story high, with a hipped roof, a belfry in the centre of the roof, and a porch or entry on the west end, towards the street. It was completed in November, at an expense of £120 Old Tenor, to each proprietor. "In honor and in memory of the generous donation" of Captain Whipple, the house received the name of WHIPPLE HALL. In the plan, still preserved, of the building, a room in each department was set apart for a library. The names of the proprietors were:

Edward Thurber, Jr.,
Benjamin Thurber,
Daniel Cahoon,
Obadiah Sprague,
Stephen Carpenter,
Dexter Brown,
Major Samuel Currie,
Joseph Wilson,
Major Simeon Thayer,
Colonel David Burr,
John Smith,
Ezekiel Burr,
Joseph Olney, Jr.,
Moses Hearne,
Levi Burr,
Nehemiah Sweet,
Charles Keene,
John E. Brown,
Captain James Olney,
William Tiler,
Aaron Mason,
Jonathan Arnold,
Captain Nathaniel Wheaton,
Samuel Thurber, Jr.,
Timothy Mason,
Coomer Haile,
George Payson,
Captain Ephraim Wheaton,
Amos Horton,
George Whipple,
Abner Thayer,
Philip Mason,
Captain Benjamin Shepard,
Benjamin Cozzens,
Joshua Burr,
Captain Amos Allen,
Comfort Wheaton,
Mrs. Comfort Wheaton,
Edward Knowles,
Benjamin Allen,
Charles Keene,
Peter Randall.

The building committee were Aaron Mason, Ephraim Wheaton, Nathaniel Wheaton, Daniel Cahoon and Comfort Wheaton. The committee to draw up regulations for the government of the school were Joseph Nash, Charles Keene, Samuel Thurber, Jr., Samuel Currie, Benjamin Cozzens, Comfort Wheaton and Jonathan Arnold. The school opened on the first day of November. It must have been a proud day for its friends and patrons. Mr. George Taylor, Jr., the first teacher in the upper grade, was compensated for his services by tuition fees, the proprietors paying him four shillings and sixpence quarterly, for each pupil they sent. An additional charge of two shillings was made to parents who were not proprietors, but filled a vacant right. Sally Jackson was teacher in the lower grade. Some of the rules to be observed by the pupils are deserving of notice. They were to be present at the devotional services in the morning, "and behave decently and soberly." They were to "take their seats without noise and disturbance." When the master or visitors entered or left the room, they were to "rise up with decent obeisence." They were not to leave their seats or communicate with each other without leave. They were not to tarry in the school-house after the school was dismissed, "unless by the special license of the master." In addressing their school-fellows, they were to use only "his or her christian or sur-name." Traffic among the pupils was not to be practised, nor were they to "play at cards, dice, or any unlawful game." When abroad, they were to "treat all men and women with civility, modesty and good manners, and especially their known superiors; and when at home their parents with all dutifulness and respect." They were not to "presume to take God's name in vain, swear, lie, steal, or use any unbecoming language or behaviour." They were not to "be seen in a tavern unless upon business." They were to "behave decently and soberly in the house of God, not whispering, laughing, or using any indecent gestures." And punishment was to be inflicted "according to the nature, desert and circumstances of the crime."

The master was required to be punctual in opening the school, and during school hours was not to engage "in business of any other kind" than that of instruction. Every Thursday afternoon, instead of the usual exercises, he was to read to the pupils "some lecture either in Natural Philosophy or some other entertaining and useful branch of science," suited to their capacities, "and explain the same so as to give them a tolerable idea of the subject," or else spend the time in teaching them "to spell and pronounce properly and distinctly, difficult words, sentences, etc." Every Saturday, before dismissing the school, he was required to "exhort his scholars to behave themselves at all times decently and soberly, teaching them both by precept and example to refrain from vice, immorality and prophaneness, and to remember the Sabbath day to keep it holy."

The parental solicitude here displayed for the morals of the young, was what we should expect from men who had witnessed the demoralizing effects of the Revolution, and who looked upon a pure, upright character as of priceless value. The oral instruction given weekly, by the teacher, upon topics outside of his daily routine, could not have failed to increase the intelligence of the pupils, by fixing in their minds certain principles of science of which they must otherwise have remained ignorant, and at the same time enhancing their enjoyment by opening to them new fields of thought.

While the committee on regulations so carefully defined the duties of teacher and pupils, they appear to have been no less mindful of those which pertain to the Board of Trustees. Besides conferring upon them plenary power in matters of finance, it was made their duty to visit the schools " and see that the rules and orders of the Society respecting the same were regularly observed and kept," both " by the proprietors, master, mistress and their pupils." They were to " see that the master and mistress do their duty towards the scholars under their care respectively; and also to see that the master and mistress are well treated by their scholars and the proprietors; and in case any uneasiness should arise, to endeavor to reconcile the differences, heal the breaches, restore unity and amity, peace and order, amongst the contending parties." All this, and whatever other business which might come before them, they were " to do and transact as faithful and honest, prudent and humane, guardians and fathers of the incorporated society of Whipple Hall, according to their best skill and ability, without fee or reward."

The teachers who succeeded Mr. Taylor were John Barrows, Nathan Downe, Sumner Wood, Joseph Balch, Solomon Bradford, Abner Tucker, and John Dexter.

Meeting Street School-House Erected.

The same year that the schools in Whipple Hall went into operation, another company of proprietors was organized, and in conjunction with the town built the brick school-house still standing on Meeting street, adjacent to the Friends' Meeting-house. The proprietors, who were chartered 1770, owned and occupied the upper story, and the town the lower. The house was built by John Smith, the carpenter work being done by Jonathan Hammond. The names of these proprietors were as follows:

John Updike,	Darius Sessions,
Thomas Greene,	Richard Jackson,
Nicholas Brown,	Ebenezer Thompson,
Ambrose Page,	Rufus Hopkins,
Joseph Russell,	Ephraim Bowen,
James Sabin,	David Harris,

Solomon Drowne,	George Corlis,
William Smith,	Nathan Jacobs,
Richard Olney,	John Smith,
Caleb Greene,	Knight Dexter,
Noah Mason,	Charles Keen,
Hayward Smith,	John Waterman,
James Lovett,	John Peck,
Joseph Carver,	Zephaniah Andrews,
Daniel Jackson,	Jonathan Hammond,
Caleb Harris,	Elijah Bacon,
Nicholas Cooke,	Benjamin Bowen,
Nathaniel Wheaton,	Joseph Tillinghast,
Henry Sterling,	Samuel Nightingale, Jr.,
George Hopkins,	Bernard Eddy,
Moses Brown,	Joseph Bucklin,
Joseph Brown,	Esek Brown,
Jabez Bowen,	Joseph Whipple,
Nathan Angell,	Gideon Crawford,
John Jeuckes,	Abraham Whipple,
Benjamin Cushing,	Jonathan Ellis,
John Brown,	Elihu Robinson.

The regulations for this school were drawn up by Stephen Hopkins, Jabez Bowen and Moses Brown. Under these the teacher was to receive his compensation from the parents of his pupils. His discipline was to be "strict, though not passionate." His pupils were to be taught to read "twice in the forenoon and twice in the afternoon." They were to be instructed "in accenting, pronouncing and proper understanding of the English tongue." They were also to devote a suitable portion of time to writing, arithmetic and spelling; "and for the raising of a laudable emulation to excel in the respective branches of learning," the master was to "range the scholars in proper classes according to their several attainments, weekly, monthly or quarterly." He was likewise to "take special care of the morals of the scholars," being careful to be exemplary in his own. Weekly, before closing the school, he was to "audibly read or pronounce a short moral lecture, either from the scriptures of truth or of his own composure, or from approved authors," and these lectures he was to present to the committee at their visits, "to be by them preserved among the papers and records of the school." To perfect this system of moral training, the pupils were to be required "on the first fourth day of every month," to "pronounce at least six verses out of Christ's sermon on the Mount, or from the Proverbs of Solomon." The committee were monthly or at least quarterly to visit the schools " to inspect the conduct of the masters, and the proficiency of those under their charge." At these visits they were to "name and notify six persons who were "parents of children at school in the time being, to visit in turn once a week, to inspect the school, and to make report to the committee if they found anything amiss, or any new regulations wanting."

These regulations show that the proprietors regarded moral instruction to be of primary importance, while the naming and notifying of parents having children in the school to visit it for the purpose indicated, expresses the value they attached to a practice which could not fail of extending and deepening an interest in the cause of education.

A New Impulse Given.

To give an additional impulse to the cause, Rev. Enos Hitchcock, D. D., pastor of the First Congregational Church in Providence, whose active efforts had given him an influential position, by request delivered a "Discourse on Education," in the meeting-house on the west side of the river, (Rev. Joseph Snow's,) November 16th, 1785. The discourse was printed, and served an excellent purpose. It is now a rare tract, and accessible to few. As a way-mark in the progress of events, a few paragraphs from it are here reproduced:

"It has ever been the opinion of the wise and the considerate, and it is a plain dictate of the Scriptures, that the serious attention of parents to the education of their children is a matter of the greatest importance—that the present and future happiness of individuals, the welfare of society, and the progress of virtue and religion, depend very much upon it.

"It is well known that the delicacy, strength and usefulness of plants, depend very much upon their early growth. If neglected, they will be infested with evil weeds, their growth stinted, their appearance pale and languid; but if cherished with due cultivation, will gain their form, size and vigor in the proper growing season. In the same manner, the form, size and qualities of the mind, depend upon the means of education being employed during the season of its growth and improvement.

"As we have just merged from a grievous and oppressive war, which obstructed the progress of science, suspended or destroyed schools, and laid waste the means of education, how can we improve the happy event, and the invaluable blessings of peace and independence, so well as by exerting ourselves for the revival and promotion of languishing science, and instituting schools founded upon the liberal and permanent footing of general usefulness!

"To be endowed with the faculty of reason and understanding, and to be ranked in the scale of being with intelligences, we justly esteem a great honor and happiness—and truly it is an invaluable blessing if rightly improved. We account it a very great privilege and happiness to have our lot cast in a land of freedom, where ignorance and superstition are not the necessary engines of government; where we may enjoy at pleasure all the means of information. 'But if a country stored with diamonds, lying in their native crust, may be denominated poor, because it is neglected, what brand of infamy shall we deserve if we take no pains to rescue our richest treasure and brightest ornaments from perpetual obscurity!'

"To suffer these powers to lay dormant, and not to draw them forth and cherish them, by the use of those means and opportunities which God hath granted us, is to 'wrap up in a napkin' a most important TALENT—a talent bestowed for use and improvement, with this injunction, 'occupy till I come.' These latent powers and qualities must be drawn forth and improved, by seasonable and diligent cultivation, as the tender plant is nourished and reared by the fostering hand of diligence and care. Hence education is called NURTURE in allusion to the culture of plants and vegetables. St. Paul calls upon parents to bring up their children 'in the NURTURE and admonition of the Lord.' This must mean to nourish and cherish the mind in its growing season, with the most useful knowledge.

"The mind, like the infant plant, is, in its first stages, feeble and tender. Like that, it is capable of growth and enlargement and may receive almost any direction or impression you please to give it. If left untutored, it becomes the sport of every passion; but if informed, and guided by a suitable education, it will produce noble and worthy fruits. As reason in its first dawn is small, so its progress is slow, but with early cultivation, diligent and persevering application, is capable of great enlargement in the wide field of science, as many brilliant genii have proved, greatly to the honor of human nature and benefit of mankind.

"It is observed of the brute creation, that they 'soon arrive at that pitch of perfection which is allotted to their nature, where they must stop short, without a possibility of going any further. Sense, which is the highest natural power they have, moves in a narrow sphere; its objects, in comparison, few; dull and gross; and therefore not only come more quickly round, but become more languid and dull at every revolution.' But man is endowed with nobler faculties, and presented with nobler objects whereon to exercise and employ them. Nothing can bound the noble range of reason, ever improving and ever improvable When we take a view of the intellectual world, how are we struck with admiration at the progress the human intellect is capable of making! How small the beginning! How slow the progress! And yet, how great the store of intellectual acquirements which some have made!

"It is in every man's power to make his life a progressive state. The faculties of the human soul are in themselves noble and excellent, and capable of continual enlargement. The more the soul thinks and reasons the more capable it becomes of that noble exercise, and it may be eternally increasing in knowledge and wisdom, making perpetual advances towards perfection—bending forward to the excellence of superior natures, unbroken by exercise and unimpaired by time,—receiving new accessions of bliss and glory from its perpetual approaches towards the fountain of all perfection. The concern which individuals have in this momentous affair, is an immediate address to personal interest and parental affection. Involved in its consequences are the honor, comfort and happiness of parents—the present and future good of their children. Therefore, the subject lays claim to your attention by all the ties of interest, affection, and humanity.

Education rescues the mind from that darkness and obscurity which is the unhappy lot of savages, and which distinguishes them from enlightened and civilized nations. Why are not we howling in the uncultivated desert, untutored as 'the wild ass's colt?' Is it not to be ascribed to the early care of our pious ancestors, in instituting schools and colleges, for the preservation and general diffusion of knowledge and science? As the chisel works the rude block into shape, so does education form the human soul, which would otherwise be filled with nothing more than a jumble of wild, unconnected ideas, incapable of forming itself into any system.' The business of education, says the great Dr. Price, is to teach 'how to think' rather than 'what to think.'

" Education opens all the secret sources of the mind; marshals all its powers; and prepares the subject for future action. * * * For want of a suitable education, how many of superior natural abilities, have sunk under the weight of untutored genius; perverted their noble faculties to base purposes; and 'fallen among the splendid ruins of human nature?' It is the judgment of the most accurate writers upon this subject, that of the men we meet, nine parts out of ten are, what they are, good or bad, according to their education. If you wish to see your children entering upon the stage under every possible advantage, cultivate their minds, direct their manners, and 'train them up in the way they should go.' This will qualify them for the part they are to act in life, of whatever station or relation; and enable them to discharge the duties and offices of the places they may fill, with honor to themselves, and usefulness to the public.

" If the means of education should be neglected, the rising generation would grow up uninformed and without principle; their ideas of freedom would degenerate into licentious independence; and they would fall a prey to their own animosities and contentions. If education is not laid open to all, and schools instituted for common benefit, of poor as well as rich, 'your posterity will be in danger of being gulled out of their liberties by an artful and insidious few, who may have all the wealth and learning in their hands.'

" Sentiments and practice depend much upon education; as that is, such in general will the man be. If the principles of virtue are early implanted in the mind, they will take deep root, and produce the most happy fruits. If a foundation is seasonably laid in the mind by regular instruction, men will learn to think rationally and soberly upon subjects of moral duty, and christian faith. They will be able to inquire candidly after truth, and determine impartially, what is their duty.

" It is not my province, in this place, to point out the particular methods to be pursued in the institution and arrangement of schools. But it is well known, that where the public have provided the means of instruction, knowledge has been more generally diffused; and the advantages to society more largely experienced, and those ill-consequences to government prevented which have been sadly experienced where they were neglected. Much credit is due, therefore, to every one who steps forth in so good a cause, and distinguishes himself by his exertions for the establishment and support of schools upon such principles and in such manner as shall be most subservient to general good."

In closing he thus addresses parents and the guardians of the young:

" By the love you bear to your tender charges, watch the first dawn of reason, beaming forth in immortal rays, and pour religious instruction into the opening genius. Follow it through the several stages of its growth, with due cultivation, to its mature state. Take the helpless creature by the hand, and lead it 'in the way it should go,' and there is the strongest probability that 'when it is old, it will not depart from it.' Let the mind be early formed to virtue. Let the principles of it be deeply rooted, before the habits of vice get possession there. Be more solicitous to see in them unaffected goodness of heart, and unsullied purity of manners, than brilliancy of wit, or beauty. Teach them the right government of their passions, and that uniform rectitude of manners which will give them the fairest claim to honor and reputation. Raise them above anxiety. Secure to them a happy tranquillity of mind, in the troubles of life. Lead them in the way to comfort and happiness in this world, with the pleasing assurance that it will be perfected in that which is to come."

From 1775 to 1783, the state of affairs in Providence was unfavorable for advancing the work which the friends of free education had at heart. The raising of troops for the continental army, the exposed condition of the colony, the campaign upon Rhode Island, the military encampment into which the town had been turned, and other excitements of war, absorbed time and thought to the exclusion of almost everything else. From 1778 to 1781, the school in Whipple Hall was suspended, and the building occupied by the Continental Committee of War for a Laboratory and Magazine. The Meeting street school-house was converted to a similar use.

The damage done to "Whipple Hall" was estimated at "one hundred and thirteen Spanish milled dollars, and one-third of a dollar." Subsequently the town set apart all sums "which should be received of the State or the United States, for damage done the brick school-house during the revolutionary war, all rents to be received for Market-house cellar, chambers and stalls, and all wharfage to be received on the Market-house lot, as a fund for the support of public schools." These sums could do little more than keep the buildings in repair; but the appropriation had an important bearing upon the public mind, by drawing attention to the distinction between free and proprietors' schools.

In 1770 the school cause received an accession of strength in Rev. James Manning, D. D., the first President of Rhode Island College, which had been established at Warren, and in the above named year was removed to Providence. He interested himself in the labors of and co-operated with those, who for twenty years had been moulding public thought, and endeavoring to secure effective action. Of his services more will be said in another place.

Second Epoch.

The experience of several years proved that town partnership in proprietors' schools, could not produce satisfactory results; and a committee appointed to draw up a plan for the government of the several schools in town, reported that in their opinion no effectual method could be devised for the encouragement of learning, and the general diffusion of knowledge and virtue among all classes of children and youth, until the town should think proper to take a matter of so much importance into their own hands, and provide and support a sufficient number of judicious persons for that purpose.

The town did not, however, adopt the proposed measure, and matters continued with little change until 1791, when a renewed effort in the right direction was made.

"At the annual town meeting held on the 6th day of June, 1791, the subject came up in the form of a petition, praying that a sufficient number of schoolmasters be appointed to instruct all the children in town, at the public expense. The petition was read and referred to the School committee, consisting, besides the Chairman, Dr. Manning, of the Rev. Dr. Hitchcock, the Rev. Joseph Snow, pastor of the Beneficent Congregational Church, the Rev. Moses Badger, pastor of St. John's Church, the Rev. Jonathan Maxcy, then the youthful pastor of the First Baptist Church, and Messrs. Jabez Bowen, Moses Brown, John J. Clark, David Howell, Theodore Foster, John Dorrance, Welcome Angell and Benjamin Bowen. The consideration of the subject, says the *Providence Gazette*, was referred to the adjournment on Monday next, (June 13,) and the School Committee were requested to report at that meeting, rules and regulations for the government of schools, etc. From the almost unanimous approbation this important measure received from all quarters, 'we anticipate,' says the *Gazette*, 'with the greatest pleasure, the happy consequences that may be reasonably expected to result from an establishment which will do honor to the town, be of infinite service to the rising generation, and which must interest every humane mind in its final success. We cannot close this article without saying, what we deem it to be just should be generally known, that a number of the most opulent gentlemen in town, who will pay largely on this establishment, have interested themselves warmly in its favor.

"At the next meeting, the Committee found themselves unprepared to report in full upon a subject of such vast importance, and again the meeting was adjourned until the first Monday in August. Meanwhile the matter was discussed in the columns of the weekly press, and the advantages of public free schools were fully and ably set forth. In the *Gazette* for Saturday, July 30, every male inhabitant, and heads of families especially, are requested to lay aside other concerns, 'and attend on the town meeting next Monday, in the afternoon, to consider and decide on the important measure of establishing town schools.'"—*Providence School Report, 1869.*

The report above referred to, was written by Dr. Manning, who died greatly lamented a few days before the town meeting was held at which it was to be presented.* It is here printed entire, as a document deserving a permanent place in the history of the free school movement:

REPORT OF THE SCHOOL COMMITTEE IN 1791.

"At a town meeting of the Freemen of the town of Providence, held, by adjournment, at the State House, on Monday, the 1st day of August, 1791.

"WHEREAS, the School Committee, who were, on the 6th and 13th days of June last, appointed and continued to make report respecting a petition pending before the meeting, for the erection of schools in this town, the expense whereof is to be paid out of the town treasury, presented the following report, to wit:

"To the Freemen of the Town of Providence, to be convened next by adjournment, the underwritten members of your School Committee, in pursuance of your resolution at your last meeting, report.

"After the most deliberate and mature consideration of the subject, we are clearly of opinion that the measure proposed by the petitioners is eligible, for many reasons:

"1st. Useful knowledge generally diffused among the people is the surest means of securing the rights of man, of promoting the public prosperity, and perpetuating the liberties of a country.

"2d. As civil community is a kind of joint tenancy, in respect to the gifts and abilities of individual members thereof, it seems not improper that the disbursements necessary to qualify those individuals for usefulness should be made from common funds.

"3d. Our lives and properties, in a free State, are so much in the power of our fellow citizens, and the reciprocal advantages of daily intercourse are so much dependent on the information and integrity of our neighbors, that no wise man can feel himself indifferent to the progress of useful learning, civilization, and the preservation of morals, in the community where he resides.

"4th. The most reasonable object of getting wealth, after our own wants are supplied, is to benefit those who need it; and it may with great propriety be demanded, in what way can those whose wealth is redundant, benefit their neighbors more certainly and permanently, than by furnishing to their children the means of qualifying them to become good and useful citizens, and of acquiring an honest livelihood?

"5th. In schools established by public authority, and whose teachers are paid by the public, there will be reason to hope for a more faithful and impartial discharge of the duties of instruction, as well as of discipline among the scholars, than can be expected when the masters are dependent on individuals for their support.

---

* Rev. Dr. Manning was born in Elizabethtown, New Jersey, October 22d, 1738, and received a liberal education at Princeton College, where he was graduated September 29th, 1762, and the same year was ordained as a Baptist Minister. He was elected President of Rhode Island College, (Brown University,) in 1765, of which he was the successful and honored head until his death which occurred suddenly, Sunday morning, July 24, 1791, in the 54th year of his age. As an educator he occupied a leading rank.

"These, among other reasons, have lead your Committee to investigate the means of accomplishing an object so desirable as the establishment of a competent number of schools in this town, to be supported at the town's expense. The Brick School House and Whipple Hall are buildings conveniently situated for our present purpose; but, as the former is, in part, and the latter wholly, private property, it will become necessary that the individual owners should be compensated, and the entire property of those buildings vested in the town.

"The large number of inhabitants on the west side of the river renders it indispensably necessary that a suitable school-house be erected on a lot to be provided for that purpose on that side of the river. It would also be proper that a fourth school-house should be provided on a convenient lot, to be procured near the lower end of the town.

"When your Committee consider that, according to the late enumeration, there are in this town twelve hundred and fifty-six white males under sixteen years of age, they cannot estimate the number of scholars lower than to require, at the Brick School-house, a principal Master and Assistants; at the School-house on the west side of the river, a principal Master and Assistants; and a principal Master and Assistants at each of the other school-houses; to be appointed by, and amenable to, a committee to be chosen by the Freemen, annually assembled according to law, to be called the Town School Committee, for the time being; by whom also the salaries of such teachers, from time to time, shall be contracted for and paid by orders by said Committee, drawn on the town treasury. The Assistants to be occasionally appointed, when need may require.

"Your Committee are further of opinion, that all the aforesaid schools be subjected to such rules and regulations, from time to time, as may be devised and formed by the School Committee, for the time being, after the same shall have received the approbation of the Freemen of this town, in town meeting legally assembled.

"And as the Society of Friends have a convenient school-room of their own, and choose to educate their children under the tuition of their own members, and the direction of committees of their own Meeting, it is recommended that they receive, from time to time, of the money raised for schooling, according as the proportion which the number of scholars in their school shall bear to the whole number educated out of the town's funds, to be ascertained by their Committee to the Town's Committee, who are to give orders on the town treasury for the same, as in the case of other schools,—their schools being open to the Town's Committee for their inspection and advice in regard to the moral conduct and learning of the children, not interfering in respect to the address or manners of the Society, in relation to their religious opinions.

"Finally your Committee recommend, as new and further powers are hereby proposed to be granted to, and exercised by, the Town's future School Committee, which were not in contemplation at the time of their appointment, that they have liberty to resign their places, and that a School Committee be appointed for the Town of Providence, to remain in office till the next annual choice of Town Officers, and instructed to report the rules and regulations aforesaid to the next town meeting; that a committee be also appointed to contract, in behalf of the town, for suitable lots where to build the two new school-houses proposed to be erected, and to form plans and an estimate of the expense of such buildings, and to report the same to the next town meeting; That said Committee last mentioned also inquire and report on what terms the proprietors of the Brick School-house and Whipple Hall will relinquish their claims to the town.

"JAMES MANNNING,   "DAVID HOWELL,
ENOS HITCHCOCK,   BENJAMIN BOURN,
MOSES BROWN,   JOHN DORRANCE,
JOSEPH SNOW,   THEODORE FOSTER,
MOSES BADGER,   WELCOME ARNOLD.
JABEZ BOWEN,

"Providence, July, (7th month,) 1791.

" And the said report having been duly considered, *It is Voted and Resolved,* That the same be received and adopted, except as to the resignation of the School Committee, who are hereby continued, and directed to draft rules and regulations for the government of said schools, and to make report at the next town meeting.

"*It is further Resolved,* That Messrs. Moses Brown, John Brown, Welcome Arnold, Edward Thurber, Charles Keene, Zephaniah Andrews and Charles Lippitt, or the major part of them be and they are hereby appointed a Committee to procure the lots in said report mentioned; to inquire the terms on which the proprietors of Whipple Hall and the Brick School-house will relinquish their rights in said buildings to the town; to estimate the expense of the two new school-houses, and to perform all other business required of the Committee last mentioned in said report; and that they also make report to the next town meeting.

"*Ordered,* That these resolutions be published in the newspapers in this town.

" A true copy—witness,

"DANIEL COOKE, *Town Clerk.*"

Between the foregoing report and the one presented to the town twenty-three years before, there is entire harmony with a single exception; and that is, the clause allowing the Society of Friends to maintain a separate school " under the tuition of their own members," and draw upon the public treasury for its support. And here rose a strong objection. It was seen that a favor like this granted to one denomination could be demanded by every other; and hence the plan of public free schools, to be attended by children of all classes without regard to theological tenets, would ultimate in a collection of sectarian schools, a great gulf between each, maintained at public charge—a system totally incompatible with the genius of Republican institutions. There is foundation for the belief, that, well intentioned as was the recommendation, it was the real cause why the action of the town through committees and otherwise, for several succeeding years, proved abortive.

THIRD EPOCH.

(1791-1800.)

THE SCHOOLS ESTABLISHED BY LAW.—MR. HOWLAND'S NARRATIVE.

THE nine years following 1791 were years of uncommon interest to the friends of public free schools. The unsuccessful attempts of the preceding twenty-three years had not been in vain. The discussions in town meetings and in private, brought the subject more prominently to view, and not a few, who, at the start, were indifferent or absolutely hostile, had become actively interested. A change was coming slowly but surely over the public mind, and those who had borne the heat and burden of the day, sometimes hoping against hope, felt their courage stimulated, and their determination to persevere, strengthened.

Near the close of the century a new and important element was brought to the aid of the cause. This was the Providence Association of Mechanics and Manufacturers, founded in 1798, and which soon became one of the most influential organizations in the town. Among the prominent members of this body was John Howland, descended in the fifth generation from John Howland of the Plymouth Pilgrim Company of 1620. He had been an attentive observer of the course of things, and, as he saw the inadequacy of the means of education, and reflected upon the privation of his early years, he was stirred to make another effort in behalf of free schools. He was peculiarly adapted to the work partly assumed by him, and partly assigned him by his fellow townsmen. He was noted for sound judgment, far-reaching discernment, skill in execution, and unconquerable persistence. There came daily to his shop men of all shades of opinion, and he was not long in becoming familiar with the peculiarities of each. His position in the community gave him a strong influence with the wealthy and with the laboring classes, and as the hostility to free schools was found largely among the latter, he was able to create a better sentiment among them. In his place of business, in the street, and by the fireside, public free schools were made by him a topic of conversation. "Most of us," he said, "have had but few advantages of education, but it will be our fault, as well as the fault of our fellow citizens, if the next generation is not better taught. Perhaps this is a subject on which we are too indifferent. It is a subject which ought to be the *lesson* of the day, and the *story* of the evening. Let it be said in all private companies; let it be asserted in all public bodies; let it be declared in all places, till it has grown into a proverb; that it is the duty of the legislature to establish free schools throughout the State. But until this can be accomplished, let us not neglect our duty. It is the duty of every man who has children, to see that they have what is called a good common education; not such a common education as permits them to grow up destitute of morals or of principles; but such as will qualify them to be respectable, as well as useful members of society."

In 1798, the Mechanics' Association committed itself to the support of these ideas. Mr. Howland, as chairman of a committee appointed for the purpose, prepared a memorial to the General Assembly soliciting that honorable body "to make legal provision for the establishment of free schools, sufficient to educate all the children in the several towns throughout the State;" and subsequently when a bill had been introduced into the legislature, he prepared, by vote of the town, a letter of instructions to its representatives, directing them to vote for it. But the story of his efforts is best told in his own words as taken down by the author during an interview in 1847.* The familiar, unstudied language of the recital, which has been literally preserved, imparts to the narrative an additional interest; and having compared it with the records, and verified the accuracy of every statement relating to the action of the town, it must ever be regarded as an invaluable contribution to the school history of Providence.

"In 1789, the Mechanics Association was formed, and in this body begun the agitation that led to the establishment of public schools. When we came together in our association, we made the discovery of our deficiencies. There were papers

---

*The reader may be surprised to find this story entire in the preliminary portion of the centennial volume. The author can only say in explanation, that he was not aware of its being thus appropriated until he saw it in print. But as it was included in his manuscript, and is necessary to the completeness of his narrative of the public schools in Providence, he has, upon consultation with friends, decided not to suppress it.

to be drawn and various kinds of writing to be done, that few of us were competent to execute. Then we began to talk. The question was asked, ought not our children to have better advantages of education than we enjoyed? And the answer was, Yes. Then it was asked, how shall these advantages be secured? The reply was, we must have better schools. So when we had talked the matter over thoroughly among ourselves we began to agitate. As I was something of a talker, and had practised writing more than most of my associates, a good deal of this work fell to my lot. And I was very willing to do it, because I felt and saw its importance. So I wrote a number of pieces for the newspaper, and tried to induce others to do the same. I prevailed, however, with only one, Grindall Reynolds. He felt as I did about the matter, and wrote a piece for the *Gazette* in favor of schools. We had, indeed, the good-will of many educated men. There were Thomas P. Ives, Thomas L. Halsey, David L. Barnes, and others, who had been educated in the schools of Massachusetts, all of whom understood our wants and favored our movements. Governor Bowen and the Bowen family, were also friendly. So was Governor William Jones. We met no opposition from the wealthy, but they having the advantages for their sons and daughters that wealth can always procure, did not feel as we poor mechanics did. They were not active. In this beginning of the movement, they seemed willing to follow, but were unwilling to lead the way. It is a curious fact, that throughout the whole work, it was the most unpopular with the common people, and met with the most opposition from the class it was designed to benefit. I suppose this was one reason why the most influential citizens did not take hold of it heartily in the beginning. They thought its success doubtful, and did not wish, in a public way, to commit themselves to an enterprise that would curtail their popularity and influence. This was not the case with all, but it was so with many. The more we discussed the subject, the greater became its importance in our eyes. After a good deal of consultation and discussion, we got the Mechanics Association to move in the matter. This was an important point gained, and an encouragement to persevere. A committee was chosen to take up the subject. Of this committee I was a member. They met at my house, and after due deliberation, it was resolved to address the General Assembly. I told them, that as neither of us were qualified to draw up a paper in a manner suited to go before that body, we had each better write a petition embodying our individual views, and bring it to our next meeting. Out of these mutual contributions we could prepare a petition that would do. This was agreed to and the committee separated. When we next met it was found that but two had been written according to previous recommendation. These were by William Richmond and myself. Richmond then read his. It was in the usual *petition* style, ending, 'as in duty bound will ever pray.' I told the committee I did not like the doctrine of that paper. It was too humble in tone. I did not believe in *petitioning* legislators to do their duty. We ought, on the contrary, in addressing that body, to assume a tone of confidence that with the case fairly stated they would decide wisely and justly for the rising generation. I then took out my memorial and read it. It was not in the shape of an 'humble petition.' It expressed briefly our destitution, and the great importance of establishing free schools to supply it. It received the approbation of the committee, and was adopted. This memorial was presented to the General Assembly in the name of our association. It was there warmly debated, and after pretty severe opposition, the Assembly referred the whole subject to a committee, with directions to report by bill. This bill, embodying a general school system, was drawn up by James Burrill, Jr., Attorney General of Rhode Island. I was with him all the while, and he readily complied with my suggestions. When the bill was reported, the Assembly was afraid to pass it, until the sense of the towns could be obtained. So it was printed, and sent out to the Freemen for instructions. The great object now was to get the towns to vote right. When the subject came before the town meeting in Providence, I moved that a committee be appointed to prepare instructions to our representatives, and report at the present meeting. This was carried, and William Richmond, Samuel W. Bridgham, afterwards our mayor, George R. Burrill, William Larned and myself, were constituted the committee. It was now late in the afternoon, and Bridgham, said, 'Mr. moderator, this is an important matter. It will require some time to draft instructions, and it is now almost night, I think the subject had better be postponed until the next town meeting.' 'Never fear,' replied Richard Jackson, the moderator. 'I guess Howland has them already written in his pocket.' 'O,' rejoined Bridgham, 'I didn't think of that — then we can go on.' The committee accordingly retired to the office of George R. Burrill for consultation. The questions then came up, what shape shall the instructions take? who shall write them? Various opinions were expressed, but I kept silent. Bridgham then turned to me and said 'what do you think Mr. Howland?' I had anticipated the course of events, and was prepared to answer the question. I had set up, the night before, till 11 o'clock, to prepare a document I intended to submit to the town meeting. I therefore said to the committee, 'I have got *my* opinion in my pocket. If you wish to hear, I will read it.' 'Let us hear, by all means,' was the reply. So I took out my document and read it. When I got through, Burrill said, 'well, that is just what we want. All we need do is to sign our names' They accordingly signed it, without suggesting any alteration, and we returned and reported it to the meeting. The paper was adopted by the town, as its instructions to its representatives.

"But though Providence was thus committed to the good work, the country towns generally were not so safe. In many, the movement was decidedly unpopular, and there was ground for apprehension that it might fail. One of the most influential men in the State councils was then a resident of Newport. I felt very anxious to secure the favorable expression of that town. I therefore wrote to the town clerk, urging him to get an article inserted in the warrant for the town meeting, to instruct their representatives to vote for the bill before the Assembly. And so fearful was I that this precaution would be neglected, that I made a special journey to Newport to secure the measure. Much to my gratification, Newport voted for the instructions, and valuable services were rendered by Mr. George Champlin, the principal representative from that town. Essential aid was also rendered by a member from Smithfield. At the autumn session, (1799,) the bill passed the House of Representatives, and was sent up to the Senate. That body was afraid to pass it, and did not dare to reject it. So with other unfinished business, they laid it over until the next session. The Assembly met in February in this town. I resolved to persevere in my efforts to get the school bill passed. I saw the secretary, and at my suggestion, he placed the deferred bill among the papers first to be called up. One day, in the early part of the session, I met Joel Metcalf, a man of strong good sense, who had interested himself in the matter of public schools. 'Come,' said I, 'you and I must go up to the Senate to day and get them to call up the school bill.' 'Well' he replied, 'I don't know as we can influence that honorable body.' 'We can try,' I responded. And so we went. We saw John Innis Clarke, a senator, and told him our errand. 'Well,' said he, 'the governor and senate are to dine with me to day, and I will do what I can to secure favorable action.' We left, and went up to the senate chamber in the afternoon. As soon as I opened the door, Clarke rose and came to me, and said 'the school bill has just passed.' Was it opposed?' I inquired. 'No,' he replied, 'I called it up, and it was passed without a word of opposition.' Thus we achieved our great State triumph—not of long duration,indeed, as the act was repealed in 1803,—but long enough to secure a permanent blessing to Providence.

"I shall not confine my narrative to the strict order of dates, as I have no minutes of the events I am relating by me. My object is to give a brief view of the part I took in this work. The town resolved to establish four schools, three on the east and one on the west side of the river. I was on a committee to carry out the design. Having made a motion in town meeting, June 3, 1799, that a committee be appointed to purchase the shares held by the proprietors of 'Whipple Hall,' and the brick school-house, standing near the State House, I was made chairman, and entered at once upon my duties. The other members of the committee were Richard Jackson, Jr., and John Carlile. Afternoon after afternoon, accompanied by Paul Allen, I traversed the north end in search of the proprietors. Sometimes we found one at home and another in the street. In this way, we picked up forty-five shares, at $10 each—I making the contract, and Allen, as justice of the peace, legalizing it. Five of the old proprietors we never could find, nor could we ascertain who were their heirs. To this day they have not been purchased. One of the proprietors, a sturdy, self-willed man, at first refused to sell. He 'wasn't going to educate other peoples children.' But after being made to see that the system would go on, and his refusal would injure nobody but himself, (the town then owning over forty shares, and thus able to control the house,) he relented, and acceeded to our terms. We next bought the brick school-house. This was more easily done, as the principal number of shares was in the hands of Moses Brown, and the town already owned the land on which the building stood. These shares were purchased at $10.50 each. It was not so easy, however, to obtain the lot for a school-house site at the south end. This land belonged to a gentleman who was unwilling to have a school of two hundred scholars so near his house and garden. I was not on the committee to make this purchase, but when I heard he had refused to sell, I went to see him. I asked the ground of his objections. He said if a school was established there, the neighborhood would be a perfect bedlam every time it was dismissed. Besides, his garden would be robbed of all its fruit. These were very natural fears. But I assured him they were groundless.

"Under our rules, the school would be dismissed by classes, and not permitted to loiter about the premises, and as to his garden, so strict a watch would be kept over the scholars, that his fruit would be safer than ever. I cannot repeat all my arguments on the occasion. It is sufficient to say, that before I left him, he consented to sell. Some time after, when the schools had gone fairly into operation, the town council, accompanied by the school committee, made their first visit to this school. When opposite his residence, I requested the company to pause till I went in and invited him to go with us. They did so. I went in and said, 'I have been deputed by the honorable town council and the school committee, to invite you to accompany them in their first visit of examination to the Transit street school.' He appeared gratified with the attention, and readily complied with our invitation. I will not say there was not a little policy in this. At all events, it had a good effect. Our skeptical friend was delighted with all he saw and heard, and was ever after a firm supporter of the public schools.

"It was clear, that to carry out our system successfully, a larger sum of money than hitherto appropriated for schools must be secured. Here we experienced the strongest opposition, and were in greatest danger of defeat. I moved, in town meeting, for an appropriation of $4,000. Some said it was too much, and others, hoping to defeat the motion, opposed on the ground that the sum was insufficient. After listening sometime to the discussion, I rose and said, that as there appeared to be a difference of opinion in the meeting, with a view to obviate the last objection, I would move the insertion of $6,000 in the place of $4,000, first proposed. This was seconded by one of the opponents, thinking thereby to give the motion its quietus. Much to his surprise, however, the motion was adopted. When the result was announced, great excitement prevailed. Two of the strongest opponents came up to me and said, 'you have taken us in—you have taken us in—we didn't intend to vote you so much money.' 'You have taken yourselves in, and I am glad of it,' I replied. This agitation of the school matter induced many of the mechanics to attend town meeting, and take an active part in town affairs, who never went before. April 16, 1800, the town appointed James Burrill, Jr., John Corliss, Richard Jackson, Jr., John Carlile, Joel Metcalf, William Richmond and myself a committee to devise and report a plan for carrying the school act into effect. This plan I drew up. It was reported to an adjourned town meeting, April 26th, and adopted.

"The first school committee under the act of the General Assembly, was chosen in August, 1800. It consisted of President Maxcy, Rev. Dr. Gano, Rev. Dr. Hitchcock, David L. Barnes, Jabez Bowen, Amos M. Atwell, James Burrill, Jr., William Jones, John Carlile and myself. The town council, in conjunction with this body, appointed a sub-committee to draw up rules and regulations for the government of the schools. On this committee were President Maxcy, Rev. Dr. Hitchcock and Rev. Dr. Gano. When nominated, Dr. Gano said the schools had his warmest wishes for success, but as he was not much acquainted with the matter, and as Mr. Howland had done so much, and understood the wants so well, he would decline in his favor. His wish was complied with, and I was placed on this important committee.

"When the work of drawing up the rules came to be done, to my surprise, the burden of the labor was assigned to me. President Maxcy, was pressed with the cares of the college, and could not conveniently attend to the duty. Dr. Hitchcock's health was declining, and though warmly devoted to the cause of education, was unable to give the subject the attention it deserved. So it was left for me to go on with it. This was rather a formidable undertaking, but as I had the approbation of the literary gentlemen, I boldly put my hand to the work. To aid me in the matter, I sent to Boston, and procured the rules established there, and also a list of the books used in school. After my rules and regulations were prepared, I submitted them to the committee and town council. They were accepted, and adopted October 16th, less than two months after my appointment.

"Up to this time, I had never seen a grammar—a sorry confession for a school committee man, some may think—but observing that 'The Young Ladies' Accidence' was used in the Boston schools, I sent to the principal book-seller in that town, and purchased one hundred copies for the use of ours. For whatever accuracy I have obtained in writing, I am indebted to observation and practice.

"The introduction of grammar was quite an advance in the system of education, as it was not taught at all except in the better class of private schools. The same was true of geography, which had never been taught before. Geographies could not be bought in this town, so I sent to Boston and purchased as many as were wanted for our schools. Dr. Morse, of Charlestown, had published the first volume of his geography, and that was the work we adopted. Many thought it an unnecessary study, and some in private objected to it because it would take off their attention from arithmetic. But it met with no public opposition."

"To some, this recital may seem egotistical. But I have no such feeling. I was so constantly connected with the school movement, that I cannot speak of it without speaking of myself. I take no improper pride in the part I acted. If better educated and more influential men had seen fit to take the lead, I should have been contented to follow. But I felt that somebody must do the work, and as others would not, I resolved that I would. I thank a kind providence, that I have been able, in my humble way, to be of service to my fellow men; and I wish to occupy no other place in their memories, or the page of history, than that which truth shall assign me."

Such is the simple recital of the part borne by Mr. Howland in laying the foundation of the Public Schools in Providence, and in its effects reaching beyond, shedding a blessing upon the entire State. The names of Hopkins, Bowen, Jones, Burrill, Brown, Jackson, Nightingale, Hitchcock, Manning, Gano, Maxcy, Bridgham, Ives, Rhodes, Smith and Barnes, with many others of like spirit, will ever be held in grateful remembrance for the interest they early exhibited in the cause of free education. Without the sympathy and coöperation of such men, little could have been accomplished. But to the mind that from its own fertile resources originated plans, combined influences, organized popular sentiment, and by its indomitable energy carried forward to its ultimate triumph this great enterprise, a distinct acknowledgement is due. And this tribute is here rendered to the memory of John Howland.*

*Mr. Howland was a native of Newport. As a member of the school committee, he for twenty years discharged the duties of his office with scrupulous fidelity, and retired

School Regulations—District Boundaries.

On the 17th day of October, 1800, the System of Instruction drawn up by Mr. Howland, was reported and adopted. It prescribed that "all children of both sexes admissible by law," should be admitted to the schools, " and faithfully instructed without preference or partiality," and that the instruction should " be uniform in the several schools, and the pronunciation as near alike as possible." The good morals of the youth, being a matter of the highest consequence, both to their own comfort, and to their progress in useful knowledge, they were strictly enjoined "to avoid idleness and profaneness, falsehood and deceitfulness, and every other wicked and disgraceful practice, and to conduct themselves in a sober, orderly and decent manner, both in and out of school." It was also enjoined upon the teachers, " That they endeavor to impress the minds of their pupils with a sense of the Being and Providence of God, and the obligation they are under to love and reverence Him ; their duty to their parents and masters ; the beauty and excellence of truth, justice and mutual love ; tenderness to brute creatures ; the happy tendency of self-government and obedience to the dictates of reason and religion ; the observance of the Sabbath as a sacred institution ; the duty which they owe to their country, and the necessity of a strict obedience to its laws ; and that they caution them against the prevailing vices."

From the third Monday in October, to the third Monday in April, the morning school sessions were to commence at 9 o'clock, A. M., and close at 12, M. The afternoon sessions were to open at 1½ oclock and close at 4 o'clock. From the third Monday in April to the third Monday in October, the morning sessions were to hold from 8 o'clock until 11½ o'clock, and the afternoon sessions from 2 o'clock until 5 o'clock. The 4th of July, Fast, Thanksgiving and Christmas days, Tuesday, Wednesday and Thursday of Commencement week, the day succeeding each quarterly visitation, and " the regimental training day in October," were made holidays. The course of instruction was to comprise " spelling, accenting and reading both prose and verse, with propriety and accuracy, and a general knowledge of English grammar and composition ; also writing a good hand, according to the most approved rules, and Arithmetic through all the previous rules, and vulgar and decimal fractions, including Tare and Tret, Fellowship, Exchange, Interest," etc. The pupils were to be classed " according to their several improvements, each sex by them-

only, when the demands upon his time as town treasurer, and treasurer of the Providence Institution for Savings, suggested the necessity of release from some of his public responsibilities.

selves," and " different hours were to be allotted to the different exercises." In the matter of discipline and good government which the committee regarded as " absolutely necessary to improvement," it was provided that " if any scholar should prove disobedient and refractory, after all reasonable means used by the master to bring him or her to order, and a just sense of duty, such offender shall be suspended from any further attendance or instruction in any school in the town until the next visitation of the committee." Pupils were required to be punctual in their attendance " at the appointed hour, and be as constant as possible in their daily attendance." Excuses for absence were to be " by a note from the parents or guardian " of the pupil. Monitors were to be appointed by the masters of each school to notice the absence or tardiness of the delinquent scholars, the list of whose names was to be preserved and exhibited to the committee at their visitation.

The books authorized to be used, were Alden's Spelling Book. 1st and 2d parts ; Caleb Bingham's Young Ladies' Accidence ; the American Preceptor ; Morse's Geography, abridged ; the Holy Bible, in select portions ; and an Arithmetic, author not named. A few years later, Daboll's Arithmetic was introduced, as were Murray's Sequel to the English Reader, and Murray's Abridgment to the English Grammar. Smith's Grammar superseded Murray's ; Farnum's took the place of Smith's, and in the course of a few years Greene's was introduced, and continues to be used. In 1828, Smith's Arithmetic was introduced. This was succeeded by Emerson's ; and, from time to time, Colburn's, Davies,' Greenleaf's, Leach and Swan's and Hagar's followed.

For the better convenience of pupils in attending school, the town was divided into four districts, the lines of which were designated as follows : " From the house of the widow Hall, [on North Main street, opposite St. John's Church] eastward up the Church lane, across Benefit street, all that part of the town lying northward of said line, to constitute the First District. The second District to include all that part of the town lying between Church lane and the lane that runs eastward by the house of the late Welcome Arnold, Esquire, and to take in part of the west side of the river, as far as Orange street. The Third District to include all that part of the town lying southward of said lane, by the late Welcome Arnold's. The Fourth District on the west side of the river to include all that part of the town lying westward of Orange street." It was at the same time directed that children are to " attend the public schools of their respective districts."

FOURTH EPOCH.

(1800—1844.)

QUARTERLY VISITATIONS—DEATH OF REV. DR. HITCHCOCK.

FOUR schools were now in successful operation, with an aggregate attendance of 988 pupils, viz.: First District, Whipple Hall, under John Dexter, 180 pupils; Second District, Brick school-house (Meeting street) under Moses Noyes, 230 pupils; Third District, Transit street house, under Royal Farnum, 240 pupils; Fourth District, west side, under Rev James Wilson, 338 pupils.* These schools sufficed for the town with a population of 7,615. The first quarterly visitation by the Town Council and the School Committee mentioned by Mr. Howland, on a preceding page, took place January 6th and 7th, 1801, and was made an occasion of more than usual importance. That all things might be conducted with propriety, and conduce to the satisfaction of the visitors, it was recommended to the several masters of said schools to prepare accordingly to receive the Committee, by complying with the following regulations, viz.:

"1st. That they enjoin upon their scholars the propriety of appearing neat and clean, and that the Committee expect a general and punctual attendance at the time appointed.

*The teachers acting as principals, from 1800 to 1828, as nearly as can be ascertained, were John Dexter, Moses Noyes, Royal Farnum, Rev. James Wilson, Richard Briggs, Oliver Angell, Liberty Ransom, William E. Richmond, Noah Kendall, Rev. Thomas Williams, Joseph W. Torrey, Christopher Hill, Elisha R. Atkins, Thomas C. Hartshorn, Thomas C. Fenner, Joseph Beverly, Edward Beverly, George Taft, Cyrus Grant, Daniel Baker, Martin Snell, Jedediah L. Stark, Richard Battle, Calvin Barnes, Sumner W. Arnold, Benjamin Allen, Stephen Rawson, Hezekiah Battle, Samuel P. Bullard, Nehemiah E. Rogers, Samuel Stetson, Daniel G. Sprague, William S. Boss, Charles Arnold, Joseph Shaw, Steuben Taylor, Jesse Hartwell, Moses Curtis, Esek Aldrich, Jr., Sylvester R. Aborn, Origin Batcheller, Joseph L. Shaw, Edward Seagrave, John Holroyd, Oliver C. Shaw, Noah Smith, Jr., Elisha W. Baker, Barnum Field, Joseph C. Gardner, Thomas Wilson. Most of these were promoted from ushers.

"2d. That the scholars of the several schools be prepared, in the first place, to exhibit their writing and cyphering books in good order.

"3d. That the masters call upon each scholar to read a short sentence in that book which may be used in the class to which such scholar belongs.

4th. That the Committee may be informed of the progress of the several scholars in the art of spelling, the masters are desired to direct them to spell one word each.

"5th. If time should permit, the Committee will hear the scholar recite passages in Geography, English Grammar and Arithmetic, and such other select pieces as may be adapted to their several capacities."

At the Transit street school, the official visitors were welcomed with a poetic address, written by Paul Allen, Esq., and spoken by a lad nine years of age. It is here given.

"GENTLEMEN OF THE HONORABLE COUNCIL AND COMMITTEE:

"Heroes of ancient and modern days
Have challenged, and received, the palm of praise,
The favored poets will their deeds rehearse,
And blazon forth their destiny in verse.
A more exalted task your time employs,
To watch the morals of the rising boys,—
To teach their wandering feet to tread the road
That leads direct to virtue's bright abode—
To check the sallies of impetuous youth,
And in their bosoms plant the seeds of truth.
No more shall avarice presume to blind
With her dark shades, the eye sight of the mind,
Nor shall presumptious ign'rance dare enslave
Those talents which the God of nature gave.
The tribute that from gratitude is due,
Our hearts rejoicing fondly pay to you;
Unostentatious virtue seeks the shade,
And by its own success is amply paid;
Thus the fair stream with steady silent force,
Through the long meadows winds its devious course,
And in its route, itself unseen the while,
Surveys the verdure spread and flow'rets smile,
Till all the meads in sweet luxuriance grow,
And tell the wonders of the stream below:
Thus, while *you* wish industrious to conceal,
Those virtues gratitude would fain reveal,
The morals of the rising youth shall tell
The names of those whose deeds deserve so well.
Why should my infant tongue these deeds relate?
Your future glory shall adorn the State,
When Patriots yet unknown shall tread the stage,
And shame the parties of the present age."

The favorable impression made upon the Council and the School Committee was entered upon the records in the following words:

"The extraordinary progress made by the scholars of the several schools, in reading, writing. arithmetic, English grammar, geography and elocution, was such as to merit great honor, and obtain the highest commendations of the gentlemen who attended. The good order, decorum, and propriety of behavior, so manifest in the several schools on this occasion, not only evince the great public utility of the institution, but reflect the highest honor on the several preceptors and assistants, who, in the short space of about two months, have established so excellent a system of instruction, and contributed so greatly to the improvement of their pupils. The thanks of the Council and Committee were also presented to the several teachers as a testimonial of the high opinion entertained of their abilities and merits."

The second quarterly visitation, April 7th and 8th, appears to have been quite as satisfactory as the first. On this occasion governor Arthur Fenner and Judge Samuel Eddy were invited to be present. For several years the schools continued to prosper under the fostering care of the town council, the school committee and men of influence generally. In 1803, the schools lost a valued friend and supporter, in the death of Rev. Dr. Enos Hitchcock.* He departed this life February 27th, and was buried on the following Wednesday afternoon. The Town Council as a token of respect for his memory, and in appreciation of his services in behalf of education, directed a suspension of the schools. They also provided that the teachers with their pupils of the first and second classes should attend the funeral, and "join in the procession according to their sizes, the smallest first, and preceding the corpse." This was done.

USHERS APPOINTED.—FUEL, INK, BOOKS FOR THE POOR.

The schools had not been long in operation, when it became apparent that a herculean task had been assigned the teachers. They were all competent and experienced men, but were not equal to the labor imposed upon them. Rev. Mr. Wilson could easily and effectively preach to an audience filling the church to its full sitting capacity, but to require him

---

* Rev. Dr. Hitchcock was a native of Springfield, Mass., and was graduated at Harvard University in 1767. In 1771 he was ordained as colleague pastor with Rev. John Chipman, over the Second Congregational Church in Beverly, Mass. He served as chaplain in the army of the Revolution, was present at the battle of Hubbardston, where his friend and parishioner, Colonel Ebenezer Francis, was killed. He was for a time stationed at West Point. After leaving the army, he was installed pastor of the First Congregational Church in Providence, and had a successful pastorate of twenty years. He was a Fellow of Brown University, and the author of several works. He was a learned divine, a good preacher, and a man of active benevolence.

to maintain order and satisfactorily instruct 338 pupils without assistance, was a demand reaching beyond the power of physical and mental endurance. And so with the other teachers. This the Town Council saw, and promptly appointed five ushers to aid the principals, viz.: First District, Ezra Leonard; Second District, William Norton; Third District, Daniel Young; Fourth District, Lucius Bowles and Gravenor Taft. The salary of each principal was $500 per annum; that of each usher, $200. This compensation to ushers was continued until 1818, when it was increased to $250 per annum.*

Among the early school arrangements was an assessment on each pupil for the supply of fuel. This practice continued until 1833, when, upon the recommendation of the school committee, it was abolished. The pupils were also required to furnish themselves with ink, those failing to do so to be " debarred the privilege of writing." In 1804, provision was made to furnish books to poor children whose parents were unable to purchase them. This course is still pursued, except that they are not given, but loaned. To be absent at a quarterly visitation was an offence which excluded the pupil from the school until permission to return had been obtained of the Town Council.

The Abrogation of the Law of 1800 harmless to Providence. Special Supervision of the Schools.

The school law of 1800, under which the public schools of Providence were organized, was met in the country by an opposition so strong that, after being in operation three years, it was abolished. It seems strange, at this day, in the light of nearly three quarters of a century, that such a step backward should have been taken. But it only adds another to

---

* The ushers from 1801 to 1828, were Ezra Leonard, Lucius Bowles, Gravenor Taft (promoted), Daniel Young (promoted), William Blanding, William Norton, Palmer Cleveland, Samuel Randall, Theopholus Hutchings, Samuel Barton, Jabez B. Whittaker, David Holman, Thomas Philbrook, Eliphalet Dyer, Frederick W. Bottom, Simon Davis, Thomas H. Sill, Jonathan Thayer, John Dunbar, J. H. Cady, Thomas A. Larned, Gideon W. Olney, ——— Whiting, William H. Smith, Rodman Starkweather, Stephen K. Rathbone, Joseph K. M'Clintock, Gardner W. Olney, Christopher Safford, Daniel H. Haskell, Levi Millard, Robert S. Holden, William C. Jones, Amos Warner, Leon Chapotin, William Alverson, Reuben Torry, George Taft (promoted), Ebenezer Colman, Stephen Rawson, (promoted,) Elias Fisk, George L. Atwell, Isaac Southwick, Samuel W. Tillinghast, Calvin Barnes, Noadiah W. Woodward, Benjamin Allen (promoted), Ebenezer Greene, Joseph Patrick, Thomas Warner, John Holroyd (promoted), William Crossman, John G. Merrill, Samuel Billings, Elisha W. Baker, Caleb G. Balch, William P. Taft, Alfred B. Lee, James H. Bugbee, Joshua S. Tweed, Joseph C. Gardner (promoted), Silas Weston, Joseph B. Pettis (promoted), John Ames, Jonn S. Phillips, Benjamin Wade, Richard Anthony.

11

the multitude of historic events showing the hostility with which important reforms have usually been resisted. Men of ideas in advance of the time in which they lived, have pretty uniformly had experiences like this. But the three years' reign of law proved a blessing, by stirring the friends of educational progress to cling with greater tenacity to the noble purpose with which they had become imbued. The abrogation of the law was harmless in its effects upon Providence. The town continued the course it had commenced, as though nothing had happened. Free schools had been established by law. Enough had been seen by discerning minds to satisfy them of their great value as an intellectual force to move and direct the machinery of private and public prosperity. And so, without the aid of law, and with no other encouragement than that which comes in the consciousness of doing a right thing, the schools were to be maintained. This decision had a reflex influence upon the neighboring towns, and upon the State, and prepared the way for certain victory in the second struggle, which was to signalize the close of the next quarter of a century.

In 1816, it being thought that a special supervision of the schools would be advantageous, they were, by vote of the committee, placed " under the superintending care of the Reverend Clergy interim between the several quarterly visitations." Under this resolution the assignments were made as follows: First District, Rev. Dr. Edes; Second District, Rev. Dr. Crocker; Third District, Rev. Dr. Gano; Fourth District, Rev. Mr. Wilson and Rev. Mr. Preston. This arrangement appears to have succeeded so well that by vote, the following year, it was continued. In this arrangement we may recognize the germ of the present system of district committees, who, besides exercising " a general supervision over all the schools in their respective districts, except the High School," are required to " visit or cause to be visited, all the schools at least once in each term."

In 1819, a stone school-house, one story high, was built on Summer street, occupying the site of the recently erected Primary and Intermediate school building. A second story was subsequently added. In October of the same year, " the west part of the town was divided into two Districts; the fourth retaining the old school-house, and the fifth occupying the new house on Pond street." In 1824, an additional teacher was provided for the first district, to take charge of a portion of the pupils removed to a separate room. The salary was fixed at $300 per annum.

In 1828, the subject of primary schools " for children from five to eight years of age," to be taught by females, was agitated, but beyond this nothing appears to have been done.

January 26, 1826, the following record was made: "It being the opinion of the committee and council that the use of profane language and swearing is increasing among the youth, it is ordered that the several preceptors be instructed to read the law on that subject in their several schools."

In July, 1827, it was decided " that no male pupil should commence the study of geography until advanced in arithmetic as far as Practice, and that no female pupil should engage in the former study until she had pursued the study of arithmetic as far as Compound Division."

RECONSTRUCTION OF THE SCHOOLS.

In 1828, a triumph for the schools was achieved. At the winter session of the General Assembly, after a severe struggle, "An act to establish public schools" throughout the State was passed. Though Providence, as already said, was not hindered in her school work by the abrogation of the law of 1800, the friends of education were highly gratified when the law was re-enacted, and accepted it as an endorsement of the principle they had so long maintained.

Twenty-five years had wrought a great change in the public opinion of Providence on the question of education. Increased intelligence made palpable the need of an advance in the course of instruction that should correspond to advances made in the practical arts of life. The school system of 1800, well adapted to the first recipients of its advantages, required some modifications to suit it to a generation standing on a higher plane in 1828 Soon after the passage of the school law, a proposition to re-organize the school system " and place the schools in a condition of greater usefulness to all classes of the community," was referred to a committee consisting of Francis Wayland, William T. Grinnell and Thomas T. Waterman, with directions to examine into and report upon the subject. Immediately after this appointment, two of the committee visited Boston, and occupied several days in the schools of that city, for the purpose of collecting such information concerning the course of studies and the general management of the schools there as might be serviceable in the work of re-construction at home. A report, written by President Wayland, was presented on the 22d of April, which was printed and very generally circulated throughout the town. This document was valuable for the able and exhaustive manner in which it discussed its theme. It is specially interesting as embodying the views of an eminent educator nearly half a century ago. Some portions of the report have more than a local bearing, and contain ideas of an enduring character; and for the purpose of preserving familiarity with the best thought of that day, copious extracts are here given:

"The principle which should mainly direct the appropriation of public money is evidently equity. In other words, money raised by a tax upon every individual should be so distributed that every individual should have an opportunity of participating in the benefits of its expenditure. Or, to apply the principle to the present case, if money is contributed by every citizen for the purpose of education, a school system should be so devised that every citizen should receive, not merely the general advantage of having his neighbors better instructed, but also an equitable share of that instruction which he assists to maintain. Now if this view of the subject be just, it will follow that there should be furnished a number of schools sufficient to accommodate all who wish to avail themselves of their advantages. Every one sees the injustice of taxing the whole community to support one or two schools, to which not more than one-tenth part of the whole number of children could find admittance. The same injustice will evidently occur if the number of scholars imposed upon a teacher be so great as to render his instructions of so little value that a large portion of the community is obliged to resort to private schools.

"The same principle would dictate that there be established the various grades of schools, suited to the wants of the public. If there be but one description of schools, it must either be so elevated that many of the parents cannot prepare their children to enter it, or else so elementary that none would avail themselves of its advantages, for any considerable length of time, or else everything would of necessity be so imperfectly taught that a very small portion would be benefited. In either case but a small portion of the community would receive the benefit of that provision, which all were taxed to support. The first was the case in Boston previous to the establishment of primary schools. The grammar schools admitted no one unless he could read in the Testament. But it was found by actual examination that a very great proportion of the poorer class, were unable or unwilling to procure at their own expense this preparatory education for their children, and that thus many thousands were growing up in utter ignorance.

"It may here be properly suggested whether equity does not demand that the system of public education in this town, should make provision for at least one school of a higher character, a school which should provide instruction in all that is necessary to a finished education. If it be said that such a school would be of advantage only to the rich, it may be answered, as the rich contribute in an equal proportion to education, why should not they be entitled to a portion of the benefit. But it is far from being the case that such a school would be only for the rich. It would be as much a public school, as open to all, and as much under the government of the public as any other. But it would evidently be of most peculiar advantage to the middling classes, and the poor. Such an education as we propose, the rich man can give, and will give to his son, by sending him to private schools. But the man in moderate circumstances cannot afford to incur the heavy expenses of a first rate school, and if no such provision be made, the education of his children must be restricted to the ordinary acquisition of a little more than reading and writing. With such a school as we have contemplated, he would be enabled to give his child an education which would qualify him for distinction in any kind of business.

"And lastly, the principles of equity to which we have alluded, would dictate that the public schools of every description, should be well and skilfully taught. If this be not done, the result will be obvious. The funds by which they are supported are contributed by the rich and by the middling classes of society. If they be badly taught the rich will derive no benefit from them. This, however, is a small matter, as they can afford to give something towards the education of the poor, and also to pay for the education of their own children elsewhere. It is otherwise with the citizen in middling circumstances. If a public school be badly taught and he is sensible of the value of a good education, he also will send his children to a private school. To him this double expense, especially if his family be large, is a serious inconvenience; he is taxed to support schools of which he will not avail himself, and in addition pays as much for the education of his children as though he had contributed nothing. It must be evident that the true interest of every citizen of moderate circumstances, must be so to elevate the character of our public schools, that he need look nowhere else for as good instruction as his family may require. Although to accomplish this he pays a somewhat heavier tax, for public education, he will in the end be greatly the gainer.

"Here, however, we are aware that another consideration will occur. It may be said, that in the distribution of funds raised for public schools, perfect equity is not to be looked for nor desired,—that this is a contribution from the rich, for the benefit of the poor, and that they are sufficiently rewarded by the improved morals and intellectual condition of the poorer classes of the community. Now granting all this to be so, we must remark that the spirit of the suggestion seems to us at variance with our republican institutions. It in reality belongs to the old world more than to the new. Why create such distinction between our fellow citizens? Why should one class of society be supposed to say to another, it is for our interest that you should have education, and we give it to you, but it shall be as useless as anything that can bear the name, so useless that for ourselves and our families, we will have nothing to do with it. We hope no man amongst us, would be willing to harbor such a thought, or utter such a sentiment.

"But, as we said before, granting all this to be true, and that perfect equity in the distribution cannot be effected, as, clearly it cannot, what then? Is not education a commodity which all classes of the community want? Why then should we not furnish it of such quality that all may enjoy it together? By furnishing a valuable course of public instruction, the rich will enjoy its advantages and surely it cannot injure the middling classes and poor. Nor do we here look towards an impracticable result. Children of every class are seen in the public schools in Boston, and they are found there because, as in several instances wealthy parents told your committee, the public were preferable to the private schools.

"And here we may remark, that there can be no doubt of the effect of a single school of the highest character, upon the discipline and improvement of all the others. Entrance to it would be conferred, as the reward of merit, upon the most deserving scholars of each grammar school, and its requirements should always be an accurate knowledge of the branches taught in these schools. It is needless to suggest that a thorough education in such a school as we propose would be the most valuable reward which could be conferred upon diligence and good conduct.

"If, then, we are not mistaken in these views, it is evident that public instruction should be provided in sufficient extent to meet the wants of the community. The course should embrace a series of instruction, from the simplest elements to the higher branches of knowledge, and the instruction in every department should be of the most valuable character. Let us, then, briefly inquire how far our present school system accomplishes these objects.

"How far the provisions for education are proportioned to the magnitude of our population, it may not be possible with perfect accuracy to decide. Judging from the few facts in our possession, it would, however, seem probable that the public good would be promoted by considerably enlarging them. The schools now number on their books as many pupils as can receive advantage from the labors of the present instructors. Yet it will not, we presume, be denied that a very considerable portion of the children about our streets attend no school whatever.

"It would therefore seem proper that the school committee, joined with such persons as the town council may add, be empowered to increase the means of instruction from time to time, as the wants of the population may require. But it has appeared to your committee that one part of this object may be accomplished immediately, and with very little additional expense, by establishing a sufficient number of primary schools in different parts of the town. The effect of these will be to provide a grade of instruction as much needed by the public as any other, to elevate the character of the grammar schools, and to enable the teachers of these schools to devote their attention to a larger portion of those who are prepared for instruction in the more advanced branches of education. We have no doubt that by providing a suitable proportion of these schools, the number of scholars under public instruction would in a short time be doubled, and the convenience to the community be immeasurably increased.

"If, in addition to these two grades of schools, a single school for the whole town be established, of a more elevated character, to enter which, it shall be necessary to have been a proficient in all the studies of the grammar schools, and in which should be taught a more perfect and scientific knowledge of geography, book-keeping, arithmetic, algebra, geometry, navigation, moral and natural philosophy, natural history, the elements of political economy, and the Constitution of the United States, and the Latin and Greek languages; we think that our system of instruction would be such as to do honor to the public spirit of this commercial and manufacturing metropolis, but not at all beyond what is demanded by the advancing intelligence of the age. Whether a high school, of somewhat the same character, for girls, might not also be desirable and expedient, would be a matter for future consideration.

"Your committee have reflected deliberately upon the question, what system of instruction should be recommended for the grammar schools now existing, or whether any alteration be necessary. It may here be proper to remark, that your committee believe that the present instructors have done every thing in their power to carry forward the course of education committed to their charge, and have richly merited the thanks of the community. But from the remarks which have been made, it will be evident that they have labored under many and peculiar embarrassments. A large portion of their pupils are occupied in the simplest elements. They are mere children. They occupy the teacher's time unprofitably to themselves and to the rest of the school, and hence the instruction to them and to the older scholars, is far less valuable than it would be under a different arrangement. Of this fact the teachers themselves are aware, and they sincerely regret it.

But while your committee are convinced of the benefit which the schools, as they now exist, have conferred upon the public, they have seriously deliberated whether they might not be greatly improved by the introduction of the monitorial system. Some of the considerations, which have had effect on their minds, are these:

" The beneficial effects of the monitorial system on the primary schools, have been already alluded to; but if such are the results upon children of from 4 to 7 years of age, why should they not be the same upon those of from 7 to 13 or 14. If children of 5, 6 and 7 years of age can teach each other, why should not children of 14, 13 or 12. But it is said a child cannot teach as well as a master—that all things being equal he could not, may be granted; but such is not the case in fact. If a master could spend ten minutes with a child that was learning to spell, he might teach it better than a monitor but little older than himself; but if the time of the master is so occupied that he can spend but one minute upon this child, and the monitor can spend ten, we think there will be but little doubt under whose tuition the child can learn most.

" But again, in teaching elements, we are far from being certain that, under proper supervision, the child may not be the best instructor. Children who associate with children learn to talk much faster than those who associate with adults; and we are not sure that the principles which govern in the one case would not govern in the other.

" But waiving this question, and granting that, if a teacher were limited to 20 or 30 pupils he would teach better by personal instruction than upon the monitorial system—what has this decision to do with the case? Are we prepared to establish such schools? Are there anywhere such public schools? The plain fact is, that we must construct a system upon the supposition that there will be from 150 to 200 scholars to a teacher, or to a teacher and an assistant. Now for such schools as these, we are inclined to believe that the monitorial system is preferable. So far as our observation has gone we frankly declare, that the proficiency of scholars, under the same circumstances in other respects, when taught under the monitorial system, has been decidedly superior to that of those taught upon the common system.

" But although these have been the views of your committee, they are far from recommending that the monitorial system be at once adopted in all our grammar schools. They are aware of the uncertainty of theory, and that many of the circumstances necessary to success in any particular place, may have been overlooked. They, however, feel fully justified in recommending, that one of the public schools be so far altered as to be established upon the monitorial system, and that thus a fair trial, open to the inspection of the public, may be made. The truth of the question can thus be easily settled, by allowing every one to judge for himself. The expense will be light, and the advantage which is hoped for, is most important.

"With regard to the improvement of the grammar schools, on the present system, your committee have but little to remark. Many of the most necessary improvements would certainly flow from the establishment of primary schools, and could not be carried into effect without it. Others will necessarily arise from a more punctual superintendence on the part of the committee.

"Benefits would result, in the opinion of your committee, from introducing into the schools some system of rewards, which should appeal continually to the emulation of the pupils. This may be arranged in a variety of ways, either of which would accomplish the same purpose, if it applied invariably and at all times to every individual. Human beings may be governed by an appeal to their love of character, or to their fears. We prefer the former, as more kind and more successful.

"As to the manner in which a high school should be conducted, we will not here hazard any opinion. The decision on this subject will depend so much upon the branches to be taught, that until the character of the school be permanently settled, any opinion would be manifestly fruitless.

"In closing this report, your committee feel obliged to assure their fellow-citizens, that it is utterly in vain to hope for a valuable course of public instruction without a thorough and active system of supervision on the part of the community. Unless the schools be visited frequently, and examined thoroughly, and unless the school committees determine to give to this subject all the attention, and reflection, and labor necessary to carry the system of education to as great a degree of perfection as the case admits, every thing will be fruitless. Without this, every plan of education will fail, and with it almost any may be made to succeed. If a sufficient number of gentlemen can be found, who will devote to the interests of the rising generation a half day every month, and who will so combine their labors as to produce the effect of a particular and general supervision, all that the most benevolent could wish can be accomplished. If such men cannot be found, nothing of value will ever be done."

The report closed with four recommendations :—

"1st. That the school committee should be so divided as to constitute a primary and a grammar school committee, and this committee in conjunction with the town council, to be charged with the whole business of the public education.

"2d. That primary schools for the instruction of children from four to seven years of age, be established in various parts of the town under the superintendence and direction of the primary school committee.

"3d. That the monitorial system be immediately tested in one of the common schools.

"4th. That a public high school be established, in which shall be taught all the branches necessary to a useful, mercantile and classical education."

In accordance with the recommendations of the foregoing report, several changes were made in the school system. Primary schools were established, embracing children between the ages of four and eight years, and placed under the instruction of female teachers, the principals being paid $175, and the assistants $100 per annum. This arrangement relieved the grammar masters of the care and tuition of a large class of small children, to whom it was impossible for them to give much personal attention. The books to be used in the primary schools were, Union Nos. 1, 2, 3, and the New Testament. The branches to be taught in the Grammar schools were to be, spelling, reading, the use of capital letters, and punctuation, writing and arithmetic, rudiments of bookkeeping, English grammar, geography and epistolary composition. The books to be used were, Union Nos. 3, 4, 5 ; American First Class Book ; Smith's Arithmetic ; Murray's abridgement of English Grammar, and Woodbridge's small Geography. Walker's Dictionary was the standard for pronunciation.

The monitorial system, after a fair trial of a few years, was abandoned.

During the year 1828, a school for colored children was established, the teacher receiving $400 per annum. This school was opened on Meeting street. At a subsequent period (1837), another school was opened on Pond street. In 1865, both schools were abolished, since which time colored children have attended school with the whites.

In 1829, Noyes's system of penmanship was introduced, and teachers were directed to instruct their pupils how to make pens. They were also directed " not to permit any scholar to learn or practice any ornamental penmanship at school in school hours."

A General View of Education—Its Methods.

There were many points touching the subject of education which had not yet been wrought into a system that might with confidence be accepted. What to teach? How to teach? and how should discipline be administered? were questions that needed further elucidation. It was believed by the friends of education that the public schools could be greatly benefited by presenting to teachers such methods of instruction and discipline as experience had proved to be successful. In this view, a meeting of gentlemen interested in the cause of education was held in the Providence Town House, in May, 1831, at which President Wayland presided. At this meeting two committees were appointed, one to consider and report upon lyceums and similar institutions, then in vogue, designed to promote the cause of popular education ; and the other to consider and report upon the then present state of schools, and what improvement, if any, could be made in discipline and instruction. At an adjourned meeting, May 17th, 1832, both committees submitted reports, which were accepted and a motion made that they be printed. The first committee withdrew their report, and that of the second committee was published. It was from the pen of Oliver Angell, an experienced educator, and is here preserved as a part of the tale of the past:

"The committee appointed 'to take into consideration the present state of schools, and to report generally thereon; and also what improvement, if any, can be made in the discipline or instruction thereof,' beg leave to report:—

"That in pursuance of the object for which they were appointed, it appeared to them necessary to obtain, if possible, from each town in the State, a statement of the number of schools, public and private; the number of scholars in each; what portion of the year the schools are continued, and what sum is annually appropriated by the town, in addition to the sum received from the State, for the purposes of education. To obtain this information, they addressed circulars to respectable individuals in each town, requesting a statement of the above mentioned particulars. Through the politeness of many of the gentlemen to whom these circulars were directed, and by personal inquiry, we are able to present the annexed detailed statement.

"The law establishing public schools in this State, is of recent date. It cannot, therefore, be expected that your committee will be able to state any facts showing the comparative increase of information farther than may be deduced from the increased number of schools. Your committee perceive, both from the reports which they have received from the several towns and from personal observation, that the system of public schools has not yet acquired that stability and uniformity which it undoubtedly will attain, after a little more experience and a more general interchange of opinions and feelings on the subject of education, between the intelligent and influential citizens of the different towns. If some regular plan could be devised by which this mutual interchange of views on this important subject might be promoted, your committee think it would greatly facilitate the progress of education through the State.

"We find that in some of the districts there are not yet convenient houses or rooms provided for the accommodation of the schools, but this deficiency will probably soon be supplied. Considerable difficulty has also been experienced in some towns in the location of school-houses so as to meet the convenience of the inhabitants. When the deficiency in school-houses shall be remedied, the difficulties attending their location removed, and a regular and systematic plan established in every town, the benefits resulting to the community from this best of all establishments of our State, will become more obvious.

"In this stage of our report, we find it necessary to advert to a subject which we deem of primary importance: we allude to the *qualifications of teachers*. However numerous may be our schools, and however munificent may be the appropriations, either by the legislature or the towns, if placed under the management of unqualified or unskilful teachers, much of the benefit which might otherwise result from them must inevitably be lost. The impropriety of placing any person of *immoral character* in charge of a school, is so obvious that we think any comments upon this point unnecessary. We believe that the good sense and virtue of the citizens of this State will be a sufficient barrier to every imposition of this nature. But a good moral character, although indispensable, is not the only qualification of a teacher. To be useful and successful, he must have a good knowledge of what he attempts to teach to others, as well as judgment and skill in the manner of teaching. We are aware of the difficulty which exists in procuring teachers possessing all the requisite qualifications. It is a difficulty not peculiar to this State, but exists in a greater or less degree in every State and probably in every town. We are sensible, also, that the compensation usually allowed to teachers, especially in country schools, is not and, from the nature of the case, cannot be such as always to command the best talents. But those who may be obtained for the moderate compensation thus allowed, might render themselves much more useful were they to take as much pains in preparing themselves, as is deemed necessary in almost any other employment in life. In one, at least, of our sister States, an institution has been established for the express purpose of qualifying young men for teaching. Perhaps this is the only feasible means of remedying the deficiency which is at present so much a matter of complaint.

"It is a position well established that, " on the early and correct education of youth, depends the ultimate success of every rational enterprise for the intellectual and moral improvement of man." On this early and correct education depend, also, in a great measure, the preservation of our liberties and the continuation of the present free institutions of our country. Deeply impressed, therefore, with the importance of the occupation, both in a moral and political point of view, your committee would present the subject of the qualifications of teachers as one deserving the most serious and attentive consideration.

"Respecting the branches to be taught in our public schools, your committee would hazard a very few remarks. While we admit that spelling, reading, writing and arithmetic are the *most essential*, and although we would by no means, have any others introduced to the exclusion or detriment of any one of these, we, nevertheless, think there is an error in limiting the schools exclusively to these branches. More than these can be successfully taught in almost every school in our State. It is true that in some of our public schools, grammar and geography are partially taught, but this is not enough; the standard of our schools should be raised; the branches should be extended, at least, so far as that those of every day use in life, may be embraced. There are but few persons who have not occasion, in the course of their lives, to express their ideas on paper, either in an epistolary, or some other form, yet how often is it the case that when a necessity exists for an attempt of this kind the task is entered upon with the greatest reluctance from a consciousness of inability to write with any degree of correctness. We submit it, therefore, as a very important question to school committees, whether in every school, excepting those for very young children, the more advanced scholars should not be taught to express their ideas in *writing*, and the proper method of arranging sentences. A very little practice in youth will render the task of writing a common letter comparatively easy. Most of us are frequent witnesses of the deplorable deficiency which exists in this particular. A proper use of the capitals and some general rules for pointing sentences, are very readily learned at school; but if not learned there, they are seldom learned at all; and whenever, in after life, a written communication is required, this deficiency in their early education is most sorely felt.

"Another essential, and as we think indispensable acquirement, is a knowledge of accounts, but of this we shall say more in connection with another subject. All these and more, it is believed by your committee, may be advantageously taught in our public schools, without detriment to the more elementary branches. Teachers frequently complain that they have *no time* for such exercises; but we would earnestly recommend to them to make the attempt. If school committees should require these branches to be taught in their schools· teachers, if not already qualified, would find it necessary to prepare themselves to teach them.

"Upon the question, 'whether any, and if any, what improvement may be made in the discipline or instruction of schools,' your committee do not hesitate to reply, that it is decidedly their opinion *much* improvement may be made both in the *discipline* and *mode* of instruction now generally adopted in our public schools. The committee are aware that this is a delicate subject, and in the few remarks they may offer they feel constrained to speak cautiously. They cannot forbear, however, suggesting a few things in relation to this part of their duty without presuming to censure, or to prescribe in what manner every school shall be taught and governed.

"There are two extremes into which communities as well as individuals are apt to fall. The one is a hasty adoption of every new thing which happens to be cried up as an improvement; the other is a pertinacious adherence to old established customs and usages, however obvious their inconvenience or their defects. To these extremes, schools for elementary education have been peculiarly subject. While in some of them, no one system has been pursued long enough to test its utility or unfitness, in others it has been deemed almost sacrilegious to depart a single step from the ancient mode of instruction and government. Either of these extremes is unspeakably injurious to the cause of education. That great improvements have been made both in the means and method of imparting instruction to youth, it is believed none who have been at all conversant with the subject will deny; but in many places, a rooted attachment to established rules and preconceived notions have prevented the benefits which might have resulted from the adoption of these improvements. Why is it, we would ask, that so many teachers have failed in their attempts to communicate instruction to the youthful mind? Why have so many parents and patrons of schools so much cause to lament the ill success of their exertions in endeavoring to promote the education of their children? Your committee think it has been owing in a great measure, to mistaken views on the subject. We think there has been a mistake both in the theory and practice of teaching. Instead of considering and treating children as rational beings, strongly actuated by the passions of shame, of pride, of emulation, of hope and despair; instead of reflecting that they possess a mind in embryo, susceptible of deep and lasting impressions made upon it through the medium of the above named passions, we very much fear they are too often considered and treated as beings entirely passive; as incapable of receiving any impressions but such as are forced upon them by a compulsory process.

"The passion of *fear* is one which children manifest earlier and more distinctly than any other. This has been seized upon as we think injudiciously by some teachers, as if it were the only avenue by which approaches could be made to the understanding of the child. Acting upon this principle, it is easy to see what must be the course of discipline and instruction. The teacher at once arrays himself in terror, and the whole business of teaching and governing must be a *system of coercion.* Our opinion is, that where this system is pursued, there is great danger of creating in the pupils a morbid sensibility, a stubbornness of temper, a hatred of the school and whatever is connected with it. It operates as a check upon all the better feelings of the scholar, and it will be a fortunate circumstance if it does not create a hardened indifference to improvement of every kind. On the subject of corporal punishment we fear to express all we feel. As a *system* of government it is decidedly objectionable, and we think if it must be used, it should be used only as a *last resort.*

"It belongs not to us to point out all that we consider faults, either in teaching or discipline, but we will briefly express our views respecting some of those faults which have a tendency to defeat the ends for which public schools have been established. We have no hesitation in stating what we consider one of the greatest faults in teaching, and the one from which almost all others spring: it is *a departure from nature.* Children may be compared to young and tender plants. When we wish to rear these in the utmost perfection what course do we pursue? We surely would not heap upon them piles of rubbish, for this we know would crush them at once. Neither would we pour upon them a constant deluge of water, which would soon destroy their vitality. Even 'the sturdy oak which defies the tempest,' springs from a tender and pliant twig, which may be easily destroyed or fashioned to an unshapely shrub. While the vital sap of the young tree is passing from its root to its branches, do we surround it with snow and ice to promote its growth? Should we not rather cherish every spontaneous effort and gently clip those excrescences which would render the tree unsightly or unfruitful? Let it not be said the two cases are not analogous. If the principle be applied to the physical powers of children we know it is correct. And why not as applicable to their mental powers?

"If parents and teachers, in their attempts to communicate knowledge to the youthful mind, and to train up children to usefulness and respectability in life, would closely adhere to the principles followed by the experienced farmer and the skilful horticulturist in rearing their grain, their plants and their trees, they could scarcely fail of success. An obvious departure from these principles is the practice too common both with parents and teachers of crowding the memory of children with a mass of unintelligible matter, answering no other purpose than to display the wonderful memory of the wonderful child, while every other faculty of the mind is left uncultivated and unfostered. We view it as a matter of the first consequence in teaching, that nothing be presented to the mind of the scholar which he cannot understand. Whatever is unintelligible is not only useless, but its effect upon his mind is decidedly bad.

"It is an axiom that those means are best which are best fitted to accomplish the end proposed. The design of education undoubtedly is, to develop, strengthen and bring to maturity the mental powers, to give them a right direction, and thus to prepare youth for the scenes and duties of active life. What then are the means best adapted to the accomplishment of this great end? Surely not those which call into exercise one single faculty of the mind only, while all the rest are left to spring up spontaneously, or to rest in total inaction. Viewing it, therefore, as absolutely essential that in teaching, all these powers should be brought into exercise, your committee would recommend *oral* instruction as best fitted to produce this important result. By this mode of teaching, children are necessarily led into the habit of thinking and reasoning upon every thing they learn. What they do learn, therefore, they learn intellectually and not mechanically.

"We think this mode of teaching furnishes many opportunities of imparting useful instruction, which are not presented by the other mode. We do not, however, by this recommendation, mean to imply that books ought to be dispensed with in teaching. On the contrary, we think them useful auxiliaries and absolutely essential in every school. But we think books are too closely adhered to, especially in the departments of arithmetic, geography and grammar. We believe these may be taught, and much more successfully and practically taught, by oral instruction, using the books merely for reference. The time devoted to committing to memory the *solid contents* of books, we think not the most usefully employed. Time, to children, is all important. In those towns where schools are continued through the year, and where children have the opportunity of attending them constantly from infancy upward, the loss of a portion of their time may not prove a very serious calamity, although even under these circumstances it ought if possible to be avoided. But in the country towns, where schools are supported but a part of the year, this loss is a very serious evil. Where a scholar has the privilege of attending school but three months in the year, and is obliged to lose a considerable portion of that time by unskilful teaching, his progress must necessarily be slow, and he will probably feel the embarrassments resulting from this loss of time, throughout his whole life. On the subject of teaching arithmetic, we would simply suggest the expediency of dispensing with the use of manuscript ciphering books, especially in schools of limited duration, and that most if not all arithmetical questions be proposed directly by the teacher; that these questions be of a practical nature, designed to habituate the pupil to a readiness of calculation in the ordinary concerns of life. When scholars are sufficiently familiar with the fundamental rules of arithmetic, and their hand-writing will admit of it, we would recommend to them the subject of book-keeping as a valuable substitute for their manuscript ciphering books. This is a branch of knowledge of so great and so general utility that we cannot forbear recommending it to school committees as a branch that should be taught in every school. Book-keeping by *single entry*, is very easily learned, and when learned will probably never be forgotten. We think much time may be saved to the pupil also, in the study of geography and grammar, by adopting the *oral* method of teaching them. This method may require more exertion and labor in the teacher, but his remuneration will be the more rapid advance of his scholars.

"In connection with what we have already stated on the subject of intellectual teaching, we take the liberty to recommend, as a most valuable auxiliary, the simple *school-apparatus*, designed to elucidate the elementary principles of astronomy, natural philosophy and mechanics. In the schools where this has been used, it has produced the happiest results.

"Our only apology for entering thus far into the details of teaching is, an earnest desire that the youth of our State may enjoy all the advantages intended by our legislators from the invaluable establishment of public schools. We have not considered ourselves as censors of the schools, neither have we intended to express our views in the spirit of dictation. The suggestions we have made have arisen from no personal or local feelings, but from a wish to discharge the duties entrusted to us under a conviction of their importance to the community.

"Upon a review of the subject, your committee find much cause for congratulation in the increased and increasing means of education in the State. There is not a town in which *all* the children may not have the means of acquiring a common school education, and when we consider the nature of our institutions, and how much their preservation depends on the general spread of information and on the correct morals of our youth, we have much cause to rejoice at the present favorable prospects, and we look forward to the period when Rhode Island shall be as celebrated for the facilities afforded to education as she now is for her industry and manufactures.

"Respectfully submitted,
"OLIVER ANGELL,
"*For the Committee.*"

THE SCHOOLS UNDER A CITY CHARTER.

In 1832, the town of Providence commenced a chartered existence as a city. The change from the more primitive forms under which its affairs had been conducted, in nowise militated against the interests of the public schools. In some respects an advantage was gained, especially in matters requiring prompt action. In the first Mayor, Hon. Samuel W. Bridgham, the cause of public education found a devoted and enlightened supporter. In his inaugural address he expressed himself in the following words:

"Under the act establishing free schools, passed by the General Assembly in January, A. D. 1828, it is necessary that an appropriation to a certain extent should be made by the city, for the purpose of supporting such schools, in order to entitle the city to receive out of the State treasury its proportion of the money appropriated by the legislature to that object. I therefore recommend this subject to your early attention. It is a subject of the deepest interest to the community. In a free government, education, which elevates the mind, diffuses virtue, and leads to virtue, is the surest foundation of freedom and public safety. Without free schools a portion of the community are cast into obscurity, and oftentimes intellect of the first order is lost to its possessor and to the world. Children of the poor as well as of the rich, ought to be instructed both in letters and in morals, and no state of society can, in my opinion, excuse the neglect of it. The opulent cannot bestow a portion of their wealth more benevolently, nor, I humbly conceive, more for their true interest than by applying it to this object. If they wish to live in a community peaceably, orderly, free from excess, outrage and crime, let them promote by their wealth and their influence the cause of education. They will find both their interest and their happiness in it. By looking over the catalogue of offenders it will be found that vice of every kind and degree most generally springs from ignorance. The want of learning and of moral instruction generally leads to idleness, to dissipation and to crime, and often ends in ruin. The town of Providence has taken a lead in the good work of education, highly honorable to the community. * * * And I hazard the assertion that few, if any, institutions of the kind in our country are better established, regulated and conducted, or prove more useful to the public."

The first school committee under the charter was composed of the following gentlemen: Samuel W. Bridgham, President; Dexter Thurber, Charles Holden, John H. Ormsbee, William T. Grinnell, Henry R. Green, Asa Messer, George Curtis, Moses B. Ives, Robert H. Ives, Peter Pratt, Thomas H. Webb, Frederick A. Farley, William Aplin, George Baker, Alexis Caswell, David Pickering, Pharcellus Church, Robert Knight, Robert E. Patteson.

"In August, 1835, a special effort was made in the school committee to improve the character and increase the number of schools under their care. It was urged by some of the members of that body, that the establishing of a high school, in which the older and more advanced boys might pursue the higher branches of an English education, would tend to improve the grammar schools. It was urged that the removal of these pupils from the grammar schools would allow the masters to devote their attention to the mass of their scholars, instead of to a few already advanced beyond the common studies, and engaged in pursuing the higher branches. It was also urged that the establishment of a high school would afford a healthful stimulus to the boys in the grammar schools, and urge them onward in their studies, in order that they might become qualified for admission to such a school.

"The subject was referred to a special committee with instructions to examine into the expediency of having a 'free high school' established, and to report the result of their examination. This committee presented a report in the form of a series of resolutions, which were adopted by a vote of two-thirds of the school committee. Among these resolutions was the following: 'That it is highly desirable and expedient that a high school should be established in this city, for the instruction of young men in the higher branches of a good English education; and that said high school be established by this committee, should a provision for the same be made by the city government.' " *

The city council appears not to have been ready to accede to this recommendation, and voted that it was then inexpedient to establish a high school.

In 1835, the salaries of masters were raised to $600, and of ushers to $300 per annum. The committee in their report to the city council this year say:

* Barnard's R. I. School Report, p.

"No measure has been omitted which they deemed necessary, and was in their power to adopt for the promotion of the good of the institutions of which they have had the superintendence. The time and labor of the committee have been largely taxed, but they do not complain of the burthen, deeming their efforts to have been made in a good cause, and trusting that those efforts will not prove to have been made in vain. They have visited the schools under their charge regularly every quarter agreeably to law, and at other times according to their own rules, regulations and by-laws. The schools are now in as good condition, and promise as much usefulness, as at any former period."

In 1836, female assistants were for the first time employed in the grammar schools. The ushers were not at once removed, but whenever vacancies occurred in their places they were filled by the appointment of two female assistants, at a salary of $175 per annum.* In the course of a year or two, all the ushers having resigned, female assistants were employed in all the grammar schools of the city. About this time Goold Brown's Grammar, Field's Geography and Atlas, and the National Reader were introduced into the grammar schools, and Emerson's First Part and the American Popular Lessons were introduced into the primary schools.†

Further Reconstruction Proposed.

The arrangements made under the reconstruction of 1828, worked satisfactorily for several years; but with the growth of population in Providence the schools became crowded to an extent requiring relief by the erection of more school houses. Certain changes to give the schools increased efficiency were also needed. The Mechanics' Association, ever watchful of these interests, brought the subject to the attention of the city council early in 1837, in an earnest memorial written by George Baker, Esq., President of the Association, and for many years an active member of the school committee. It was a clear-sighted paper, looking to present and future wants, and as a part of the history of the public schools specially valuable, showing as it does the common sentiment of the body he represented, and the readiness of its members, who com-

---

*The first female appointed to this position was Miss Avis W. Lockwood. She had been preceptress of the girls' school established in the fourth district in 1827, and was continued in the same place when that school was made a primary, in 1828.

†From 1828 to 1836, the teachers of the primary schools, so far as ascertained, were: —— Carr, Ann J. Ware, Sarah P. Church, Mary Ann Davis, Avis W. Lockwood, Harriet Fisher, Eliza P. Delano, Sarah Pratt, Abby R. Thornton, Mary Godfrey, Emily Phillips, Hannah Farnum, Ann Page, Rosa A. Grafton, Elizabeth E. Brown, Sarah A. Hayford, Eliza Thurber, Ruth Winchester, Abby S. Cooke, Abby B. Hayford, W. Walker, Elizabeth R. Little, —— Tillinghast (colored school), Almy E. Spaulding, Diana Bragg, Sarah W. Arnold, Emeline A. Vinton, Harriet Wood, Mary C. Bragg, L. G. Lincoln, Susan Lincoln.

posed "a large portion of the heads of families of the city," to cheerfully meet the increased expense to be incurred in carrying out the desired change. The memorial is as follows:

"TO THE CITY COUNCIL OF THE CITY OF PROVIDENCE:

"The undersigned, in behalf of the Providence Association of Mechanics and Manufacturers, respectfully represent : That

"At a meeting of the Association, held on Monday evening, January 30, 1837, the accompanying resolutions were unanimously adopted :

"*Resolved*, That no subject can be of more importance to the inhabitants of this city, than the education of the rising generation.

"*Resolved*, That as the members of this Association were the pioneers in the establishment of the public schools, they manifested a most laudable zeal on that subject.

"*Resolved*, That the public schools of this city come far short of the wants of the community, and are much inferior in their character to the public schools in the neighboring cities.

"*Resolved*, That the public schools can and ought to be made equal to the private schools, so far as relates to the common branches now taught.

"*Resolved*, That two of the greatest evils now existing, as respects public school instruction, are the great number of scholars in each school, and the small salaries paid to the teachers.

"*Resolved*, That an increased number of public schools ought to be established in this city as soon as practicable.

"*Resolved*, That a committee be appointed to draft a memorial to the city council, on the subject of public schools, in conformity with the recommendation of the select committee, to report at an adjourned meeting, to be held on Saturday evening next.

"In accordance with said resolutions, the following memorial was reported and approved at the adjourned meeting, and directed to be signed by the President and Secretary, and presented to the city council.

"Your memorialists have long considered that public schools, as at present conducted in this city, are wholly inadequate to the wants of the community, and fall far short of what might be expected from its present opulence. It is the opinion of this Association, that unless a more liberal system of public education is pursued, the children of the poorer classes must grow up in comparative ignorance; and that the laxity of morals, and loss of an honest pride in their own capacities, which would result from this state of things, would more than outweigh the increased expense which would be necessary to arrest it.

"Your memorialists have been struck with one fact, to which they would respectfully solicit particular attention. It has been argued by some, (and perhaps the argument has attracted the consideration of your honorable body), that the instruction of youth in the public schools is a heavy tax upon the middling classes, without an adequate return, as they do not participate in the benefit of this public instruction. This argument, which is evidently weighty in the present condition of these schools, would be destroyed if they were raised to the condition desired by your memorialists. Why is it that the middling classes do not become participants in this instruction? There is evidently but one reason. They perceive that the crowded state of the schools alone, would prevent proper attention to the pupil; and they are aware that with the small sum which the instructors receive, it is difficult to procure and retain the services of competent persons to fill the station. But let the schools be made so numerous that the scholars may receive as much attention as they do in the private schools, and let the salaries be so large as to induce men of equal ability to take charge of them, and that which is now considered as a tax, would then be viewed as an alleviation of one of the heaviest burdens put upon the middling classes.

"Your honorable body have, no doubt, in the consideration which you have given this subject, perceived how far we are behind our neighboring cities in this particular. Whilst they are constantly aiming at perfection in their free school system, we have been at a stand, or retrograding. To us, this is a matter of serious concern, inasmuch as in proportion to our inferiority in this particular we are liable to become inferior in every other matter which requires intelligence, industry and enterprise.

"In evidence of these statements, it is found that the number attending public schools in this city, in 1836, was, - - - - - - 1,456
Private schools, - - - - - - - 3,235
Attending no school, - - - - - - - 1,604
Amount actually paid for public schools from June, 1835, to
  June, 1836, by the city, - - - - $5,936 34
  By the State, - - - - - - 1,524 65
                                              ——————— $7,461 99
"Amount paid for private school instruction, over - - 20,000 00
Number attending public schools in Boston, in 1836, - 8,847
Number attending private schools, - - - - 4,000
Amount paid for public schools, - - - - - 88,000 00
Amount paid for private schools, - - - - 100,000 00

"There are about 50 per cent. more attending private school instruction than public, in this city; while in Boston, *three-fifths* of the whole number, 12,848, are attending the public schools.

"Boston, containing a population of about 80,000, pays $88,000; and Providence, whose population is about 20,000, pays $7,461. Should Providence pay $22,000, instead of the sum above stated, her public schools might then be equal in standing, and perhaps nearly adequate to the actual wants of the community.

"To remedy the defect in our present system, your memorialists would suggest that a grade of schools be established between the primary and writing schools, for reading, writing and arithmetic only, the design of which is to give a thorough instruction in these branches to those children whose parents need their services at as early an age as twelve or thirteen years, and who, under the present arrangement, are compelled to leave school with a very superficial knowledge of those branches which are so necessary for obtaining a livelihood in any business. It must be obvious, that without a thorough knowledge of reading, writing and arithmetic, the purposes of education are not, in any important degree, answered. And they would further suggest, that in addition to grammar and geography, now taught in the writing schools, such of the higher branches should be added as might be deemed most useful.

"To effect an essential reform in our public school system, great expense must necessarily be incurred; and your memorialists, who represent a large portion of the heads of families of the city, would meet this increased expense with hearty encouragement. They need but the assurance that the schools shall be adequate to the purposes of education, to stimulate them to unremitting efforts for their support and maintenance; and they feel confident that they would be met with corresponding efforts on the part of the inhabitants of the city generally.

"Your memorialists are convinced that the present is the time to commence this work of reform. The amount which will be received from the government, and devoted to education, will considerably alleviate the expense in the outset; and the inhabitants of the city are now so well convinced of the necessity of effort, that any appropriations for this object would no doubt meet with their approbation.

"GEORGE BAKER, President.

"SAMUEL TINGLEY, JR., Secretary."

This memorial, replete with just views, was received by the city council with marked respect, and referred to a committee who subsequently reported a plan for the improvement of the schools; but the provisions of it being unsatisfactory, a second plan was presented, comprehending twelve primary, eight intermediate, and four upper schools—the primary to occupy the place of those now bearing that name, the intermediate to rank with grammar schools, and the "upper schools" to be practically equivalents for a high school. A salary bill was agreed upon, which, with the school plan, was sent to the board of aldermen for their concurrence. By that body the schools were diminished to twenty, and the salaries reduced about ten per cent.

With these modifications the bill was returned to the common council, who refused to concur. After frequent meetings and protracted debates, with no approximation to unity, the board of aldermen devised a plan embracing ten primary schools, six intermediate schools, two upper schools, and two schools for colored children. This, when presented to the common council, was voted down by a large majority, and without any final decision the municipal year closed.

The feeling on the school question was now stronger than ever. The election of aldermen and councilmen for the year 1837-38 turned somewhat upon this question, and resulted in returning to the two boards a majority in favor of an entire reörganization of the public schools. Shortly after the organization of the city government a joint committee of both boards was appointed to take the subject of a new organization of the schools into consideration. A sub-committee from this committee visited Boston, Salem, Lowell and New Bedford to gain such information as might be helpful in arriving at correct conclusions. On their return they made a report to the city council as follows:

"To The City Council of the City of Providence:

"The Committee appointed to take into consideration the expediency of a new organization of the public schools, beg leave to report:

"That the important subject presented to the consideration of your committee, has ever been one of great and constant interest. In no former period of our history, has it excited more universal attention than at the present time. In this country, such has been the interest felt in the cause of education, that in aid of individual efforts, there have been legislative enactments establishing public schools.

"The true wealth of a community should always be deemed to be the mind and intelligence of its children. Other treasures are as dross compared with this. By means of the public schools, the poor boy of to-day, the orphan perhaps, may become the man of influence of to-morrow, and what legacy so good, so fraught with lasting benefits as education!

"Our public schools should be sustained, if sustained at all, by a liberal policy. Neither the indigent nor the sick have higher claims upon us than the ignorant. On a subject of such vital importance to this community, may we not reasonably indulge the hope, that it will yet become the ambition of its citizens to emulate each other in the good work.

"The system of public instruction in this country, generally commences at the age of four years. Whether it ought not to begin at an earlier period, is a question which has been more or less discussed. Certain it is, that the earliest moment should be seized for imparting moral and intellectual culture to the infant mind. Experiments which have been made, show that instruction may be given at an age much earlier than that recognized for the admission of children into our public schools. Whether it would be an improvement in the system of instruction adopted in this city, to create a certain number of infant schools, is a consideration worthy of public attention. The free operation of our schools is doubtless impeded, and the instruction of the pupils greatly restricted, in consequence of the number of those who are continually entering the writing schools, with but a partial knowledge of the first rudiments. If infant schools, for the benefit of children from the age of three to five years, were established, a positive advantage would be gained to the primary and writing schools. Many of us have spent an occasional hour in an infant school. In those cradles of learning, the eye views nothing that is depraved; the ear is there unassailed by by the language of impiety; a universal glow of pleasure is depicted on every countenance. Children are there made happy, because they are instructed to be good. Into such schools are introduced children of the tenderest age, who become at once the recipients of kindness, and who are led along by gentle steps to the portals of knowledge.

"To have good schools, it is necessary they be provided with good teachers. We fear the office of teacher will never attain to that rank in society which it ought, until it is rewarded by the best salaries, in order that it may be coveted by the best talents. For the purpose of improving their pecuniary condition, educated men will ever be ready to abandon a calling which subjects them to severe duties, without an adequate reward. Pay to teachers something more than the means of a bare subsistence for their labors, and their services will be secured, their ambition stimulated, and your schools improved.

"Every thing connected with education, should be made attractive to the child. The school-house, to which he is accustomed to go, should be such as to harmonize with the nature of his mind. In its exterior or interior aspect, it should never present a repulsive character. Instead of being unsightly and unclean, it should be the reverse. Consecrate the spot where your children are to spend so many hours of their existence, to good order, beauty of arrangement, and general neatness, and they will be grateful for the attention bestowed, and will be seen resorting there for pastime as well as for study.

"In the opinion of your committee, it will be found eminently useful to establish a superintendent of the public schools. In the plan of instruction herewith submitted for consideration, such an officer is incorporated. It must be obvious to every one, that an individual well qualified for such a station, might carefully survey the whole ground, and understand from time to time its actual condition. It should be the duty of such an officer, to have a knowledge of all the children in the city, especially those of the poorer classes. It would be within the sphere of his influence, to lead the minds of parents and guardians to a more comprehensive sense of their duty. It should be his province to confer with the teachers, and to submit to the school committee a quarterly report, exhibiting the condition of the schools, and of all such matters relating to the general subject, as its importance would suggest. Create such an officer, with a salary sufficient to enable him to devote his whole time to the duties of his office, and much will have been done towards sustaining the character of the plan of instruction which may be adopted.

"In conclusion, the committee offer the following resolutions:

"1st. That it is expedient that the number of schools in this city be increased to seventeen, not including the schools for children of color.

"2d. That it is expedient that said schools be of the following descriptions, viz.:

"One high school, six grammar and writing schools, ten primary schools.

"3d. That in the opinion of the city council, no child ought to be admitted into the primary schools at a less age than four years; into the grammar and writing schools at a less age than seven years; nor into the high school at a less age than twelve years, unless by special permission of the school committee.

"4th. That in the opinion of the city council, no pupil ought to remain in the high school, longer than three years unless by special permission of the school committee and in no case unless the same is not full.

"5th. That in the opinion of the city council, the principal of the high school, should be paid one thousand dollars per annum; the assistant teacher seven hundred and fifty dollars per annum; the masters of the grammar and writing schools, eight hundred dollars per annum; two assistant female teachers, two hundred dollars per annum; the principals of the primary schools, two hundred and fifty dollars per annum; the assistant teachers, one hundred and seventy-five dollars per annum.

"6th. That in the opinion of the city council, it is expedient to establish a superintendent of the public schools.

"7th. That in the opinion of the city council, the superintendent of the public schools, should be paid a salary of eight hundred dollars per annum.

"8th. That the high school should be instituted for the purpose of fitting young men for college, and for perfecting those who are not intended for a collegiate course of study, in the branches of a good English education.

"9th. That it is expedient that the high school shall be open for candidates from all the schools in the city, once a year, viz.: on the   next succeeding the exhibition of the schools in   ; and that for admission into the high school, candidates from the public schools shall have preference over all others.

"All of which is respectfully submitted,

"J. L. HUGHES,
STEPHEN T. OLNEY,
HENRY ANTHONY,
AMHERST EVERETT,
SETH PADELFORD,
JAMES E. BUTTS,
} Committee.

"September 25, 1837."

This report, which was printed and widely distributed among the freemen of the city, was the signal for a renewal of the discussion, both of the advantages and disadvantages of a reconstruction of the public free school system, bringing out the strongest arguments of friends and opponents. These discussions were propitious. "The advocates of a new organization insisted on a radical change in the whole system. They asked for a new classification of the schools into primary and grammar schools, and a high school. They likewise urged the necessity of new plans for the instruction and supervision of the schools. Elaborate arguments were adduced to show that it would be more economical for the city to make liberal provisions for very good public schools, than to continue to expend small sums for very poor schools."*

Conspicuous in these discussions and labors were John L. Hughes and Simon Henry Greene, the former a member of the school committee, and both members of the common council. Hon. Seth Padelford, then also a member of the common council, and subsequently for fifteen years a member of the school committee, and always a devoted friend to popular education, rendered valuable services during this contest. These gentlemen, and others not named associated with them, succeeded in securing the adoption of "A bill providing for a new organization and the future government of the public schools in the city of Providence." The bill is here presented as an important part of this narrative:

* It is due to the opponents of reörganization to say, that their hostility appears to have been based mainly upon the increased expense involved in the change.

Providence.

"An Ordinance in relation to Public Schools.

"Section 1. Be it ordained by the city council of the city of Providence, that from and after the 7th day of September, A. D. 1838, the number of public schools in said city shall be seventeen; (not including schools for colored children,) and that said schools shall be of the following description, to wit: one high school, six grammar and writing schools, ten primary schools. And that free instruction shall be therein given to the children of all the inhabitants of said city who may see fit to avail themselves thereof; subject only to the rules and regulations hereinafter contained and provided for.

"Sec. 2. That each primary school shall be under the care of a principal, and one assistant teacher, and the rudiments of an English education shall be taught therein. That each grammar and writing school shall be under the care of a master, and at least two female assistant teachers, or one male assistant teacher, at the discretion of the school committee; and the ordinary branches of an English education shall be taught therein. That the high school shall be under the care of a preceptor, and one or more assistant teachers, and thorough instruction shall be given therein in all the branches of a good English education; and instruction shall also be given therein to all the pupils whose parents or guardians may desire it, in all the preparatory branches of a classical education.

"Sec. 3. The high school shall not at any time contain more than two hundred pupils; of which number, not more than one hundred shall be females, except when the number of male pupils shall be less than one hundred; in which case, an additional number of females may be admitted, until the school shall be filled, under such conditions as the school committee may prescribe.

"Sec. 4. That no child who shall not have attained the age of four years, shall be admitted as a pupil into a primary school.

"That no child who shall not have attained the age of seven years, shall be admitted as a pupil into a grammar and writing school, nor unless qualified immediately to enter upon the course of studies pursued therein.

"That no child who shall not have attained the age of twelve years, shall be admitted as a pupil into the high school, nor unless qualified immediately to enter upon the course of studies pursued therein. That no pupil shall remain in the high school more than three years.

"No child who shall not have attended a grammar and writing school for at least three years, shall be admitted to the high school when there is a sufficient number of candidates in the grammar and writing schools qualified for admission therein. But whenever there shall not be a sufficient number of such candidates, any child over the age of twelve years, may, if qualified, be admitted for such time as the school committee may determine.

"Sec. 5. That the school committee be, and they are hereby authorized and requested to appoint annually a superintendent of the public schools, who shall perform such duties in relation to the public schools as said committee may from time to time prescribe. Said superintendent to be subject to removal at any time by the school committee, in case of inability or mismanagement.

"Sec. 6. That there shall be a public exhibition in the last week of each school year, in some place to be designated by the school committee, by so many pupils of the highest class of each of the grammar and writing schools as may be selected, in such manner as the school committee shall prescribe. There shall also be an annual public exhibition by the graduating class, and such other pupils of the high school as may be selected by the school committee, or under their direction; which exhibition shall take place on the Monday next preceding the first Wednesday in September.

"SEC. 7. That the first regular term of all the schools in each school year, shall commence on the Monday next succeeding the second Wednesday in September.

"SEC. 8. That there shall be two public schools maintained exclusively for the instruction of colored children; each of which shall be under the care of a principal, and also of an assistant teacher, whenever, in the opinion of the school committee, the services of such assistant may be necessary; and that free instruction shall be therein given in the ordinary branches of an English education, to the children of all the colord inhabitants of the city who may see fit to avail themselves thereof, subject only to the rules and regulations herein contained and provided for.

"SEC. 9. That the following annual salaries shall be paid to the superintendent and instructors of the schools, respectively, in equal quarterly payments, to wit:

"To the superintendent, twelve hundred and fifty dollars.

"To the preceptor of the high school, twelve hundred and fifty dollars.

"To each male assistant teacher of the high school, seven hundred and fifty dollars.

"To each female assistant teacher of the high school, five hundred dollars.

"To each master of a grammar and writing school, eight hundred dollars.

"To each male assistant teacher of a grammar and writing school, four hundred dollars.

"To each female assistant teacher of a grammar and writing school, two hundred and twenty-five dollars.

"To each principal of a primary school, two hundred and fifty dollars.

"To each assistant teacher of a primary school, two hundred dollars.

"To each male principal of a school for colored children, five hundred dollars.

"To each female principal of a school for colored children, two hundred dollars.

"To each male assistant teacher of a school for colored children, two hundred and fifty dollars.

"To each female assistant teacher of a school for colored children, one hundred and fifty dollars.

"SEC. 10. That all moneys appropriated for the support of the public schools, shall be subject to the exclusive control of the school committee, who shall have full power to cause the same, or any part thereof, to be expended in any manner which they may deem most advisable, for the benefit and welfare of the schools, excepting so much thereof as will be from time to time required for the payment of the salaries established by this ordinance, and excepting also all such appropriations as may be made for a specific purpose or purposes. Said committee shall also have full power and authority to alter, from time to time, as they may deem expedient, the bounds of the several school districts, in order to provide suitable locations for such new schools as may hereafter be established by the city council, or to make a more equal apportionment of pupils to the several schools. It shall be their duty to see that the school houses and estates are kept in proper repair; to select and designate the best text books, and to provide all such apparatus, and all other means of instruction for all the schools, as may be necessary for keeping the same in efficient operation, and for enabling the pupils to receive all the advantages therefrom which it is the intention of this ordinance to provide and secure. Said committee shall have and exercise a general discretionary power in all matters and things relating to the public schools, which are not specially provided for by this ordinance, or by the laws of this State, and not repugnant to said laws, or to the provisions of this ordinance.

"SEC. 11. That it shall be the duty of the aldermen and members of the common council from each of the wards in the city, on or before the first Monday in May in each year, to recommend to the city council three candidates for election as members of the school committee for the ensuing municipal year, which recommendation shall be made by filing a list of the names of such candidates in the office of the city clerk.

"SEC. 12. That this ordinance be published three weeks successively in the semi-weekly *Morning Courier, Manufacturers' and Farmers' Journal*, and *Republican Herald*.

"Passed April 9, 1838. A true copy: witness,

"RICHARD M. FIELD, City Clerk."

Under this ordinance the primary and grammar schools went immediately into operation. Subsequently an intermediate grade, such as recommended by the Mechanics' Association, was introduced. The high school, concerning which more will be said hereafter, was at a latter day added, and gave completeness to the course of study.

"Immediately after the adoption of this ordinance, the city council appointed a committee to examine all the public school-houses and estates, and instructed them to report at an early day, what alterations and additions would be necessary in order to carry the whole system into effect. This committee pursuant to their instructions, made a thorough examination of all the old school-houses, and reported that they were 'all unfit for use in their present condition, and were all either too small, too dilapidated, or too badly constructed to be worth repairing.' In June, 1838, another joint committee was appointed, with instructions to report plans for new school-houses, and also to present estimates of the cost of erecting them on the different plans which the committee might lay before the city council in connection with a bill recommending the appointment of a building committee. This recommendation was adopted, and the building committee were authorized to cause such of the present public school-houses to be removed or taken down, and such new school-houses to be erected and furnished, as may be necessary to carry into full operation the provisions of the ordinance."

This liberal provision was at once improved, and within two years thirteen new school-houses were completed. "The first day on which the new system went into operation, more than a thousand pupils entered the public schools who had never been to one before. All the rooms were soon so crowded that it became necessary to establish additional primary schools, and erect houses for their accommodation. Within two years the number of scholars in the public schools was more than double that in attendance under the old system. The grammar schools were so full that many pupils who were prepared to enter upon the course of studies therein pursued, could not be admitted."

The first school committee chosen under the reörganization of 1838, comprised the following gentlemen:

Samuel W. Bridgham,	Thomas C. Hoppin,
William Aplin,	Usher Parsons,
William C. Barker,	Caleb Williams,
George Curtis,	Hezekiah Anthony,
Moses B. Ives,	Jesse Metcalf,
Robert H. Ives,	Joseph Cady,
William G. Goddard,	Richard E. Eddy,
John F. Phillips,	Joseph Veazie,
Edward B. Hall,	John S. Eddy,
Thomas W. Dorr,	Nathan Tyler,
Seth Padelford,	Rufus Claggett,
John L Hughes,	John Ames,
Thomas R. Holden,	Amherst Everett,
Mark Tucker,	Thomas R. Ripley,
Benjamin Clifford,	Henry Anthony.

This year the committee report that "all the schools maintain a fair and respectable standing as at any former period, and though susceptable of improvement still continue a source of much usefulness to the public." The next two years the schools are reported as follows:

1839. "The schools in the opinion of the committee, still maintain as fair and respectable standing as at any time heretofore. * * * The schools are more numerously attended than at any former period; more room is therefore required. * * * The annual increase of scholars must be expected to produce, correspondently, an annual increase of the expenses of the school."

1840. "Much additional time and attention of the committee have been occupied in the measures taken and pursued to carry into effect the revised plan of popular education adopted by the city council. The execution of that plan is now in a great state of forwardness. All the schools have been visited and examined every quarter agreeably to the rules and regulations of the committee. In the opinion of the committee very considerable general improvement has been recently made under the new system, and everything promises still further results favorable to the progress of useful knowledge and moral discipline. * * * The committee deeming females to be preferable to males, for both principals and assistants in primary schools, and for assistants in the grammar schools, all teachers of those descriptions are now females. The character and reputation of the schools are advancing, and that the confidence of the public in their usefulness is increasing, is evinced by the extraordinary increase in the number of pupils.

More scholars now belong to the schools than at any time since their establishment, and their increase far exceeds the increase of population."

This year (1840,) the schools were deprived of another of their most reliable friends, by the death of Hon. Samuel W. Bridgham, who departed this life on the morning of December 29th. He was graduated at Brown University in 1794, and in 1828 was elected chancellor. He chose the law for his profession, was admitted to practice in 1796, and at the time of his decease was the oldest member at the bar in Rhode Island. He was for several years attorney general, and speaker of the house of representatives. At the organization of the city government of Providence in 1832, he was chosen mayor, to which office he was annually re-elected for eight consecutive years. During the same period he was president of the school committee. Through a long life he maintained a character for integrity and probity which secured him the confidence of all who knew him. The school committee, in a series of resolutions lamenting his death, say: "That while we pay a passing tribute to his exemplary virtues as a man, and to his tried fidelity as a magistrate, we desire more especially to recognize the relation in which he stood to the committee, and to express our sense of the impartiality with which for many years he presided over its deliberations, and of the cordial and efficient service which he rendered to the cause of public education in this city." As a further mark of respect for his character and services, the committee voted to attend his funeral in a body, and ordered all the public schools of the city to be closed on that occasion. The funeral took place on Thursday, December 31st, and was attended by the city government, by the bar, and by a large number of citizens desirous of testifying their respect for his memory.

The report of the school committee for 1841 is minute in its details. Extracts from it are here copied, as showing the status of the schools at the close of the official year:

"REPORT FOR 1841.

" In rendering the account of their proceedings for the past year, prescribed by law, the school committee have great pleasure in being able to state to the city government, that our improved system of public education, so far as it has been carried into effect, has answered the just expectations of its friends, and has strongly recommended itself to the public favor. The most satisfactory evidence of this is a large and continual increase of pupils in the schools. The pleasure which we take in making this communication is enhanced by the gratifying assurance, that a portion of this system, deemed of very great importance,

Fourth Epoch.

and indispensable to the best success of the other parts of the system, after great delays, is about to be reduced to practice, by the erection of a high school; which we hope to see in operation before the end of another year, ample provision, as it is understood, having been made for the cost of the building.

"In addition to the regular quarterly meetings for the visitation and examination of the grammar schools, the committee have held nine adjourned, or special meetings in the course of this year,—five less than in the year preceding;—a difference which is explained by the unusual demand upon the time of the committee in that year, for the consideration in detail, of a new code of by-laws and regulations, adapted to the changes that have been made in our plan of education. The average attendance at the meetings has been twenty-two of the thirty members, who compose the committee.

"The whole number of school districts is six, and of schools nineteen, viz., six grammar schools, twelve primary schools, and one school for colored children, which combines the instruction both of the grammar and primary schools. The grammar schools have been transferred to the new and commodious buildings erected for them, with the exception of the school in the second district, which remains in the old building. This building has undergone considerable repairs to render its occupation less inconvenient to scholars and teachers; and it is to be hoped, that before the end of the next year, the new house now in contemplation, at the corner of Angell and Prospect streets, will be completed, and that thus the inhabitants of the second ward will equally participate in the improvements designed for the whole city.

"In consequence of a pressure of pupils upon some of the grammar schools, it was deemed necessary, in December last, to apply to the city council for leave to make use of the ward-rooms, for school purposes; and a portion of the pupils in the third, fifth and sixth districts, were placed in these rooms, under the charge of an additional assistant for each, and with the supervision of the principal teacher. In the third district, it is believed that the difficulty will be obviated by the erection of a larger building in the second district, and by altering the boundaries of the two districts, so as to equalize the attendance in each. In the fifth district the pressure has so far diminished, that the branch-school in the ward-room has been discontinued; and it is doubted whether it will be necessary to make use of the ward-room in the sixth district during the next quarter. It will be seen from this statement, that the attendance upon our schools is somewhat fluctuating, though the number of scholars is largely on the increase. The high school will, in part, prevent the accumulation which now takes place in the grammar schools, by withdrawing, at stated periods, a considerable portion of their scholars; so that the buildings now erected for these schools may furnish the necessary accommodations for some years to come. But the time is probably not far distant, when it will be thought advisable to devote the ward-rooms to the primary schools, some of which are already too much crowded. The occupation of these rooms, by classes intermediate between the primary and grammar schools, will afford relief to the latter; and may be found advantageous to both.

"The primary school in India street having been removed to the new house in East street, the building in which it was kept has been put in good repair, and surrendered to the proprietor, Hon. Nicholas Brown, to whose liberality we have been indebted for its occupation, without rent, for several years past.

"For the accommodation of the fourth and a part of the fifth district, a primary school was opened in Mathewson street; and it has recently, for greater convenience, been removed to the old school-house in Richmond street.

"The whole number of school-houses belonging to the city is eleven. The school for colored children and the primary school on Federal Hill, are kept in hired houses.

"The number of teachers in the schools is forty-three—seven males and thirty-six females; of whom it is due to justice to say, although of course they manifest various degrees of excellence, that, taken as a body, for the useful and faithful discharge of their laborious duties, they are entitled to great praise; and, so far as we are able to speak from our own observation, will compare honorably with teachers of the same class in those places of New England, which are considered as having made the greatest advances in public education.

"In the course of the year several changes have been made among the teachers, in consequence of resignations; and it has become necessary to supply the places of the grammar master in the second district, of two assistants in grammar schools, of two preceptresses of primary schools, and of three assistants in the same.

"The whole number of scholars whose names have been entered on the books in the schools, during the last quarter, is 3486, viz., 1363 in the primary schools, and 1623 in the grammar schools. The whole number at present belonging to the schools is 3035, viz., 1674 to the primary, and 1361 to the grammar schools. The whole number present at the last quarterly examinations was 2791, viz., 1537 in the primary, and 1254 in the grammar schools. The average daily attendance in all the schools is 2419, viz., 1260 in the primary, and 1159 in the grammar schools, leaving of course an average daily absence of 414 in the former, and of 202 in the latter; in other words, of 25 per cent. in the primary, and over 15 per cent. in the grammar schools. In the last annual report of the committee to the city government, it was stated, that at the quarterly examinations in May, 1840, the number of pupils in attendance was 1977; which, when compared with the attendance at the examinations in May, 1841, already given, makes a gain in one year of 814.

"In some of the best private schools, for larger children of both sexes, which we may adopt as standards of comparison in this case, the amount of daily absences is from ten to twelve per cent. of the whole number of pupils; which makes a difference of from three to five per cent. against our grammar schools. So large an amount of absences is highly censurable, and can be justified by no excuses of sickness or necessity; and it becomes a matter of great regret and concern, that so many parents and guardians should thus undervalue and throw away the liberal provisions for public education made by the city. Besides the detriment to the pupils, thus unwarrantably absenting themselves, a serious injury is inflicted by them upon those who punctually and regularly attend the schools, by deranging the classification, and by interrupting the uniform progress in the same studies which are so essential to success, and without which the best plans, and the most ample endowments may be set at naught and rendered comparatively inefficient. The remedy for the evil complained of, is with the people themselves. Such a thing as compulsory education forms no part of our legal system. When the extent of the duties imposed on the school committee is considered it cannot be reasonably expected that they should undertake the additional task of going from house to house, to urge the delinquent to come in, and partake of the neglected advantages of public instruction. All that the members of the committee can do in this way, they will do cheerfully: but they must mainly depend upon the good sense and good feelings of the mass of their fellow citizens for the just appreciation and hearty adoption of a school system, which tends, without partiality or exclusion, to the public welfare, and is thus commended to the voluntary and cheerful support of the whole community.

"It would be interesting, if possible, to ascertain what portion of the youthful population of Providence are receiving instruction in all the schools, both public and private. The number of children in this city between the ages of four and fifteen years, as nearly as it can be obtained from the census of the United States for 1840, is 5267. The whole number of scholars at present belonging to our public schools, as before stated, is 3035, leaving 2232 children, a part of whom are receiving instruction at private expense. A resolution was communicated some time since by the committee, suggesting a small appropriation for the expense of making the requisite inquiry, but it received attention from only one branch of the city council.

"The whole amount received from the city during the past year for the expenses of the public schools is $12,377.67; from the State $3,818.20—total $16,195.87. Of this amount $13,175 have been expended for instruction, including the compensation of the superintendent; and $3,020.87 for rent, fuel and other items, including about $1,200 for repairs on school-houses, and for fixtures. The expenditure of the city, as aforesaid, for education is at the rate of $1.33½ a quarter, or $5.34 per annum for each scholar belonging to the schools. The rate in the city of New York, as appears by a recent statement, is $5 per annum for each scholar. In Boston it is much larger; and, in general, the expenses of the larger towns in Massachusetts, on the same account, are much greater in proportion to population than those of this city. Before the close of another year we hope to obtain more precise information on the subject of the comparative cost of education in different places, and to communicate the same in our next report.

"Under the new census of 1840 the sum to be received by this city from the State for public instruction will exceed $5,000.

"Considering all circumstances, the committee recommend that an appropriation of not less than $12,000 be made by the city council for school expenses in the ensuing year.

"The annual return to the secretary of state, and also the certificate to the general treasurer, that the money received from the State has been expended in the prescribed manner, have been duly furnished, according to law.

HIGH SCHOOL BUILDING ERECTED—THE SCHOOL ESTABLISHED.

FROM 1841 to 1844, was a period of great interest to the friends of popular education. For more than twelve years a high school had been contemplated by them as necessary to give completeness to the public school system. "The difficulties encountered in establishing this school, and the efforts made to prevent its going into operation, are matters of recorded history, and would excite surprise did we not remember how slow has been the advance of all real improvements. It was opposed by some because it was an ' aristocratic' institution; by others, ' because it was unconstitutional to tax property for a city college;' by others, ' because it would educate children above working for their support;' and by still others, ' because a poor boy or girl would never be seen in it.' One writer, in a printed communication, went so far as to pronounce the proposed school an excrescence on the school system. But the majority of citizens did not recognize the validity of these objections." * After surmounting numerous obstacles, their will was expressed by the city government ordering a high school building to be erected.† A site, fronting on Benefit street, and bounded on the north by Angell street, and on the south by Waterman street, was purchased, and a house fifty-six feet by seventy-six feet put immediately under contract. The basement (the front standing several feet above the level of the street,) contained a large room designed for lectures and scientific experiments, office and private room for the superintendent, and a room for storage or other purposes. The second story contained four rooms for the girls' department. The third story was divided into three apartments for the uses of the English and classical departments, and so arranged that when necessary they could be thrown into one. The entrance for girls was in front; that for the boys on the north end. Ten or twelve years later, another entrance was provided at the south end of the building.

But the spirit of hostility had not yet been effectually subdued. When the house was nearly completed, a second effort was made to prevent the school going into operation. It was proposed by its opponents to convert the building into a city hall, a convenience then much needed. A petition addressed to the city council, praying for the repeal of that portion of the ordinance which established a high school, and to appropriate the new building to the purposes of a city hall, was circulated for signatures, but received so few that it was never presented.

The question in its final form, of school or no school, excited lively discussions in private and in the public prints. The opponents of the measure produced their strong reasons with an earnestness that left no doubt of their sincerity. On the other hand, the friends of the school rushed to the front, and fought its battle with a vigor that no opposition could repress. The *Providence Journal* gave to the cause its powerful aid. "We

---

* Providence School Report, 1875, p. 12.

† The question had previously been put out to the people and decided in the affirmative by a majority larger than the most sanguine anticipated.

go for the schools, and for the high school," said the editor.* "We have seen nothing which induces us to think that public opinion has changed upon this subject." Through the same medium "A Parent" said: "Should we give up the contemplated high school, and convert the edifice erected for its accommodation to some other purpose, we should, in my humble opinion, be greatly disgraced, and the language be justly applied to us, ' this man began to build, but was not able to finish.' I have, however, no fears for the result. I have confidence in my fellow citizens, to believe that they will carry forward what they have proposed to accomplish, and that the school will soon be in successful operation, filled with the cheerful faces and glad hearts of our youth."

Another writer,† who had been active in the cause of public education, said : " The perversion of this new school house from the use for which it was intended, would be a virtual breach of good faith. The city government has, at various periods of its existence, taken unwearied pains to ascertain the sentiments of the citizens upon the question of the high school. The reply of the citizens has been at all periods, in its favor ; and on the last trial, by a greater majority than ever before. They have repeatedly called for, and now confidently expect, the establishment of a high school. Let their expectations be met by a becoming respect for their opinions. At least, let nothing be done to defeat the object, without a new and formal appeal to the freemen, to be answered through the ballot boxes."

In the discussion of the high school question, the friends of that feature in our system of public education found an important auxiliary in Professor William Giles Goddard. He believed it the true policy of the city to give the greatest possible efficiency to its schools, by providing such instruction as would prepare its youth for any course of life they might choose, whether agricultural, mechanical, mercantile, scientific, or professional. In a series of thoughtful and well digested papers, printed in the *Providence Journal*, he recited the history of the high school movement from its inception, and then in strong, positive words, appealed to his fellow citizens to sustain it.

The earnest and eloquent words of Professor Goddard were not lost upon a community so largely ripe to receive them. They served as a stimulus to exertions which were crowned with complete success. On Monday, March 20th, 1843, the high school was opened with appropriate services. One hundred and sixty-four pupils were admitted during the year—eighty boys and eighty-four girls. The original design of the

---

*Hon. Henry B. Anthony.   †William E. Richmond.

school has been steadily pursued, and during the thirty-three years of its existence, upwards of forty-five hundred pupils have received instruction within its walls. The policy of selecting teachers for the lower grades from its graduates, which was very early adopted, has been continued. All things else being equal, the high school graduate has received the preference. Of more than three hundred teachers employed in 1876, a large proportion were educated in this school. Thus, in the higher culture and more exact training of those to whom the instruction of the young is intrusted, has the city, year by year, received back rich returns for the generous expenditures made.

The high school gives completeness to the system of public free instruction, and its practical value is perhaps best seen in the thousands of its graduates who have engaged in the various industries which constitute the material prosperity of the State.

FIFTH EPOCH.

(1844—1876.)

SUPERINTENDENT OF PUBLIC SCHOOLS CHOSEN.

AGREEABLY to the school ordinance of 1838, providing for a superintendent of public schools, the committee, in 1839, proceeded to fill that office. They made choice of Mr. Nathan Bishop, who had been a tutor in Brown University.* Mr. Bishop entered upon the duties of his office August 1st, which he discharged with great benefit to the schools, and to the entire satisfaction of the committee, until 1851, when he resigned to accept a similar position in Boston. The beneficial effect of this appointment was reported to the common council by the school committee, May 28th, 1841, in the following words: "The labors of the superintendent have put a new face upon our business meetings. If the question was to be taken upon the abolition of this office or of the committee, there could be but little hesitation in saving the office with those who regard the best interests of public education."

The experience of subsequent years was in confirmation of the above expressed opinion.

Mr. Bishop was succeeded by Mr. Samuel S. Greene, who brought to his work a large experience as a teacher in the Boston public schools. Among his earliest arrangements was one for bringing the teachers of the various schools together, at stated times, to receive from him such instruction as might be of essential service to them in their daily work. He also suggested a normal class, to be formed out of such graduates

---

* So far as is known, Providence was the first city in this country to provide for a superintendent. The example was afterwards adopted by other cities and towns.

of the schools as wished to become teachers, in which they would "go through a systematic drill in the art of teaching," as an "important step forward in the elevation of our schools." He likewise commenced a course of written examinations as the best test of the quality of the work done by pupils in the grammar schools—a course that is still continued, and producing excellent results. Mr. Greene discharged the duties of superintendent for four years with signal advantage to the public schools, and to the general interests of education in the city, when, having been appointed to a professorship in Brown University, he resigned.

Immediately on the resignation of Professor Greene, the present incumbent, Rev. Daniel Leach, D. D., was elected to the office, and for twenty-one years has performed the services devolved upon him with marked industry and singleness of purpose. During these years many important changes have been made in methods of instruction, tending to elevate the character of the schools and to attract attention to them from abroad. His reports have been much sought by educators in every part of the country, for the important views and valuable hints they contain.

In his first quarterly report Superintendent Leach recommended that provision be made for a "Mixed or Ungraded School," for a numerous class of children having too little education to be qualified to enter the grammar schools, and too old to be willing to attend the primary or intermediate schools.

In his report for the next year (1856), the superintendent suggested "the propriety of having an annual course of lectures adapted to the higher classes in our schools, and those who have recently left them," showing, "by familiar illustrations, the intimate relation of science to art, and how every species of knowledge can be made productive, and so applied as to secure the greatest results."

Instruction in physiology so far as necessary to give to the young a knowledge of the fundamental laws of health, was also commended to the attention of the school committee, together with the introduction of sewing into the schools as an important element of female education. This latter suggestion was subsequently adopted, and for many years needle work has been successfully taught without detriment to the usual book studies. Already thousands of girls have left school with a competent knowledge of the use of the needle who could never have received the instruction at home, and hundreds are known, in consequence of this acquisition, to have obtained remunerative employment in the way of self-support.

FIFTH EPOCH.

Until the office of superintendent of public buildings was established a few years since, the superintendent of public schools, in addition to his ordinary duties, had the care of all the school-houses, estates and school apparatus, and under the executive committee attended to making repairs and furnishing school-rooms with furniture, etc.

GRADES—CLASSIFICATION—PROMOTIONS.

Previous to the reörganization of 1828, the schools were ungraded, and much of the time of the principals was employed in instructing young children in alphabet and other elementary lessons, an arrangement neither satisfactory nor economical. The reörganization of 1838, suggested by the experience of ten years, provided for four grades of schools — primary, intermediate, grammar and high, and when the latter went into operation, the original idea of a public free school system was as well developed as the suggestions of a carefully tried method, and the light of the hour rendered possible. But this advance upon the past fell short of completeness. To make these grades answer best the purpose for which they were created, specific classification became necessary. On the recommendation of the superintendent such a classification was made, and a uniform course of study in the corresponding classes of the same grade throughout the city, secured.

When the grammar school-houses on Benefit, Prospect, Arnold, Elm, Summer and Fountain streets were built, accommodations were provided in the first story of each for a primary and an intermediate school. The second story was thrown into one large hall, to be occupied by the grammar, or third grade pupils. These soon averaged in each school about two hundred, under the charge of a male principal and several female assistants who heard recitations in adjacent ante-rooms. But this arrangement while affording some advantages, was open to serious objections. The large size of the room enabled pupils remote from the principal's desk to escape his constant observation, and afforded them opportunity to shirk study without detection, while the noise and confusion caused by classes passing continually to and from the recitation rooms, distracted attention, and tended to disturb the order of the school. It was believed that were this mass of pupils placed in separate rooms to the number of fifty or sixty in each, and each teacher made responsible for her own room, better results would be obtained. As an experiment, the Benefit street and Elm street houses were altered, and the pupils graded and classified according to their attainments. This succeeded so well, that other houses were altered to correspond, and in the building of new grammar school-houses the same plan was pursued.

The benefit derived from adopting the foregoing plan, was soon perceptible, and attracted the attention of educators in our own State and elsewhere, who visited the public schools to acquaint themselves with the Providence system. The State commissioner of public schools in his report to the legislature at its January session in 1859, said: "During the interval between the winter and summer schools of the rural districts, I visited all the schools in the city of Providence. Afterwards I made short visits to Boston and New York, for the purpose of making myself better acquainted with the schools of those cities. The results of these visits was such as to give me increased confidence in the system now established, and which has so long been in operation in this city. The changes which have been recently made in the classification and gradation of the schools, will add greatly to their efficiency and success. The friends of public schools in all parts of the State, especially in the villages and larger towns, in attempting to improve their schools, will do well to give the schools of Providence a careful examination before they proceed far in their attempted improvement." Following out this system, an exactness and uniformity never before attained has been reached, and is scarcely open to future modification, certainly not to radical change.

Another important method connected with gradation and classification, is this:—that while promotions take place in the grammar schools semi-annually, and from the grammar schools to the high school annually, every pupil in the former who can advance faster than his class is allowed so to do, forestalling all cause for complaint that bright, studious pupils are compelled to wait the slow progress of idlers or dullards; and as each by this course finds a stimulant to industry, individuality is more distinctly developed.*

The exactness with which this system of classification works, is seen in the following statement: The average age of the first or lowest grade of pupils in all the grammar schools in the city, is 11 years and 4 months; the second grade, 12 years and 11 months; the third grade, 13 years and 11 months; the fourth grade, 14 years and 11 months; and the lowest, or entering grade in the high school, 15 years and 11 months.

---

* "At Providence the school system seems to be remarkably complete."—*Report U. S. Commissioner of Education*, 1873.

Improvement in Spelling.—Geography.—Drawing.—Centennial Exhibition.

About 1860, the superintendent made an effort to improve the spelling in the public schools. By a " group method," as it may be called, introduced first into a colored school, the most remarkable results were obtained. As the other schools entered heartily into the superintendent's views, the success became so marked as to attract attention and call forth encomiums from abroad.* Quarterly written examinations in this department have for many years been practised, which tend to strengthen the memory and ensure exactness.

In the study of geography, a similar improvement has been made. Every lesson recited is required to be illustrated with a map drawn by the pupil from memory, upon the blackboard, showing the courses of rivers, mountain ranges, the location of the principal towns and cities, and other points of importance embraced in a topographical description. By this method the pupil obtains a clear perception of the relation of different parts of a country and of the world to each other. The skill and exactness thus acquired in free hand drawing, gives a charm to a study important, but usually dry and unattractive to the young. To the Rhode Island department of the great Centennial Exhibition of 1876, at Philadelphia, specimens of maps were sent from the Providence schools, drawn entirely from memory, which for accuracy and beauty of finish could scarcely have been surpassed had the pupils been permitted to copy from an atlas. In this line of free hand drawing the schools of Providence occupy a foremost rank.† Accompanying these, were a large number of architectural and mechanical drawings and ornamental designs, made by pupils in the polytechnic school, as a part of their regular work. The specimens were finely executed, and many of them would have been creditable to a practised draughtsman. In the same connection were

---

* "The Providence schools have a high character for the accuracy of their spelling. One of the professors of Brown University told me that he noticed a marked superiority in this respect in students who had been educated in the Providence schools to those educated elsewhere. There is a colored intermediate school whose performances are quite wonderful in this way. Mr. Northrop, the agent of the board of education in Massachusetts, has mentioned in one of his reports the fact of setting the children in this school seventy-five of the hardest words he could find in their spelling book, and of their being spelt without mistake. I saw something of a similar kind myself."—*Report of Rev. Dr. Fraser to the English Parliament*, 1866.

† Walter Smith's system of drawing has been introduced into the public schools, and a teacher employed to give instruction. The lessons take their appropriate place in school routine.

sent, in neatly bound volumes, a large collection of papers comprising written examinations made in the customary way, in writing, spelling, arithmetic, grammar, geography, history and music, showing the daily work of all the schools.

School Houses.—School Attendance.

Commencing in 1800, as already seen, with four school-houses, the number has increased, as the growth of population required, to fifty-one, in 1876. "Whipple Hall" was purchased of the proprietors for $500, to which was added $450, paid to Darius Allen and Samuel Staples for alterations and repairs. For the brick school-house on Meeting street the proprietors were paid $892.50.* A school-house was the same year built on "Transit lane," and another on the west side of the river, at a cost of $2,097 each. The price paid for the land on which the former stood, was $610. Between 1838 and 1844 Thomas R. Holden, Edward P. Knowles, Joseph Cady, Henry Anthony, and Seth Padelford, under authority of the city council, supervised the building of a high school, six grammar and six primary school-houses, at an aggregate cost of $100,060. The high school-house, including $5,500 paid for the land, and $98.08 for curbing, grading, etc., cost $21,484.79. Of the thirty-seven houses since built, the best specimens of the primary and intermediate are the Summer street, Messer street, Warren street and Jackson avenue; and of the grammar, Doyle avenue, Thayer street, Federal street and Point street, all of which are fine specimens of school architecture. Of these, the Point street house covers the most ground, and presents a highly imposing appearance. The internal arrangements are such as to leave little or nothing to be desired. The annexation of the tenth ward to Providence, added seven school-houses to the previous number. Two have since been built. The assessors' valuation of school property, exclusive of houses and land in the tenth ward, is $714,380.

For the first twelve years, after the schools were established the attendance rarely exceeded 800. From 1819 to 1827 the attendance ranged from 744 to 886. In 1836, the number reported attending the public schools was 1,456; the number attending no school, 1,604; while 3,235 attended private schools. In 1828, the absences reported amounted to one-quarter of all the pupils registered. The average attendance that year was 1,000. In 1838, it was 1,717; in 1848, it had increased to

---

* The proprietorship of "Whipple Hall" was divided into fifty rights, at £100 old tenor (not £120 as inadvertently stated on page 137), or £4.10.9 "lawful money," each. The brick school-house on Meeting street, comprised eighty-five rights at £3.10 each.

6,005; in 1858, the register showed an attendance of 7,257; in 1868, the number had increased to 7,892. In 1875, the whole number registered was 12,507.

School Expenditures.—Moral Supervision.

The first appropriation made for the support of the public schools, was, as already related, $6,000. From that time, as the necessity for additional school accommodations was met, expenditures in this department advanced. In 1848, the cost of maintaining the schools was thirty per cent. of the whole city expenses. In ten years (1858), the proportion had diminished to fourteen per cent. In 1874, they were reduced to 2.7 per cent. for school instruction, and including "general expenses," 3.1 per cent. In few New England or other cities is the cost of free school education so low as in Providence. In Boston, the expense of the public schools, is more than fifty per cent. greater. "No private academy or seminary can give to the children of this city an education so thorough and advanced as our public schools furnish, at less than three or four times the cost now charged upon the public treasury; nor, so far as is known, does any other principal New England city receive larger or better returns for its outlay." *

By reference to preceding pages it will be seen how careful were the early guardians of the public schools to protect the morals of the young. They did not believe that dogmatic theology or sectarian peculiarities should constitute a part of public school instruction, but they did believe that every pupil should be impressed with the value of a pure character, and taught that virtue and integrity as underlying principles of christianity, were of higher moment than mere intellectual attainments. And in this unexceptionable spirit are the schools still supervised.

Evening and Vacation Schools.

Evening schools were commenced in Providence in 1842, under the auspices of the Ministry-at-large, to meet a large class of wants not reached by the day schools, and were continued for thirteen years with gratifying success. In the meantime this class of schools attracted public attention, and in 1849 two were opened by the city, and with the exception of three winters (one during the war of the rebellion,) have been regularly continued to the present day. In 1856 they had attained

---

* School Report for 1875.

a popularity and usefulness that authorized their recognition as a part of the public school system. For several years past the schools have been seven in number, including a polytechnic school. The two schools opened in 1849 registered 210 pupils. In 1875 the total enrollment was 2,228. The pupils embraced both sexes, none being received under twelve years of age. These schools have been found of great value in two respects: They withdraw from the streets five evenings in the week a large class of boys and girls who would otherwise be exposed to out-door temptations, and afford opportunities for acquiring an education to many operatives and others who by age and other causes are precluded attending the day schools. To the immigrant population, every year increasing in the city, these schools have proved an invaluable blessing. In 1856 an additional school for girls was opened in the high school building, in which gratuitous instruction was given by superintendent Leach and William G. Crosby. The efficiency of these schools have commended them to the friends of education in different parts of the State, and upwards of fifty have been established in different manufacturing villages.*

Vacation schools were opened in 1871, for the benefit of children who during the summer vacation of the public schools remain in the city exposed daily to the dangers and temptations of the streets. The pupils are mostly of the primary and intermediate grades. The schools are commenced about two weeks after the close of the public schools and closed one week previously to their opening in the autumn. The number of children enrolled in 1875 was 1,150. Besides the usual course of study, a large amount of oral instruction is given, for the purpose of acquainting the pupils with the names and uses of the various products of agriculture and of manufactures, and also those which constitute the main features of domestic and foreign commerce. By this process much useful knowledge is acquired which school books do not furnish, while at the same time, without any strain upon the brain, they are pleasantly preparing pupils for the more exact studies of the autumn term.

Vacation schools, as connected with our public school system, and carried on under the supervision of the public school committee, are peculiar to Providence. Their success here has attracted the attention of educators and philanthrophists in other principal cities of our country, and it is believed that the year is not far distant when the example here set, will be very generally adopted in all thickly populated places.

---

*Mr. Samuel Austin, of Providence, as agent of "The Rhode Island Educational Union," has been largely instrumental by his personal labors, in awakening an interest in this class of schools.

Music in the Schools.

Music "as an important branch of learning," was introduced into the public schools of Providence, in 1844. The first male teacher was Mr. Jason White, the second Mr. Charles M. Clarke, and the third Mr. Seth Sumner. For a single year (1866,) a portion of the schools were placed under the charge of Mr. Walter S. Meade. The fourth teacher was Mr. Henry Carter, who was succeeded by the present incumbent, Mr. Benjamin W. Hood. As the duties of the principal from year to year increased, female assistants to take charge of the lower grades of school, were appointed. These have been Eliza Lewis, Charlotte O. Doyle, (resigned in 1875,) Mary E. Rawson, Charlotte R. Hoswell and Sarah M. Farmer. Mrs. Rawson and Miss Farmer are the present assistants.

Under the several successive principals and assistants above named, constant and satisfactory progress in the knowledge of music has been made, and the study found to be helpful rather than a hindrance to other studies. The course of instruction is substantially this: In the lowest grade of the primary schools rote singing is principally practised, with a few characters given to the pupils, acquainting them with the staff, names of lines, spaces, notes and rests. In the next higher grade, reading notes and singing by note is added to rote singing. The intermediate grade is drilled in singing by note, and receives instruction in rhythm. In the grammar schools the pupils are taught music in two parts, and as they advance to higher grades (the high school) they are taught more elaborate music, at the same time paying attention to quality of tone and exactness of time. At an exhibition of grammar school pupils in Music Hall, in 1875, under the direction of Mr. Hood, they showed a thoroughness in culture that drew forth unqualified commendation. The music was of a more difficult character than is usually heard in public schools, and the time and rendition were so exact as to excite the surprise of the large audience present. The annual exhibition of the high school pupils, which for many years has filled Music Hall to its entire capacity with interested friends, has, in the fine music of the occasion, furnished an attraction second only to the essays and forensic efforts of the graduating classes. The study of music, however, has been for its advantages as a vocal drill and for its practical utility in other respects, rather than for display; and at no time have other studies been curtailed or suspended for its advantage. The specimens of musical composition, elsewhere referred to, sent by the schools to the Centennial Exhibition, are proofs of the thorough instruction given, and of the progress made in the study as a science.

Presidents and Secretaries of the School Committee — Standing Committees.

The successive presidents of the school committee have been as follows:

Rev. Asa Messer,	from 1828 to 1832.
Hon. Samuel W. Bridgham,	" 1832 to 1840.
Thomas W. Dorr, Esq.,	" 1841 to 1842.
Hon. Thomas W. Burgess,	" 1842 to 1852.
Hon. Amos C. Barstow,	" 1852 to 1853.
Hon. Walter R. Danforth,	" 1853 to 1854.
Hon. Edward P. Knowles,	" 1854 to 1855.
Hon. James Y. Smith,	" 1855 to 1857.
Hon. William M. Rodman,	" 1857 to 1859.
Hon. Jabez C. Knight,	" 1859 to 1864.
Hon. Thomas A. Doyle,	" 1864 to 1869.
Hon. George L. Clarke,	" 1869 to 1870.
Hon. Thomas A. Doyle,	" 1870 to 1875.
Rev. Henry W. Rugg,	" 1875 to

All the above named gentlemen, except Rev. Mr. Rugg, were *ex-officio* members of the school committee, and from 1832 to 1875, it had been customary to elect the mayor to preside over the deliberations of that body.

The secretaries of the board have been Walter R. Danforth, George Curtis, Robert H. Ives, William Aplin, Edward R. Young, Charles H. Parkhurst, Reuben A. Guild, Amos M. Bowen, and Sarah H. Ballou, the present incumbent.

The standing committees are ten in number, viz.: executive committee, committee on qualifications, committee on high school, committee on evening schools, committee on music, committee on drawing and penmanship, committee on finance, committee on by-laws, committee on vacation schools, committee on text-books.

School Hygiene.—Ventilation—Dr. Leach's System.

In the early period of public schools in Providence, little attention was paid to the hygiene of the school-room, and particularly to ventilation in its relation to health. For twenty-five or thirty years after the schools were established, open fire-places (the best kind of ventilation,) were in vogue, and these with the fresh air forcing its way through the crannies of windows, doors and floors, prevented an accumulation of impure atmosphere noticeable as detrimental to the health of pupils; and it was only when anthracite coal was introduced as a fuel, throwing a portion of its unconsumed gas into the room, consuming its oxygen, and by the dryness of the atmosphere accelerating the outflow of insensible perspiration from the human body, that improvement in the construction of school-houses came to be considered necessary.

The first advance upon the past was made between 1838 and 1842, when the new primary and intermediate, grammar and high school buildings were erected. But even in these dependence was placed solely on lowering the upper sashes of windows and a small trap opening in the ceiling of the room for the escape of heated air into the attic of the building, to escape again through a small oriole window. Such was the kind of ventilation provided for the high school until within a few years, when a Robinson apparatus was applied to a single room, and for the first time direct communication by a ventiduct was had with the external air. Previously to this the grammar schools had been partially relieved by the use of Emerson's ventilators, but in all the old primary and intermediate buildings teachers and pupils continued to suffer from breathing mephitic air.

To the need of better ventilation, and to other causes injuriously affecting health, the superintendent at different times called attention, and in 1870 a special committee made a report to the school board on "Health in relation to Education," in which the same need was urged. Perfect ventilation, it was said, should be secured "at whatever pecuniary cost." To this should be added such an arrangement of seats in the school-room as would " secure pupils from the discomfort of sitting facing the light, or of suffering the dazzle of cross-lights," which strain the optic nerve, and affect the brain. Shorter and less exhaustive lessons for pupils troubled with myopia or near-sightedness, and physical exercise as a part of the daily routine of the school, were recommended as helps in securing "strong, healthy and thoroughly cultured bodies and minds."

No marked opportunity for improvement occurred until the erection of the Thayer street grammar school-house in 1867, when the superintendent of schools was authorized to introduce a system invented by him in 1854, while employed by the Massachusetts Board of Education to examine into the location and construction of school-houses in that State. It consists of four ventiducts or shafts in the building, extending from the cellar through the roof. The dimensions of these shafts are $4\frac{1}{2}$ by $3\frac{1}{2}$ feet, and made perfectly smooth. There are two openings from each room into one of these ventiducts 3 feet by 2 feet, one at the bottom, the other close to the ceiling. The temperature in the ventiduct is raised several degrees higher than it is in the school-rooms. This is absolutely necessary to success. The higher the temperature, -the more effective the ventilation. The heat may be applied by means of a smoke pipe, by a steam radiator, by gas, or by a small stove at the bottom. In this house a stove is used whenever the condition of the atmosphere requires.

The success of this system has been so complete, that after a session of two hours or more, there is no perceptible difference in the quality of the air in the rooms or out. The same system was subsequently applied to the Warren street primary and intermediate school building, with equal success. Since then, in the erection of new school-houses, ventilation has received the attention its importance demands, and pure air in sufficient quantity obtained.

Several years ago, the superintendent devised another plan of an economical character, for relieving school rooms of foul air that have no adequate means of ventilation, and upon which it is inexpedient to lay out any considerable sums. As an experiment it was applied to two rooms in the East street school-house. The plan embraces four openings of suitable length and width, two on each side of the room and opposite each other; the upper openings being about one foot below the ceiling, and the lower ones near the floor. Into each of these openings is inserted a frame of slats, placed at a very acute angle,—the upper ones forcing the inflowing current directly against the ceiling, causing its rapid diffusion through the upper atmosphere of the room, without detriment to the comfort of the pupils. This fact was satisfactorily determined by very accurate chemical tests. The slats above mentioned should be about one foot in width, one-fourth of an inch thick, and not more than three-eighths of an inch apart.

These openings are covered with slides moved at will, and held in place by weights suspended over pulleys. The slides enable the teacher to regulate the inflow of pure air, so as to preserve uniformity in quantity, whatever may be the force of the wind. The lower openings are used only for expelling the noxious air which at times forms a stratum near the floor. But one of the openings is used at a time, and that opposite the direction of the wind.

This description is enough to give a general idea of the plan of ventilation which has been on trial nearly three years. According to the testimony of the teachers, it has been entirely successful. A pure air has been obtained, and the use of open windows for ventilation has been entirely superseded.

Gentlemen interested in the subject of ventilation who have visited the East street school have borne testimony to the purity of the air in these rooms, and to the wide awake appearance of the children; and they have been equally emphatic in stating the foul condition of the air in the other rooms, and its unmistakeable effects upon the children, even though the windows were lowered more than it was safe to have them.

Recently, a number of medical sanitarians* examined into the workings of this system, and in a valuable report on the Hygiene of the school room, give it their hearty sanction. They say: "The system, which we have carefully investigated, possesses the following advantages over its competitors, which seem to us strong ones: It is cheap and readily applied to any building, old or new. It is independent of light supply and directly under the control of the teacher of the room. It has double apertures for entrance of fresh and exit of exhausted air, close to both floor and ceiling. By the upward angle of the broad slats, composing the entry flue, the air is directed away from the floor and ground currents avoided. By the close proximity of the slats to each other, the air enters the room in thin sheets, in which condition it mixes with and is heated by that which it meets with greater ease than if projected into the apartment in one mass. We believe that the method applied in East street combines more valuable features than any other which has fallen under our notice. It therefore gives us great pleasure to express our hearty approval of this system."

This plan admits of various modifications, and can be applied to windows when the original method would be less convenient and more expensive. In this way it has been successfully used in school-rooms, hospital and other buildings. The inventor having neglected to take out a patent, while he has freely explained it to inquirers, the principle has been used by persons in different parts of the country, and claimed to be original with them; and this since it was applied to the East street school-house in 1873!

According to the most approved authorities, the laws of health demand for each pupil at least twenty-five square feet of standing room, and not less than two hundred and forty cubic feet of pure air per hour. Three hundred feet would be better. In the erection of new school-houses, and in the alteration of old ones, these conditions should be observed.

THE CLOSE.

It has been a favorable circumstance in the history of the public schools, that the successive chief magistrates of Providence have been their helpful friends. Both in their private and official character they have given them unqualified support, and sanctioned liberal appropriations for their support. His Honor, Mayor Doyle, whose long connec-

---

*William F. Hutchinson, M. D., William H. Traver, M. D., J. Morrow, M. D., L. R. Col. Ed., Oliver C. Wiggin, M. D.

tion with them as a member of the school committee has made him familiar with their wants, represented the spirit of his predecessors no less than his own, when at the dedication of the Thayer street grammar school-house in 1868, he said: "As a representative of the common school, I have felt a deep interest in whatever relates to the cause of free education; and as a member of the city government, I have advocated a liberal policy towards this most important department of the municipality." And again, when at the dedication of the Hughes grammar school-house, in 1870, he said: "Fellow citizens, before we unite in singing the dedication hymn, let me, as your representative, speaking in your behalf, utter the wish and the hope that the day is far distant when a narrow and a contracted policy shall rule the councils of this city in regard to common school education. Be the day far distant when, in the eyes of the city representatives, her highways, her lamps, her other departments, will be of more consequence than the education of her youth. When that day arrives, darkness will have settled upon this city."

From 1800 to 1828, there was but little apparent change in methods of instruction. The school routine was each successive year essentially the same. Teaching was more mechanical than intellectual. The author of the text-book had done all the necessary thinking, and the teacher who could instruct only with book in hand, and determine the correctness of a pupil's answer only by reference to it, and who like a sailor adrift in a long-boat without oars or sail, would be helplessly afloat without it, was considered sufficiently qualified for his office. New and better methods were not thought of. Progress beyond the stereotype lesson was not expected in the schools. Professor Goddard, in one of his admirable papers in support of the high school, printed in 1839, says: "I was a pupil in one of them more than thirty years ago, and in comparing the school which I then attended with the schools which now exist, I am unable to note any signal improvement—none, certainly, at all answerable to the demands of the present time, or to the improvement which, in parallel institutions, has been accomplished elsewhere."

But that period is not to be undervalued. That day of small things is not to be despised. The friends of free school education builded as well as they knew. They gave out all the light they had received, and their earnest, persistent labors prepared the way for better things to come. Gradually advances were made. Under the reform of 1828, an encouraging change was perceived. In the ten years following a clearer insight into the wants of the schools was obtained. In 1847, the committee could say of the schools: "We believe that they rank at the present moment, with the very best public schools in the country." The next year they said: "The great cause for congratulation in regard to our school system, in the opinion of your committee, is that we have begun well, and have laid a good foundation. We shall never be obliged to tear down, but only to build higher. The base is firm enough and broad enough to support the loftiest superstructure. Our future progress will not require a change, but merely a development of principles."

From that time forward the annual reports have been records of improvement. With no blind devotion to the past, the schools, in methods of instruction, have kept abreast with the times, and whatever experience has proved to be of practical worth has been adopted. The written examinations for 1876 show a higher scholarship for the schools of Providence than they have ever before attained. This result was obtained, not by any forcing process but by the faithfulness of teachers and the healthful industry of pupils. In the grammar schools, improved methods in teaching arithmetic, geography, grammar and history, have enabled scholars to accomplish in a single term, what formerly would have been impossible. In the high school the course of study has been, in successive years, adapted to the practical needs of pupils intending to become teachers, or designing to enter different departments of business. The advantages of this comprehensive system of education, are seen alike in the pulpit, at the bar, in the school-room, in the halls of science, in the office of the civil engineer, in the improved products of the manufactory, in the skilled labor and inventive genius of the machine shop, in intelligent horticulture, and in the successful enterprise of trade and commerce.

That the system of public education devised in the reconstruction of 1839, and brought step by step to its present state of perfection, is susceptible of further advancement is undoubtedly true. In the century upon which the schools have now entered, the true relations of the home to them will come to be better understood, and the cordial coöperation of parents with teachers will become more general. A stronger stress will be laid upon primary instruction, and the wisdom of placing children at the most impressible age under the molding hand and mind of teachers of broad culture and large experience, will be acknowledged and become the rule. Fewer pupils will be assigned to a teacher in all the schools, so that those slow to apprehend can receive the personal attention that class instruction forbids. Smaller and more inexpensive school-houses will be built, as increased accommodations shall be required, avoiding thereby the evils which spring from massing large numbers of children under one roof. The laws of health will be more carefully studied, and in the construction of school-houses rigidly enforced. Aptitude for teaching not less than competent literary qualifications, will more than ever guide in the selection of teachers. Changes in courses of study and in methods of instruction, to harmonize with the ever-changing condition and new wants of society, will be made. Plans tending to create an aristocracy in education by limiting free instruction to grammar school studies, will be repudiated as consistent only with monarchical institutions, and as antagonistic to the spirit of a republic. The duty of the appropriate authorities to see that every child in the community is educated, will be made paramount. Methods of supervising schools adapted to the progress of the age, will be devised, and every influence which a liberal, just and statesman-like policy can bring into activity, will be employed in carrying forward to the highest ideal of perfection the free school system of 1876. Such is our prediction.

In closing this brief history of the progress of public free school education in Providence, from the crystalization of the thought in 1767 to the present time, words recently spoken in another connection, may not be considered inappropriate :

" Our schools are among the most attractive institutions of our city. Enterprise, capital and a better population are drawn to it by the superior advantages they afford for the education of the young, and by the reputation which intelligence and culture always give to a community. The enlightened spirit in which they have been conducted, and the liberal support they have ever received, has enabled them not only to give tone to the educational sentiment of the State, but to maintain a front rank with other States in educational progress. No city in the country has stronger reasons for so fostering public schools as that their influence shall be perceptible among every class of the population, than our own. Her varied industries demand intelligent labor such as the schools only can provide. Her influence in State and Nation is to be perpetuated by the potency of mind which has received its development and culture in her educational institutions. Let it be the wisdom of the future as it has been of the past, to render them all the support that the broadest views of public free education shall require, or that can honor the Rhode Island name."

ERRATA.—Page 137. For Captain John Whipple read Captain Joseph Whipple.

UNIVERSITY GRAMMAR SCHOOL.

This is undoubtedly the oldest institution of learning in the State, not excepting even the University, of which it was the germ and origin. In the month of April, 1764, the Rev. James Manning, afterwards the distinguished president of Rhode Island College, removed with his family to the town of Warren, and at once opened a Latin School, with a view to the beginning of college instruction. During the latter part of the year he was chosen pastor of a church, which had been organized mainly through his instrumentality. The following year, 1765, he was formally chosen president of the infant college. He thus sustained the threefold relation of president, pastor and principal. The first commencement of the college, now Brown University, was held in Warren in 1769, at which seven young men were graduated, most of whom had been trained by Manning in the Latin School. In the contest that afterwards ensued for the final location of the College, Providence was successful, and the foundations for the College Building, now called "University Hall," were accordingly laid on College Hill, Providence, in May, 1770. Meanwhile instruction was given in the upper part of the "Brick School-house," so called, on Meeting street, the College occupying one chamber, and the Latin School the other. This schoolhouse, as appears from Staples' Annals of Providence, was built during the year 1768, partly by the town and partly by subscription. By this compound arrangement the town owned the lower story, while the upper story was owned by the subscribers, among whom the friends and guardians of the College and the Latin School were largely represented. This was in the days of beginnings, or small things.

The first allusion that we find concerning the Latin or Grammar School, after its removal from Warren, appears in the *Gazette* in connection with an account of the college commencement for 1770, this being the first commencement held in Providence. "The business of the day being concluded, and before the assembly broke up, a piece from Homer was pronounced by Master Billy Edwards, one of the Grammar School boys, not nine years old." This Edwards was a son of the Rev. Morgan Edwards, one of the principal founders of the college. He was graduated in 1776, at the early age, it appears, of fourteen. In 1772 the School was removed to a room on the lower floor of the new college edifice, the president, as appears from the following advertisement in the *Gazette*, still retaining charge of the same, in connection with his other duties :—

"Whereas several gentlemen have requested me to take and educate their sons, this may inform them, and others disposed to put their children under my care, that the Latin School is now removed, and set up in the College edifice; where proper attention shall be given, by a master duly qualified, and those found to be the most effectual methods to obtain a competent knowledge of Grammar, steadily pursued. At the same time, Spelling, Reading, and speaking English with propriety, will be particularly attended to. Any who choose their sons should board in commons, may be accommodated at the same rate with the students, six shillings per week being the price. And I flatter myself that such attention will be paid to their learning and morals, as will entirely satisfy all who may send their children. All books for the school, as well as the classical authors read in College, may be had, at the lowest rate, of the subscriber.

JAMES MANNING.

Providence, July 10, 1772."

In the following year, May 20, 1773, President Manning thus writes to his friend and correspondent, Rev. John Ryland, of Northampton, England : "I have a Latin School under my care, taught by one of our graduates, of about twenty boys." This graduate was the Rev. Ebenezer David, of the class of 1772, a most accurate and excellent teacher, whom the Hon. Judge Howell, who for many years was associated with President Manning as Assistant Tutor and Professor, always claimed the honor of having instructed. How long he continued in charge of the school we are not informed. Probably until the breaking out of the Revolutionary War. In Judge Pitman's address before the Alumni Association of Brown University, we find the following paragraph :—" In 1774, fifteen entered the Freshman Class ; eight of them were from the Latin School in Providence, under the tuition of the Rev. Ebenezer David, of the class of 1772, one of the best instructors," says Mr. William Wilkinson, who was one of the eight, "that I have ever known." The next mention of the school appears in the *Gazette* for 1776, as follows :—

"A Grammar School was opened in the school-room within the College edifice on Monday the 11th instant, in which the same mode of teaching the Learned Languages is pursued, which has given such great satisfaction to the inhabitants of this town. The scholars are also instructed in Spelling, Reading and Speaking the English language with propriety, as well as in Writing and Arithmetic, such part of their time as their parents or guardians direct.
"College Library, March 22, 1776."

Under date of November 8, 1773, President Manning, in renewing his correspondence with Rev. Dr. Stennett, of London, which had been interrupted during the war of the revolution, thus writes : "I have the assistance of a Tutor, and a Grammar Master keeps school in the College edifice." This was the late William Wilkinson, of Providence, who had just graduated at the commencement in September. In another letter Manning adds :—"He is a good Master. The School is nearly up to twenty." Mr. Wilkinson retained his position as principal of the school eleven years, during which time he prepared many young men for a collegiate course, and trained them for the responsible and active duties of life. Among his pupils may be mentioned the names of Hon. Samuel Eddy, LL. D., Secretary of State and Judge of the Supreme Court of Rhode Island, Hon. James Burrill, LL. D., United States Senator, Hon. James Fenner, LL. D., United States Senator and also Governor of the State, and His Honor Samuel W. Bridgham, first Mayor of Providence. In connection with his duties as principal he was also librarian of the college, residing with his family in rooms in the college building. He died in May, 1852, at the advanced age of ninety-two. For many years he presided over the Masonic Institution in Rhode Island, as Grand Master of the Grand Lodge, Grand High Priest of the Grand Chapter, and Grand Commander of the Grand Commandery of Massachusetts and Rhode Island. A fine portrait of him has recently been placed in Masons Hall, by his surviving daughter, Mrs. Tibbits.

In 1786, the School was removed from the College edifice, back to the Brick School House on Meeting Street, as appears from the following advertisement, published in the *Gazette:*—

"William Wilkinson informs the public, that by the advice of the School Committee, he proposes removing his School from the College edifice, on Monday next, to the Brick School House; and sensible of the many advantages resulting from a proper method of instruction in the English language, he has, by the Committee's approbation, associated with him Mr. Asa Learned, as an English instructor. Those gentlemen and ladies who may wish to employ them in the several branches of Greek, Latin and English languages taught grammatically, Arithmetic and Writing, may depend on the utmost attention being paid to their children. Greek and Latin at twenty-four shillings per quarter; English at sixteen shillings.

WILKINSON AND LEARNED.

Providence, October 20, 1786."

The first mention of the school in the records of the corporation of the University, appears under date of September 4, 1794, as follows:—

"*Voted.* That the President use his influence to establish a grammar school in this town, as an appendage to the college, to be under the immediate visitation of the President and the general inspection of the town's school committee, and that the President also procure a suitable master for such school."

In accordance with the foregoing vote the school was again established in the college. In a recent notice of the late Hon. Philip Allen, a graduate in the class of 1803, it is stated that he was "prepared for college in the Latin School, then kept in the northwest corner room of the lower story of the old college building, by Jeremiah Chaplin, afterwards President of Waterville College." Under date of September 7, 1809, we find upon the records of the Corporation the following:—

"*Voted.* That a suitable building in which to keep a Grammar School, be erected on the college lands, provided a sum sufficient to defray the expense of erecting said building can be raised by subscription; that said school be under the management and control of the President of the College; and that Thomas P. Ives, Moses Lippitt, and Thomas Lloyd Halsey, Esqrs., be a committee to raise said sum and cause said building to be erected; and that they erect the same on the west line of the Steward's garden."

"*Voted.* That the President be authorized to procure a Master to teach the Grammar School ordered at this meeting, and that if a sufficient sum be not raised from the scholars to pay the salary of the Master, the deficiency be paid out of the funds of the University."

In accordance with the foregoing instructions the committee, consisting of Messrs. Ives, Lippitt and Halsey, proceeded at once to procure subscriptions, and to erect a house suitable for the purpose in view, directly opposite the present Mansion House on College street. It was built of brick, twenty-four by thirty-three feet, and two stories in height. The whole expense was fifteen hundred dollars, which amount was obtained from one hundred and eighteen persons, mostly citizens of the town, in sums ranging from one hundred dollars down to five, three and two dollars. The names of the subscribers are given in Guild's Documentary History of Brown University, a quarto volume published by subscription, in 1867.

We should be glad in this connection to present a list of all the masters, preceptors, or principals of the Latin or grammar school from the beginning; the means for this, however, are not at hand, no records or files of the school, until a comparatively recent period, having been kept. In the catalogues of the university from 1808 to 1824, the names of the " Preceptors" are appended to the names of the president and faculty. Whether the school was continued with regularity from this date is uncertain. Very likely there were interruptions. For many years after the completion of the building, in 1810, the upper story was used for the medical lectures, that were formerly given in connection with the university. In 1837, Mr. Benjamin H. Rhodes, the present popular and efficient librarian of the Redwood Library, at Newport, took charge of the school, and continued it two years. He was succeeded by Gen. Joseph S. Pitman, a son of the late Judge Pitman, who taught it, however, but a short time. In 1843, Mr. Elbridge Smith, who had been a tutor in college during the two preceding years, assumed the charge, and the following year Mr. Henry S. Frieze, a graduate in the class of 1841, was associated with him. In 1845, Mr. Smith left the School, and his place was supplied by Merrick Lyon, LL. D., also a graduate in the class of 1841. Under their joint management the UNIVERSITY GRAMMAR SCHOOL had a brilliant and successful career. The number of scholars was greatly increased, so that in the year 1852, Messrs. Lyon and Frieze were encouraged to make, at their own expense, an addition to the building of thirty-five feet, and to supply the commodious halls and rooms thus obtained, with all the conveniences and appointments of a first-class school.

In 1854, Mr. Frieze accepted a Latin Professorship in the University of Michigan, at Ann Arbor, and his place was supplied by Emory Lyon, M. D., a successful principal of an academy in an adjoining State. Under their skillful and efficient management the school has increased in usefulness and reputation. Dr. Emory Lyon has had charge of the English and Mathematical Departments, while his brother, Dr. Merrick Lyon, has had charge of the Classical Department, teaching Greek and Latin exclusively. As it was in the beginning, so is it now, a most important preparatory school for the college, training for entrance thereto large numbers of youth who take high rank in their respective classes, and thus do honor to their early instructors. As an illustration it may be stated, that during the past quarter of a century, between two and three hundred young men have been admitted to the University, who were prepared for College at the UNIVERSITY GRAMMAR SCHOOL.

We close this imperfect sketch with the following list of all the instructors of the School, as nearly as can be ascertained, from the beginning down to the present time :—

INSTRUCTORS.—1764–1876.

Rev. James Manning, D. D., Hon. David Howell, LL. D., Rev. Ebenezer David, A. M., William Wilkinson, A. M., Mr. Asa Learned, Rev. Jeremiah Chaplin, D. D., Hon. Tristam Burges, LL. D., Wood Furman, A. M., Rev. Ebenezer Burgess, D. D., Rev. Hervey Jenks, A. M., David Avery, A M., George Fisher, A. M., Rev. Solomon Peck, D. D., Isaac Kimball, A. M., Rev. Willard Pierce, A. M., Rev. Jesse Hartwell, D. D., Rev. Rufus Babcock, D. D., Hon. Isaac Davis, LL. D., Rev. Silas A. Crane, D. D., Prof. George W. Keely, D. D., Benjamin H. Rhodes, A. M., Rev. George Ware Briggs, D. D., Prof. George W. Greene, A. M., Hon. Samuel Curry, A. M., Asa Drury, Rhodes B. Chapman, Hon. Thomas A. Jencks, LL. D., Gen. Joseph S. Pitman, A. B., Christopher Greene, Prof. Henry Day, D. D., Prof. Henry Warren Torrey, A. M., Elbridge Smith, A. M. Prof. Henry S. Frieze, LL. D., Merrick Lyon, LL. D., Emory Lyon, A. M., M. D., Alfred Lawton, A. B., Benjamin Braman, A. M., Howard M. Rice, A. M., Rev. Elisha B. Andrews, A. M., James R. Corthell, Frederick B. Byram, A. M., William V. Kellen, A. B., Harmon S. Babcock, A. B.

INSTRUCTORS IN SPECIAL STUDIES.

Felix Aucaine, Alfred Gaudelet, Charles H. Gates, A. B., Rev. George E. Horr, William F. Hammond, Stephen A. Potter, George H. Rogers, Ellery C. Davis, Miss Mary A. Potter.

R. A. G.

BROWN UNIVERSITY.

This venerable seat of learning, the oldest of all the colleges under the control of the Baptist denomination, was formally incorporated in February, 1764. The plan of the institution originated with the Philadelphia Association, which, at its meeting in October, 1762, " obtained," says the historian Backus, " such an acquaintance with the affairs of Rhode Island as to bring themselves to an apprehension that it was practicable and expedient to erect a college in the Colony of Rhode Island, under the chief direction of the Baptists, in which education might be promoted and superior learning obtained, free from any sectarian tests." In this little colony Roger Williams had first recognized and practically enforced the grand principle of "soul liberty," or entire freedom in all religious concernments. Here the Legislature was chiefly in the hands of the Baptists, " and here, therefore," says Morgan Edwards, " was the likeliest place to have a Baptist college established by law." The establishment of an academy at Hopewell, New Jersey, in 1756, for the literary and theological training of young men suggested, doubtless, the idea of a higher institution of learning. Although founded by the Rev. Isaac Eaton, who for eleven years was the honored and successful principal, it was under the supervision and control of the Philadelphia and Charleston Associations, who appointed certain trustees to have the general oversight of its affairs, and to attend its quarterly and annual examinations.

In the month of July, 1763, the Rev. James Manning, who the year previous had graduated with the second honors of his class, at the College of New Jersey, Princeton, arrived at Newport, Rhode Island, on the business of the great educational work, with which he had been especially entrusted by a committee of the association. The details of his mission have been related in full by his biographers. Through his personal influence, and that of the Rev. Morgan Edwards, a charter reflecting the liberal sentiments of the colony and of the denomination was obtained from the General Assembly, not, however, without a severe and protracted struggle on the part of those who opposed the enterprise. In the spring of 1764, a preparatory or latin school was opened in the town of Warren, and the year following, Manning was formally appointed " President of the College, Professor of Languages and other branches of learning, with full power to act in these capacities at Warren or elsewhere." He was, therefore, principal of the latin school, president of the infant college, and pastor of a large and flourishing church, which had been gathered and organized mainly through his eloquence and faithfulness. Thus the interests of learning and religion, in the days of the fathers, were most intimate and friendly. Far distant be the day when "what hath been joined together" evidently by the Divine favor, shall be ruthlessly " put asunder."

In 1766, Mr. Edwards was appointed an agent to solicit funds for the college in England and Ireland. He was quite successful, considering how " angry the mother country was with her dependent colonies," obtaining eight hundred and eighty-eight pounds sterling, or about four thousand five hundred dollars. The original document, containing the names of the subscribers in their own handwriting, has been placed among the archives of the college library. About the same time Rev. Hezekiah Smith, of Haverhill, Massachusetts, a classmate and intimate friend of the president, obtained subscriptions for the college in South Carolina and Georgia, amounting to about twenty-five hundred dollars. Subscriptions were also taken up in all the Baptist churches, every member, in the language of the records of the various associations, being recommended to pay six pence sterling annually to the treasurer of the college. The gifts and offerings thus contributed were from the "*res angusta domi*," from " pious enlightened penury," to the noblest of all causes, the advancement of " religion and sound learning."

The first commencement of the college was held in the meeting-house at Warren, on the 7th of September, 1769. Four years had elapsed since the President with a solitary pupil commenced his collegiate duties as an instructor. Through toils and difficulties and opposition even, he had quietly persevered in his work until " Rhode Island College " had won its way to public favor. And now his first pupils, seven in number, were about to take their diplomas and go forth to the duties of life. They were young men of promise. Some of them were destined to fill conspicuous places in the approaching struggle for independence ; others were to be leaders in the church and distinguished educators of youth. One, Charles Thompson, who delivered the valedictory address, afterwards succeeded President Manning in the pastorate of the Warren church. Another, William Rogers, attained to eminence as a divine, and was the successor of Morgan Edwards in the pastorate of the First Baptist Church of Philadelphia. He was also a professor in the University of Pensylvania, and an intimate friend of Washington. His nephew, the late William Sanford Rogers, has recently bequeathed to the University the sum of fifty thousand dollars to found the "Newport Rogers Professorship." Another, William Williams, was for many years pastor of a Baptist church in Wrentham, Massachusetts, and the instructor of many young men in theology. This was before the founding of the Theological Institution at Newton. A fourth member of the class was James Mitchell Varnum, afterwards distinguished as a lawyer and a judge, and who served as a brigadier-general in the war of the revolution. Probably no class that has gone forth from the University, in her palmiest days of prosperity, has exerted so widely extended and beneficial an influence, the times and circumstances being taken into consideration, as this first class of 1769. A full and extremely interesting account of the commencement is given in the *Providence Gazette*, of which the following is the closing part:—

"The President concluded the exercises with prayer. The whole was conducted with a propriety and solemnity suitable to the occasion. The audience (consisting of the principal gentlemen and ladies of this colony, and many from the neighboring governments,) though large and crowded, behaved with the utmost decorum. Not only the candidates, but even the President, were dressed in American manufactures. Finally, be it observed, that *this class are the first sons of that college* which has existed for more than four years, during all which time it has labored under great disadvantages, notwithstanding the warm patronage and encouragement of many worthy men of fortune and benevolence; and it is hoped, from the disposition which many discovered on that day, and other favorable circumstances, that these disadvantages will soon in part be happily removed."

As the place for the permanent location of the college was yet undetermined, the four towns of Warren, Providence, Newport and East Greenwich, in four different counties of the State, all preferred their claims as being, each respectively, the most eligible and desirable situation. The consequence was that the public mind was greatly agitated by the contentions which grew out of these conflicting claims. Mr. Edwards, in referring to the subject, says: "Warren was at first agreed on as a proper situation, where a small wing was to be erected in the spring of 1770, and about eight hundred pounds raised toward effecting it. But soon afterwards, some who were unwilling it should be there, and some who were unwilling it should be anywhere, did so far agree as to lay aside the said location and propose that the county which should raise the most money should have the college." A full account of this remarkable contest is given in the "Documentary History of Brown University." The two ablest competitors were Providence and Newport. The latter town raised by subscription four thousand pounds lawful money, but Providence, says Manning in his correspondence, raised four thousand two hundred and eighty pounds lawful money, and advantages superior to Newport in other respects. After an earnest discussion on the merits of the conflicting claims, the corporation, on the 7th of February, 1770, decided by a vote of twenty-one to fourteen, "that the edifice be built in the town of Providence, and that there the college be continued forever." Accordingly, in May following, the President removed with his students from Warren, and occupied for a time the old brick school-house on Meeting street.

We have thus given in brief the outlines of the early history of Brown University. The details of its progress and continued growth would crowd the pages of a volume. We can only add a few words respecting its grounds, buildings, resources and present condition. The location is admirable, being the summit of a hill, easy of ascent, and commanding a delightful view of Narragansett Bay, studded with islands, and of the country around, variegated with hills and dales, woods and plains. "Surely," says Edwards, "this spot was made for the seat of the muses." The grounds, comprising some fifteen acres, are tastefully laid out and shaded with magnificent elms, some of them having been growing for nearly half a century. The college enclosure, including the "green" in front and the "campus" in the rear, comprises a square area of about ten acres, bounded by Waterman street on the north, George street on the south, Prospect street on the west or front, and Brown street in part on the east. Beyond this enclosure is the "College Park," extending east to Thayer street, and still further on, extending to Hope street, is a strip of land comprising upwards of three acres, bequeathed to the University in 1841 by the Hon. Nicholas Brown, from whom the institution derives its name. The total valuation of its lands, situated as they are in the most delightful part of a wealthy and growing city, can not be far from a million of dollars. Of course they are unproductive, with the exception of the strip referred to, which may perhaps eventually be sold and the proceeds applied to the erection of a new dormitory, of which the college stands greatly in need.

Of its six buildings the oldest is "University Hall," the corner stone of which was laid by the celebrated John Brown of "Gaspee" fame, on the 27th of March, 1770. The plan of this venerated pile was that of "Nassau Hall," Princeton, which was regarded at the time as one of the finest structures in the country. It is of brick, four stories high, one hundred and fifty feet long and forty-six feet wide, with a projection in the centre on the east and west sides of ten by thirty-three feet, and an entry of twelve feet extending through the centre of each story. It has fifty-six rooms for officers and students, including various recitation rooms. The "Grammar School Building," erected in 1810 for the accommodation of the preparatory or Latin School, was originally a small brick structure, twenty-four by thirty-three feet, and two stories in height. "Hope College," erected in 1822, was presented to the Corporation by the Hon. Nicholas Brown, and named by him in honor of his only surviving sister, Mrs. Hope Ives. It is of brick, four stories high, one hundred and twenty feet long by forty feet wide, and contains fifty rooms for officers and students. This building is sadly in want of repairs. "Manning Hall" was erected in 1834, at the expense also of Mr. Brown, and by him presented to the Corporation with a request that it might be named "in honor of his distinguished instructor and revered friend, President Manning." This beautiful building is an exact model of the temple of Diana Propylea, in Elusis, being just twice the size of the original. It is of stone, covered with cement, and of the pure Doric order. Including the portico it is ninety feet in length by forty-two feet in width, and of two stories. The height from the top of the basement is forty feet. The library occupies the lower hall, which is sixty-four by thirty-eight feet, with a height of thirteen feet. The upper hall is used for the chapel. The front of the edifice is ornamented with four immense fluted columns, resting on a platform projecting thirteen feet from the walls. "Rhode Island Hall," erected by subscription in 1840, is of stone, covered with cement, seventy feet long by forty-two feet wide, with a projection in front of twelve by twenty-six. The first floor is divided into two lecture rooms, one for the Professor of Chemistry and the other for the Professor of Natural Philosophy. The second story is thrown into a beautiful hall for the Cabinet of Mineralogy, Geology and Natural History. During the past year a wing has been built on the east side, giving additional accommodations for the professors on the first floor, while the second floor is occupied as a "portrait gallery." The "Mansion House," built in 1840 for the use of the president, is a commodious dwelling of wood, forty-six by thirty-seven feet, with an octagonal projection in front, forming a vestibule. Over the front door is an Ionic portico, eight by seven feet. The addition is twenty one by eighteen feet. The "Chemical Laboratory," erected in 1862, is a neat and substantial building of brick, two stories in height, forty by fifty feet, with a projection on the east side, thirty-five by fifty-five feet.

The late Mr. John Carter Brown, for many years a member of the Board of Fellows, and a distinguished benefactor of the library, gave to the University, some years since, the sum of fifteen thousand dollars, to be on interest, and the accumulated amount to be eventually used in the erection of a fire-proof library building. At his death, in 1874, he bequeathed the additional sum of fifty thousand dollars, and also a valuable lot of land, for the same purpose. This lot, which is one hundred and twenty feet square, is on the corner of Prospect and Waterman streets, overlooking the lawn in front of the college buildings. The erection of the building has already been commenced under the direction of a committee of the corporation, consisting of Rowland Hazard, Esq., of the class of 1849, Joseph C. Hartshorn, Esq., of the class of 1841, and ex-President Caswell. The foundation walls have been laid and good progress has been made on the main building. The building is to be two stories in height, in addition to the basement, which is high and well lighted. The style of architecture is the Italian Gothic, the plans adopted being those of General William R. Walker, architect. The exterior walls are to be of brick, with olive stone decorations. Accommodations are to be provided for one hundred and fifty thousand volumes.

The Library for the present is in the lower part of Manning Hall. It contains forty-five thousand well bound and carefully selected volumes. In its early history it received additions from donations and legacies made by friends of the college, both in this country and in England. During the presidency of Dr. Wayland a permanent library fund of twenty-five thousand dollars was raised by subscription.. Since that time the income of this fund has been expended, under the direction of a joint committee of six, appointed annually by the corporation and the faculty of the university. During the years 1844-6, the foundations of the French, German and Italian departments of the library were laid, through the generosity of Mr. Brown. At this time, also, a special fund of five thousand dollars was raised by subscription, and was expended in the purchase of English books. The greater part of the library, therefore, has been procured within the last thirty years, with special reference to the wants of professors and students and of other persons engaged in literary and scientific research. Besides being well supplied with works illustrating the various courses of college study, it has a large number of the collections pertaining to civil and ecclesiastical history, antiquity, literature, and the Greek and Latin classics. The library is especially rich in bibliography and and patristics, and in the pamphlet literature of New England. It has also a large number of works on architecture. Upon the library table may be found the most important American and English periodicals, and also periodicals in the German and French languages pertaining to science, history, literature, bibliography, philology and the classics.

The invested funds of the institution, according to the last annual report of the treasurer, amount to $640,834. These funds are thus classified:—"Common Fund," $365,215; "Scholarship Fund," $57,725; "Aid Fund," $8,428; "Library Fund," $27,000; "Agricultural Fund," $50,000; "Premium and Prize Funds," $21,012; "Hazard Professorship," $40,931; "Romeo Elton Professorship," $16,674; "Newport-Rogers Professorship," $50,000; "Marshall Woods Lectureship," $3,849. In addition to this is the sum subscribed by Mr. Brown for the erection of a library building, amounting with interest to $21,708, and the $50,000 bequeathed by him for this purpose.

The faculty of Brown University consists of a president, ten professors, three instructors, one assistant instructor, a librarian and a registrar. The following are their names and titles as given in the latest annual catalogue: Rev. Ezekiel G. Robinson, D. D., LL D., President, Professor of Moral and Intellectual Philosophy; John L. Lincoln, LL. D., Professor of the Latin Language and Literature and Instructor in German; Samuel S. Greene, LL. D., Professor of Mathematics and Astronomy; Albert Harkness, Ph. D., LL. D., Professor of the Greek Language and Literature; Rev. J. Lewis Diman, D. D., Professor of History and Political Economy; Benjamin F. Clarke, A. M., Professor of Mathematics and Civil Engineering; John H. Appleton, A. M., Newport-Rogers.Professor of Chemistry; T. Whiting Bancroft, A. M., Professor of Rhetoric and English Literature and Instructor in Elocution; Eli W. Blake, A. M., Hazard Professor of Physics; —— ——, Elton Professor of Natural Theology (at present instruction in Natural Theology is given by the President of the University); John W. P. Jenks, A. M., Professor of Agricultural Zoölogy and Curator of the Museum of Natural History; Charles W. Parsons, M. D., Professor of Physiology; Nathaniel F. Davis, A. M., Instructor in Mathematics; William Ashmore, Jr., A. M., Instructor in Latin and Greek; Charles H. Gates, A. B., Instructor in French; Edwin E. Calder, assistant Instructor in Analytical Chemistry; Reuben A. Guild, LL. D., Librarian; Rev. William Douglas, A. M., Registrar.

The number of students connected with the University is at present, 255. The triennial catalogue, published in 1873, gives the names of 2,540 graduates, more than one-fourth of whom have been ordained and set apart for the work of the Christian ministry. This enumeration does not include the three classes which have graduated since the Spring of 1873. Of the graduates from the beginning, upwards of one hundred have been honored with the degree of Doctor in Divinity, including bishops eminent for their piety and learning, missionaries at home and abroad, presidents of colleges and theological schools, and religious teachers whose names are conspicuous in the republic of letters, and whose virtues and deeds will be held in grateful remembrance by the manifold churches of our common Lord.

R. A. G.

DR. STOCKBRIDGE'S SCHOOL FOR YOUNG LADIES.

The founder of this school was the late Hon. John Kingsbury, LL. D. In age, it takes precedence of all the private female schools of the city, having been established in 1828. Mr. Kingsbury was born at South Coventry, Ct., May 26th, 1801. He graduated from Brown University, in 1826, with the second honors, in a class of which the late Bishop Burgess, of Maine, and Professor Edwards A. Park, of Andover, were members. Mr Kingsbury commenced his undertaking with the earnestness and zeal which were such marked features in his character, and soon had the satisfaction of seeing his experiment a complete success. The time and the place were both favorable for embarking in such an enterprise. The public school system, which now furnishes such facilities for higher education, was then in its infancy, and citizens of wealth and refinement were prepared to encourage an undertaking which promised to afford a better intellectual training for their daughters. Moreover the influence of Brown University in raising the tone of the community, had long been acknowledged, and parents felt that their daughters ought to be put on a footing with their sons, in the matter of their mental culture. The number of pupils was at first limited to thirty-six, which was soon extended to forty. The school was under the charge of Mr. Kingsbury for thirty years, the admissions during this period being five hundred and fifty-seven.

At the close of his long term of service Mr. Kingsbury had a re-union of his pupils, in the chapel of Brown University. The occasion was one of great interest and proved how warm a place the retiring principal held in the affections of his pupils, and in the regards of the community. Dr. Wayland presided on the occasion and paid a warm tribute to the successful instructor who had been both guide and friend of so many of the ladies of Providence. Mr. Kingsbury, in his reply, gave a brief historical sketch of the school which had so long been under his care, and dwelt at some length on the principles which had governed him in its management.

Mr. Kingsbury's term of service closed February 5, 1858, when the school passed into the hands of Hon. Amos Perry, and by him was soon transferred to Professor J. L. Lincoln, LL. D., who commenced the school year 1858-59, in the month of September. For eight years, Professor Lincoln carried on the school, which, under his administration, enjoyed a prosperity similar to that which it had had under his predecessor. The present Principal, Rev. Dr. Stockbridge, took charge of the school in the fall of 1867, and has endeavored to keep up the standard of previous years. During the forty-eight years of its existence, not far from one thousand young ladies have received their education, in part or wholly in this school. How great a blessing it has been in training so many who have filled important positions as wives, mothers and teachers of the young, it would not be possible to estimate. Among the educational institutions of Providence it holds a high rank, and if encouraged by the patronage of its citizens, will continue to be in the future, as it has been in the past, a power for good in the community where it has so long had its home.

SCHOLFIELD'S COMMERCIAL COLLEGE.

A Brief History of its Rise and Progress.

This institution was founded by its present proprietor, Albert G. Scholfield, in June, 1846. This was the first commercial school established in Rhode Island, and the patronage for its first year was secured by great exertions on the part of the principal, so skeptical were the citizens of the State in regard to the necessity for such a school and the advantages to accrue therefrom.

The primary object of this institution was to cultivate a taste for writing, and awaken a greater interest in the science of accounts. Hence writing and book-keeping were the leading branches taught. For the first three years its patronage was drawn mainly from men in actual business, either as accountants or their employers. It soon became apparent that it were wise to introduce other branches, the common English department, and mechanical drawing, which latter study has been almost exclusively confined to professional mechanics.

As occasion demanded, there have been added to the studies formerly pursued, the higher English, languages, surveying and navigation. The patronage of the school has ranged since its establishment, from fifty to five hundred students per annum.

The teachers have ranged from one to twelve, as occasion has demanded. During the thirty years of its existence it has enjoyed a patronage of ten thousand students, and has graduated three thousand in the business or book-keeping course.

ENGLISH AND CLASSICAL SCHOOL.

WILLIAM A. MOWRY, A. M., AND CHARLES B. GOFF, A. M., PRINCIPALS.

NAME AND OBJECT.

THIS school is called the ENGLISH AND CLASSICAL SCHOOL, for boys, and is located at No. 49 Snow street, Providence. It was first opened February 22, 1864.

As its name indicates, it is an *English* and a *Classical* school. Its English department is designed to give the most thorough, and practical preparation for scientific schools or for business. Its classical department aims to furnish the best facilities to prepare boys for any of our New England colleges.

DEPARTMENTS.

The school is divided into five rooms, which are comprised in three departments.

1. *The Preparatory Department*, which prepares the younger boys for either of the following:

2. *The English Department*, which embraces two rooms, the *Junior English* and the *English and Scientific Room*, and is designed to give the best preparation for technical schools or for business life.

3. *The Classical Department*, which also has two rooms, the *Junior Classical* and the *Senior Classical*, and designs to furnish the most adequate and thorough preparation for any college.

COURSES OF STUDY.

Its courses of study begin with the elements of reading, writing, spelling, geography and arithmetic, with boys of about eight years of age, and after completing the common English studies, pursue the higher mathematics, natural sciences, the modern languages, rhetoric and English literature and authors, metaphysics, and other practical studies. The classical course of study is full and thorough, and is varied from time to time, as the requirements for admission to our American colleges demand.

The entire course of study extends through nine years. The pupils pursue arithmetic five years, algebra one year, geometry one year, trigonometry and surveying six months, geography four years, English grammar three years, English composition and rhetoric two years, English and American literature one year, spelling, reading and elocution through the course, writing seven years, drawing five years, history two years, natural philosophy one year, chemistry and astronomy one year, physiology and geology one year, book-keeping six months, political economy six months, constitution United States six months, intellectual philosophy six months, German two years, French three years, Latin seven years, and Greek four years.

The Growth of the School.

The growth of the school has indeed been a marvel to its friends and most sanguine supporters. It began with about 50 pupils and two teachers, and has steadily grown until it has reached 85, 100, 125, 150, 175, 200, 225, and now numbers 250 pupils. It has from time to time improved its course of study, and added to it, as the occasion seemed to require. It has, however, ever followed the motto :—

"Nulla Vestigia Retrorsum."

In addition to its regular corps of teachers it has special instructors in elocution, penmanship, vocal music, physiology and military drill. From the very beginning it has had regular and systematic exercises for all the pupils in a system of light gymnastics, and for more than eleven years it has furnished also to all regular military instruction and drill. These exercises in gymnastics and drill have proved eminently successful and beneficial. They have always been popular and pleasing as well as healthful and otherwise advantageous to the pupils.

Its Numbers and Graduates.

About 1000 pupils have been members of the school, of whom over 100 have graduated and received the school diploma. Of these about 75 have entered Brown University, and have taken one-third of all the prizes offered for excellence in Latin and Greek on entering. Pupils have also been sent to Yale, Harvard and other colleges. Among the graduates may be found railroad superintendents, architects, engineers, merchants, manufacturers, accountants, bankers, teachers, lawyers, doctors, and ministers.

THE SCHOOL BUILDING.

The school commenced in a modest way, in two leased rooms, in the fourth story of the Lyceum building, where it remained one year. For the next five years it was located in the then new Narragansett block, on Westminster street. Having outgrown the capacity of the rooms there, it removed to the new and elegant Fletcher building, where it was well accommodated for six years more. Finding its wants still but imperfectly supplied, and needing a home of its own, the proprietors have now built a large brick school building on Snow and Moulton streets, which furnishes, perhaps, as many substantial advantages as are possessed by any school in New England. In lighting, heating and ventilation, visitors from all parts of the country have uniformly pronounced it superior to anything they have known. The light is over the left shoulder, and the surface of the glass is ten per cent. of the surface of the floor. The floor divided by the number of pupils, gives twenty-five square feet to each, and the cubical contents of each room divided by the number of pupils gives about 300 cubic feet of air to each. The value of the building and land is estimated at $100,000.

NEW SCHOOL DESK.

The school is supplied with a new school desk upon an original model, with a patent arrangement for folding the lid, by which a rest is made for the book in studying, which obliges the pupil to sit upright, and which brings the book at the right distance and angle from the eye.

LABORATORY AND APPARATUS.

The chemical laboratory is complete and well arranged for practical use. The philosophical, astronomical and other apparatus is large and valuable. The library of reference books is of great value and practical service to the school.

ENGLISH AND CLASSICAL SCHOOL.

INSTRUCTORS.

The present corps of instructors is as follows:—

William A. Mowry, A. M., Metaphysics, U. S. Constitution and Book-keeping.
Charles B. Goff, A. M., Senior Latin and Greek.
Howard M. Rice, A. M., Modern Languages and English Literature.
Rev. James W. Colwell, A. M., Mathematics.
Richard W. Smith, A. M., Junior English Studies.
William S. Liscomb, A. M., Latin and Greek.
George B. F. Hinckley, A. M., Junior Classical Studies.
Frank P. Whitman, A. B., Natural Science and Mathematics.
Mrs. H. M. Miller, Elocution and Voice Culture.
Mrs. Harriet A. Dean, Preparatory Department.
Prof J. W. P. Jenks, A. M., Physiology.
Ellery C. Davis, Penmanship.
Benjamin W. Hood, Vocal Music.
Mrs. Mary E. Rawson, Vocal Music, Preparatory Department.
Gen. Charles R. Dennis, Military Drill.

MOUNT PLEASANT ACADEMY.

ESTABLISHED 1865. PRINCIPALS: JENCKS MOWRY, JOSEPH E. MOWRY, A. M.

THIS school had its origin in the opening, by the senior principal, of the Mount Pleasant Select School, for affording a more thorough and extended course of study in the English branches than was at the time pursued in the public schools in the immediate vicinity. It was soon found that the school met a requirement of a class of scholars whose age or diversity of attainments in different branches, prevented from following the routine of the public schools, and that such a school was needed to supplement those schools. Scholars also from the small ungraded schools in our rural districts found opportunities for studying branches not taught at their schools. There was no fixed schedule of studies, but the studies pursued were the common English branches, and sometimes algebra, and the elements of geometry and physics. Especial attention was given to the explanation of the principles of arithmetic and to their practical application.

The number of scholars increased and there arose a demand for a more extensive course of study. In 1872, a new school building was erected, and the course of study was so extended as to include the higher mathematics and French, and the college preparatory classics, and it became the aim of the principals to afford a thorough, disciplinary, and complete preparation for ordinary business pursuits or for admission to our colleges.

The views which suggested its establishment are still adhered to:— That all scholars can not with advantage pursue exactly the same course of study, nor should their progress in all branches be made uniform; but that beyond a knowledge of the rudiments, which all should possess, and which should be thorough, the scholar may best pursue those studies for which he has a natural inclination; that a thorough knowledge of a few subjects, or of a few topics connected with one is better than a smattering of many subjects, or a superficial view of much of any one. Thus scholars entering upon a liberal course of study form habits of incalculable advantage, while those whose advantages have been limited, and whose time for the completion of their education is short, have facilities offered, which of necessity cannot be enjoyed in our rigidly graded public schools.

It has also been the aim of the school to afford equal advantages to scholars of both sexes, the entire course being open to both, and both having the same privileges in selecting the studies to be pursued. The influence of the two classes is believed to be mutually beneficial, both intellectually and morally.

There is then at present two departments, a preparatory and an academic. The latter has two parallel courses of study, extending for most pupils over four years. The scientific includes the higher English, mathematics, and a modern and ancient language; the classical is limited to the college preparatory studies.

The number of pupils in attendance for the past year has been one hundred and twelve.

PROVIDENCE ASSOCIATION OF MECHANICS AND MANUFACTURERS.

On the 27th of February, 1789, a number of the principal mechanics and manufacturers of the town of Providence, met at the house of Captain Elijah Bacon, on Union street, and " voted, that we will form ourselves, with such others as may join us, into an association for the promotion of home manufactures, the cementing of the mechanic interest, and for raising a fund to support the distressed." At this meeting Col. William Barton,—so well known in our country's history as the capturer of the British General Prescott at his quarters on Rhode Island in the revolutionary war,—was chosen chairman, and Bennett Wheeler, clerk. At the same meeting a committee, consisting of Amos Atwell, Charles Keene, John Davis, Robert Newell, Bennett Wheeler, Elijah Bacon and Nicholas Easton, was appointed to draft the form of a constitution for the association. This committee reported at an adjourned meeting, held at the house of Daniel Jackson, March 4th, and the constitution presented by them was, after being debated paragraph by paragraph and amended, unanimously agreed to. The following officers were then elected: Barzillai Richmond, president; Charles Keene, vice president; Amos Atwell, treasurer, and Bennett Wheeler, secretary. A committee of correspondence was also elected, consisting of Aaron Mason, Levi Hall, Robert Newell, Daniel Stillwell, John Davis, William Richmond, Zephaniah Andrews, Thomas Hazard, Elijah Bacon, Charles Holden and Nicholas Easton. At the same meeting a committee was appointed, composed of Charles Keene, Amos Atwell, Bennett Wheeler, Thomas Hazard and Amasa Gray, to draft the form of a petition to the honorable General Assembly for an act of incorporation. Levi Hall was requested to present the petition to the Assembly, and "use his influence to get the prayer of it granted." The Assembly granted a charter, which, on the 16th of March, received the signature of governor John Collins. The thanks of the Association were presented to Mr. Hall and to David Howell, Esq., for their services in the matter, and also to Governor Collins " for his politeness in signing the charter of the Association without the usual fee."

The Association thus formed was one of the very earliest organizations in the country for the promotion of the mechanic arts; probably the earliest which had any long-continued existence. The only previously existing society of which we have any knowledge was an association of tradesmen and manufacturers in the town of Boston, which was, "owing to some party political measures," dissolved about the year 1788.

In the commencement of its corporate existence, the Association, in matters pertaining to social life, personal expenses, and business obligations, assumed high moral ground. At a meeting held March 30, 1789, the following recommendations were adopted:—

"On motion, resolved unanimously, that it be and hereby is, earnestly recommended to all the members of this Association, to discourage as far as possible, all foreign manufactures, by using in their families and business those of our own country; and that each member avoid all extravagance in dress or other expenses, in themselves or those under their care, whereby an emulation may be excited.

"It is also earnestly recommended, that each member be careful not to contract debts or enter into engagements beyond their ability to perform with the utmost punctuality, that their families may escape the distress, and the society the disgrace, attending a different line of conduct.

"It is also recommended in the most serious manner, that all law suits be avoided by the members of this Association; that they do not enter into them until they have endeavored to have their disputes settled by referees; and that no member take advantage of laws which are, or may hereafter be made, either to distress an honest debtor, or defraud an honest creditor.

"It is also recommended that the members of this Association very carefully inspect into the conduct of their apprentices, and those under their care, that they be not strolling in the streets late in the night season, and disturbing the inhabitants by revels.

"It is voted and resolved, that on application being made to this society at any of their meetings, by an inhabitant of this town who may think himself defrauded by bad manufactures being sold him by any member thereof, or by any member not completing his contracts in a workmanlike manner, or by extravagant charges, they will immediately appoint a committee to examine into the facts, and endeavor that justice be done to the parties."

At a subsequent period, in the revision of the by-laws, the Association expressed its sense of the value of character, as follows:

"As the reputation of every society must in a great degree depend on the character of its individual members, and the estimation in which they may be held by their fellow citizens, therefore if any member of this Association shall fall into profligacy of manners, base and immoral habits, or be chargeable with intemperance or fraudulent practices, it shall be the duty of the select committee to examine the case of such member, and report thereon to the Association, that measures may be taken for his exclusion therefrom. But, in order as far as may be, to prevent the necessity of the exercise of this power, it shall be the duty of the committee, by any member or members whom they may designate, to advise or admonish any member of the Association who may be declining to vicious or base courses, or who may appear to be falling into any habit or practice which may affect his reputable standing in society, to the end that by faithful counsel and admonition he may be preserved from such a course as would render his expulsion necessary."

The Association was quick to sustain its members in the free exercise of the elective franchise, as appears by the following vote, passed April 5, 1790:

"It having been suggested, that several worthy members of this Association have been dismissed from their employ, in consequence of voting their sentiments at the last town meeting, they being contrary to the sentiments of their employers: *Voted*, that the following gentlemen be, and they are hereby appointed a committee to inquire into, and report such facts concerning this matter as may come to their knowledge, as soon as may be, viz.: Colonel William Barton, Mr. William Richmond, Robert Newell, Esq., Mr. Samuel Thurber, Jr., and Mr. Nicholas Easton."

The humane spirit of the Association is shown in the following report, made on the 28th of May, 1790, by a committee to whom had been referred the subject of rendering advice and assistance to the widows and orphans of deceased members:

"Whereas, the well-being of all societies depends on a proper care being taken of the education of the rising generation, and as individuals and families under many circumstances, are not in a situation to pay proper attention thereto, it behoves all associated bodies of people to aid and assist in the accomplishment of that important object: Be it therefore voted and resolved, that a committee be annually appointed, of this Association, from different parts of the town, whose duty it shall be to advise and assist the widows and children of all deceased members thereof, and where circumstances require it, endeavor to provide suitable places for education in the mechanic arts, or otherwise, as in their judgment is best suited to the genius of such children. And if anything impedes their well-meant endeavors, or any further assistance may be found wanting, (after consulting in committee) they shall lay the same before the Association, for their aid and support, as circumstances may require."

This report was adopted, and made the basis of a by-law, authorizing pecuniary aid to members reduced to indigence by sickness or misfortune, and to widows and orphans, to an amount not exceeding forty dollars, to be applied to any one case during the year. And a committe of nine members, three for the north part of the town, three for the south part, and three for the west side of the river, were appointed to carry the by-law into effect.

When the Providence Association of Mechanics and Manufacturers came into existence no settled public opinion touching the industrial interests of the country had been formed. The need of such an opinion, governed by a just regard to mutual rights became obvious; and one of the first steps taken by the society was to impress the mechanics of Rhode Island and also of other States, with the importance of forming similar organizations, for concerted action in regard to the protection and encouragement of home productions. With this view, the committee of correspondence addressed letters to the mechanics and tradesmen of Newport, East Greenwich, Warren and Bristol, in Rhode Island; and also to those of Boston, Worcester, Salem, Newburyport, Portsmouth, New London, Norwich, Hartford, New Haven, New York, Albany, Trenton, Philadelphia, Baltimore, Alexandria, Wilmington, Norfolk and Charleston. From most of these places prompt and cordial responses were received. And it appears that the efforts of the Association resulted in the formation of similar organizations, both in Rhode Island and other States.

The letters from the Providence mechanics exhibit the patriotic spirit by which they were actuated, and their ardent desire to be identified with the Union of States into which Rhode Island had not yet entered. It was a natural feeling. Some of the leading men of the Association had bravely fought for civil freedom. They were men of practical minds, and well knew that the perpetuity of the blessing for which they had hazarded life and fortune, could be secured only by the fostering care of a central government. To them, a nationality of thirteen hundred square miles, and United States custom houses in border States along the line of its territory, presented no charms; and with praiseworthy devotion, they labored to effect a better condition. The feeling with which they were oppressed appears in their correspondence; and while they lament the unfortunate position of their State, they look hopefully towards the future. Without doubt, the popular sentiment of the State which resulted in the adoption of the constitution, was in large degree, the creation of the mechanics of Rhode Island ; and there is ground for the belief that the action of the Providence Association of Mechanics and Manufacturers, the earliest chartered body of the kind in New England, did much to stimulate this sentiment to successful action.

When the news arrived that Rhode Island had become a member of the Union, the Association partook of the general joy. At a meeting held June 4, 1790, a congratulatory address to the President of the United States was reported and adopted, expressing their regard and attachment to him, and their confidence that Congress would do " all in their power to promote the manufactures, as well as the agriculture and commerce of our country." The address was forwarded through the senators from this State, and an appropriate reply was returned to the Association by President Washington.

When the President visited Providence, August 18, 1790, the Association, by formal vote, joined as a body in the procession that escorted him and suite from the wharf to his lodgings, at the Golden Ball Inn (now known as the Mansion House), kept by Abner Daggett. They also participated in the public solemnities in commemoration of the lamented death of General Washington, and appeared in the procession with their standard and wardens' wands draped in mourning.

From its organization to 1825, the business meetings of the Association were generally held in the State House. Occasionally they met at the Golden Ball Inn, and elsewhere. Very early, a strong feeling was expressed in favor of building a hall for its use, but this was never carried out. In 1824, when the Franklin building, on Market Square, was erected, provision was made for a hall for the Association, and when the walls were up, the front was surmounted with the emblems of the mechanic arts, to identify it as an abiding home. It was formally taken possession of, and an historical address in commemoration of the event delivered by the President John Howland. After a few years, objections to the place were raised, and a new home was found in the hall of Washington buildings. In 1853, the Association removed to the hall in Dyer's block, on Westminster street, and in 1860 to the bank building, then erected by Mr. Amos C. Barstow, on Weybosset street, being on the site of the former residence of Amos Atwell, the first treasurer and third president of the Association, which location it has continued to occupy to the present time.

Early in 1791, Alexander Hamilton, secretary of the treasury of the United States, was directed by the house of representatives, to report to that body "a plan for promoting manufactures." In pursuance of this direction, he issued a circular calling upon individuals and associations, in every part of the country for information upon which to base his plan. A copy of this circular was addressed to Col. John S. Dexter, then supervisor of the district of Rhode Island, who referred the letter to this Association, requesting them to furnish the information desired. The Association cordially responded to the Secretary's circular, and in July, 1791, appointed a committee, who, after making a careful investigation into the manufactures of the town, presented in October following, their final report, which was transmitted to Mr. Hamilton, through Col. Dexter, giving an exhibit of the products of industry in Providence, from January 1, 1790 to October 10, 1791, being a valuable contribution to the history of manufactures, at a period when the population of the town was less than seven thousand souls.

With a view to self-improvement among the members of the Association, Mr. Isaac Greenwood proposed, at a meeting held January 10, 1798, that a lecture be delivered at each quarterly meeting, by a member, on subjects relating to improvements in the mechanic arts, the practical means of encouraging the manufactures of the country, and the advantages resulting from social or corporate connections in promoting the interests of the manufacturing branches in union with the general prosperity of the United States. The proposition was adopted, and lectures were delivered by Mr. Greenwood, Grindall Reynolds, John Howland and Mr. Greene. The practice was afterwards discontinued, but the idea was never wholly lost sight of. The fact held a place in the memory of more than one, who recognized its importance, and sympathized with the spirit that gave it form. After a lapse of more than thirty years, the original plan was revived with satisfactory success. In 1831, a series of lectures was delivered before the Association alone. To this, George Baker, Walter R. Danforth, Isaac Thurber, Leonard Blodget and Stanford Newell, Esqs., contributed. The first of the series was by Mr. Baker, and was designed to stimulate the moral and intellectual faculties to worthy endeavors. Mr. Danforth's lecture was on General Industry; Mr. Thurber's on Hydraulics and Dynamics; Mr. Blodget's on Building, and Mr. Newell's on Metals.

The influence of these lectures was not limited to the hours of their delivery. They awakened a desire for continued instruction. Additional courses were delivered by the Providence Franklin Society, Professors Griscom, Chace, Caswell and Elton, Mr. Evans and others; and thus was paved the way for the public courses, under the auspices of the Association, commenced in 1844, which have maintained their popularity and held the interest alike of the Association and the community, continuing almost without interruption down to the present time. For some years past the society has united with the Providence Franklin Society in the care of these lectures, and they have been devoted mainly to scientific subjects.

In 1799 the subject of education engaged the attention of the Association, and the want of a better system of school instruction being deeply felt by the members, a memorial was prepared and presented to the General Assembly, forcibly urging the establishment of free schools throughout the State, and reminding that body "that liberty and security under a republican form of government, depend on a general diffusion of knowledge among the people."

This question was thus, we believe, for the first time since the existence of the State, pressed upon the deliberations of the legislature ; and the measure proposed, though met with considerable hesitation, was finally incorporated into law.

In 1799, a practice had sprung up of supplying the wants of the United States navy, by enlisting indentured apprentices of mechanics and manufacturers. The evils of this procedure were severely felt, and the Association addressed a letter to the Secretary of the Treasury on the subject, deprecating the practice as "injurious and unjust" in its operations, and as a sacrifice not required of those classes by the exigencies of the times.

In 1800, the depressed condition of the mechanic and manufacturing interests engaged the attention of the Association. It was deemed important that these interests should receive suitable encouragement from the government. And the Association adopted a memorial to Congress, drawn up by John Howland, urging the importance of securing the revival and extension of the mechanic arts and the promotion of improvements in various branches of domestic manufacture. Letters were also addressed by the society to kindred associations in Newport, Boston, New York and Albany, soliciting their coöperation in obtaining its object. The memorial was presented to Congress, together with a similar one from New York, and referred to the committee of commerce, who reported unfavorably thereon in 1801, which report the house approved. In 1815, the Association made common cause with the community in seeking the abrogation of the revenue laws then recently passed, and which were deemed to operate injuriously to the manufacturing interests. A memorial was drawn up complaining of the "unjust and oppressive operation of the laws," and earnestly soliciting Congress for their repeal. It was placed in the hands of Hon. James B. Mason, a representative from Rhode Island, for presentation. In August, 1837, a general convention of mechanics and manufacturers of the country, was held at New York, to consider the causes of the distress and embarrassments that seriously affected all classes of the community, and to devise means of relief, and in response to the letter of invitation received by the Association, a delegation was appointed to represent it in the convention. In 1842, the Association again gave its active influence to securing the adequate protection of American manufacturing industry. A declaration relative to increasing the duties on foreign manufactures was adopted, and a copy, signed by the president and secretary, directed to be transmitted to each of our senators and representatives in Congress, with a request that it should be laid before that body, which was done.

At the annual meeting of the Association in 1809, the society expressed their sense of appreciation of " the essential service rendered the United States by Mr. Samuel Slater, of North Providence, in the introduction of the complicated machinery for the manufacture of cotton," and " as a testimony of the high consideration and regard with which this Association view Mr. Slater as the founder of an extensive and valuable branch of manufacture which will furnish employment and subsistence to thousands, and be the means of eventually saving millions of property in the country," elected Mr. Slater, by a spontaneous vote, a member of the society " without the intervention of the usual forms."

In September, 1819, the subject of the establishment of a savings bank in the town was introduced in a meeting of the select committee of the Association, and after consideration, " being convinced that such an institution would be advantageous to a great number of persons, by promoting economy and frugality, and thereby enabling them to save a part of their earnings till age or infirmities should render the use of it indispensable," the committee requested the secretary, John Howland, to take such preliminary measures as would lead to the establishment of a savings bank. In pursuance of this request, and with the concurrence of gentlemen not of the Association, a public meeting was notified and held at the Washington Insurance Company's office, from which resulted the establishment of the Providence Institution for Savings, of which Mr. Howland was chosen the first treasurer.

In January, 1821, the Association voted to establish a library for the use of its members and their apprentices. It was commenced by voluntary donations, and in the following April four hundred volumes had been collected, when a code of rules for its government was adopted and steps were taken for putting it into immediate operation. At a later period a reading room was established in connection with the library.

Continual additions of books have been made from time to time by appriations from the treasury as well as by donation, until a library of some seven thousand volumes has been accumulated; and the issue of books has amounted to as many as twenty thousand in a single year.

At a meeting of the society, April 20, 1827, a committee was appointed " to take into consideration the subject of promoting temperance, and that they report at a special meeting to be called by the president, and further, that said committee procure an address to be made by one of the Association at the time of presenting their report." The special meeting contemplated by this vote, was held May 29, 1827, and a meeting of citizens having been held in the vestry of the First Baptist Church since the last previous meeting of the Association, to consider the same subject, the resolutions adopted by the citizens at that meeting were approved and recommended " to the serious attention of all our members for their cordial coöperation." It was also resolved: " That it be recommended to the several trades and professions composing this Association to call separate meetings, to consider and adopt such measures respecting the practice of furnishing ardent spirits to workmen and apprentices in their employ in the course of their business, or in manufacturing establishments, as they may judge most effectual to restrain or abolish their use." At this meeting, on invitation of the committee, an address on promoting temperance was delivered by George Baker, being the first service of the kind known to have been performed in Providence. It was favorably received, and a resolution was adopted by the Association thanking Mr. Baker for his " excellent and well adapted address," and requesting a copy for publication.

In 1844 efforts were made to obtain funds for founding an asylum for the insane, and at a meeting in September of that year, the Association voted to contribute the sum of one thousand dollars towards that object. The name of the asylum was subsequently changed to the " Butler Hospital for the Insane," to which organization the subscription of the Association was paid over in April, 1845.

At the quarterly meeting of the Association in January, 1847, the importance and need of the establishment of a house of correction or reformation in this city was brought up by the select committee, and after discussion was referred to a special committee to consider and report thereon at a future meeting. The committee reported at a meeting in April and presented the following resolution:—

"*Resolved*, That in the opinion of this Association the wants of our city demand the erection of a " *House of Reformation*," within a convenient distance from the city, whose objects shall be the confinement, instruction and reformation of such persons as may be placed in it; and we would earnestly and seriously urge the consideration of this subject upon the authorities of this city, as the constituted guardians of the welfare and happiness of all the inhabitants thereof."

The report and resolution were received, and the committee was instructed to draft the form of a memorial in accordance with that resolution, to be presented to the city council. At a meeting held May 11th, the committee reported the draft of a memorial urging the matter upon the attention and serious consideration of the council, and suggesting weighty reasons for the action desired. The memorial was adopted by the Association, and ordered to be signed by the president and secretary and presented to the city council.

In January, 1850, a communication was received from a committee of the corporation of Brown University, stating that that body had under consideration the expediency of enlarging the course of study in that institution, with a view of promoting the more general diffusion of knowledge and the practical application of science to the useful arts; and desiring the advice and coöperation of this Association in regard to the same. The communication was referred to a special committee, of which Isaac Thurber was chairman, who presented, at a meeting in February, a carefully prepared report, approving cordially the proposed enlargement, enforcing the importance of uniting theoretical knowledge with practical skill, and stating that "our mechanics need an education that will inspire confidence in themselves; that will make them acquainted with the science of their arts, and the properties of matter with which they have to deal; that will enable them better to judge of the pursuits of others and estimate their value; that will qualify them to lead, as well as to follow, in the business transactions of life. And this they should have an opportunity of acquiring, without being compelled to devote so many years to other and more classical studies." The report also suggested the expediency of establishing a normal school in connection with Brown University, and closed as follows: "The enlargement of the course of studies in our literary institutions, so as to extend its benefits to a more numerous class of our fellow citizens, that they may be better trained to observe and judge, not by blind conjecture, but with reference to laws or principles, which should have their proper weight, is, in the opinion of your committee, the dictate of wisdom, and calculated to confer on mankind lasting and beneficial results. Your committee would therefore recommend a most cordial compliance with the request, to coöperate with the corporation of Brown University in the promotion of an object so desirable as a more general diffusion of knowledge."

The report of the committee was accepted and adopted, and a copy thereof with a copy of the adopting vote of the Association, was transmitted to the committee of the corporation of Brown University.

In the autumn of 1850, a movement was made to procure a course of lectures by gentlemen of our own city and State on subjects connected with Rhode Island history, its manufactures, agricultural and mineral products. etc., the proceeds, if any, to be set apart as a fund towards the erection of a monument to the memory of Roger Williams. Lectures in this course were delivered gratuitously by Rev. Francis Wayland, D. D., president of Brown University, Hon. William R. Staples, Samuel Ames, Esq., Charles S. Bradley, Esq., Abraham Payne, Esq., Hon. Samuel G. Arnold, Prof. William Gammell, of Brown University, Rev. Charles T. Brooks, of Newport, Rev. James M. Hoppin, of Salem, and George W. Curtis, Esq., of New York; but not resulting in pecuniary success, a subscription was started and circulated among the members, and a sum of money obtained which was deposited in the Providence Institution for Savings, to be held as the nucleus of a fund for the erection of a monument to the memory of Roger Williams, subject to the order of the Association.

On the 27th February, 1860, the Association celebrated the seventy-first anniversary of its founding by a festival in Howard Hall. The hall was splendidly decorated with banners, streamers, mechanical designs, etc., and nearly 800 ladies and gentlemen partook of a sumptuous repast. Hon. Amos C. Barstow, president of the Association, presided, and after the viands had been disposed of, toasts and sentiments were offered, which were responded to by Mr. Charles Akerman, Mayor Knight, Rev. Dr. Sears, president of Brown University, Ex-Governor Dyer, Hon. Thomas Davis, Rev. G. T. Day, Rev. E. B. Hall, Ex-Governor Hoppin, Ex-Mayor Rodman, Rev. A. H. Clapp, Rev. L. Whiting, and Rev. E. M. Stone. The entertainment was enlivened with music by the American Brass Band, and closed by singing a good night song, composed for the occasion by Hon. William M. Rodman.

In 1870 a movement was made for the establishment of a free public library in this city. The Association voted their hearty approval of the project, and appointed their president, Zachariah Allen, Esq. to act with other gentlemen as a committee to procure an act of incorporation, and to take measures to carry the plan into effect. They also appointed a committee to assist in raising funds for the purpose. The subject was frequently considered in meetings of the Association thereafter, a deep interest being felt therein, and the zealous endeavors of their president being constantly exerted in its behalf. In April, 1874, the Association voted to appoint a committee " to solicit contributions from the members of the society to create a fund to the amount of ten thousand dollars, for the proposed free library, and to enable this Association to have a trusteeship in said library." In 1875 they voted to donate their library to the trustees of the public library, to be estimated at a fair valuation as a part of the amount contemplated in the above vote. In January, 1876, the committee on subscriptions reported that the amount of subscriptions required to make up the sum of $10,000 had been obtained; and the Association is now prepared to make a transfer of the same whenever the trustees of the public library are ready to receive it and open the library to the public.

PROVIDENCE FRANKLIN SOCIETY.

The Providence Franklin Society should not be overlooked in naming the educational institutions of this State. The idea of a society in this city for the cultivation of the knowledge of physical science, was conceived by William T. Grinnell, who interested others in his design, and in response to their petition, the "Providence Franklin Society" was chartered by the General Assembly, at the January session, 1823.

The interests of the Society were afterwards diligently studied by its founder, who made it several liberal donations, and to this day, it is indebted to him for its continued secure, if economical, existence. From its organization to the present time, the objects of its pursuits have embraced nearly every department of physical science. It has a cabinet of miscellaneous curiosities and specimens of much scientific interest, including an extensive geological collection, in which are representatives of nearly all the minerals and fossils found in the State. It has also a fine collection of war and other implements from the South Sea Islands. It has also an interesting zoölogical collection, including birds, beasts, fishes, reptiles and insects. It has a small but valuable scientific library, to which additions are made from time to time as its funds will justify.

It has ever been its purpose to awaken interest among its members by scientific discussions, and it has sought to extend this interest to the public by popular scientific lectures. It is believed to have been the first society organization in this city to institute a course of popular lectures for public entertainment and instruction. Through its lectures it has introduced to the citizens some of the most noted scientists of the world. It has sought, and not without success, to cultivate a love for the study of natural science, by encouraging excursions of small parties into the country, under the conduct of competent naturalists. It has also organized "field meetings," which are open to all who desire to hold communion with nature in her "visible forms."

A microscopical department has been organized and carried on with commendable zeal and success for several years past.

The members of the society now number over three hundred, among whom there appears to exist a good degree of *esprit de corps*.

FRANKLIN LYCEUM.

1876.

The Franklin Lyceum was established in the summer of 1831, by Levi M. Holden, Daniel A. Jackson and William B. Shove. By the records of the twenty-first of April, 1832, the society then consisted of Messrs. Holden, Jackson and Shove, together with Charles Cushing, Frank Cushing, Crawford Nightingale and Geronimo Urmeneta. These were all scholars in Mr. De Witt's school on Waterman street, at the time of the organization of the society, and the first meetings were held at their homes on Friday evenings, after the labors of the school were over. The officers were elected quarterly. The exercises consisted of lectures and debates. The first regular room occupied by the Lyceum was in the basement of Mr. Shove's house on Benefit street, nearly opposite the Central Congregational Church, where a library and a cabinet of minerals, shells, chemical apparatus and antiquities were commenced. The first room hired by the society was in a small building opposite Dr. Hall's church, on Benefit street. Their next room was in the third story of the arcade, which they occupied until April, 1835, when they removed to the De Witt building, on Waterman street, where the meetings were held regularly until 1849. At the meeting held April 28, 1832, the name of "Providence Lyceum," was adopted, which, on the twenty-second of the following December, was changed to that of the "Franklin Lyceum," the name retained ever since. The first recorded annual meeting was held on the fifth of January, 1833, at which the officers were elected. Between the years 1839 and 1842, "The Franklin Lyceum Review and Miscellany," appeared, under various editors, and the copies have been preserved. In July, 1833, there were thirteen active, and two corresponding members. In the latter part of this year steps were taken towards the formation of a library. The first public anniversary was held on the first of January, 1836, at which Henry C. Whitaker delivered an address, and William M. Rodman a poem. The first public lecture before the

Lyceum was delivered in 1839, by Ralph Waldo Emerson. In January, 1843, the legislature granted an act of incorporation, under which the Lyceum now exists. The society at this time, contained thirty-one active, and twenty-four corresponding members. In the autumn of 1848, the Lyceum received an important accession to its numbers by its union with the Westminster Lyceum, a newly formed society, which merged its separate name and existence in the Franklin Lyceum.

On the first of January following, the society, desiring a more central location, removed to the hall No. 19 Westminster street, which they continued to occupy until November, 1858. On the nineteenth of November, 1858, formal possession was taken of the present rooms. The dedicatory exercises consisted of a procession; the uncovering of the statue of Franklin, the first public statue in Rhode Island; an oration by Francis E. Hoppin, and a poem by Henry C. Whitaker, delivered in Dr. Hall's church, and concluded with a supper in Railroad hall. In the autumn of 1859, a catalogue of the library, which then numbered about three thousand volumes, was published. In the war for the Union a large number of the members of the Lyceum enlisted in the army or the navy; many of whom attained high positions of honor and of command. During the past ten years the growth of the society has been rapid in every department. For several years members' courses of lectures were held in Lyceum hall, all the lecturers being members of the Lyceum, which were largely attended and of great interest. The debates have been earnest, spirited, and, at times, exciting. The library has increased from three, to upwards of nine thousand volumes, and many new magazines and newspapers have been added to the reading room. Recently, a change was made in the by-laws, so that women may be admitted as members, on the same terms and conditions, and with the same rights and privileges as men, and several have become members,

Such is a brief sketch of the more important events and principal landmarks in the history of a society, which has risen from the very humblest of beginnings to be recognized as an honor to our city, and one of its most valuable institutions. There are, at present, belonging to the Lyceum, eight hundred and forty-seven active members, besides a large number on the corresponding list. The library contains upwards of nine thousand volumes, and is constantly increasing by the addition of the best books in every department. The reading-room is well supplied with all the leading newspapers and periodicals. The meetings are held in a hall devoted to the exercises of the Lyceum, while the library occupies a separate room. A room handsomely furnished has recently been opened for social conversation, chess, etc., which has become a popular feature. Earnest and spirited debates are regularly held every Monday evening, from October to June, in whichall the members are cordially invited to participate. Many of those who have been active in these debates, now occupy high places in our city, state and national councils. As a school in which to gain an accurate knowledge of parliamentary law and a ready skill in parliamentary tactics the Lyceum probably has no equal. From the ex-officers of the Lyceum have been chosen several governors of Rhode Island, mayors of Providence, members of Congress, secretaries of State, professors of Brown University, law officers of Rhode Island cities, etc., while in both city and State governments many members of the Lyceum are always to be found.

The membership includes many of the leading lawyers, editors, teachers and merchants of Providence, and the annual election of officers creates as great excitement as an ordinary municipal election.

The system of annual public lectures and entertainments is one of the oldest and most successful in the entire country. The lectures are usually by the most eloquent and famous orators; the readings by distinguished elocutionists, and the concerts by the highest musical talent that can be secured. To these the members are furnished with free tickets and the general public are admitted at reasonable rates.

A SKETCH

OF THE

PUBLIC SCHOOLS

IN THE

CITY OF NEWPORT.

BY

THOMAS WENTWORTH HIGGINSON AND THOMAS H. CLARKE.

PUBLIC SCHOOLS.

The early school history of Newport is detailed with sufficient fullness in the " History of the Common Schools of Rhode Island." It is necessary only to continue that sketch from the time when local schools were absorbed into the general school system, in 1828. It will, however, be better to go back three years earlier than this, to the time when the town was authorized by the assembly to raise a tax of $800 " for educating the white children of the town who are not otherwise provided with the means of instruction," and to apply to this purpose the avails of certain lands which had been bequeathed to the town.*

By vote of a town meeting held in February, 1826, a lot in Mill street was bought for a school-house and a committee was appointed to erect a building. This committee reported in March, 1827, as follows:

"The committee appointed by the town to superintend the building of a public school-house respectfully report: That, having purchased a very eligible lot in Mill street, they have erected thereon a school-house 60 feet long and 36 feet wide, of brick and stone, two stories high, which is now so far completed that the upper room intended for boys is nearly ready for the reception of the school; the cost of the lot and building up to this period is about $2,750. To defray this expenditure has absorbed the funds placed at the disposal of the committee, consisting of the following items, viz.:

Net sales of Gallow field,	$891 24
Appropriation by tax of 1825,	800 00
Net balance of rent of theatre,	180 00
Donation of Mr. Wm. Vernon,	100 00
Appropriation for 1826,	800 00
	$2,771 24

* See ante, p. 42.

"The committee are of opinion that to finish the upper room for the accommodation of the boy's school, and fence in the lot will require about $200 additional resources."

At the same time measures were taken by the town to establish a fund from the sale and rents of school land, the avails of licenses, etc., in aid of the public school of the town.

At the same meeting, March 25th, 1827, the following resolution was adopted, which was the opening of the first public school in Newport on the present system :

"Resolved that a school for boys on the Lancasterian or monitorial system be commenced as soon as may be under the following regulations, viz. :

"1st. That a committee (to be hereafter annually chosen at our June town meeting) consisting of five persons, one of whom shall be a resident in each of the town wards, be immediately appointed to be denominated the 'public school committee,' who shall have power to appoint school masters and assistants, fix their compensation, regulate the admission and discharge of scholars, (having a special regard to the laws of the State on this subject,) provide books, stationery, etc., and in general superintend and manage the schools in conformity to the laws and orders of the town.

"2nd. The school committee shall be, and they are, hereby authorized to draw on the town treasurer for any sum necessary to meet their expenditures, not exceeding the annual appropriation for school purposes, and they shall also receive the tuition money hereinafter named, and apply it to the current expenses of the school, and shall present their accounts to be audited by the town council on the first Monday in June in each year.

"3d. In order that the benefits of the school may be extended not only to the most indigent of our citizens, but those also whom industry and economy place above want, the following very low rates of prices for tuition shall be established, viz. : For the alphabet, spelling and writing on slates, 25 cents per quarter. Continuance of ditto with reading or arithmetical tables, 50 cents per quarter. Continuance of the last with writing on paper, arithmetic, and definitions, $1. The preceding, with grammar, geography, with the use of maps and globes, book-keeping, etc., $2. No additional charge for fuel, books or stationery.

"4th. Scholars shall be admitted at any time, on application to the committee and payment of the tuition money.

"5th. The regular quarter days, however, shall be the first school days in February, May, August and November, on which days payment will be required in advance, of every child in school for the ensuing quarter.

"6th. Of scholars admitted on other than the regular quarter days a ratable payment will be required until the end of the current quarter, unless the admission be within the first two weeks of the quarter, in which case the whole quarter must be paid for, or within the last two weeks, when the coming quarter must be paid for, without including the fortnight.

"7th. The object of the foregoing scale of prices for tuition is to foster and encourage the honorable feeling of independence in those parents who wish to educate their children at their own expense, but whose limited means are insufficient to pay the customary rates. But it is at the same time hereby expressly provided, that no child shall be excluded from the benefits of the school merely from inability to pay for his tuition.

"8th. The public school committee shall perform their duty gratuitously, the honor of the station and the gratitude of their townsmen is to be their only reward.

"9th. Until recurrence of the June town meeting the following persons shall compose the committee, viz.: Nicholas G. Boss, Edward W. Lawton, George Engs, James B. Phillips, Theophilus C. Dunn."*

The following is the first report of a Newport School Committee:

"REPORT FOR 1828.

"The public school committee of the town of Newport respectfully report, that since the commencement of the public school in Mill street on the 21st day of May, 1827, the number of applications for admission has been 337;

Of which there has been rejected as not coming within the provisions of the law, ...	33
Suspended for further consideration, .	25
Admitted, ...	279
	337

Of the scholars admitted 67 have been withdrawn or dismissed, leaving the present number 212.

"In the selection of the scholars the committee have endeavored strictly to comply with the resolution of the town, and the law of the State, in admitting those only who were 'not otherwise provided with the means of education.' In considering the list of applicants the most needy, according to their best information, were first admitted, and it is gratifying to them to state that, although at first some apprehensions were entertained that the room would not accommodate all who were entitled to admission, they have been able (after every exertion on their part, both by public advertisements and personal representation to obtain suitable applications) to receive all those candidates whose cases came within the spirit of the law. The pupils have generally been attentive to the duties of the school, and have made considerable progress in their several studies. The greatest difficulty the committee has met has been in enforcing constant attendance at school, and the same culpable indifference to the benefits of education which prevented some parents from making application for admission of their children, has been shown by other parents in not using their persuasion and authority to compel the punctual attendance of their children after they were admitted, instances in the later class have been comparatively very few, and wherever remonstrance or representation on the part of the instructor or committee has been ineffectual, a suspension of the delinquent from school

---

*Barnard's Journal of R. I. School Institute, III, 147-8.

has been resorted to. The small amount required quarterly of each scholar has been found to have a very salutary effect, for those who pay are, generally speaking, the most attentive—there are some exceptions, and the school in some instances is a blessing to those who are quite destitute of the means of payment. The committee consider it advantageous to the school to require payment of all those who can by any means afford it (as the sum required is insufficient to defray the expenses of books, slates, etc.,) and they are fully of opinion that if the school was rendered quite free it would be less beneficial, and would probably be regarded like other common bounties of very little value. The Lancasterian system adopted under the resolution of the town, was, to most of our fellow citizens, as well as to ourselves, a novel mode of instruction. But whatever doubts may have been entertained as to its efficiency they have been entirely dispelled by the success of the school during the past year, which has surpassed the expectations of its most decided advocates, and has satisfied them of the superiority of the monitorial system for a large school, over all others. The school, under the superintendence of its present able instructor (to whose abilities, attention and perseverance the town is greatly indebted for its success,) bids fair soon to be numbered among the most useful of the system, and to be the means of educating and training to habits of industry that part of our population who so much need, and who are so well entitled to the opportunity of obtaining instruction. The lower room in the building is nearly completed for the reception of pupils and the committee, believing it to be the wish of the town, have engaged a young lady who is well qualified for the business to take charge of the girls' school, who will probably be ready to commence in about three weeks, and the committee take the liberty to recommend the same plan of discipline and instruction for that school as has qeen practiced in the boys' department.

"The accounts and vouchers for the past year were presented to the town council yesterday, and by them audited, leaving a balance due to the committee of $202.01, as will appear by the following abstract:

Received from town treasury under the appropriation of 1827,	$600 00
Scholars' pay, first quarter,	56 96
Scholars' pay, second quarter,	61 37
Scholars' pay, third quarter,	68 53
Balance,	202 01
	$988 87
Paid Instructor's salary,	600 00
Printing, advertisements, &c.,	11 04
Interest on acceptances,	9 47
Books, slates, stationery, &c.,	187 35
Stovepipe, fuel, benches, book-case, painting, &c.,	181 01
	$988 87

"The balance of the appropriation of 1827, being $200, was expended by the building committee in completing the building.

"For the committee,

"NICHOLAS G. BOSS, *Secretary.*

"Newport, June 3d, 1829."

"Condition of the public school fund in 1828:

Donation by Governor Fenner,	$100 00
Donation by Governor Collins,	50 00
Licenses,	154 37
Legacy of Constant Taber,	1,500 00
Sale of Warden (school) lot,	325 00
Estate I. Begna, having no being in the United States,	23 63
	$2,153 00"*

In 1844, a committee made a report from which the following extracts are taken:

"The committee have been astonished to learn that there are nearly 900 children in this town, between the ages of five and fifteen, for whom no schooling is provided. Mr. Manchester reports the whole number of children in town, over five and less than fifteen years of age, to be nearly 2,000; of these 680 are provided for by the existing public schools; and the 30 private schools which they have ascertained to exist, averaging 15 pupils, give 450 more, making in all 1,130 capable of being seated in the existing schools, and leaving 870 unprovided for. Evidently, then, there is an irresistible call for schools, and the committee consider that two primary schools are immediately wanted, one in the lower part of the town, near the factories, and the other in Broad street, whence too many children now seek admission into the Point schools. The committee also feel that another intermediate school is needed for those pupils who have to leave the primaries, and yet are not fit for the grammar schools. But this they do not at present so strenuously insist upon, as on the increase of primary schools, for which they have been inundated with applications they could not meet.

"In relation to the other point suggested, namely, the character of the schooling given, the committee feel bound to express the opinion, that the time is come for an advancement in our upper schools, upon higher branches of study than have yet been pursued. In one or two of the schools many of the scholars have for some time been expressing a strong desire to remain at school longer, and go on with certain of the more interesting and important of the advanced branches. And the committee would respectfully ask if it is not time that something of natural and mental philosophy, of political economy and of the important subject (particularly in this country) of the science of government, and the duties of citizenship, should be taught to our pupils before leaving schools, at which most of them may receive their last instructions, except the bitter ones of experience? The committee would ask, if such subjects as these they have named are not something more than mere accomplishments—if they are not essential parts of a common school education; essential parts of that education which every free community ought to be trying, at least, to devise some way of furnishing its rising generation? Is it not time, in short, that we began to think seriously of carrying our school system to its proper height, while we attend to the enlargement and expansion of the base."

* Barnard's Journal, III, 148-9.

"If any ask why these higher branches, to which the committee have alluded, are not already taught in the upper schools, they reply, that it would be crowding too much upon the teachers and depriving the lower studies and students of the attention due to them. They cannot be pursued without some additional provision being made. * * *

"With a few specific statements and suggestions, the committee will now close their report. The treasurer reports the receipt during the past year, of $1,766.59 from the State; $1,600 from the town, and $203.21 from the tax levied on the scholars, amounting in all to $3,569.80. Of this sum, $3,000 have been paid for salaries; $113 for fuel; $228.24 for stationery in 1842-3; and $228.41 for incidental expenses; $196.54 remain in the town treasury, and the outstanding debts amount to about $400.

"The committee close, therefore, with recommending—That two new primary schools be established, one in Broad street, or thereabouts; and the other in the extreme lower part of the town; and that the sum of $2,000 be appropriated by the town for the coming (town) year to the purposes of public education.

"All of which is respectfully submitted, by

R. J. TAYLOR,   C. G. PERRY,
WILLIAM BROWNELL,   WILLIAM GILPIN,
C. T. BROOKS,   AUGUSTUS BUSH,
JOSEPH SMITH,   THATCHER THAYER,
DAVID KING,   JAMES A. GREENE,
C. F. NEWTON,

School Committee."*

Four years later (1848), the committee reported in part as follows:

" The school committee of the town of Newport, in rendering the account of their stewardship for the year now closed, respectfully report: That there are under their care, seven primary schools, a school for colored children, three intermediate or grammar schools, and a boys' and girls' senior department; the last of which, from necessity, embraces in it an intermediate school and is taught by a principal and assistant, and has accommodations for ninety pupils. These schools, containing nearly nine hundred pupils, are under the direction of qualified and diligent instructors. They have not only maintained their former good standing, but most of them have made advances. Since the last report, the course of studies has been enlarged in every department, a more rigid classification of scholars instituted, and a more close and careful examination exacted for admission to the higher schools. (For the details of which, the committee refer to the rules and regulations recently published and distributed). The result of these arrangements is seen in the high appreciation of the schools by our townsmen; and the increased desire and more numerous applications for admission to a share of their advantages.

"For the first time since the establishment of the public schools, the committee have found themselves so straitened for accommodations and means, as to be compelled to refuse admission to some applicants, while at the same time a parochial school, attached to one of the religious societies, has withdrawn a large number of boys who were formerly in our schools. Private schools, which have heretofore met the wants of the wealthier classes, no longer compete with

*Barnard's Journal, III, 141-3. This report was also printed in pamphlet form.

those of the town. The advantages afforded by the latter, in the nicer classification of pupils, in the uniformity of school books, as well as in the constant and zealous supervision of the school committee, are all understood by the people.

"In this condition of things the committee believe that their fellow-citizens will not only justify them in the suggestion of measures for greater improvement, but that they will meet these suggestions with a response.

"The first step, and not the least important in the economy of education, is the provision of convenient and comfortable school-rooms. The essential elements in these are location and space. * * *

"In view of these circumstances, with the most careful consideration of the best means of providing for present exigencies, the committee earnestly recommend to the town, the erection of a school house large enough for two hundred pupils, in some place which shall be found most expedient.

"The committee are fully persuaded, that this is not only the best course, but that it will prove to be altogether the most economical in a pecuniary point of view. It is not meet or just that any child in the town should be denied its lawful share of the moneys appropriated to public schools, yet this must be done, unless there be provided ample accommodations.

"The committee append the report of their returns, from which it will be seen that they are compelled to ask of the town an increased appropriation of five hundred dollars.

"Amount on hand from last year,	. . . . .	$2 83
Received from the State,	. . . . .	1,766 02
" " town,	. . . . .	2,500 00
" " registry tax,	. . . . .	259 83
" " school tax,	. . . . .	447 09
		$4,975 77
"Amount paid for salaries of teachers,	. . .	$3,737 37
Stationery,	. . . .	419 30
Rent,	. . . .	223 00
Fuel,	. . . .	148 20
Repairs,	. . . .	36 84
Incidentals,	. . . .	397 29
Cash on hand.	. . . .	13 77
		$4,975 77
Mr. Barber's bill unpaid,	. . . . .	$282 00

JOHN STERNE,   A. H. DUMONT,
S. WARD,   A. BUSH,
ED. CLARK,   I. SMITH,
C. L. BROOKS,   C G. PERRY,
WILLIAM BROWNELL,   T. C. DUNN,
WILLIAM GILPIN,   JOSEPH B. WEAVER,
School Committee.

"Newport, June, 1848." *

* Barnard's Journal, III, 153–6,

There apparently exists no full series of State reports, even at the office of the Commissioner of Education; and the early reports moreover gave, in respect to local school systems, only the statistics, and not always even those. The full report of the Newport school committee appears for the first time in the State report issued January, 1856; and there are similar local reports in the State reports for January, 1861, 1864, 1865 and 1866; since which time the Newport reports have been annually printed in pamphlet form, for the use of the citizens.

Going back to the earliest of the above reports, we shall find that in April, 1855, there were in Newport 873 public school pupils distributed among 17 schools, these being taught by 22 teachers. There were two high schools, four grammar, (two of these having an intermediate department,) two intermediate and seven primary; besides separate primary and grammar schools for colored children. The receipts were $9,729.25, leaving a deficit of $696.28. The school committee recommended a city appropriation of $10,000, instead of $6,500 as before.

At that time the Farewell street school-house had been for some time in use, having been built about 1833, while that on Clarke street had been built in 1852. No others remain to us of the school-houses of that day. The Thames street building was finished in 1860; those on Willow street and Edward street and the Parish school-house in 1863; that on Cranston street in 1867, the Coddington in 1870, and the Rogers high school in 1873. It has just been voted (April, 1876) to erect a new brick school-house on or near Broad street.

The high school seems to have undergone a varied and fluctuating existence, having been originally established under that name; then reduced for economy, to a "senior department" of the grammar schools; then re-organized, in 1863, as a high school, the sexes being separated; then consolidated into a "mixed school" in 1864–5; then expanded, in 1873, by the aid of the munificent Rogers bequest, to its present proportions.

With the consolidation of the high schools into one, there came a general movement to unite the sexes where this had not been previously done; and there has not been, for ten years, a separate school in the town, for either sex, at the public expense. So entire has been the success of this change that there never has been any movement to revoke it, nor has there been so much as a petition, from any source, to that effect.

Another important change, that occurred about the same time, was the introduction of individual ownership of school books instead of their being supplied by the city, as previously. This met with some opposition, but there has never been the slightest effort to revive the earlier plan. Precisely the same occurred in regard to the abandonment of separate schools for colored children, which was effected in 1865, before the passage of the State law on the subject.

The most important event in the history of our schools was, however, the introduction of the school superintendency. This office was created in 1865, the first incumbent being Rev. M. J. Talbot. He was succeeded, after one year, by F. W. Tilton, Esq., since principal of the Rogers high school. He effected a great work in the grading and elevation of the schools ; a work industriously carried on by his successors, A. D. Small, Esq., and T. H. Clarke, Esq.

COURSE OF STUDY.

The schools are now graded as follows : primary, intermediate or secondary, grammar, and high. There are three grades primary, two intermediate, and four grammar, making with the high school, 10 grades. The course pursued in the various grades is as follows :—

TENTH GRADE.

To be admitted to this grade a child must be five years old.

Reading. Alphabet and simple words from blackboards and word cards; formation of words and sentences by the use of the composing stick; printing on slate and blackboards, and reading in Analytical First Reader. Counting from 1 to 100 by use of abacus and objects prepared for the purpose.

Writing and reading numbers containing two figures, and addition of numbers below 10.

Drawing. Definitions of lines, angles, triangles, drawing them and naming when drawn by the teacher, drawing lines of different lengths, as, one inch, two inches, five inches, etc. Cultivation of perception in regard to form and size of objects.

Music. Rote singing. Use of National Chart No. 1. *Oral lessons on general topics daily.*

NINTH GRADE.—SECOND PRIMARY.

Reading. Analytical Second Reader completed, and Third Reader, same series, taken up.

Special points: expresssion, clear enunciation; distinct utterance; interest or enthusiasm.

A thorough comprehension of the lesson. Exercise never prolonged to weariness.

(*The above points apply to all grades.*)

Writing and reading numbers below one hundred. Addition and subtraction of units and tens. Tables of addition, and subtraction written upon blackboard involving the 9 digits. Simple examples in mental arithmetic. Exercises on slate, and oral lessons as in previous grade.

Drawing. Free hand from copy on cards, enlarged on slates; dictation and memory drawing; definitions of lines, angles, etc.

Music. Sounds, long and short; idea of measure; development of measure; beating and counting measures; rests, long and short; the scale; the staff. G cleff and six sounds of G scale. Singing by note, using pitch names; idea of pitch; names of notes; signs; beating time; component parts of scale.

EIGHTH GRADE.—PRIMARY.

Analytical Third Reader completed. Questions on lessons; analysis of same; general information.

Spelling. Words from reading lessons, Worcester's Elementary Speller, selections of words in common use, names of trees, flowers, articles of manufacture and commerce, and implements of industry. Use of capital letters, name and use of each of the following points : , ; : . ? !

Arithmetic. Thorough drill on first two processes involving numbers of first period. In next two processes with easy numbers; multiplication table, measures of weight, value, capacity, extension, time. Eaton's Primary Arithmetic completed. Analysis of examples involving dollars and cents, making change, etc.; examples constructed by pupils.

Geography. Cornell's First Steps. Form, size, motions of the earth; component parts; natural divisions; definitions; examples; naming those seen; location of natural divisions; points of the compass; political divisions of North America—physical divisions, mountain systems, river systems—formation of river systems.

New England States; outline; capitals; occupation of inhabitants. Agriculture, manufactures, commerce, defined and examples given. Oral lessons.

Writing. Duntonian Writing Primer No. 1. Thorough drill on method of holding the pencil, requiring the letters to be made by the movement of the fingers rather than by the movement of the hand; tracing copy; formation of letters in marked spaces; drill on curves; word tracing and the writing of words.

Drawing. Practice same as in previous grade, with thorough drill on lines, angles, and definitions of the same together with the formations of right line figures. Occasional attempts at designs.

Music. Primary Music Reader. Review of previous grade. Key of C. Middle, upper and lower scale, the chromatic scale, ascending and descending; singing by note, using syllables through several keys for cultivation of voice; signs for ending, repeating, and abbreviation used in common music.

SEVENTH GRADE.—SECOND INTERMEDIATE.

Reading. Analytical Intermediate Reader. Thorough drill in expression as in previous grades; emphasis; pauses; inflections. Analysis of lessons; general information, etc.

Spelling as in previous grades, words from lessons—speller and words in common use.

Arithmetic. Work of previous grades reviewed. Thorough drill in writing and reading numbers of three periods, and in addition and subtraction. Construction of examples. Primary arithmetic completed. Mental arithmetic to accompany the written.

Geography. Thorough review of previous grade. Motions of the earth—what they cause; why; mathematical geography; climate; plants; animals; races of men; conditions; occupations. General outline.

Writing. Duntonian Freehand Series, No. 1.

Drawing. Free hand from copy on cards to be enlarged; blackboard exercises; dictation and drawing from memory; definition of plane geometry; simplest forms of designs, combining previously drawn forms to form new designs.

Music. Review of previous grades. Thorough drill in science of music—Key of C. Time; movements; one part finished.

SIXTH GRADE.—FIRST INTERMEDIATE.

Reading and Spelling, from the whole of First Intermediate Reader. Thorough drill in analysis and spelling; practice on combination of consonant sounds. Use of capital letters and punctuation marks. Dictation exercises. Lessons in Language. Construction of sentences.

Written Arithmetic to reduction. Thorough drill in general principles with practical applications. Roman notation; principles; uses; review of tables, weights, measures, etc., class exercise on blackboard. Mental arithmetic to correspond with the above.

Geography. Warren's Primary, through the United States. Oral lessons on general topics.

Writing. Duntonian Freehand Series, No. 2.

Drawing. Work of previous grade advanced, blackboard dictation and memory drawing, and simplest form of designs.

Music. Practice singing at sight in key of C. Ascending and descending forms of chromatic scale explained. Science of music. Thorough drill in definitions, reading music, use of terms, and writing measures.

FIFTH GRADE.—FOURTH GRAMMAR.

Reading. Analytical Fourth Reader; Exercises in phonic analysis. Exercises in concert for elocutionary drill. Thorough understanding of the lessons. General information on various topics.

Arithmetic. Reduction; definitions; measures of value, weight, capacity, extension, surface or area, volume, time, and circular. The difference and uses of measures of weight and capacity. Thorough drill in examples involving the above. Examples prepared by pupils. Mental arithmetic to accompany the written through the various processes. Drill on general principles; relation of numbers, factoring, greatest common divisor and least common multiple.

Grammar. Language. Sentence making, principal parts of a sentence, modifiers; parts of speech, properties, examples, sentences involving examples, dictation exercises, use of capitals and punctuation marks; drill on definitions; number of nouns, gender, elements of parsing, drill from reading book.

Geography. Thorough review of preceding work; climate, races of mankind, conditions of society; productions of different zones; government, different forms; most preferable, analysis of republican form; United States, state, city, town, district. Mathematical geography. Political geography—North America and its divisions.

Writing. Duntonian Freehand Series, Nos. 3 and 4.

Drawing. Freehand from copy, using Walter Smith's Intermediate Drawing Book, Nos. 1 and 2—exercises as in previous grades; definitions of plane geometry; design.

Music. Key of G. Reading at sight. Blackboard exercises and drill, composition. First Transposition.

Fourth Grade.—Third Grammar.

Reading, with exercises, as in fourth grade.

General Information. Familiar science, etc.

Written and Mental Arithmetic through common and decimal fractions. Thorough drill in analysis of principles. Work of previous grades reviewed.

Geography, Warren's Common School. Plants—distribution, uses, food, clothing, medicine, other uses. Animals—distribution, most useful, classification. Inhabitants—races of mankind, condition, occupations. Minerals—distribution, most useful, etc. Study to include general outline and political division of North and South America and part of Europe. General information.

Grammar, construction of easy sentences, sentences containing parts of speech having certain properties; compound sentences, complex; corrections of false syntax; dictation exercises, composition.

Writing in writing books Nos. 4 and 5 and other drill, twenty minutes daily.

Drawing. Same as in previous grades, advanced.

Music. First and second, third and fourth transposition by sharps. Drill on terms, signs, abbreviations and musical composition. Singing at sight, keys of G, D and E.

Third Grade.—Second Grammar.

Reading. Analytical Fifth Reader; particular attention to variety of expression, occasional recitations and declamations, elocutionary drill, spelling from reader and speller; words, selections, etc. Words defined.

Written and Mental Arithmetic through denominate numbers, United States money; duodecimals, longitude and time, percentage to exchange. The pupil to be familiar with business forms, principles of interest and discount and to construct examples involving principles of any of the preceding rules. Thorough analysis of problems required.

Course in geography completed at the end of second quarter. History of United States taken up at the beginning of third quarter.

Grammar. Construction of sentences as in previous grades. Thorough drill in syntax, and analysis of simple sentences. Dictation exercises, composition, general information.

Writing daily. Writing books, Duntonian Freehand, Nos. 5 and 6, and *general exercises on paper, notes, letters* and *other* drill.

Drawing. Freehand from copy in book No. 4, plane and geometrical drawing. Analysis of forms, definitions, design.

Music. Transposition, four keys, singing at sight, key of F, E flat, B flat, A flat. Musical composition in the above keys. Review of definitions, terms, etc.

SECOND GRADE.—FIRST GRAMMAR.

Reading. Analytical Fifth, Sixth and other readers. Thorough drill in articulation, enunciation, and analysis. Elocutionary drill, recitation, declamation.

Arithmetic, through mensuration of surfaces and solids. The pupil to be thoroughly acquainted with general principles, powers of numbers, and able to construct, solve and analyze problems under any process in common or high school arithmetic. To be thoroughly acquainted with business forms, concise and most approved methods of discount; construction and discussion of notes; exchange, reason of different rates, etc., partnership and companies and other organizations, involving capital or stock; dividends; assessments; measurements of lumber; walls of a house; areas of triangles, circles and other geometrical figures. A thorough analysis of the principles of arithmetic.

Grammar. Analysis and construction of sentences, simple, compound and complex, etc. Dictation exercises, composition, etc. English grammar completed.

Writing. Nos. 7 and 8 of freehand series, daily drill in writing books or on paper. Exercises in arithmetic, grammar, etc., to be marked, taking penmanship into account.

History of United States completed. Study of the constitution of the United States. State constitution, etc.

Drawing. Freehand drawing from copy in book; blackboard, dictation and memory drawing, alternating with the freehand; model and object drawing; also definitions of plane and solid geometry, and design.

Music. Singing and reading music in any key. Three parts, chords, triads, common chords of fifth, fourth, second, sixth and third degrees. Harmonies in the various keys, definitions, terms, etc., musical composition in any key.

FIRST GRADE.—HIGH SCHOOL.

JUNIOR CLASS.

English History; Hitchcock's Anatomy and Physiology; Harkness' Latin Grammar, coarse print; Harkness' Latin Reader, 40 pages; Bradbury's Algebra, 187 pages; Otto's French Grammar, part I; Translation of "Mère Michel et son Chat;" Book-keeping, (no text book); English composition, reading, drawing, vocal music.

SECOND MIDDLE CLASS.

Bradbury's Geometry, plane; Ganot's Physics, with constant use of apparatus; Harkness' Latin Reader completed, grammar continued; Cæsar's Gallic war, four books; Otto's French Grammar, part II, to lesson XVIII; translation of "Le Conscrit," exercises in conversation; English composition, elocution, drawing, vocal music; in the classical department students commence Greek at the middle of this year; Goodwin's Greek Grammar; Xenophon's Anabasis commenced; two extra recitations per week in Latin. Students taking Greek may drop philosophy or part of the work in French, at their option. In the scientific department, students who desire to enter a scientific school at the end of their third year, will be allowed to take extra work in mathematics.

FIRST MIDDLE CLASS.

French History; Ancient History; Roscoe's Chemistry; Eliot and Storer's Manual of chemistry, used in the laboratory; Gilman's English Literature, with study of choice selections; Cicero, four orations; Virgil's Æneid, books I, II, and VI; Otto's French grammar finished; exercises in conversation; translation of "La Poudre aux Yeux," "Athalie;" Otto's German Grammar to lesson XXVI; English composition, elocution, drawing, vocal music. In the classical department three extra recitations per week in Latin; Sallust's Catiline; three orations of Cicero; Goodwin's Greek Grammar; Xenophon's Anabasis, three books; Latin composition; Ancient History. Students taking this course are allowed to omit the work assigned for this year in French, German, English Literature and French history. In the scientific department, students are allowed to substitute extra work in mathematics for parts of the regular course.

Senior Class.

Astronomy by lectures, with frequent use of the telescope; Eliot and Storer's Chemical Analysis, pursued in the laboratory; Bradbury's Trigonometry; Botany; English Literature—critical study of parts of the writings of Milton, Shakspeare and Goldsmith; also of extracts from Chaucer and other writers of early English; Abercrombie's Intellectual Philosophy; Moral Philosophy, by lectures; Mrs. Fawcett's Elements of Political Economy; Rhetoric, by lectures; translation of "Les Doigts de Fée;" one of Moliere's plays; exercises in French conversation; translation of a part of the Odes of Horace; Otto's German Grammar completed; translation of Eigensinn; two acts of Wilhelm Tell; English composition, drawing, elocution, vocal music. In the classical department, substitutions are made for all the above work, except English composition, elocution, and music, as follows:—Virgil, Æneid continued, Eclogues; Cicero's orations continued; Xenophon's Anabasis continued; Homer's Iliad, three books; Greek and Latin composition; Ancient Geography and History; review of mathematics, and of Latin and Greek authors. In the scientific department, students are allowed to substitute extra work in mathematics for parts of the regular course. The requirement for admission to the Junior class is the ability to pass a satisfactory examination in arithmetic, English grammar, geography, United States history and spelling.

There is one feature of the course of study for the high school, as given above, to which especial attention is called. A portion of every class leaves the school before the beginning of the second year, and the number is farther reduced before the beginning of the third year. It is very important that each scholar's connection with the school shall be a source of direct and lasting benefit to him, be the period long or short. With this end in view, the strictly practical and disciplinary studies have been very evenly distributed throughout the four years. There is no point in this course at which it can be fairly said that a pupil, leaving the school at that point, has spent his time upon studies valuable, in the main, only as preparatory to higher work.

HISTORICAL SKETCH

OF THE

REDWOOD LIBRARY AND ATHENÆUM.

By David King, M. D.

Among the causes of American civilization, the formation of early colonial libraries, naturally occupies a prominent place. The early libraries were connected with the churches, or with the universities, or were formed by associations of gentlemen in the different colonies. Among the former, the society for the propagation of the gospel in foreign parts, undoubtedly effected much for the general enlightenment *of the colonies* by the distribution of books and tracts, and by the establishment of Libraries in connection with the principal Episcopal churches.

Thus, from 1702 to 1728 that society had distributed among the inhabitants of the colonies above eight thousand volumes of books, and above one hundred thousand small tracts of devotion and instruction. The other churches and the various colleges by their libraries must have likewise contributed to promote the early intellectual and moral improvement of the people. Indeed the best portion of English literature, in that age, was presented to the American mind, and grasping it, as it did with eagerness, all its powers were quickened by the learning and genius of the mother country.

Among the libraries that accomplished a good work for American civilization was the Redwood Library, founded in 1747, at Newport, Rhode Island. Its members had formed an association for literary purposes in 1730 under the auspices of Bishop Berkley, who resided at Newport from 1729 to 1731. The association gradually aspired to the formation of a library company. In 1747, through the generosity of

Abraham Redwood, Esq., there was placed at their disposal the large sum of £500 sterling for the purchase of standard books in London. From Henry Collins, Esq., they received an appropriate building site for their library, then called Bowling Green. For the erection of a library building five thousand pounds were almost immediately subscribed by one hundred gentlemen, who constituted the association. The library building, which was a beautiful specimen of the Doric order, was begun in 1748, and completed in 1750, from a plan furnished by Peter Harrison, Esq., the assistant architect of Blenheim house, England. While the library was in process of building, the catalogue which had received much careful consideration from its members, was transmitted to London, where with a few alterations by Peter Collinson, Esq., it was, immediately, at the full cost of £500 sterling, purchased. In 1750, it had arrived and was placed on the shelves of the library, and, was generally considered by American scholars as the finest collection of works on theology, history, the arts and sciences, at that time in the American colonies. An examination of the statistics of American libraries, shows, that the Redwood *Library* stands in the front ranks, as a colonial library, which, from the first, was endowed with a charter of incorporation, possessed of an appropriate and well-designed library building, and furnished with books, that involved the expenditure in London, of a larger sum of money, than, had at any time previously, been transmitted from any of the colonies, for that purpose. It would be interesting to give here, the catalogue of the English and classical works which were deemed at that time, a complete and well-appointed library—did space permit our so doing. The names of the liberal founders of the Redwood Library—a colonial one, at an early period of our civilization, should at least be preserved.*

The beneficial influences of this library in colonial times, must have been great. The Rev. Dr. Ezra Stiles has acknowledged his indebted-

---

* Abraham Redwood, Rev. James Honyman, Edward Scott, Simon Pease, Thomas Moffatt, M. D., John Brett, M. D., William Paul, John Channing, Jahleel Brenton, David Cheeseborough, William Vernon, John Brown, Daniel Updike, Daniel Ayrault, Jr., Abraham Borden, Henry Collins, Joseph Jacob, Samuel Rodman, Samuel Wickham, Thomas Ward, Josias Lyndon, Peter Bours, Charles Wickham, John Easton, Joseph Sylvester, Thomas Wickham, John Tillinghast, Joseph Harrison, Clark Rodman M. D., Rev. William Vinal, Walter Rodman, M. D., James Honyman, Jr., Samuel Ward, Rev. John Callender, John Bennet, Joseph Scott, Ebenezer Gray, M. D., Joseph Phillips, Benjamin Hazard, Rev. James Searing, Samuel Vernon, Benjamin Wickham, John Gardner, Jonathan Nichols, Stephen Wanton, Patrick Grant.

November 4, 1747. Gideon Wanton, Joseph Wanton, Joseph Whipple, Jr., William Ellery, Walter Chaloner, Jonathan Thurston, Samuel Holmes, Godfrey Malbone, Jr., Charles Bowler, Gideon Cornell, Robert Crooke, John Collins, John Dennis, Abraham Hart, Matthew Robinson, William Dunbar, John Chaloner, John Jepson.

ness to it for his useful, curious, and recondite bearing. It was from this library that he furnished himself with armor for the great and growing contest in American colonies. The late Dr. William Ellery Channing, says of him. " To the influences of this distinguished man, in the circle in which I was brought up, I may owe in part, the indignation which I feel towards every invasion of human rights. In my earliest years I regarded no one with equal reverence." A similar auspicious influence, on the character, intelligence and public spirit of the town, on her rising statesmen, her liberal merchants, her cultured scholars and her able lawyers, must be attributed to the Redwood library. It should likewise be recollected that it attracted many of our literary men in the English colonies, who availed themselves of its treasures, while enjoying the delights of our climate. From the Carolinas, from the West Indies, from New York and Boston, they came here as to a paradise on earth to replenish their stock of health and their stores of knowledge, ere they returned to their native climes. " The library of Rhode Island though built of wood," says a fellow of Trinity College, Dublin, who passed his youth at Newport before the revolution, in the " still air of delightful studies," was a structure of uncommon beauty. I remember it with admiration, and I could once appeal to the known taste of an old school-fellow (Stuart the painter) who had the same feeling towards it."

From 1778 to 1785 the tumults of war interrupted the meetings of the library company, while the town was occupied successively by the English, the American and the French forces.

The library undoubtedly suffered some losses by the occasional purloining of books, but considering its exposed position, from the dispersion and occupation of its natural guardians, it was remarkably preserved from injury and depredation. But at the close of the war it was discovered that many of the books were missing from the shelves, that the building and fences had fallen into decay; that in consequence of death or removal from the State, thirty-three members and proprietors only, were left to manage the affairs of the company, and to carry out the generous and noble intentions of its founder and of its other generous benefactors. With a view to restore the institution, an able committee was appointed in September, 1785, to apply to the legislature for a renewal of the charter. They were not successful till October, 1790, when the charter was renewed, and still farther amended in May, 1791.

In September, 1806 it was resolved to apply to the legislature for a lottery to raise three thousand dollars, and for the admission of thirty new members on paying twenty-five dollars each for a share in the library. On the 13th of March, 1810, the company adopted a successful measure for the revival of the institution, in the admission of so many new members, on the payment of fifteen dollars each, as should carry the whole number of proprietors to one hundred. This number was long considered as fulfilling Mr. Redwood's ideal of a library company. In October, 1810, the proprietors appointed a committee consisting of William Hunter, Benjamin Hazard, Edmund Waring, David King, William Marchant and John L. Boss, Jr., to prepare an address, and to present the same to the public, for the purpose of obtaining donations of books to the library. This direct appeal to the public contributed to revive the interest, already directed towards the Library, and to encourage the spirit of liberality now re-awakened by the example of generous and high-minded individuals.

In January, 1810, James Ogilvie, Esq., a great rhetorician of that day, visited the town and delivered several lectures on the advantages of public libraries, which contributed essentially to awaken the public to the claims to the Redwood Library on their generosity and support.

In 1813 Solomon Southwick, Esq., of Albany, gave to the library one hundred and twenty acres of land in the State of New York, for the purpose of advancing the institution, and thereby perpetuating the memory of Henry Collins, Esq., one of its principal founders.

In 1834 Abraham Redwood, Esq., of Dorset Place, Marylebone, England, being desirous of promoting the institution founded by his honored grandfather, gave to the company, the homestead estate, situated in Newport which he inherited from his father Jonas L. Redwood, Esq. Through the instrumentality of Robert Johnston, Esq., the public records of England, as far as then published consisting of 84 volumes, viz.: 72 large folios and 12 octavos were presented by the British government. It is to be regretted that the volumes subsequently published have not been obtained by the library.

In 1837, Baron Hobbing, a distinguished banker of Paris, who was connected by marriage with the Redwood family, presented to the company 1,000 francs for the restoration of the building.

In 1840 the honorable Christopher G. Champlin bequeathed to the company 100 dollars and some valuable books.

In 1844, the library company received from Judah Touro, Esq., of New Orleans, (a native of Newport), the gift of 2,000 dollars, which sum according to the wish of the donor, was appropriated to the repairs of the portico of the building and to the laying of a sidewalk in East Touro street from the library building to the corner of Kay street. Mr. Touro at his death in 1854, left a bequest of three thousand dollars to promote the interests of the institution. The Centennial Anniversary of the incorporation of the Redwood Library company was celebrated August 24, 1847 by the delivery of an able and eloquent discourse by the Hon. William Hunter, and by an appropriate and beautiful poem by the Rev. Charles T. Brooks.

In September, 1855, it was resolved to promote the usefulness of the institution by increasing its resources, viz.: by the sale of four hundred new shares at twenty-five dollars a share for the purpose of enlarging the library building, increasing the number of books, attaching a reading room to the Library, and opening it daily to the public. A circular was prepared by Dr. King, the president, exhibiting the condition and resources of the institution and presenting the proposed plan for improving the Redwood Library and Athenæum, and the terms of admission to its present and prospective privileges.

In January, 1856, the charter was amended, so that the company were enabled to elect from the members, at the annual meetings, a president and *eleven* directors, instead of *five* directors, as formerly. In 1861, an additional act was passed by the legislature, authorizing the corporation, annually, to elect a vice-president, and not exceeding, eight additional directors. In January, 1867, an act was adopted by the legislature, allowing the Library company to issue "preferred" shares, and to increase the number of directors to twenty-five. It was not till September, 1858, that the whole stock of new shares was taken. It is not more than just to mention with praise the zeal and energy of the Hon. William C. Cozzens and on this occasion the liberality of subscriptions of Messrs. Charles H. Russell, Edward King, William S. Wetmore, Sidney Brooks and James Lenox. The whole subscription was highly creditable to all the proprietors who then participated in increasing the power and resources of the institution. With these funds, the directors proceeded to enlarge the building, preserving as far as possible the original design of Mr. Peter Harrison, the first architect. By the aid of Mr. Snell, of Boston, the architect, they were enabled to add a principal room, fifty feet long, twenty-eight feet wide and nineteen feet high, lighted by six windows on the north and south façades and by an octagonal dome, or lantern light, the whole beautifully frescoed, supplied with gas lights and warmed by a furnace. The room for books was still further increased by the extension of the original wings and by central openings into the old Library room. The corporation also expended in the purchase of valuable books about 4,000 dollars with the assistance of Joseph G. Cogswell, Esq., of the Astor Library. They added a gallery of paintings, being enabled to enrich the gallery, by the munificent donation of Charles B. King, Esq., a native of Newport with upwards of 200 valuable paintings, many of them by his own hand, and some by other distinguished artists. In the gallery of pictures are to to be found paintings given by David Melville, Miss J. Stuart, Mrs. Catharine Allen, Usher Parsons, M. D., Augustus N. Littlefield, C. H. Olmstead, of New Haven, Russell Coggeshall, George C. Mason, William N. Mercer, M. D., and John Purssord, Esq., of London. The library building was opened to the public in July, 1859.

In the winter of 1859-60 an inaugural discourse on the advantages of public libraries was delivered by the Hon. Geo. G. King, president of the institution, who was followed by various gentlemen, in a course of free lectures instituted at that period by the directors.

In 1860 was presented to the Library by Sidney Brooks, Esq., a valuable collection of French books, illustrative of art and military life, embracing a donation of eighty-one volumes—3 folios, 3 quartos and 75 octavos.

A donation was presented by the Hon. David Sears, consisting of seven volumes quarto of Plymouth colony records ; 6 volumes quarto of Massachusetts records, and eighteen volumes octavo of Massachusetts Historical Society collection. Also by James Lenox, Esq , his privately printed copy of the "Opusculum de Insulis Nuper Inventis" by Nicolaus Lyllacius, first published in 1494. Also was presented by John Purssord of London, a portrait of Abraham Redwood, the grandson of the founder.

In August, 1862, twenty pictures were received from the executor of the estate of Charles B. King, Esq., in addition to a donation of forty-two made by Mr. King the year before. Also a specific donation of the Library of Charles B. King, Esq., consisting of 391 volumes of books, of which 31 volumes are illustrated works ; 14 volumes of bound engravings of various sizes from large quarto to large folio. Also three portfolios of unbound engravings. Also Mr. King bequeathed to the Redwood Library one-quarter of the residuary portion of his estate, real and personal.

In 1864, it was announced by the President, the Hon. George G. King, that the whole sum received by Library from the late Charles B. King, Esq., was in cash, $8,913.70 ; the whole sum being paid in 1863 and 1864. And that in addition to this sum must be added, the estimated value of books, engravings and paintings—the mere inventory price of which was $2,000. Among the donations received this year, were two hundred and nine volumes of the best authors, from James Lenox, Esq., some of these are rare reprints relating to the early history of our country. From the widow of Dr. Benjamin Waterhouse, the bequest of the portrait of her late husband and the portrait of Gilbert Stuart the artist, both by Stuart, were received.

In April, 1865, Dr. William I. Walker, a temporary resident of Newport, left the generous bequest of ten thousand dollars to the library. This year the Clarke estate was purchased for the sum of fifteen thousand dollars, toward the purchase of which the library received $500—the generous gift of Alfred Smith, Esq.

In 1867, cork models of the coliseum, models of the fragments of two Roman temples, and a model of the arch of Constantine, all from the estate of Miss Sarah Gibbs, were presented through the instrumentality of Hon. W. C. Gibbs, administrator.

In 1868, Mr. Charles H. Russell and Mr. H. Hoppin, presented plans for the enlargement of the Library edifice, as devised by Mr. R. II. Hunt. In 1869, Dr. David King, in behalf of Miss Elizabeth F. Thomas and other descendants of Peter Harrison, Esq., the first architect of the Redwood Library, presented the portraits of Mr. Harrison and his wife.

In 1863, Mr. Edward King had offered his valuable collection of statuary to the Library, on condition that a suitable place should be provided for it. This year, he consented to place the statuary in the Library building; hoping that more room would be given when the building should be enlarged. The subjects are copies in marble from the antique, of the "Dying Gladiator," and the busts of the "Venus of Milo," "Ariadne," "Demosthenes," "Cicero," and the "Young Marcellus,"—all being the work of Paul Akers; also an original work by James Mozier, the "American School-boy." The president and eighteen members raised at this time, $1,600 to pay off a debt of the institution.

Hon. George G. King, the president, at his death, July 17, 1870, left the Society a bequest of one thousand dollars, to constitute a part of the permanent fund for the purchase of books. In December, 1869, through Henry Ledyard, Esq., the Library received two noble offers from George W. Gibbs, Esq.; first, that if the Directors would raise by subscription the sum of five hundred dollars for the purchase of books, he would subscribe five hundred dollars more. Whereupon in the course of 1870, twenty-five individuals subscribed nine hundred and fifty dollars, which, added to Mr. Gibbs' five hundred made, a fund of $1,450 for the purchase of books. The second proposition was, that if the Library would raise by subscription ten thousand dollars for enlarging the building, he would contribute an additional ten thousand dollars.

In 1871, the Library received a benefaction from Mrs. Maria D'Wolf Rogers, consisting of three thousand dollars' worth of rare and valuable books, and a special fund of one thousand dollars, the income to be used only for the purchase of books. The benefaction is to be perpetually held as a memorial of the late Robert Rogers, Esq., of Bristol. It was announced that Edward King, Esq., the executor of the late Hon. George G. King, had paid over the legacy in full, and that it had been invested in the savings bank as the nucleus of a book fund. Twenty-eight shares had been converted into $100 shares, the holders surrendering the $25 shares, and paying in cash, $75 each, and four shares were taken by new parties, at $100 each. Seven of the "preferred" shares had been taken in the previous years.

During the year 1872, two special shares were taken at $100 each, and fourteen were taken by original shareholders, on the payment of seventy-five dollars and a surrender of a present twenty-five dollar share, thus making the special share fund on deposit in the savings bank $4,075. The Gibbs building fund was made up this year, and placed in the Trust Company on deposit, the whole sum being $20,025. William Sanford Rogers, Esq., of Boston, a native of Newport, left a bequest of four thousand dollars, the income to be applied to the purchase of books.

In 1874, a generous bequest of $5,000 was left to the library by John Carter Brown, Esq., as a library fund. The library company adopted this year a plan presented by George C. Mason, architect for the enlargement of the building. They appointed C. H. Russell, Sidney Brooks, and John T. Bush, Esqs., the building committee to superintend the erection of the new structure. The master builders, Perry G. Case & Co., contracted to have the new building constructed of stone and brick, and to have it completed by December 1, 1875, according to the plans and specifications, for which purpose $25,000 were appropriated.

In 1875, Mrs. Lucy K. Tuckerman presented to the Library the works of the late Henry T. Tuckerman, Esq., also a framed photograph of Mr. Tuckerman. These volumes, enclosed in a casket of ebony and cedar, will be perpetually preserved in the library in memory of that accomplished scholar and good man. During this year, the society seem to have been saddened and appalled by the frequent demise of many of their prominent friends; among whom were John Carter Brown, Robert H. Ives and Edward King.

From 1861 to 1875, inclusive, the additions to the Library have been constant and numerous, ranging each year from four hundred to fifteen hundred volumes, besides many pamphlets. During these fifteen years the total acquisitions have been nearly twelve thousand volumes, for the larger portion of which, by far, the Library stands indebted to generous donors, prominent among whom are Messrs. Robert H. Ives, James T. Rhodes, George A. Hammett, David Sears, Sidney Brooks, James Lenox, Henry Ledyard, J. Carter Brown, R. C. Winthrop, George Calvert, J. R. Bartlett, William Hunter, E. D. Morgan, H. B. Anthony and T. A. Jenckes.

During these years, also, valuable and interesting additions have been made to the art treasures of the Library, including statuary, paintings and engravings. The paintings are mostly portraits of persons having either a local or national fame, thus rendering the gallery one of rich historical interest.

In the early part of the year 1876, the new structure of stone and brick was completed. It furnishes an admirable room for library and gallery purposes, 36 feet wide, by 48 feet long, and thirty feet high; and a room on the south, 17 feet by 22 feet, for the use of the directors. Thus ample room is supplied for pictures, statuary, and library purposes for many years to come. The whole structure may be considered as classical and ornate; and though planned by three successive artists, has been made to conform as much as possible to the design of the original architect. The library company has expended $31,696.03, to which sum must be added the subsequent expenses of re-arranging the gallery and library, of repairing the fences and of ornamenting the grounds, and now offers to the public admirable galleries of painting and sculpture; and a library of twenty-one thousand volumes, many of them costly works, and the rare acquisitions of generations of growth.

We have traced in few and brief words, the career of one of the oldest institutions in the country. The liberality of individuals has sustained it through periods of adversity and prosperity, through changes in political and social life, and vicissitudes in the fortune and character of individuals and families. From the beginning to the present time, the Redwood Library, always from the first, highly respectable in the public eye, has gradually increased in true power and in growing adaptation to the wants and necessities of the community. It is now placed on a firm foundation, with ample means of progressive improvement. It sprung at first almost full armed, from a period of great commercial prosperity. It is associated with our first attempts in America at culture and scholarship, with early recollections of learning and piety, and with splendid memories that may never die. Whatever may be its position and resources in the future, it can never forget the debt it owes to the thoughtfulness, the learning and the intelligence of the past. We conclude with a list of the presidents from 1747 to 1876:

Abraham Redwood,	from 1747 to 1788.
Henry-Marchant,	" 1791 to 1796.
William Vernon,	" 1796 to 1801.
John Bours,	" 1801 to 1809.
Jonathan Easton,	" 1809 to 1813.
Robert Stevens,	" 1813 to 1830.
David King,	" 1830 to 1836.
Audley Clarke,	" 1836 to 1844.
George G. King,	" 1844 to 1846.
William Hunter,	" 1846 to 1849.
David King,	" 1849 to 1859.
George G. King,	" 1859 to 1870.
William C. Cozzens,	" 1870 to 1872.
Henry Ledyard,	" 1872 to 1874.
Edward King,	" 1874 to 1875.
Francis Brinley,	" 1875 to 1876.

ERRATA.—On page 260, for "hearing" read "learning." On page 270, for "Hobbing," read "Hottinguer."

THE PEOPLE'S LIBRARY.

Mr. Christopher Townsend, while in the prime of life and in the enjoyment of his usual health, conceived the purpose of appropriating a considerable share of the property which he had acquired by his industry, and saved by his prudence, to objects of public charity. He first gave liberally to The Association of Aid for the Aged, and then provided and endowed A Home for Friendless Children.

Aware of the benefits received by General Greene from books borrowed of Dr. Stiles, and that Channing "studied theology in the Redwood Library without an instructor," he resolved to establish a Free Library for the benefit of the people of this, his native city.

He matured his plan after years of deliberation, and finally devoted upwards of fifty thousand dollars of his fortune in carrying that plan into effect.

With this sum he purchased and fitted up the substantial edifice which contains the library, and selected and purchased, with rare discretion and judgment, seven thousand volumes of standard books.

With a modesty only surpassed by his generosity and public spirit, he has declined to have his name in any way associated with the name of the charity which he has thus established. He has donated the library to the use of the people of Newport, has given it their name, and has enjoined upon the trustees whom he has charged with carrying his charity into effect, to see to it that the Library is made what its name denotes, *The People's Library and nothing else.* While Mr. Townsend was deliberating upon the project of founding the The People's Library, other charitably disposed persons, by generous and disinterested efforts, (aided somewhat by Mr. Townsend,) became incorporated for the purpose of establishing a free library. They leased a room and gathered a miscellaneous collection of books, containing some three thousand volumes, which they magnanimously turned over to the custody of "The People's Library," thus making with the volumes donated by Mr. Townsend a collection of about ten thousand volumes.

Ample provisions have been made for regular additions to the library, and at the present time the whole number of volumes is over sixteen thousand.

As an evidence of the need of such an institution, and also of its appreciation by those for whose benefit it was founded, the report of the librarian for the past year shows that the whole number of volumes circulated within that time was 29,995.

SKETCHES

OF THE

PROGRESS OF EDUCATION

IN THE

TOWNS

OF

RHODE ISLAND.

BARRINGTON.

By Isaac F. Cady,

Superintendent Public Schools.

The first settlers of the present town of Barrington brought with them the true Puritan spirit on the subject of education. Coming, as they did from Plymouth and neighboring towns in Massachusetts, the picture of the school-house standing in the shadow of the church held a vivid place in their imaginations, and served as a powerful incentive in the moulding of their social character and civil polity. Hence the establishment of " a godly ministry " and an efficient arrangement for the education of the young was a subject which received their early and earnest attention.

Soon after obtaining from the Indians a deed of " Sowams and parts adjacent," they proceeded to set apart certain lands called pastors' and teachers' lands, the proceeds of which were to aid in the support of the ministry and the schools. The deed referred to, bears the date of March 29, 1653, and is signed by Ousamequin, generally known as Massasoit, and his son Wamsetto. This is supposed to be the last deed signed by Massasoit, who, to the last, remained an unwavering and invaluable friend to the early settlers of New England.

The lands obtained under this deed were held by the purchasers under the title of proprietors. They embraced the present towns of Somerset and Swansea in Massachusetts, and of Warren and Barrington in Rhode Island, all of which were originally included in the town of New Swansea, which was established by the court of New Plymouth in the year 1667. The history of Barrington, is therefore included in that of Swansea until it became a separate town in 1717.

"In 1673, this town voted to establish a school for the 'teaching of grammar, rhetoric, and the tongues of Latin, Greek and Hebrew, also to read English, and to write.'"

Its first teacher was Rev. John Myles, a native of Wales. He was a Baptist clergyman, and is represented as the ablest and most successful preacher in his country; but he was virtually compelled to become an exile by the acts which followed the restoration of 1662. He emigrated to America, and came to Swansea, where, at a salary of "forty pounds per annum," he rendered services in the capacity of both minister and teacher until the breaking out of King Philip's war in 1675.

From this humble school one pupil entered Harvard College, and graduated with the degree of A. M. in 1684. He afterwards became rector of King's Chapel, Boston, where he remained during a period of forty years.

Among the successors of Rev. Mr. Myles, as teacher, we find the names of Jonathan Bosworth, engaged at a salary of £18 per annum, in the year 1698, and of Mr. John Devotion in 1702, at a salary of £12, "current money of New England, to be paid quarterly, and the town to pay for his diet; and they also allow him £20 to be paid by the town for the keeping of his horse." In 1709 he was re-engaged for a term of six years. His services proved so satisfactory that the selectmen were authorized to engage him for an additional period of twenty years, "to teach our youth to read English and Latin, and cipher as there may be occasions." The school was to be kept five months each year, and he was required "diligently and steadily" to attend to his duties. He can hardly have completed this long term of service, since, in 1722, "the select men were authorized to see that the town be provided with a schoolmaster to teach to read, write and arithmetic, for four months from the first of November." Twenty pounds were raised in 1723, to pay a Mr. Andrews for twelve months' teaching. In 1724, twenty-five pounds were raised for the payment of the teacher's wages for one year. John Webber was school-master in 1729 and 1730. For this last year his wages were five pounds per month for nine months.

With occasional interruptions, one or more schools have been maintained at public expense, from the last named date until the present. The schools were somewhat itinerant in character, being maintained for a series of months in one quarter of the town, and then removed to another for the purpose of furnishing equal chances for improvement to the youth in all parts of the town.

I have not been able to ascertain the precise date of the division of the town into districts. It was probably made soon after the final separation of the town, in 1770, from Warren, with which it had been blended in 1747 by the formation of the town of Warren from a portion of Rehoboth and Swansea, in Massachusetts, and the whole of Barrington in Rhode Island. The original number of three districts remained unchanged until 1873, when, owing to the increase of population in Drownville and vicinity, a fourth district was formed to accommodate the citizens in that quarter of the town.

The buildings in which the schools were kept belonged to individuals, and were held by joint ownership. I think no buildings were owned by districts previous to 1840. The best of the older school buildings, that in the first district, was transferred to the district by its proprietors in 1846.

It is a well-known fact that Rhode Island was tardy, compared with the other New England States, in establishing an efficient system of public schools. It was not until what may be called the awakening of 1843 that the subject received a degree of general attention at all proportioned to its importance. The movement then inaugurated in the State Legislature by the Hon. Wilkins Updike, and the appointment of Hon. Henry Barnard, as school commissioner of the State, by Governor Fenner, lie at the foundation of nearly all, in the history of public schools in our State at large, that can be reviewed with any high degree of satisfaction. Since that period, no friend of education in our State need be ashamed of the progress made and the success that has been achieved.

Of this movement, Barrington was one of the first to reap the advantage. Two new school-buildings were soon erected, and a third was repaired and refitted. The new building in the second district was one of the best of its grade in New England. Its furniture and fixtures were after the best models of the time. Through the efforts, chiefly, of two members of the district, the school was furnished with an excellent library of five hundred volumes, which, in connection with other influences, ushered in an era of unwonted success.

A comparison of a few items in the statistics of the town in 1844 with those of 1875 will throw some light upon the progress of the cause of education during the intervening period.

In 1844, the population of the town was 549 ; the number of children under fifteen years of age, 188 ; the aggregate value of property in the town, $316,733 ; the amount expended for public schools, $241.56, of which $115 was raised by taxation.

In 1875, the population of the town was 1,185 ; the number of children under fifteen years of age 332 ; the aggregate value of property in the town, $1,494,805; the amount expended for public schools, $1,501.93, of which $1,107.55 was raised by taxation.

From this comparison it will be seen that the amount expended for each pupil in 1875 is more than three times as great as in 1844. The difference arises chiefly from two sources; first, from an increased length of the schools, and second, from the increased compensation of teachers.

Within the last two years, two new school buildings have been erected at an expense of nearly $3,000 each. These are very complete in all their appointments. The school-rooms are large for the number of pupils to be accommodated, are supplied with elegant furniture and fixtures and with ample means for warming and ventilation; and, what is a matter of primary importance, with a separate seat and desk for each pupil.

During the last year the schools have been under the charge of specially faithful and competent teachers. Two of these are graduates of our State Normal school, and a third, of the Normal school in Bridgewater, Massachusetts. The fourth, although not a graduate of any Normal school, is doing excellent service in the school where she is employed.

For several years, ladies have been almost exclusively employed as teachers in our schools, and have won a measure of success which confirms the wisdom of their employment.

During the last five years, a private school has afforded an opportunity for pupils to pursue an advanced course of study at a moderate expense. During this period upwards of one hundred pupils in the town, have been in attendance for periods varying from a single term to five years. Four have graduated to enter college, three have pursued a course of study in our State Normal school, and one is at present a teacher in the Normal school in New Hampshire.

BRISTOL.

By Eleanor R. Luther.

The history of the public schools of Bristol, as of most New England towns, dates almost as far back as the history of the town itself. Indeed, for the first half century or so, the most conspicuous items in its annals are the minister and the school-master, the "meeting-house" and the school. The irrepressible school-master appears at every conceivable point; sometimes leading the van of the whipping-post and stocks, sometimes bringing up the rear of a procession of "Gunpowder, Lead, Flints, Muskets, Drums and Colors"—like the citizens and strangers in a Fourth of July parade, with this difference, that he was always there, and they are usually not.

On the 14th of September, 1680, John Walley, Nathaniel Byfield, Nathan Oliver and Stephen Burton, bought of Josiah Winslow, Thomas Hinckley and William Bradford, the tract of land known as Bristol, for £1,100. This tract included the two peninsulas, Bristol Neck and Poppasquash, lying between Taunton—now Mount Hope—Bay on the east, and Narragansett Bay on the west, and extending from Bristol Ferry some six miles to the north, together with a few small islands in the vicinity, of which the one at the mouth of the harbor, long known as "Hog Island," but now by its more musical Indian name "Chessawanock," is the largest. This island is now part of the town of Portsmouth.

The first town meeting of the newly erected borough was held November 10, 1681. At the fourth town meeting, held September 7, 1682, the following vote was passed:

" *Voted*, That each person that hath Children in town ready to go to School shall pay 3d. the week for each Child's Schooling to a School master, and the Town by Rate according to each Rateable Estate shall make the wages amount to twenty-four pounds the year. The Select Men to look out a Grammar School master and use their endeavour to atain five pounds of the Cape Money granted for such an end."

In accordance with this vote, Mr. Samuel Cobbitt was engaged to take charge of the school. A house-lot, ten acre lot and "commonage" were bought for the use of the "school-master," as he is invariably called. Mr. Cobbitt held his position from 1685 to 1694. From time to time during this period of nine years he appears as constable, rater of estates and grand juryman. In 1694 a committee appointed for that purpose agreed with Mr. Josiah Hervey to the effect that he would take the position left vacant by Mr. Cobbitt. His salary was fixed at £25, and he was to have whatever benefit might accrue from the school land, which was to be considered his by virtue of his office. It is to be feared that during his first year of service, this added nothing to his regular salary, for it was not until August, 1695, that Mr. Cobbitt appeared before the town meeting, and then and there "did renounce" his office and the school property.

Mr. Hervey's stay among the youth of the town seems to have been short, for it stands recorded that in 1699 Mr. Easterbrooks was "re-elected" school-master with a salary of £30. Part of this was to be paid by the scholars themselves, "3d. a week for reading and writing, and 4d. for Latin;" the remainder to be made up by the town. Towards the end of this year, it was thought desirable, on account of the increase of inhabitants on the outskirts, to divide the town into two school districts, the "North Creek," over which the town bridge now stands, being the dividing line. The success of this plan depended upon Mr. Easterbrooks's willingness to "condescend to be and abide with Mr. Allen or thereabouts," one-third of the year and the remainder of the year in town. This proposal met an absolute and uncompromising refusal from Mr. Easterbrooks, and the plan came to nothing that year. But the farmers and others who lived north of the bridge complained that they paid taxes for the support of a school in town, and yet lived at such a distance from it, that their children received no benefit from it. It was only fair that they should have a school of their own at least three months of the year. So effectual were their representations, that in a town meeting held in November, 1700, a vote was passed that £20 should be given to that part of the town south of North Creek, provided they maintained a school, or in the quaint phrase of the town records "improved a school-master" eight months of the year, and £10 to the part north of the North Creek, on condition that they "improved a school-master" four months of the year. Either party failing to observe this condition was to forfeit to the other. Mr. Easterbrooks was elected to the south district and Mr. Williams to the north.

In 1701 Mr. Severs succeeded Mr. Easterbrooks. In 1702 steps were taken for the first time towards the erection of a school-house within the limits of the compact part of the town. For this object £20 were appropriated. Previous to this time, the school had been taught in private rooms hired for the purpose, the town records showing that at various times, certain sums of money were paid for "the use of the west lower room in Mrs. Wilkins her house," and also for a "room in Mr. Berge his house." It is by no means clear, however, that such a school-house was built.

Mr. Severs remained until 1705, and was succeeded by Mr. Pease, who in his turn was succeeded by Mr. Samuel Howland, in 1709. Mr. Howland proved more manageable than Mr. Easterbrooks in the matter of "abiding at Mr. Allen's or thereabout." He taught on the neck during the three winter months, and in town the remainder of the year. He was "persuaded to tarry" until 1712. Upon his resignation of office, Mr. Timothy Fales was installed "school-master." The total expense of maintaining the town government at this time was £60, forty of which went to the school-master. Mr. Howland was afterwards town clerk for many years.

In 1714 Mr. Byfield, "for and in consideration of a due regard which he had for the advancement of learning and good education," conveyed to John Nutting, who was the teacher of the grammar school at that time, for the use of the schools forever, certain land known ever since as the "school lands." These are in four lots or parcels; a lot lying between Church and Byfield streets and extending west of High street to the estate of the late John Hoard; a lot at the east of the town, bounded on the west by the old burying ground and the estate of the late Leonard Waldron, on the north by State street, on the south by the Mount road, and extending east as far as the property of Mr. John Barney; a lot between State street and Bradford street, extending west from Wood street one hundred and sixty-five feet; a lot on the main road to Warren. A part of this land was rented the very next year, and most of it has been productive of more or less income ever since, much of it being at present leased for a long term of years. For a very long time the school was mainly supported by this income. The people were never taxed directly for this purpose after this gift, until far into the present century. It must have been some time between 1830 and 1840 that the committee first asked for a special appropriation from the town for the support of the school. The sum asked was $500. The request was granted without difficulty. Year by year this sum has increased with the growth of the town and the needs of the schools. The amount received from the rent of the lands was, previous to this appropriation, eked out in various ways. In 1718 a source of revenue was developed, in allowing certain persons to keep houses of entertainment on condition of their paying certain sums of money for the benefit of the school. These licenses varied from 21s. to £4.

In 1729, the school-master was instructed to receive from each scholar 4s., or in default of the money, which was not always easily obtained, its value in firewood. The money thus raised was called " wood money." Whether this practice of carrying " wood money " was kept up year after year cannot be determined, but it certainly was a common one in Captain Noyes's time. Again, in 1818, a vote was passed that all money which was due to the town from the property of " strangers deceased and actually resident in the town " should be for the increase of the school fund. By this act, if a man not a native of the town died and left no heirs, his property was devoted to school purposes. From time to time, considerable sums came into the treasury in this way. In the same year, the following appears on the records :

" *Voted*, That the town council be instructed to exact a reasonable sum from all persons who may dance the Slack rope or wire or perform any feats of Activity, or exhibit any animal or Wax figures or other Shew in this town who exact pay from their spectators, and to collect double the sum exacted in case any Person shall presume to exhibit without their permission, and that the money arising under this act be appropriated to the support of free schools."

Still again, in 1832, the committee was instructed to demand of each scholar a small sum of money, to be paid before he could be entitled to a seat for the term. This sum was not to exceed twenty-five cents, and even this was remitted to those whose parents were unable to pay it. This act remained in force until 1867. The money thus obtained was used to purchase books, paper, and such other articles as were necessary for the use of the scholars. At the time of the abolition of this practice, this sum was sufficient to supply all the books and stationery needed in the schools. Notwithstanding that this source of revenue has ceased to be available, all articles of this kind are now supplied by the town without any expense to the pupil, so that a scholar may go the whole course from the first year in the primary to the last year in the High school, without the direct outlay of a single cent. Our schools are consequently precisely what their name purports, free schools. Besides Bristol, there are few, if any, towns in New England where the members of schools are not expected to provide their own books.

In the year 1724, it was "ye mind of ye town" to settle a schoolmaster for a term of years—to take a lease of him, as it were. The time fixed upon was seven years, the salary to be £50 if he was single, sixty if married. Mr. Amos Throope was invited to take the school and was persuaded to do so in consideration of an addition of £10 to the salary and the use of the school lands, and the fathers of the town breathed freely in the belief that that business was off their hands for seven years at least. But alas! for human hopes, in seven months Mr. Throope appeared in town meeting and asked a release from his engagement, having received a call to the work of the ministry in Woodstock. He offered to accept his salary at the rate of £50 a year in view of the trouble caused by his withdrawal. His proposal was accepted, and again the town found the vexed question of the "Grammar schoolmaster" before them. All along the early history of the schools, there are intervals sometimes extending over months, between the going of one teacher and the coming of the next, which are probably to be accounted for by the delay unavoidably attendant upon the filling of the vacancy. Teachers were not as numerous then as now, communication between distant settlements by no means easy, and the school system not so elaborate as at present, when a vacancy is hardly made before it is filled. It was in January, 1726, that Mr. Throope retired from office, and it was not until some time in 1728 that his successor appeared upon the stage of action. This was Mr. John Wight, of Dedham. He was put upon probation a year. Having in this year approved himself to the town, he was engaged for seven years.

Some years previous to this time some private individuals had, at their own expense, erected on the school land on the Neck, a school-house for the use of the north district. In 1727 the town bought it for £20. In 1750 a vote was passed in town meeting, which does not seem to be very intelligible, "that a committee be appointed to regulate the town school with respect to its being removed to the Neck and to provide a teacher," and in 1765 the town sold the building which they had bought in 1727, for what it would bring, sum not stated. In 1727 they also appropriated £50 for a school-house in town. It was to be twenty-six feet by twenty, and twelve feet between joints. It was to be located on King street between the Court House and High street. This was in "good old colony times when we were under the king," when Church street was Charles, State street, King, and Bradford street, Queen street. The Court House—which was doubtless a stately structure in those days, but which is now a tenement house near the eastern extremity of Bradford street—stood in the middle of the street, about half way between Hope and High. What idea possessed the minds of our forefathers when they selected such a site, is open to question. Whether it was, that educated, as the early settlers of the colony necessarily were, in principles of rigid economy, they regarded the broad streets of the town an extravagance not to be tolerated, or that they foresaw a time when Bristol should be an emporium of commerce and close packing would be necessary, or simply that they thought that a building thus situated could not fail to be conspicuous, it is quite certain that more than once they erected buildings in the middle of the street. The school-house, whose bearings were taken from the Court House did not, however, stand in the middle of the street, but on the north side, a short distance east of the present Methodist church. While it was in process of erection, the school sessions were held in the Court House.

Mr. Wight's seven years of service were satisfactory, and he was invited to remain seven years longer. But in 1738 he was brought before the town meeting, charged with not doing his duty as a teacher. The records, which are not always clear in their statements, leave the settlement of the matter in doubt. It would seem, however, that he remained until 1740. In that year, Captain Timothy Fales, who was himself a former teacher, was sent to Cambridge to procure a suitable teacher for a year or less, the seven years plan not having proved a success. The result was Mr. Hovey was elected on a salary of £130. In 1742 he was succeeded by Shearjashub Bourn. From 1747, at which time Mr. Bourn's term of service seems to have expired, until 1772, the school-master is a very uncertain person, coming and going with a rapidity quite bewildering, sometimes staying no longer than two months. The school on the Neck, too, which had hitherto shared the teacher with the town school, here asserts itself and employs one of its own. The list of these teachers comprises Daniel Bradford, John Throope, Bosworth Kinnicut, John Coomer and Samuel Pearse. Meantime the school in town was taught at various times by Shearjashub Bourn, Israel Nichols, Leverett Hubbard, Bellamy Bosworth, Nathaniel Lindall, John Throope, Josiah Brown, Haile Turner, John Barrows, and Rev. John Usher. These teachers have a trick of appearing spasmodically, so although the same one may have taught two or three years, he rarely taught two in succession. It is recorded that in 1763, £1,050 were paid to Parson Usher for teaching the town school a year and a half.

In 1751 a committee was chosen to manage the prudential affairs of the schools. Hitherto this had fallen to the town as a part of their yearly business. This committee consisted of Shearjashub Bourn, John Howland and Nathaniel Fales, and although at various times previous to this, persons had been appointed to engage a school-master, whose appointment expired when that business was disposed of, this may be considered as the first regular school committee.

In 1772 the school-master disappears entirely for a period of nine years. This was within three years of the breaking out of the Revolution and already the approaching struggle loomed on the sight. Doubtless in those " times that tried men's souls," there were more pressing affairs to be looked after than the education of the young even, and the peaceful school-master gives way to warlike preparations of guns, powder and barracks and the no less warlike, although apparently more peaceful ones, of provisions of grain and beef. In the year 1781 the school was re-opened for four months under Samuel Bosworth. The school-house, either from long disuse or the chances of war—which came very distinctly to our town in the shape of a bombardment in 1775—or both, was so badly out of repair, that it was necessary to procure a room in which to hold the school until the school-house could be made fit for occupancy. For years school was held, at the most, but five months of each year. Samuel Bosworth's name appears for the last time in 1788, after which the town records give no clue to the name of the teacher, and the committee, although some years consisting of the Town Council, kept no record.

At the June session of the State Legislature of 1799, a bill entitled " An Act to establish Free Schools " was presented. The representatives to the General Assembly from Bristol, were instructed to vote for its passage. Among other things, this bill provided for the apportionment of a certain sum of money from the State to each town, to be used in addition to that raised by the town for the support of free schools. The sum received from this source for the year 1875, was $1,864.58.

In 1802 Peter Church, William DeWolf, William Coggeshall and others living on the Neck, presented a petition in town meeting, praying to be allowed to build a school-house on the ten-acre school lot on the main road to Warren. This petition was granted and a brick building twenty-two feet by twenty was erected. This was used for public school until 1841, when a new school-house was built much nearer the town, on the west side of the road on a part of the land belonging to the Asylum Farm. The town had appropriated $500 for this purpose and in 1843 they sold the old brick house and laid out the proceeds on the new one. The old building still stands, without doors and windows, and only ministers to the instruction of the mind through the medium of posters and bills. It belongs to the estate of the late Charles Fales.

In 1803 a committee of five was appointed to take measures in regard to the building of a new school-house in the South District, the old one having been a constant bill of expense since the Revolution. But it was not until the next year that active measures were taken for its accomplishment. John DeWolf, Moses Van Doorn, and Charles Collins were directed to solicit subscriptions for this object. With that disregard for details which was chronic in the earlier annals, the town records fail to give any information of the sum obtained. Some money was obtained, however, and the town in company with the St. Alban's Lodge of Free Masons, erected the brick school-house which stands at the northwest corner of the common, but were obliged to ask for an appropriation to complete it. This was in 1809. Originally it was about two-thirds of its present size.

The school lands had thus far been rented annually, being sold at auction at town meeting. For obvious reasons it was thought better that some other plan of disposing of them should be adopted, and in 1811 a committee consisting of James DeWolf, Samuel Wardwell, John Bourn, Hezekiah Munro and Richard Smith, was appointed to prepare a plan for leasing them for a term of from twenty to fifty years.

They were also empowered to divide the town into three or more school districts for the purpose of having the proceeds of the school lands distributed more justly. At the next meeting they reported that in their judgment the following was the best plan : that the lands be leased for fifty years from March 25, 1812—the land in town being parcelled into eighteen lots and that on the Neck remaining unchanged ; that they be sold at auction on or before October 7, 1811 ; one-fourth of the purchase money to be paid in six or nine months after March 25, the balance to remain on interest paid annually, under penalty of forfeiting twenty-five per cent. of the price, and the improvement of the land if interest were not paid within nine months of March 25. They recommended that the proceeds of the sales should be invested in bank stock, the revenue thereof, together with the interest of the notes, to be applied to the support of the schools. In order that the money thus obtained should be distributed justly, they had divided the town into three districts, to be known as the North, Middle and South districts. The North District extended from "Peck's Hill" to Warren; the Middle began at Peck's Hill and extended to Poppasquash Corner and included Poppasquash; the South District comprised the remainder of the town. All of these districts stretched from shore to shore. This plan was accepted and the sale of the lands made. All of the land was rented except a small lot at the corner of High and Church streets and one on the Neck near Mr. John Fales's house. Arrangements were afterwards made for letting these annually.

Four years later the inhabitants of the North District erected a school-house at their own expense, on the "sixteen acre lot" on the East road. This "sixteen acre" lot was not school land, but town land, and the town gave them the rent of so much of it as was sufficient for their purpose. It has since been known as the "school lot." This was the first school-house in this district. In the same year in which it was built the office of School Treasurer was created, and the President of the Town Council was appointed Treasurer *ex-officio*. It was not until 1844, that the school-house known of late years as the North District School-house was built. For this purpose the committee bought a small lot of land at the north end of the town, on the east side of the main road, a short distance south of Crane's Lane.

After 1788, as has been before said, the town records do not hold themselves responsible for the name of the schoolmaster. About the the year 1835, the committee began to issue a yearly report of the condition of the schools. Of these none is known to exist of a date earlier than 1838. There is, then, an interval of fifty years, from 1788 to 1838, of which there is no written record whatever, and which must therefore be filled—as far as it is filled at all—from memory. This portion of school history will of necessity be somewhat unsatisfactory. No successful attempt can be made to fix any date before 1825, and there is not wanting a reasonably strong suspicion that the list of teachers, especially the earlier ones, is not perfect. Daniel Bradford, mentioned before as having taught on the Neck—or perhaps his son—is the most remote name that it is possible to lay hold upon with any degree of certainty, and he must have come a long time after Samuel Bosworth, as he is within the memory of people living now. He was succeeded by Mr. Swan, who in his turn gave place to Mr. Rawson, and he again to Captain William R. Noyes. Of the first three there is nothing to be said but that they taught the school, managed it with more or less success, and were themselves more or less managed by unruly boys who would stuff seaweed into the stovepipe, and thought it was a fine thing to "thrash" the schoolmaster. But the name of Captain Noyes is a familiar one to the older inhabitants of the town, many of whom were his scholars. He was as successful as it was possible for any one to be in the days when everything seems to have been arranged with a view to hindering and nothing for helping the teacher. Text-books were very scarce, one or two of a kind doing duty through the whole school. A scholar commenced his education with Alden's Speller. When he had mastered this he was expected to learn a lesson twice a week from the New Testament. From this he passed to the English Speaker. These, together with Daboll's Arithmetic, made up the list of text-books. Occasionally, to lighten the labors of the teacher, monitors were employed for the more advanced scholars, but not systematically. Captain Noyes was a remarkably fine penman, the copies which he wrote being almost as fine as copper plate. He set all the copies and mended all the pens. He taught navigation to young men going to sea, but this was quite separate and distinct from his regular work. He was succeeded by Otis Storrs.

At this point we reach a reliable date. About the year 1826, Mr. Storrs came to Bristol and opened a private school in the Academy, on what is known as the Lancasterian system. His success was so great, that in 1828 the committee asked him to take the town school and allow girls to go and share his instructions with the boys. Before this, girls did not go to the public school. Upon his acceptance, they enlarged the brick school-house and fitted it up with reference to the workings of this peculiar system. The teacher's desk stood on a raised platform at the west end of the room. Down the length of the school-room, through the middle, ran a single aisle. On each side of this, were arranged semi-circular desks, with seats on the outer curve for the scholars. The desks did not have lids but were open in front, and each accommodated eight scholars. On the inner curve was a bench, where they sat to recite. The monitor who heard the recitations, had a stool in the centre of the circle. The teacher heard the monitors recite and had the supervision of the school. This system was very popular at the time. Mr. Storrs was succeeded by John Cross, and he by James E. Hidden. Mary Allen was Mr. Hidden's assistant.

In 1836 Dennis S. Gushee became teacher of the Grammar School. The lower part of the Academy was hired for the use of the school, but the number of scholars became so large that in the spring of 1837. it was removed to the brick school-house, which was again altered, Mr. Gushee not being a supporter of the Lancasterian system. The teacher's desk was placed on the north side of the room. There were four rows of desks running east and west, with aisles from north to south, separating them into four groups. At the rear was a narrow, raised platform for classes. The east room was partitioned off from the main room for a recitation room and used by both assistant teachers. These were at this time Hannah H. Easterbrooks and Sarah G. Munro. In the summer of the same year, Martha Diman was appointed third assistant and used the unfinished room above for her classes. At the beginning of the winter term, so many more scholars entered that the room proved too small for their accommodation, and the younger ones, in charge of Miss Diman, were placed in Dr. Briggs's hall at the rear of his house on State street. In the spring of the following year the schools were reunited.

At this time the committee were working with much vigor and interest to reduce the schools to something approaching system. These efforts were much crippled by want of means and by lack of general personal interest on the part of the towns-people. Nevertheless, the foundation of the present school organization was laid at that time. The orders of the schools were the Select, the Intermediate and the Primary, besides the district schools.

Mr. Gushee's school was called the Select School, until the formation, in 1848, of a more advanced one, which received that name, and this one was always after known as the Grammar School. It was so large that one assistant was always employed, often two, and sometimes three. Mr. Gushee and his assistants did not always teach in the same room or even in the same building. Sometimes he was in the lower part of the Academy and they in the upper; sometimes they were in the brick school-house. Finally, however, he settled down with one assistant in this building, where he remained until he left Bristol. He had the charge mainly of the larger and more advanced boys, while his assistants taught the advanced girls, and it happened more than once that his assistant teachers were really conducting a higher grade of school than he himself.

I have by me a copy of one of the earliest committee's reports. It is a very modest affair; a single small sheet of paper folded twice, like a Lilliputian *New York Tribune*, and signed by William Throop, Francis Peck, Thomas Shepard and Zalmon Toby. Judge Throop was "moderator" of the body, according to the custom of that time, having been the first member chosen at town meeting. This report is for the year ending April, 1838, and records an average attendance of 240 scholars in the "Grammar School," from which we may judge that the exact grade of the school was not settled, since this is the same one that is elsewhere known as the "Select School."

In considering this number of scholars, it must be borne in mind that it includes all the school children of the town, there being neither Intermediate nor Primary school in 1838, and, although on account of its great numbers, it was often separated and kept in different places, it was one school.

After disposing of the necessary statistics, the committee present for consideration the opinion that it would be much better that the boys and girls should be accommodated in separate rooms. This state of affairs was brought about to a certain extent, although lack of room prevented a thorough accomplishment of the plan. Still, even when they were in the same room, conversation between them, even upon lessons was so discouraged, and so strict a watch was kept upon them, that they were virtually educated apart from each other. Even as late as Dr. Cooke was at the head of the High School, this theory was acted upon, and the most trifling intercourse interdicted.

This report shows the following teachers: Select School—Mr. Gushee, with two, sometimes three, assistants; Middle District—Hannah B. Church, five months; North District—Miss Cole, five months, Nelson B. Tanner, four months; North East District—Mr. Mason and Mr. Boutelle; Poppasquash—Martha Taylor. The committee's reports were afterwards published with considerable regularity in the *Bristol Phœnix*, until it again began to be customary to issue them in pamphlet form.

In the year 1840, Bennett Munro was delegated to purchase the Academy of Captain James DeWolf. The town had hired part of it from time to time, and although it was unfinished and in anything but good condition, they determined to buy it and fit it up for a public school. Upon Mr. Munro's application for a deed of it, Captain DeWolf presented it to the town. With a number of alterations and additions, it was used by various schools until 1873, when the occupation of the Byfield School, made it of no farther use. It was therefore sold at auction. The belfry was purchased by Bishop Howe, and, surrounded by shrubbery, ornaments the lawn near his house, looking like a small summer house. The building itself was sold in two parts, one of which stands at the corner of High and Franklin streets and the other near the head of Catherine street. Both of them are now dwelling houses. About the time of this purchase of the Academy, primary schools were organized.

There had always been, since there had been any committee at all, a general committee to regulate the affairs of all the schools. But in 1847 they were instructed to allow the North and Middle districts to manage their own affairs, without any reference to those of the South District.

The North District was allowed one committee man and the Middle, two. In 1853 the North District was divided, and a portion of it set off and known thereafter as the Northeast District, and managed by a committee of one. This general arrangement remained in operation until 1864, when the plan of consolidating the interests of the schools by placing them all under the whole committee was resumed and has been retained to the present time. This committee was to consist of nine, three of whom were to retire at the end of their first year, three at the end of the second, and three at the end of the third. The places of those retiring were to be filled by others chosen for a term of three years. The number of these was afterwards increased to fifteen. From the beginning, certain ones have been set apart as an examining committee. This at present consists of five, including the Superintendent, *ex-officio*.

The year 1848 seems to have been a year of exceptional activity in educational matters. No less than four school-houses were in contemplation, with more or less prospect of completion. Byron Diman, Samuel Sparks, Ephraim Gifford and George B. Monro were instructed to procure a lot of land on a long lease, or else to purchase one, on which to erect a one-story wooden school-house large enough to accommodate one hundred scholars. This was to be for the use of the South Primary School, which was at that time holding its sessions in a little building belonging to Governor Byron Diman, near the corner of Hope and Constitution streets. At the same meeting Rowse Potter, William Pearse John Peckham and Hezekiah Wardwell received like instructions with regard to the North Primary School, which was then occupying a small building formerly used as a store, standing in the yard south of Mrs. Ruth Bosworth's house.

Oliver Mason, Elijah Gray and John C. Rich were appointed a committee to erect a one-story wooden school-house in the Northeast District, capable of seating fifty scholars ; and Joseph L. Gardner, William B. Spooner, John Norris and Nathaniel Bullock were commissioned to inquire into the expediency of building a new one in the South District for the more advanced scholars. This last committee reported the project inexpedient for the present, and the matter rested. But with the addition of the School Committee to the committee on building in the South District, and the change in the material of the two school-houses in that district from wood to stone, the other plans were carried out to their accomplishment. These buildings stand, one on the north side of Franklin street, a short distance west of High ; the other on the east side of High street, north of Union. They were erected at an expense of twelve hundred dollars each. That in the Northeast District cost something over three hundred dollars.

The next year, 1849, the School Committee was authorized to elect a Superintendent of Schools and to pay him a salary not exceeding two hundred dollars. Rev. Thomas Shepard was the first to hold this office, and he immediately commenced keeping a quarterly report of the condition of each school. The following is a list of the Superintendents: Rev. Thomas Shepard, 1849–1855; George B. Monro, 1855–1859; Robert S. Andrews, 1859–1862; John N. Burgess, 1862–1864; Robert S. Andrews, 1864–1876.

In this same year of 1849, the following entry was made in the town record:

"*Voted*, That the encouraging condition and prospects of our Public Schools are a source of honest pride and satisfaction, and that we will use every effort consistent with wise legislation and sound judgment, in sustaining them with zeal and fidelity."

Doubtless much of this encouraging condition was due to the fact that three of the schools were then occupying their new quarters.

For a long time some of the more liberal minded of the citizens of Bristol had felt the need of a higher course of study than that pursued in the Grammar School. But the least suggestion of such a thing was met by violent opposition. It was much the same story that is to be found in many newspapers to-day, with this difference, that in addition to the opinion that it is not possible to educate all up to a high standard, and therefore that the many should not be taxed for the benefit of the few, there was an aristocratic feeling on the part of a large number that such an advantage for the mass of the people was an infringement on the privileges—not to say the rights—of the select few. And so the war of words was long and sometimes bitter. But the project had among its supporters three men of culture and influence, whose own liberal education enabled them to appreciate more clearly than most, the influence of a higher system of study, not only upon the students themselves, but also on the general intelligence and cultivation. These were Rev. Thomas Shepard, Rev. James W. Cook and Rev. James Sykes. Supported by the other members of the School Committee, they did valiant service for the cause, and although met on all sides by persistent and unreasoning opposition, they at length won the victory—won it but did not dare to acknowledge that they had.

In the autumn of 1848, the Committee were holding their regular meeting in Mr. Shepard's study. They had debated whether it was possible to establish a High School. There had been expressed a good deal of doubt, both on account of want of means and lack of general friendliness towards the undertaking. All present were strongly in favor of it, yet all were taken by surprise when Mr. William B. Spooner rose and moved that such a school should be organized. The subject was now fairly before them, and although they were frightened almost by the audacity of the scheme, when it came to assume a tangible shape, the motion was seconded and carried without a dissenting voice, and the " Select School " became a fixed fact—the " Select School," for they did not choose to offend the prejudices of the town by calling it the " High School." They were contented for the present with the fact, the name would come all in good time.

The scholars who were to constitute this school were selected from the various schools in the town. They were forty-five in number, and they occupied the lower part of the Academy. The school opened auspiciously, with William E. Jillson at the head. The committee were most fortunate in the selection of this, the first teacher. He was a man of genial disposition, easily accessible, and regarded his pupils as his personal friends. His success was such as to win the admiration of even the enemies of the school. To the extreme regret of the committee and of the school, the connection came to an end in the Fall of 1849. Mr. Jillson was afterwards Assistant Librarian at the Congressional Library, at Washington, and later, Librarian at the Public Library, Boston. He was succeeded by Lafayette Burr, under whom the school went on prosperously something over two years.

In the Spring of 1851, Dr. Nathan B. Cooke was elected to fill the place left vacant by Mr. Burr. Doctor Cooke was a Doctor of Medicine and a minister of the Baptist Society, but owing to an affection of the throat, he was obliged to give up preaching for a number of years ; during which time, the committee were so fortunate as to secure his services. A more faithful, thorough and interested teacher no school ever had. While it was under his charge a systematic plan of study was adopted. This, together with the fact that the school had increased greatly in numbers, rendered an assistant teacher necessary, and created a demand for more room. The Academy was therefore enlarged in 1852, and the school moved up stairs. The east end of the upper part had been separated from the main room by a partition and sliding doors, and was used for a recitation room, and Mary W. Shepard was installed assistant. Not long after, a small sum of money was expended by the committee for philosophical apparatus. For the space of nine years Dr. Cooke remained in the position. At the end of this time, he removed to Newton, Massachusetts, where he taught two years. While there he met Professor Lewis Monroe, the elocutionist, who encouraged him to think that it was possible for him to resume preaching. It had always been a source of deep sorrow to him that he was debarred from following his chosen calling, and upon Professor Monroe's decision, he removed to Leicester to take charge of a parish, and thence to Lonsdale, Rhode Island, where he remained until his death in 1871. His remains were brought to Bristol and laid in Juniper Hill Cemetery.

Upon Dr. Cooke's withdrawal, in 1860, Thomas W. Bicknell, of Barrington, was elected to the office. He remained three years, and then left to accept the principalship of one of the grammar schools of Providence. Henry S. Latham, a most accomplished scholar, succeeded him. At the end of four years, the committee paid Mr. Bicknell the deserved compliment of asking him to become the principal of the school again. He accepted the invitation and remained two years. In 1867, the year of Mr. Bicknell's return, a case of valuable minerals was presented to the school by Mr. Allen J. Gladding, a native of Bristol, residing in California. Mr. Bicknell received the office of Commissioner of Public Schools in 1869, which he retained several years. He is now editor of the *New England Journal of Education*.

In 1869, Frank G. Morley was chosen principal. Although young, he developed a remarkable ability for imparting information and unusual talent for controlling the school. Dr. Shepard used to remark that "the machinery ran easily." He was especially genial in the school-room; in that respect resembling Mr. Jillson more than any other of his predecessors. He spared no pains to make school attractive, believing that if a scholar loved school he would be a better scholar for it. For nearly six years he labored with his whole heart and strength for the school. At the end of this time his health failed, and he sent his resignation to the committee, to take effect at the end of the term. But so rapid were the inroads of disease, that he was forced to leave soon after the middle. He went to Pittsfield, Massachusetts, where he died of consumption at the residence of his father, Rev. J. B. Morley, August 1st, 1875. The following is a copy of the resolutions drawn up by the committee upon the occasion of his leaving:

"*Whereas*, Mr. Frank G. Morley, on account of ill health, necessitating rest from active labor, has tendered his resignation as principal of the High School, to take effect at the close of the present term;

"*Therefore, Resolved*, That we regretfully accept the same, and express our cordial sympathy with him in his affliction.

"*Resolved*, That we bear cheerful testimony to the zeal, fidelity, and success which have characterized his labors in the position which he has held here for the last six years, and we commend him to the sympathy and confidence of any with whom his lot may hereafter be cast.

"*Resolved*, That a copy of these resolutions be sent to Mr. Morley."

During the remainder of the term the school was without a principal. Miss Anna Andrews kindly volunteered her services to the assistant teacher, upon whom the school devolved, which were most gratefully accepted. The summer term of 1875 Charles Fish taught the school, and at the beginning of the fall term he was succeeded by the present principal, Walter F. Marston.

It may be a matter of interest to note, that before the higher course of study was introduced into our schools, all or nearly all of their teachers came from abroad. There was in truth, no one in town capable of filling such a position. But it was not long after the first really advanced school under the Misses Sanderson was organized, before there were more applications from our own townspeople for schools than there were schools for them. At this present time, of the fifteen teachers in the schools of the compact part of the town, with the exception of the principal of the High School, all are former members of the High School, and all but four graduates.

For six months of each year, from 1850 to 1854 inclusive, a school was taught on Poppasquash by Harriet E. Norris. This school was really in the Middle District, but was called the Point Pleasant District School, and was held in a small wooden building which stands upon the road leading to the North Point.

There had always been a prejudice against Latin as a study in the Select School. Where the whole school was an object of distrust, this much-abused study might be expected to receive at least its full share of dislike. The town yielded at length to the popular feeling, and in 1850 instructed the committee in town meeting to exclude it from the school. It was afterwards permitted the principal to teach it, together with Greek, to such as were fitting for college, and gradually it was reinstated and came back to its own. In 1852, the name of the school was changed from "Select" to "High."

In 1851 a school for colored children was opened in a building on Wood street erected for a Methodist Church by the colored people. The town hired this building for this purpose several years. Afterwards the school was held in the Advent Chapel on State street. In 1864, by an act of the State Legislature, this distinction of color in the public schools was abolished. In 1867 the town bought the Advent Chapel for $1,200. It has been in use nearly ever since for a primary school.

In 1853 a Second Grammar school was formed—second only in point of time, however, scholars passing from it immediately to the High School, as from the first. The two schools were quite as often called the North and South Grammar, as the First and Second. The South Grammar was accommodated in the lower part of the Academy. In the autumn of 1856 a junior department of the Grammar School was organized, and held its sessions in the upper east end of the brick schoolhouse. It would seem that this was partially intended to take the place of the Intermediate School, since this was dispensed with during this year. It certainly was inferior in grade to the Grammar School, although it was known as the Branch Grammar. In 1863 its character was somewhat changed, although it remained under the same teacher, and it was known until 1866 as the Ungraded School. Since then it has been reduced to the grade of Third Grammar.

For many reasons it was thought best that the State Normal School should be removed from Providence. Many towns of the State made advantageous offers for its location, Bristol among others. The Congregational Society had lately erected a new church, and several of the proprietors of the former one offered to surrender all their interest in it for the use of the school. A committee, consisting of Byron Diman, W. H. S. Bayley, John Norris, Samuel W. Church, Nathaniel Bullock, Robert Rogers, William B. Spooner and Messadore T. Bennett, was appointed to confer with them and to make all necessary arrangements for the reception of the school. The building in question stood in Bradford street, just east of Hope. The committee bought a lot of land on the north side of Bradford street of Allen T. Usher for which they paid $2,067.50. The building was moved upon this land and the upper part fitted up for the use of the school. It was divided into four rooms, a school-room, with two recitation rooms and a library at the rear. The total expense, including the lot, was $2,496.65. In May, 1858, the committee was discharged and the rooms put in charge of the School Committee. In the same year the General Assembly of the State removed the school to Bristol. Dana P. Colburn was at that time principal. At his death, Joshua Kendall was appointed to fill the office, and in 1862 was elected Chairman of the School Committee. At the end of the summer term of 1863, the schools of the South District were regraded under his superintendence. The primary schools remained unchanged, but in place of the two grammar schools, with two teachers each, three were established with one teacher each, and known as the First, Second and Third. Two Intermediate schools were also organized. In 1870 a third was created. In 1868 the great number of children in the primary schools made another school of that grade necessary, and one was established, known as the Advanced Primary. In 1875 still another was formed. Its sessions are held in the school-house on State street. The schools of the South District are now: one High School, three Grammar, three Intermediate, one Advanced Primary, and four Primary Schools.

Mr. Kendall retained the office of Chairman until his removal to Cambridgeport in 1864, where he still resides, and where he is at the head of a school for training boys for Harvard. With Mr. Kendall's resignation of the principalship of the Normal School, the school came to an end for several years and the rooms which it had occupied were left vacant. The High School at this time was held in the upper rooms of the Academy. In the spring of 1865 the committee decided to place it in Normal Hall, where it remained until its removal to the Byfield Building in 1873.

In 1859, by vote take in town meeting, the particular course of study to be pursued in the different schools, was left to the discretion of the committee. In 1862 Dr. Shepard, who for twenty-five years had been an active member of this body, sent into town meeting a message declining a re-election. Once before, in 1849, he had sent a similar message, but had, at the urgent solicitation of the town through a committee appointed for that purpose, consented to remain. The town, therefore, at this time, felt compelled, however unwilling, to accept his decision. John B. Munro, Charles Sherry and James DeWolf Perry were instructed to frame a set of resolutions expressive of regret at his withdrawal and of appreciation of his services in behalf of education. They reported the following:

"*Whereas*, Thomas Shepard, D. D., having in a written communication to the electors of Bristol, declined being a candidate for re-election to the School Committee; and

"*Whereas*, He has served actively and faithfully for a term of twenty-five years in that capacity;

Therefore, Resolved, That the citizens hereby express their grateful appreciation of his services, and regret that he feels compelled to withdraw from a field of duty which he he had so long, ably and acceptably occupied.

"*Resolved*, That these resolutions be entered on the Records of the Town, and a copy be presented to the Rev. Dr. Shepard, and that the same be published in the *Bristol Phenix*.

JOHN B. MUNRO,
J. D'W PERRY, *Committee.*"
CHARLES SHERRY, JR.,

Dr. Shepard's interest in the schools remained the same, notwithstanding his withdrawal from the committee, and in 1867, under great pressure, he was again induced to accept an election to that body. He remained a member of it two years, doing a great deal of work in the way of visiting schools—much more indeed than during any previous time of the same length. In 1869 he retired finally.

It is impossible to estimate too highly Dr. Shepard's influence upon the public schools and the interests of education generally in the town. It is rare that a man remains long in a position, at once so laborious, responsible and thankless as that of an active member of a school committee. Yet for nearly thirty years Dr. Shepard was on this committee, sometimes as Superintendent, sometimes as Chairman, sometimes with no office at all, but always foremost in every good work and word for the schools. For more than a quarter of a century they had his cordial personal support and the benefit of his large experience, sound wisdom and reliable judgment. He found a single school, impeded in its work by lack of a well regulated plan of operations; he left a system of schools that do honor to him.

Mr. Gushee, of the First Grammar School, was succeeded by Mr. E. Rich. He had previously taught in the North District, and also in the Second Grammar School. In all he taught seventeen years, with one or two short intervals of rest on account of delicate health. During one of these intervals, the first term of 1856, the two schools were consolidated under the care of Aaron Porter, the teacher of the Second Grammar School. Mr. Rich's health forced him to leave altogether in 1867. Upon his resignation the town passed the following resolution:

"*Whereas*, The citizens of the Town of Bristol, in town meeting assembled, have heard with deep regret of the resignation of Mr. E. Rich as teacher of one of our schools, on account of failing health;

"*Therefore, Resolved*, That the citizens of the town do hereby tender to Mr. Rich a vote of thanks for the very faithful and earnest services he has rendered the town during seventeen years of labor as a teacher."

At a committee meeting held in October, 1871, the subject of evening schools was considered, and it was decided to be most desirable that two such schools should be established, one for boys and one for girls. On the 6th of November these schools commenced their sessions, the boys' school in the school-house on State street, under Henry C. Sayles and Hattie Frisbie, and the girls' school in the brick school-house, under H. Augusta Coggeshall and Annie P. Waldron. More teachers were soon needed, and sometimes as many as six have been employed at once.

These schools have been held regularly every winter since. The sessions last from seven to nine, and are held four evenings in the week, for five months of the year. This is a much longer term than is common in schools of this kind, three months being the usual time. No children under twelve years of age are admitted, except under peculiar circumstances; the theory being that up to that age they are not in any of the factories and are in some of the day schools—a theory which, like a great many others, is not wholly sustained by facts. These scholars are mostly operatives in the manufacturing establishments of the town, and considering the disadvantages of the long interval of seven months between two successive terms, their progress in some instances has been very gratifying. This is especially true of the advanced classes of young men of 1872–'73–'74. The studies pursued are Arithmetic, Reading and Spelling. Oral instruction in Geography is given, and the advanced class studied English and American history, higher Arithmetic and Algebra.

As long ago as 1848 the subject of a new school-house, to be situated on the Common was discussed, and the town went so far as to appoint a Committee to inquire into the expediency of building one. They reported unfavorably to the project. Since that time the subject has come up several times in a desultory way. But it was not until 1871, that the citizens of Bristol really girded themselves up for the undertaking. At a town meeting held on the 18th of March of that year Mr. William J. Miller, after some discussion, introduced the following resolution which was passed unanimously:

"*Resolved*, That there is urgent need of more and improved accommodations for the public schools of this town."

In consequence of the passage of this resolution, the School Committee were appointed a special committee to take the subject into consideration, to ascertain the condition of the school buildings and to report upon the advisability of erecting a new building centrally located, and capable of accommodating all the schools in the compact part of the town, together with an estimate of the probable expense of the same, and such other suggestions as might be of interest in the premises, and report at the town meeting to be held on the first Wednesday of the following month.

On the 5th of April this committee, in the person of the Chairman, Rev. George L. Locke, reported to the following effect: That after thorough consideration and careful investigation, they were forced to say that the condition of the school buildings of the town was far from what they could wish; that the High School was the most favorably situated, having large, airy and well lighted rooms, but that its location was objectionable on account of the Town Hall below, and that any plan for a new school building should include this school; that the three primary school-houses, although by no means all that could be desired, were not as bad as the remaining two; that these—the old brick school-house and the Academy—were too far gone to be put into proper repair; besides this, that they were badly defaced by scratches and coarse figures cut either by the scholars or by outside loungers. The committee submitted that not only the taste, but also the morals of the pupils, must be lowered by continual contact with such coarseness, and while they were far from advocating needless expenditure, they believed that a judiciously liberal sum expended on a new school-house would be better for the health, the minds and the morals of the pupils and the town generally.

The report was long, exhaustive and very carefully prepared, and met the approbation of those assembled to hear it. A sub-committee of five had been appointed to inquire into the expenses of such a building as was required. They visited and carefully examined school buildings in Providence, Fall River and Newport, and finally decided that, all things considered, the Coddington School-house, in Newport, most nearly met their needs. They would have liked to recommend a two-story brick building with a French roof, but decided that three stories were needed, as they wished to put the Primary School into it. They recommended that a brick building containing twelve rooms and a hall, on the general plan of the Coddington School-house, be immediately erected on the southwest corner of the Common, and asked for an appropriation of $40,000 for the purpose.

The town, in special town meeting, voted the amount asked for, $40,000, though not without considerable opposition. The opponents of the measure offered a resolution for a special tax to be levied, covering the whole amount of the appropriation, and that it be assessed previously to June 6th, 1871, and payable on October 1st of the same year. This, the friends of the new school-house, readily accepted, and the resolution was adopted. A Building Committee consisting of five citizens was elected, and things seemed to be in train now for a new school-house speedily. But the affair was not yet settled beyond a peradventure. The opposition, taking advantage of their own proposition, used the fact of the large special tax that was to be levied upon the tax-payers, to increase the discontent, and at a special town meeting, held April 22d, rescinded the vote, and discharged the committee.

The friends of education were too thoroughly in earnest to let the matter rest here. They were satisfied that a large majority of the tax-payers of the town were in favor of the new school-house, and they took prompt measures by the circulation of a petition for another special town meeting, to show this. This meeting was held on the 6th of June, and a resolution was adopted to appropriate $25,000 for the erection of a new school building, two-stories high, with a French roof, to be paid for in not less than five years. James Lawless, John R. Slade, Solon H. Smith, John B. Munro, William H. West, James M. Gifford and Alfred Pierce were chosen as a Building Committee. The Town Treasurer was instructed to hire money from time to time on the town's notes, to meet their requisitions. The armory (formerly the Methodist Meeting House) now occupied by the Light Infantry, was removed as soon as possible, in order that work might commence at once. The plan submitted by C. T. Emerson, architect, of Lawrence, Massachusetts, was adopted, and proposals for contract received. That of J. W. Osgood, of Pawtucket, was accepted, being in all respects the most favorable; but before commencing operations, the committee were obliged to ask a farther appropriation of $15,000, making the sum forty thousand, as originally proposed. This was granted, and obtained on the same terms as the first appropriation. The furnishing of the building cost $4,700 additional. On the 30th of August, 1873, the first day of the Fall term, the schools which were to hold their sessions in it, moved into their respective rooms. These were the High School, the three Grammar, the three Intermediate Schools and the Advanced Primary School. The building was formally dedicated to school purposes Saturday, September 6th, 1873. The following account of the dedication services is taken from the Superintendent's report for 1873:

"Saturday morning at eleven o'clock, September the 6th, the exercises commenced by an introductory address by R. S. Andrews, Chairman of the Committee of Arrangements, after which the 'Jubilate Deo,' was chanted by a select choir.

"Selections from Scripture were read by Rev. H. M. Jones; Dedicatory prayer, by Rev. James P. Lane; address and delivery of the keys by Captain James Lawless, Chairman of the Building Committee; response by Rev. George L. Locke, Chairman of School Committee; an address by Rev. Thomas Shepard, D. D.

A fine portrait of Col. Nathaniel Byfield was then unveiled. As no mention of this was found upon the programme, William J. Miller, Esq., was called upon for an explanation. Mr. Miller, after speaking of the character of Judge Byfield and stating why it was eminently proper to call the building the 'Byfield School,' stated that after seeing the original painting in the house of the Hon. Francis Brinley, in Newport, he thought it very desirable to have a copy placed in the new school-house. A few citizens of Bristol contributed the necessary amount and the work was accomplished.

"Addresses were made by Gen. Ambrose E. Burnside, formerly of this town, and Hon. Francis Brinley, of Newport, a descendant of Judge Byfield. 'America' was then sung by the choir and by the audience. Right Rev. M. A. D'W. Howe, D. D., of Pennsylvania, a native of Bristol, made an interesting address. The Bishop was followed by Hon. T. W. Bicknell, Commissioner of Public Schools.

"The 'Dedication Ode,' written for this occasion by Right Rev. Dr. Howe, was then sung:

"DEDICATION ODE.

" When first upon this rock-bound strand
  Our pilgrim fathers made their home,
Beside their huts with pious hand
  They built for prayer an humble dome.

Soon in the forest-clearing rose
  The Village School of logs unhewn,
The roof was green with hemlock boughs,
  Through creviced wall the light was strewn.

The fathers toiled and fought by turns
  To break the soil—repel the foe;—
Th' heroic fire that inly burns,
  Was fanned to flame that roof below.

The House of Prayer, the Village School,
  These were the muniments of power,
The strength to hold—the skill to rule,
  Were drawn from these in needful hour.

O, shades of holy men and brave,
  Whose dust lies buried round these walls—
Wake from your tranquill rest we crave,
  And hover o'er these votive halls.

The full-grown Village School behold,
  Planted in faith by works displayed!
Your logs have sprouted, and we hold
  Our festal day beneath their shade.

Come, thronging generations, come,
  Here gird your souls for generous strife,
Beneath this roof find Learning's home,
  And near it seek the Tree of Life!

God of our Fathers, still maintain
  The heritage their prowess gave!
Churches and Schools henceforth remain
  Th' armories of the free and brave!

"Addresses were afterwards made by Professor J. Lewis Diman, D. D., of Brown University, and by His Honor Lieutenant-Governor Van Zandt.

"The Doxology was then sung, and Rev. William T. Harlow pronounced the Benediction.

"Messrs. R. S. Andrews, George L. Locke, and John B. Munro were the Committee of Arrangements.

"The day was remarkably fine; the large hall was completely filled with an attentive and an intelligent audience, and the exercises proved of an interesting character. One of the most pleasing incidents of the occasion was the vigorous, earnest and appropriate address of the venerable Thomas Shepard, D. D., to whose watchful care, judicious management and deep interest, during the last thirty-five years, the Public Schools of Bristol are largely indebted for whatever merit they possess.

"The opening of the Byfield School-House was considered extremely propitious by those who were present at the Dedication exercises.

"For the Committee,—
"R. S. ANDREWS, *Superintendent.*"

At the same time that the schools moved into the new school-house, the Centre Primary School was removed from State street to the brick school-house. On the 8th of December, the committee for the first time held their meeting in the Superintendent's office. They had been in the habit for many years, of using the Town Council's room for their meetings. Mr. William J. Miller announced that a portrait of Dr. Shepard had been presented to the school. It hangs in the hall, on the east side, near the stage. It was painted by Miss Jane Stuart, of Newport, who also painted the Byfield portrait. She is the daughter of Gilbert Stuart, so renowned as the painter of the portraits of WASHINGTON.

The Town Treasurer's report for this year, 1873, shows the following condition of the school funds:

Fifteen shares Bank of Bristol..$75 00
Thirty-eight shares Commercial Bank........................ Value unknown.
Savings Bank 628 00
Town Treasurer's note... 750 00

Bristol now comprises three school districts: the Northeast, containing one school; the Middle, containing one; and the South, containing twelve. The whole number of scholars is 766; of schools 14; of teachers 18. The following is the list of the committee under whose control the schools are: Rev. George L. Locke, Chairman; Rev. James P. Lane, Rev. Howard M. Jones, Rev. Charles J. Rogers; Robert S. Andrews, Superintendent; Isaac F. Williams, William J. Miller, John B. Munro, Jonathan D. Waldron, John Turner, Lemuel A. Bishop, LeBaron Bradford, William Kimball, William Manchester, Seth W. Thayer.

BURRILLVILLE.

BY REV. WILLIAM FITZ.

SUPERINTENDENT.

THIS town is seventy years old, the act incorporating it having passed in the year 1806. By a line drawn from east to west through the middle of the town of Glocester that town was divided; the southern half retaining its original name, and the northern half taking the name which it now bears, to the perpetuating of the memory of Hon. James Burrill, who after serving his native State of Rhode Island at the bar, on the bench, in the General Assembly and in the Senate of the United States, closed his earthly life in 1820.

In the year 1799 a memorial respecting the "establishment of Free Schools throughout the State," was presented to the Legislature by its author, John Howland Esq., of Providence. The Legislature referred the subject to a Committee, who reported a bill at the October session of the same year. "This bill," says Mr. Howland, "embodying a general school system, was drawn up by James Burrill, Jr., Attorney General of the State." Here in this scrap of history Burrillville is united with the cause and patrons of public education, and she is thus placed under an historical, as well as other bonds, to maintain the union.

That there were schools within the territory which took the Attorney General's name, previous to the division, is probable. The earliest date at which any school-house was built was the year of the division, 1806. Other houses were doubtless erected about that time, though the *exact* date does not appear. Within eight or ten years after, a few other school-buildings were put up, of whose history we have obtained some facts, though by no means so many as to make anything like a complete record. Some schools in the earlier history of the town were held in dwellings, corn-cribs and shops. Quite a number of the older citizens attended such schools, traveling miles in some instances in order to "read, spell and cipher."

Some of these citizens too, incline to the opinion that those days of "doing the chores and going to school" two or three months only in a year, were better than the present, because of the physical exercise necessarily required, and the closer application of mind to the fewer studies. A few dwellings in which schools were kept are standing today, and the sites of others are pointed out. Hon. John Walling of Pascoag, now of more than four-score years, went as a scholar to a school kept in the house of Welcome Sayles, Esq., situated east of the Pascoag Reservoir, and near the dividing line of the town. Into that school-room the woman of the establishment would come once a week, in school time, to do the baking for her family in the long brick oven, built by the side of the ten-feet wide fire-place. The scene thus pictured for us, may be looked upon as a specimen of the olden time.

There were also "Proprietors' Schools" in buildings used for school purposes only, and owned by one person or by several persons of a neighborhood, in whom dwelt, and by whom were exercised, all the rights and powers of Commissioner, Superintendent, Committee and Trustee. But with the growth of the idea that every child in a community should be aided freely in the elementary principles of a thorough education, these limited opportunities of instruction disappeared, as but ripples on the Lake Superior of our Public School system. In certain districts there were nevertheless what were called *free*-schools, but they were made such through the enlightened liberality of the districts, rather than by conformity with the laws of the State enacted as early as 1800 and re-enacted with revisions in 1828, 1839 and 1845.

Nothing relating to schools appears upon the records of the town until the year 1828. At the June town meeting of that year, two Committees were chosen. One, consisting of twenty-three men for dividing the town into districts. Another of twenty-one (the largest number allowed by the act of the Legislature passed in the same year) to constitute the School Committee. September 8th, 1828 town appropriated for schools $300. Money received from the State in 1828, $199.80. The Committee were authorized to make alterations in any dissatisfied district, "the expense to be borne by the district that complains." "Voted that James Paine's house be a bound in district No. 8, and said Paine has his liberty to go where he pleases." Eleven school-houses with schools in all, in winter, only one kept all the year, were reported.

Number of inhabitants in 1828, 2,164. In the following year, 1829, sixteen persons were elected as School Committee, and the same number was annually chosen until the year 1846, when the number was reduced to six. From 1847 to the present time, the number has been three. The yearly appropriation for schools by the town from 1828 to 1846 inclusive, was $300. In 1847 one hundred dollars was added. In November, 1846, the Committee were authorized " so to divide the districts as not to divide any man's home farm," and the home farms were included with the houses in the several districts. In June 1847, the working Committee of six reported : 500 copies of the report were ordered printed, and the Committee were allowed " one dollar a day for their services the past year." This Committee was a favored one. No record of any allowance for the Committee appears again until 1855, when they were allowed " one dollar a day and the expense of visiting the schools." In the same year the town appropriated as in the year preceeding $600. From 1847 to 1857 the reports of School Committees were "read, accepted, and ordered to be filed." Since 1857 they have been printed each year. To Francis H. Inman, Esq., of Worcester, the writer of the first printed report, whose father was a member of the Committee of 1828, we owe the pleasure of its perusal. Among the good things in it we extract the following :

"Although the Committee have found many things not as they would wish in the schools, and the place they occupy in the feelings of the people; yet there are some redeeming qualities which have come to light during the past year. Among these they would mention, as not the least, the increased sobriety and consequent industry of the people. By the returns they see that all the schools have been visited much more frequently than heretofore. The increase of the school-fund from the town of one hundred dollars is also a move in the right direction."

DISTRICT NO. 1.

A more extended investigation than has been made for this paper, might have revealed the location of the *first* school-house in town. It may have been in District No. 1, known as the " White School House," from the color of its paint. Just in front of the present house, in this District, there stood on the "Commons," surrounded by the highway, a one story house, of antique architecture, and old fashioned arrangements ; its seats on three sides, and an open fire-place. This served until 1823, when the one-story having been raised up, a lower was added, and a house with two-stories, a belfry and steeple was dedicated both to sound learning and the worship of God. Then and there, surely, religion and learning were joined together. The citizens of the district were assisted, says Mr. H. A. Keach, the author of " Burrillville as it was and as it is," by Nicholas Brown, Esq., of Providence.

"He gave the glass and nails, the cash articles, for the White School House." Here taught in their turn, and in their own way, several citizens of the town who are now living, together with others who have passed away. Among these were Rufus Smith and his son Jarvis, afterward a physician in Chepachet. Of this man we learn that he was much esteemed. Though enforcing his authority in school by a liberal use of the ferule, yet he would play ball with the scholars when study time was over. Israel Tucker, Charles Mowry and Miss Betsey Brown also directed the minds of the youth who gathered there. "My first school," says Miss Brown, "was taught in the White School House, in the summer of 1840. This building, besides being used for a meeting-house, also contained the Burrillville Library; teachers were not then required to pass an examination, or have a certificate. I think that the Trustee was the only school officer, and there was no law requiring him to visit the school, consequently it was not officially visited during the term. My pay was one dollar and a half a week, and board round." The library thus brought to notice is further described by Mr. H. A. Keach, who himself taught in this district, as did also his father, Eddy Keach, Esq.: "In 1823, the farmers collected a library of three hundred volumes. Rufus Smith was the first librarian. For a while it was kept at his hotel, which was the old red house in the corner of the roads near the Tar Kiln Saw Mill. It was afterwards kept at the Smith Academy (or the school-house), and finally removed to the dwelling of Coomer Smith, who for many years had it in charge. In 1845 it was divided, and the shareholders took the books to their homes." This school-house, library, academy and meeting-house combined, was at length removed. The house now used for a school, is located on a spacious lot, bounded on *one* side only by the highway. It was erected and occupied in 1863 at a cost of $760. Whole number of scholars in 1847 was 42, average attendance, 28; whole number of scholars in 1875. 28, average attendance, 23.

Had the Democratic prox of 1876 been successful, the town would have been related to another Attorney General of the State, in the person of Oscar Lapham, Esq., a native of this town, and a former teacher in District No. 1.

District No. 2.

This District, called the "Mount Pleasant," probably because of its elevated situation, pleasantly overlooking the village of Slatersville, is in the eastern part of the town. The school-house formerly stood on the "commons." The School Committee in their report for 1857 say: "The location of the school-house, with a highway on four sides of it and no play-grounds, is decidedly bad." In 1858 they say "the benches ought to 'front face' to the teacher." In 1860 they felt compelled to state that "the highway still surrounds the school-house, occupying the play-grounds which the scholars ought to enjoy. Some unsuccessful efforts have been made to remedy this evil. If nothing better can be done, the Committee respectfully recommend that prompt and efficient means be taken *to move the highway from the house.*" In 1866 the district voted both to move and repair the house.

The Committee of 1867 say: "In No. 2 a most excellent work has been accomplished. The school-house has been removed from the highway, and placed on a pleasant site surrounded with a substantial and ornamental fence. The inside of the building has been entirely remodeled, and furnished with seats and desks for the pupils, and also for the teacher's platform, made after the latest and most approved pattern. Large blackboards and convenient recitation seats have been supplied. The exterior of the building has also been repaired, repainted and furnished with blinds, making it an ornament to the district." More recent efforts have further contributed to make this a neat and well furnished school-house. It is the only one ever owned by the district.

Here excellent teachers have labored. One of them who taught twenty-five years ago, was such a strict disciplinarian that having two large boys to punish he procured a large hickory stick, and ordering the offending parties to join hands through the elevated oven of the stove, which was heated several times hotter than usual, he stood by with uplifted hickory, threatening its use if they unclasped. Thus were they *melted* into penitence. Whole number in 1847 was 21, average 13; whole number in 1875 was 14, average 7; size of house 20x20, 11 feet high in the arch.

District No. 3.

The district which first bore this number was known as the "Eston," the house belonging to it standing in the vicinity of "Cripple Corner." This house is still standing, though it is as old as the town itself, having been built in 1806. The dimensions are 18x18, 8 feet high. The internal arrangements were of the old style. In 1847 (though we sincerely wish we had its history previously) the whole number of pupils was 48, average 30. In the winter of 1848–9, we find William A. Mowry, then 19 years of age, teaching in this school, having 31 pupils, 20 boys, 11 girls. He showed their "young ideas how to shoot" through the alphabet, spelling, reading, geography, grammar, mental and written arithmetic, penmanship, book-keeping, algebra, natural philosophy, compositions and declamation, showing plainly that he was even then possessed of many and varied attainments.

He reported the house as "ventilated in *every* part." Mr. Mowry was from Uxbridge, Massachusetts. One of his sisters, who, in the report of 1857, is called "a teacher of experience and good attainments," taught in this district. For several years the teachers came mostly from the same, or adjoining towns in Massachusetts. Mr. M. L. Esten gave "*perfect satisfaction* for several terms," though he was a native of Burrillville. In years subsequent to 1860 there was a rapid decrease in attendance, so that in 1863 the whole number was 20, the average 8. 1864, total 15, average 7.

In 1867 the house needed thorough repairing. In 1868 the committee briefly state that it "needs some repair and should be remodeled." Total for the same year, for the Summer term, 17, average 6 ; for the Winter term, whole number, 6, average, 2. The next Winter, 1868, the average attendance was only *one*, and the Committee thought it advisable to discontinue the district.

In 1871, No. 3 was given to District No. 16, known as the "Nasonville," which number it still has. Reviewing the history previous to the erection of the present school building, we learn that schools were kept in private houses and shops. One building used for a school was consumed by fire thirty-five years ago. James O. Inman, Esq., went to school in this village, since which time he has taught school as well as acquired the enviable reputation of manufacturing *all wool* goods of a superior quality. Here too, we believe, Mr. Mowry taught his *first* school, in a room which he describes as 22x12 and 8 feet high with five long desks and benches for smaller scholars, having registered 53, with an average daily attendance of 35. He was not then teaching such a variety of studies as we afterwards found him engaged in, for his term *here* ran from December 6th, 1847 to April 7th, 1848, and in the other district through the winter of 1848-9. *Here*, he had in money, $12 a month, *there*, $15, and perhaps felt that he could afford to teach three more branches, for the extra three dollars. The size of the blackboard in each place was 3x3½ feet. It may encourage youthful and aspiring teachers to know that Mr. Mowry did not attain eminence without some *crying* as well as trying, and the tears which he shed over the dullness and demerits of his pupils, are carefully bottled in their memories.

For the following, Mr. Mowry merits and will please accept, our hearty, thanks.

PROVIDENCE, April 1, 1876.

REV. WM. FITZ, *Superintendent Public Schools:*

DEAR SIR:—You ask me to give you some reminiscences of my teaching in Burrillville.

I have a vivid recollection of my first crude attempts at teaching school, of my inexperience, and ignorance of methods, but of honest purpose and earnest desire to do my best, and to win success by deserving it.

My first school was at Mohegan in the winter of 1847-8. I had been encouraged by my teacher, Alexander Meggett, Esq., now of Wisconsin, to "*keep school.*" In accordance with his suggestion, I made application in November 1847, in several districts of that vicinity, but in most of them found that the "master" had already been "hired." Failing elsewhere I applied to Mr. Isaac Walling, the Trustee in the district which comprised Nasonville and Mohegan. I gave him my references, and he was to inform me of his decision. A few days later he called at the school-house where I was a pupil, in Slatersville, and said that he had concluded to give me a trial. The school was to commence on the "Monday after Thanksgiving," according to custom. I was to have $12.00 a month and board.

On the morning to begin I presented myself at the school-house in Mohegan, armed with my "certificate of approbation," signed by Rev. Mr. Lord and Lyman Copeland, Esq.

The school was a large one, numbering over fifty, and was kept in a room in Mr. Harvey Thayer's house, just over his boot shop. Imagine a school of that number, of all ages from four to twenty, in all studies, and in all parts of the several books, from a large class in A B C's to parsing, cube root, and history; packed into a room 11×22 feet, and about 7 feet high, over a shop where a *deaf and dumb man made boots.* There was one good thing about the arrangement. We could not disturb him by our noise.

There, with temporary long desks and plank seats, we labored with the utmost fidelity—teacher and scholars—through the long winter term of sixteen weeks.

General good feeling prevailed between pupils and teacher, and I have often thought, that in spite of my youth and inexperience, it was the best school I ever kept. We worked *hard.* We cyphered through the rule of three, square and cube root, we bounded every country on the globe, we attended spelling schools, speaking schools and parties, indulged in sliding, snow balling and skating. The pupils tried to give the "master" a "sum" that he could not "do," and in turn the teacher would try to find words that the big girls and boys could not spell and conundrums that they could not guess. I was but eighteen, not large, wore a cap and a circular cloak.

As I passed through the village on my way to the school-house the first morning of the school, some one who saw me, remarked to the Trustee: "Is that *boy* going to keep our school? *He* never will succeed." It was very gratifying, however, when the Trustee told me the circumstance at the close of the four months' term, in the spring, to hear him emphatically say: "But nobody says anything about the *boy* now. Everybody says it is the best school we ever had."

I boarded through the winter at Mr. George Walling's, in the old house, at what was known as "Cripple Corner." It was a pleasant family and a good home.

The following winter I taught the school in the "Esten Neighborhood," the district adjoining.

The school-house was an old one, having been built, I think, in 1806. On the west side was the entry, the great chimney and the clothes closet. On each of the other sides was a long desk, reaching the whole length of the room, with a seat behind it, the wall forming the back, and a low seat in front, for the little children. The seats were two inch chestnut plank, as black, and some portions as smooth, as polished ebony.

The stove stood in the centre of the floor. When one wished to leave his seat, he must jump over the desk, or make all the others between him and the end of the seat move out to let him pass.

There was a black-board nearly two feet wide and three feet long. The teacher's desk was perhaps a foot wide and eighteen inches long, and was nailed up against the wall.

Windows, with no curtains, let in the light on the three sides, and the sun aided the fire in the stove in keeping the room warm. This was quite necessary on account of the generous provision for ventilation. Many holes and large cracks were visible in the floor, and as the underpinning on either side was quite open there was always a good draft of air upward through the floor. There were holes also in the sides of the building, especially along the edge of the seat next the wall. And there were openings in the ceilings above, giving a good draft when you did not want it.

The school was not as large as that at Mohegan, but numbered, if I remember rightly, about thirty. The scholars were of a very respectable class, generally intelligent, coming from families of sober, honest, New England yeomanry of the old stock. The descendants of Hon. John Esten, formerly judge of the old time court, formed a majority of the families and the scholars.

The history of this district furnishes a striking illustration of the change that has come over New England during the last twenty-five or thirty years.

Of the children of Hon. John Esten, the following settled on farms, either upon, or adjoining, the old homestead, and there passed their days, died and were buried, only one of them, I think, being alive at the present time: John, Jr., Benjamin, Buffum, and Amasa. I cannot now recall a single family in the district at that time, whose parents did not live in that immediate vicinity; showing the general disposition in those days to remain near the old homestead and to follow farming. Now nearly all of the children of these four sterling men have gone away, to the east and the west, to the factory villages or the cities, and are engaged in the various callings and professions of life. Among them may be found teachers, doctors, merchants, manufacturers, mechanics. etc., but *very few* of them are cultivating the land; while the old school district, which forty years ago numbered between forty and fifty scholars in school, I understand is now abolished, there being only three or four children of proper school age in its borders.

After finishing the long term of four months in this school, during which time I "boarded around," and became well acquainted with the families of the district, and receiving my salary, $15.00 a month; I was invited to "keep out," *i. e.*, to finish the term in the Mohegan district; the master whom they had hired not having been able to carry on the school, by reason of the superior physical strength of some of the larger and older boys. I accepted the offer, and finished the school, "keeping out" the money. Here, also, I boarded around, to make the money last the longer. When the money was expended, I remained through the spring and into the early summer, keeping a private school and receiving 10 cents a week tuition for the younger pupils and, I believe, 16⅔ cents a week for the older ones. During the summer and fall following I taught in the Mount Pleasant District—a very agreeable school, though smaller than either of the others and consisting of a younger set of pupils. This completed my experience in the schools of Burrillville.

In those days there were but *very* few foreigners in the rural districts, nearly all the families being of the good old sturdy class so well known as the New England yeomanry. A single winter following the experience above mentioned, completed my teaching in district schools, but rarely have ever I met more earnest minds, or witnessed greater progress than among those boys and girls of the three north-eastern districts of Burrillville.

Very respectfully,
WILLIAM A. MOWRY.

In consideration of his " desire to assist in diffusing the benefits of a good common school education among the inhabitants " of this district, Leonard Nason, Esq., deeded to them a lot of land for a school-house in December, 1849. There is a tradition that he also contracted to build the house for a stated price. He built larger than the specifications required, intending to donate what was in excess of the contract. But the district would not accept the gratuitous enlargement, wherewith Mr. Nason proceeded to tear it down, confining himself strictly to the dimensions of the contract. *He* would, but *they* would not. The present house in the district, which is the one he built, was completed in 1850 at an expense of $800 or $1,000. In the winter of 1852–3, J. O. Inman taught for $18 a month, boarding around; pupils, 45 — average, 37. Report of School Committee for 1857 refers to removals from the district as lessening the attendance at school. Parents declared themselves satisfied with the school and therefore did not visit it. Mr. Thomas B. Staples, of this town, taught successfully in 1858–9. " The district is in possession of a very good house. Its location is pleasant and its internal arrangements very convenient." 1862.—" The morals of the pupils were sadly neglected." " It has been intimated to the Committee that the parents in this district objected to having their children properly corrected; if so, the blame is not wholly with the teacher." 1864.—Ellen M. Steere, " one of our good teachers." 1867.—Summer school; whole number, 96—average, 56 ; "the house will soon need enlarging to accommodate a graded school." 1872.—The number not so large since 1870. Mrs Ellen M. Walling had been employed for two years ; Committee speak in her praise and regret that she was to retire from her profession. 1873.—Committee announce death of Mr. George D. Colwell, " one of our most promising teachers," who taught a spring term. 1874.—Winter term taught by Miss Dora Walling. Whole number, 33.

District No. 4.

Formerly called " Newell's Mills," there being a grist mill here at the time; subsequently it was the " Hines " district, now " Glendale." In 1814 Mrs. Lydia Brown taught there, being then eighteen, and now eighty years of age, yet still bright, active and good. She states that on the last day of her school the parents, being duly notified, came together at the school-house to pay her for her services. She received in money, eight shillings a week, her daughter Betsey, of whom we have already spoken, received only one shilling more in 1840. How much to be preferred was the custom of that day than that other method, which compels one to collect his own salary. The return for 1848 describes as follows : " Date when school-house was built?" "not known." "First cost?" " do." "Arrangement of seats?" " on the most approved plan." " Play ground?" " the highway." " Size of school-room?" " 20 x 20, 13 feet high."

The returns for 1847 and 1849 differ from this, as also from each other in the height, one giving 11 feet, the other 12 feet. The reporter for 1856 disagrees still further, giving size of room 19x19, 8 feet high. The same in answer to the question, when the house was built, says, " I should think in the year 1." How ventilated? " By cracks and other open places." It remained, however, for the writer of the Committee's report for 1857 (the next printed after 1847), which writer was undoubtedly Doctor S. O. Griffin, to convey to coming generations the most graphic description of the place where the school was held : " Both terms were taught by Miss Mary R. Sayles," (afterwards Mrs. J. L. Phillips, having already, 1876, served ten years as a Christian Missionary in India, but just now in this country,) " who performed her part in a very satisfactory manner. Her mode of discipline was good, and she manifested a readiness to teach, a thoroughness and degree of ease in imparting instruction, seldom excelled. The scholars, too, were active, well disposed and made very respectable proficiency in their studies. But when we consider the place where the school was kept, we are utterly at a loss to understand how teacher or scholars did anything at all. It is a little '7 by 9' structure, jutting into the lots from the road side, forming a very respectable rod of fence to the highway, presenting the appearance of a necessary appendage to its neighbor opposite, with capacity inadequate to the accommodation of ten scholars, and not a foot of play-ground not liable to be encroached upon at any moment by whatever may travel the road; in short, minus all the attractions that ought to grace a modern school-house, and in this sad plight, set apart as a fit place to educate fifty-two human beings." Mrs. Phillips also mentions a time when, on account of water which had risen over the floor of the school-room, herself and pupils were obliged to circumnavigate on the benches and desks. Mrs. Martha Wilcox also taught in 1847. In other districts of the town, also, this lady performed efficient services as a teacher. Mr. S. B. Keach, in 1854, at 18 years of age, was an instructor there. Since then he has obtained a good report in the world of letters, and his flag, bearing the motto, "The friend of all—the servant of none," floats for the *special* protection of the Prohibitory party, over " Town and Country." From the report of the Committee, 1858, we learn that the house was condemned in July of the preceding year. The vote, however, was revoked, on account of the financial crisis, in the hope that a more commodious house could be secured in more prosperous times. In 1859, there was a "proposition to form a new district from the villages of Plainville and Oakland and their immediate surroundings."

In 1860, the Committee say: "In our last annual report we alluded to the action of the Committee in relation to the division of the district. That decision was appealed from by the district, and overruled by the State Commissioner. Under the present state of affairs the district is erecting a new house, centrally located, sufficient for all the pupils and in every respect creditable to all concerned." In 1861, this district had erected "a beautiful and commodious house." Whole number, 99; average attendance, 70. This is the house which is being used by the district now. The "Patriarch," against which so many shots were fired, still stands on the original site, having been converted into a dwelling house. Within three years the present school-house has been well repaired and painted. In 1867, an enlargement was thought of, in order to establish a graded school, the whole number being 82, average, 51.

In 1868, the district was divided by the Committee, an appeal was taken, and the Committee sustained by the Commissioner. There was no public school in the district this year, the house being let for a private school. The voters being dissatisfied with the decision of the Com-

MAPLEVILLE DISTRICT. 321

missioner, applied to the Court. In 1870, the report says: "We are gratified that a final decision has been reached on the appeal of parties in District No. 4, which settles so far as judicial authority can, the questions involved in the division of that district. This decision harmonizes with that previously given by the Commissioner, and sustains the action of the Committee." The Committee opened a school in No. 4, May 31, 1869, which was continued during the year. Since 1870, though the attendance has not been as large as previous to the division, yet the facilities for an education have been regularly furnished.

DISTRICT NO. 5.

This is the "Mapleville" District, once called the "Friends," because the Friends' meeting-house is situated within its boundaries. The original school-house is still standing, altered and used as a dwelling. From what date this building was used does not appear exactly, though the probable year is 1830. Mr. Nelson Armstrong states that previous to that year a school was kept in the small building belonging now to him, and standing near the roadside in front of his present residence. In 1847 the older part of the house now used, was built at an expense of $800 or $1,000, including fence. The land belonging to it was given by D. S. Whipple, Esq., on condition that it should revert if used for other than school purposes. A "dance" which came off in the house about the time of its dedication raised the question whether that was not a diversion from the original intent. In 1849 two terms were sustained; one third of the money for the Summer, and two-thirds for the Winter. It was customary in this district for several years to prolong the school by levying a tax equal to one cent a day on each scholar. Another act of this people showed the grateful politeness which they felt oward their school officers, for in 1864-5 thanks were voted to Trustees and Clerks for their efficient services; the only instance discovered of "thanks" being voted to any school officers. For some time this was esteemed the best school in town, and especially so during Miss Lydia C. Armstrong's connection with it. Her name is honorably mentioned by the Committee. Much interest was shown on the part of the parents. In 1847 the whole number registered was fifty-one. In 1857, the whole number registered was one hundred and six, and an enlargement of the school-house was recommended. Through several successive years the school sustained its well earned reputation chiefly under the instruction of Miss Armstrong. In 1864, the Committee speak of the leading business men as not only attending meetings of the district, but as subscribing liberally for the purchase of standard books and apparatus used in the school-room.

In 1867, the matter of enlargement was again agitated, the whole number in the summer term being 105.

In 1870, the Committee report an addition to the school-house, at a cost of about $1,300.

In 1872, the school was a success, giving evidence of faithfulness on the part of teachers, and application on the part of the pupils. The average attendance in the winter term reached 95 per cent. of the whole number." Miss Emma F. Bullock and Miss Alice B. Clarke were teachers.

District No. 6.

This is the most northern and one of the oldest districts. It is said to derive its name, " Round Top," from the shape of a grist mill which formerly stood in it. Only one school-house is remembered which is the one now in use, built in 1808 at a cost of $300. At first it occupied the corner now covered by the house belonging to Mr. Judson Sherman, but was removed to its present location a few rods to the north of the old site. The reason for the change may have been that a corner-lot in the village was regarded as too valuable for a school. In 1867, the Committee report the house condemned as unfit for use. In 1868, " great improvement had been made. The house had been remodeled, painted and furnished with new windows and blinds at an expense of $300." Former customs and teachers are mentioned, which show some things curiously done in by-gone days. It is said that some teachers imbibed too freely and would go to sleep in the school-room, and while they took their rest the scholars had their fun. On one occasion of this sort a moderator was chosen and a motion for adjournment put. Both teachers and pupils would sometimes devote the school hours to games of chance and cheat, in an adjoining building, going out with impunity. Unruly girls were punished by seating them between two boys, the boys being told by the teacher to " crowd up." This, however, was no punishment to the girl if she was sandwiched between those boys who were her favorites. Girls were made to stand on the desks with a boy's cap on, in order to improve their deportment. Holding nails down was also assigned to disobedient boys, though one of them thought aloud that it was useless, as the nail was " already down." Asa Paine, Esq., one of the Committee of 1846, went to this school sixty years ago. In his school days teachers brought sticks eight and ten feet long into school, so long that the offending scholars could sometimes be reached by the teacher, without leaving his desk. Heads have been struck together, doubtless for the purpose of kindling a fire among the brains, and blisters raised on hands by a ferule so that the possessor might "take hold" with the mind, and palm off no more tricks. Very few girls studied arithmetic in his boy-hood. The Bible was read twice a day by the school, but there were no devotional exercises at the opening of the morning session. "Boarding round" was the fashion, according to the number of children. One man told a teacher that his proportion would be paid when the dinner was half eaten. Mrs. Martha Wilcox, to whom we are indebted for some of these recollections, is of the opinion that "boarding round" was conducive to a better acquaintance between teachers and parents than the present system, though it had its disadvantages; other persons speak of the narrow seats, "about as wide as a handsaw," on which the little children would go to sleep, often rolling off on the floor, to be picked up and soothed by older pupils or teachers. Children have been sent to this school as early as three years of age, and for whose sleepy heads, pillows were sent to, and kept at, the school-room. Of the teachers, Edward Babcock, Catherine Harris, the Misses Sayles, Annie Shumway, and others, are among the long and worthy list. In 1847, the whole number registered was 26. In 1875, 14. One of the earlier Trustees of this district, Daniel M. Salisbury, Esq., shows a large manuscript volume filled with problems from Daboll's Arithmetic, with ornamental headings and adorned throughout with plain and colored drawings of things in heaven, earth and under the earth, which he executed when a boy in another district. Mr. Archer Thayer also executed a similar work, which has been shown us by Mrs. Thayer, to whom we owe additional thanks for the use of six copies of the School Committee's Reports for as many different years.

Mrs. Emeline Eddy Salisbury recalls the days of her schooling in the old house when it stood on the corner. Here at noon the scholars (the master usually being respected enough to have cooked food put into his pail) would procure a forked stick from the surrounding birches and roast their sausages, holding them before the open fire. "Up into the Arch" was the aim of the large boys, i. e., standing on desk or bench they would spring upward with outstretched arm and extended fingers in order to touch the centre of the arched ceiling. In this way the father of the present Trustee, Stephen Arnold, "made his mark," both upon that ceiling and the memory of those of his fellow students who witnessed the transfer of blood from the end of his fingers to the arch, as an infallible proof that he had touched it.

DISTRICT NO. 7.

This is the Harrisville District. The original house stood where the "Air Line" railroad intended to cross the carriage road leading south from the depot of the Providence and Springfield Railroad, then " in the woods." Moved out of the woods it took a situation in the highway or "forks of the road," fronting the present school-houses in this village. Whole number registered in 1847 was sixty-seven. This first building was standing and in use in 1848, being described as 20 by 20, 8 feet high, with the old style arrangements within. The territorial extent of the district, as given in return of 1850, was, " length, 2½ milds;" "breadth, 2 milds." In 1849 a new building was erected on the site of the residence now owned by Mr. J Eagan. This was 32 x 26, 10 feet high. The location not being satisfactory to all parties this building never was occupied there, and at length was moved to the lot now holding the Primary school-house. It was afterwards raised up and a new story added as it is to-day. As far back as 1831-2, Miss Abby Owen (who became the wife of Whipple Sayles, Esq., in after time) introduced grammar and geography into the school for the first time. Several persons bear cheerful testimony to Miss Owen as a model teacher in those days. Females were not then employed in winter schools. Mr. Dike is named also as a very good teacher, highly respected for his piety and high-toned moral character. Thayer Bellows, son of Dr. Bellows, of Glocester, though "small in stature," was considered " enough " for the largest pugilist who went to school. Having chastised one of the larger girls on a time, the larger boys were inclined to take her part against him; but using his ferule with rapid severity until it broke over the backs of the rescuers, he sprang to the stove and seizing a stick of wood, assumed such a warlike attitude that the rebellion was completely crushed; and as if he would have a fair trial, he told the boys he would meet them in the woods, through which he was obliged to go for a mile or two on his way home. Those were days when physical courage was essential in a teacher.

For the following sketch of another teacher, of more than usual prominence, we are indebted to Charles L. Steere, Esq. of this town:

> Among the most noted and longest to be remembered teachers of this town, was Calvin S. Keep. Noted for his zeal in the cause of education, his versatility of talent, and the peculiar and thorough method of transmitting his knowledge to others, as well as his modesty of manners, purity of morals, and great love of science, he is remembered for his tall, gaunt person, stretching, when erect, to

upwards of six feet, and being so slender and loosely put together as to give him the appearance of being much taller than he really was,—so tall he seemed, that it was said, he had to stoop to hear it thunder. But above all, he is remembered for his extreme oddities, not only odd in appearance, but odd in everything that appertained to him; every word and movement being original. His legs and arms were long and bony, his neck after the same pattern, always incased in one of those contrivances (doubtless of the inquisition), a stock, that came plump to his chin, as if to add firmness to the foundation of his head, the crowning glory of all.

The head as remembered now, after thirty years, was somewhat peculiar. It was small and oddly shaped, with eyes large and prominent, a retiring chin, largely overshadowed by the under lip which, to his pupils possessed peculiar interest, for to them this lip was as the barometer to the signal service, or *its* signals to our merchant marine; when that fell, every urchin understood they must look out for squalls. He was a rigid Congregationalist of the old Puritanic stock, and believed implicitly in the sayings of Solomon, especially in this, "spare the rod and spoil the child," which was often recited in school, doubtless in order to give accent and dignity to the many occasions when he felt called upon to obey its sentiments.

Mr. Keep came to Burrillville, if our memory serves us, in the Winter of 1842–3, from the town of Monson, Massachusetts, and commenced his labors in District No. 8, one of the smaller, and at that time, not the farthest advanced in the sciences, in the town. It would be interesting to know with what feelings this singular man, then at the age of about thirty, a stranger in that sparsely settled, uninviting territory, on the confines of Wallum Pond, and the forests of Buck Hill and Douglass, commenced teaching the rude ideas of this region the paths to eminence, in that little school-house, dropped in the forks of two rough country roads, innocent of paint or enclosure, and little larger than the adjacent corn-crib. But whatever his feelings might have been, we know that his spirit was equal to every emergency. Did the door lack a hinge, or the window-sash its glazing, or the chimney refuse to conduct its smoke upward, his ingenuity remedied the evil in the most effectual and speedy manner, and no carpenter's, blacksmith's, or machine shop in the vicinity where he happened to be located but contributed its facilities to further his plans. He was original and eminently progressive in his modes of teaching, and here was a rugged field for the exercise of his abilities. No map or chart hung on the walls of this school-room, no blackboard added its conveniences. It must be remembered, however, that this was more than thirty years ago, when our public school system was in its infancy, and before Henry Barnard improved and developed it.

It is difficult to comprehend at this day how a school could be conducted without a blackboard or its substitute, and so thought Mr. Keep then, therefore, with his own hands he constructed one, *the first introduced into the schools of this town*, and it was done, we imagine, with no small degree of satisfaction, as he was exceedingly skillful in the art of drawing, and made good use of it withal. But it seems the introduction of this "new fangled contrivance" was not very highly appreciated by the simple yeomanry of this section, and he was severely taken to do for spending so much time in figuring and marking on this board when there were several slates owned by the older scholars. Whether this was the cause of his early departure from this field we know not, but he remained there but one term, when he applied for and obtained the school in District No. 7, where he commenced at the next Winter term, teaching about four years. In this district there was a better and more congenial field for the prosecution of his calling, the school was larger and no opposition was made to any branch or mode that he chose to pursue, the people seeming rather to enjoy his peculiarities. Here he introduced the blackboard without opposition, as well as many other modern aids to instruction. With the help of some mechanical contrivance of his own construction, he made outline maps that would do no discredit to those hanging in our schools to-day—and from an old brass clock he built a very serviceable Morse telegraphic machine, the first seen in these parts by any resident. He was wont to operate it across the school-room with wires, for the admiration of parents and scholars, explaining at the same time its whole *modus operandi*. Electricity was his hobby, and many were the ingenious and interesting arrangements he devised to illustrate it.

At one time the eye and its functions, with the theory of light, was the subject of investigation. Eyes of different animals were dissected and the uses of its various parts illustrated by such admirable drawings upon the blackboard as to impress the whole matter upon our minds so vividly as never to be erased.

Mr. Keep was not given to levity, seeming to look upon life as of too serious a matter to be trifled away, yet he enjoyed a certain kind of fun, especially what partook largely of the ludicrous. One source of amusement as well as instruction was a magic lantern or stereopticon, which Mr. Keep procured, no one knew where or how, but he had the lantern, and many pictures, a considerable portion of which were made by his own hands and in a masterly manner. These were exhibited at the evening meetings of the school, which were held as often as a sufficient number would attend. But of all sources of recreation or diversion known to him, the violin was the most complete. Did life become burdened with discouragements and disappointments it was the charm of the violin that dispelled the cloud. Did everything go wrong in school, and scholars, as they often will, become restless and inattentive, the spirit of the viol was invoked and with school song, in which all were required to join, the demon discontent was speedily cast out.

In conclusion, we will relate a snow-balling incident wherein our hero was somewhat conspicuous. There had been considerable difficulty experienced during the snow-balling season, from the abuse of this amusement; it had become quite a serious evil and one very difficult to remedy. However, it was determined by the teacher to make certain bounds around the school-house, inside of which should be a perfect asylum for all non-combatants of whatever sex or condition, "but," said the teacher, "whoever is hit with a snow-ball while outside these bounds, except when going to, or returning from school, must not complain even though it be myself who is the sufferer." Now there was a boy among the larger scholars who never forgot a wrong or an opportunity to retaliate, and who had been nursing a little grudge for sometime. It so happened a few days after, at noon time, all the school were coasting down a steep hill, near by the school-house. It was a glorious day, and the track was hard and glassy, while the sleds went like the wind; it was a day to be enjoyed, thought the children, and doubtless so thought Mr. Keep, as he appeared upon the scene and asked the loan of a sled for a ride. The largest and best was freely offered for his use, by its owner, the young rebel who had been watching an opportunity which now seemed to have presented itself for revenge. So, while the victim was stowing his long frame upon the sled, word had been given by the avenger, and behind his back twenty boys were preparing for action, and as soon as he had passed beyond the *bounds*, hostilities commenced, and such a shower of snowballs as rained upon that luckless back might have pounded the breath from an ox. There was some anxiety felt for the result among the more timid ones for a while, but Mr. Keep had too much good sense to treat it as anything more than a joke.

Hon. George H. Browne is also remembered as a teacher of great thoroughness and patience in this district. He has kindly furnished the following reminiscences:

PROVIDENCE, April 9, 1876.

DEAR SIR:—I have little to communicate about the Harrisville school, except the mere fact that I did "keep school" in that district once, so long since that I cannot recall the exact time, much less anything of interest that occurred. I think it must have been forty years ago; at any rate, most of those who now are the fathers, magistrates, legislators and prominent citizens of your town and community were school boys and school girls, and many of them were my pupils. I wish I could flatter myself that some of them, at least, owed, in some small degree, the eminence they have since attained and the usefulness they have exemplified, to my teachings or the precepts I endeavored to inculcate.

It was in those good old days when the "schoolmaster boarded round," and I have never been reconciled to the abolition of that most beneficial custom. It carried the teacher to the fireside of every family. He learned to take an interest in the children from the interest and anxiety the parents displayed. In the long winter evenings, by the blazing open fireplace, he had much time to question and talk with his pupils, discover what were the peculiarities and needs of each, and if he had any tact, awaken in them a love for their studies and for books, which the school-room furnished comparatively little opportunity for doing. The feelings and opinions of the parents, too, were freely observed, and events or processes of teaching in the school explained and thus a thousand of the petty difficulties of "school keeping" avoided.

But, as I have said, I do not remember anything of note that occurred, save a great snow storm, and which made me realize vividly that touching description of a man perishing in the snow which used to be in the old school readers.

The Laphams, the Woods, (both Otis' and Fenner's children,) the Clarks, Smiths, Harrises, Mowrys, Steeres, and many others, were constant, and before the school closed, interested and studious scholars. Your town clerk, trial justice, senator and others, who have since acquired distinction and wealth and reflected honor on their town, were pupils of mine and whom I am proud to call my life long friends.

I formed also in "boarding round" an intimate acquaintance in each family, which in almost every instance, endured as long as they lived.

One other feature of the old school machinery we practiced quite thoroughly that winter, viz., the "spelling-school," on moonlight evenings. It was a feature that I always touched with much hesitation. Unless a "lively" interest and emulation in the exercises of the evening could be awakened, they were apt to affect the discipline of the day school. In this case I do not remember that any such result followed, on the contrary my recollections are that they were a decided success.

Yours, etc.,
George H. Browne.

Miss Betsey Brown taught here as in several other districts. Such service as she has given to the town cannot have been otherwise than useful, both to the cause of education and religion. She recalls sixteen of her scholars who have become teachers; two manufacturers, one lawyer, one editor, and one military officer. The first set of outline maps used in Harrisville were placed there by her in 1851 or '52. From 1850 to 1856 this district was disturbed by differences which, however, were happily adjusted, so that the Committee of 1857 congratulate the people upon the return of an amicable state of affairs, and "trust that the same friendly feeling will continue to exist, and that the school will continue to rank, *as it really does now*, among the first in town." Mr. William Wilcox was Trustee and Misses N. R. and Ellen J. Sayles were teachers. In 1860 both terms were taught by Mrs. F. M. Steere, an excellent teacher, who has "seen service," not only in this but other districts of the town, which has been pronounced "acceptable." In 1867 there were scholars enough for three departments and room for only two. Whole number in Summer, 159; Winter term, 176. In 1869, whole number, Summer, 183; Winter, 187. In 1870, the larger of the two houses now in use was completed, at a cost of about $4,500. The report of 1872 speaks of Miss Emily A. King as having had "large experience, and a thorough disciplinarian." This is the first district in town which established *three* grades of schools in as many rooms. For the last year the Primary has been in charge of Miss Dora Walling; the Intermediate, of Miss Evelyn Steere, and the Grammar, of Miss Ellen F. Knight, whose work has been rewarded by the devotion of the school, as well as by her appreciation in the minds of all concerned.

District No. 8.

In this, the "Logee" District, there was a school before the present school building was occupied as the property of the district. The number in attendance in 1847 was 29, with 27 in the year following. The history of the present house seems to be, that it was originally a store situated near Wallum Lake, and was subsequently purchased by Mr. Dorphin Logee and moved at such great expense and trouble that those engaged in the work called it "The teacher's sinking fund." This was about the year 1825, and cost $300. In 1848, there was some talk of building a new house, but finally this house was purchased, moved about, and an addition of 6 × 18 made to it. Mr. Logee proposed to plant trees about it, but they have not been set out yet. It is interesting to read with what particularity the agreement was drawn up between Charles F. Albee, who put on the addition, and the parties acting for the district. A reading of this document leads one to think it to have been rather hard for Charles and quite easy for the district. The attendance in this district has been variable; sometimes equal to the number in 1848, but oftener less. The reports from 1857 run on with brief notices. Some excellent teachers have had their first experience here. They could not have commenced in a more quiet and well disposed neighborhood. Here Mrs. J. L. Phillips taught for $1.50 a week, and so anxious was she to teach that rather than have been disappointed, she would have taught for less. In 1867 the house was reported in tolerable repair. In 1869 it was thought large enough for the scholars of district No. 9, and a consolidation recommended. For the remaining years until the last the attendance has been small, yet the school has been uniformly successful.

District No. 9.

The house now used for a school in Wallum Pond District, is believed to have been preceded by one other in the early part of the century. When this present one was erected is a matter of some doubt. The writer of the return for 1848, says it was built in 1838, and cost $400. In 1850 a return says it was built in 1842, and cost $250. This return also states that the school was 20 weeks long. Number of pupils registered, 37; average attendance, 21. The return for 1855, reports the house as built in 1841, at a cost of $300. Attendance of pupils for this year, registered 21; average 9. This return is for a school of 29 weeks. A petition protesting against the setting off of certain residents of the district, to District No. 8, presented to the town committee in 1846, assigns as a reason for the protest, "that a new schoolhouse has been recently erected in the district and these certain residents have not paid their tax on the same." So much for the date of the building. There is also a variety of statements in regard to the size of the building. One authority gives the size as "15 × 15, and *archt*," another as "20 × 20, and 10 feet high."

Report for 1860, speaks well of the teachers, also notes improved attendance of pupils, but still complains of want of interest on part of parents. Also, says " the house is unfit for school purposes. It is out of repair, location is any thing but desirable, and all its surroundings are unpleasant. It is hoped the district will at once adopt measures to improve the condition of things. If this matter is not attended to soon, it will become the duty of the committee to condemn the house."

In 1869, the house was condemned, and consolidation recommended with No. 8.

In 1872, committee report the school as the least satisfactory of any in town. The school for the last two or three years has been as good as could be expected, considering house and location. The attendance, as for several years previous, has been small, ranging from 16 to 27 registered, with the average from 10 to 16. During this time it has been under the care of Mrs. Mary M. Prouty, a motherly instructress.

DISTRICT No. 10.

Overlooking Wilson's Pond, at the corner of a road about one mile north of the school-house in " Laurel Hill " District stands the building which was used for school purposes in earlier days, known as the " Jonah Steere house." The present house, or one-half of it, was built in 1847, costing $700. Size of room then finished was 35 × 25 and 10 feet high. Whole number in attendance in 1849 was 56. The character of the school in previous years is hinted at in the report of the year 1857, which says: " This has of late been considered a hard school to govern, but during the last year no difficulty occurred. The summer term was taught by Miss S. M. Steele, a teacher of fine literary acquirements." " At the close of the winter term considerable time was spent in preparing for an exhibition. This is a matter of doubtful propriety, for we are disposed to think the time could be more profitably spent in the regular studies of the school." The number registered in 1858, was 80. In the winter term there were many large scholars who did what no scholar ought to do, viz.: " questioned the authority of the teacher in regard to the assignment of lessons. The teacher was sustained by both the committee and commissioner, though the committee kindly suggest that more firmness and activity on her part would have made her position more acceptable. The following winter saw a master installed as the head of the school, but failing to maintain order he was succeeded by a mistress, under whom orderly and studious habits were secured. Miss Ann E. Cruff, the successful teacher, was retained through the next year, in which pupils and parents showed a good degree of interest; whole number 63. Two more than this number are reported for 1861, who were instructed by Miss A. M. Shumway who had a "happy faculty of imparting instruction," and Miss L. M. Smith a graduate of the Providence High School. "She required thorough recitations, and close study." The same person was in charge the following year. It is not said that she was too strict and thorough for the good of the school, but too much so for popularity. In 1863 we find the whole number to have been 173, with an average of 82, and the house is declared too small and poor. Other accommodation was provided and Miss H. N. Bates who was a "faithful" teacher, took the grammar department. From this time till 1871 everything was pronounced "good," though the committee were not forgetful of the *better* and the *best*, and consequently they say : "The school at Laurel Ridge, one of the best in the town, is worthy of a better house, and a better location than the present. Aside from its uninviting aspect, within and without, its muddy surroundings, and its cramped accommodations, it is so arranged as to be especially perilous to the eyes of the pupils. An opinion shared by subsequent committees. The report of the following year, 1872, announced the names of Miss Ida M. Gardner, since graduated at the State Normal School, and Miss Dora V. Brown (now Mowry), " whose employment in the same school for a series of years is the best evidence that she merits the approval of her patrons." A shadow rested on the school this year in consequence of the death of three of its members of small pox, which invaded the town, and shortened the term. In 1874, the shaky building and unsuitable furniture are mentioned as in keeping with the location, which is "altogether too much on one side of the villages furnishing nearly all its scholars." In 1875 slight, but insufficient, repairs were made. Number in Fall term, 61 in Primary ; 26 in Grammar school.

District No. 11.

This is the Pascoag District. The children of this neighborhood in the early part of this century in some cases attended school in private houses. In other cases they went to a school-house which stood near the farm of Welcome Sayles. This, however, was not much used after the division of the town. About the year 1824, the house which has long been known as the " old red," was built in the village, not far from the residence of the late Joel Paine, Esq. That the date is correct the following copy of a paper written fifty-two years ago will show.

"BURRILLVILLE, December 24th, 1824.

"Mr. James Irons we have got in warm debate about a school-house to be sot near Henry Andrews, And we want you should write how much you will give towards Building the same. Our western nabours want to git it on the hill by Nicholas Sayles, but if you will Sine pritaliberly we can have it near your house. We have sent you a copy of the Siners and how much cash has sined."

It is fair to infer that the recipient of this epistle did "*Sine pritaliberly*," for the writer and his coadjutors gained their point. Twenty-one years later, the house having attained its majority, was reported as "very bad." Mr. Emor Smith, in that year, reports himself as thirty-six years old, having taught sixteen years, mostly in this State. Whole number, 68; average, 40. From 1857 to 1863, schools were held as a variable attendance required, either in the "old red," in school-house No. 2, situated on the opposite side of the same road westward, but used for a brief period only, or in the vestry of the Baptist church. The report of 1862 informs us that "District No. 11 is entirely destitute of a house that will accommodate more than a fraction of its scholars." Immediately following, without waiting for a formal vote of condemnation of the old house, the citizens of the district took hold of the matter, and a new house arose with ample room for the time, costing about $3,000. The committee, in speaking of this house, make some very judicious remarks in relation to the planting of shade trees around, but not too near school-houses. In most instances the people have been very careful about not planting them *too near*. The effect of this house erected in 1862–3, then the best in town, was beneficial. The year after, the committee are warm in words of commendation. both of teachers and scholars. Emily A. King of Southbridge, Massachusetts, and Lucy W. Smith, were the happy teachers. Total, 133; average, 96. From this year this district, and to its honor let the fact be rehearsed, has voluntarily taxed itself to lengthen the terms beyond the limit allowed by the State and Town appropriations. This tax was for a while approved by the whole Committee, but in February, 1872. the chairman or clerk were authorized to approve any such tax provided that no school should be kept longer than ten months. For several terms Miss C. Pierce, a teacher of some celebrity, instructed in the grammar department. She is still a resident of the town, teaching in a select way, and interested in the practical questions relating to the better education of the attendants upon our public schools. In 1871 appears the name of Mrs. E. F. Harris, for most of the time since, and at present, the much esteemed and efficient teacher in the grammar school. The primary department has also been adorned by well chosen and laborious teachers; one of whom, Miss Alice Logee, (Angell,) has recently ended her labors on earth.

For some time the primary required an assistant teacher, and the growth of the school made a larger place for it an imperative necessity. In the month of October, 1874, a new house with three stories, in modern style, and with modern furniture, costing about $7,500, was dedicated by appropriate services, there being in attendance, and delivering addresses, the outgoing and the incoming Commissioners, Hon. T. W. Bicknell and Hon. T. B. Stockwell. The occupancy of the second story of this house by the grammar school, allowed an intermediate grade to be constituted in the room vacated, and thus afforded the needed relief to the Primary. This change increased the number of *schools* in the town to *twenty-one*, the number of *districts* being *fifteen*.

There have been four school-houses proper built and used by this district, besides the use of the Baptist vestry, which was fitted for a school in which Rev. D. P. Harriman was the first teacher, who was also chairman of the committee of 1846. He was succeeded in the vestry by Rev. A. R. Bradbury, Mowry Arnold, Emeline E. Arnold, (now Steere,) and others.

Mr. Moses Salisbury, the "General," by which title he is familiarly known, himself well skilled in *naming* things, furnishes some facts out of his clear and retentive memory, for which we are grateful. He first attended school in "Clark" Daniel Smith's shop, having Rufus Boulster for a teacher, who in the use of his rod one day struck off a steel button from an urchin's coat, which, spinning across the room, came so near the "General's" knowledge box, that he never forgot it, though he was then only six years old. Nicholas Jenks, John W. Wood, Mr. Clark, William Colwell, Caleb Crosby are named among his other masters. The last-mentioned taught in "Daniel Sayles' Shop," in which was a large oven, and beneath, according to the custom, a wood hole. During a brief absence of Crosby, one Smith S., "a good scholar, but a great rogue," mounting the back of the negro boy Pollock, rode him around the school-room. The master's coming being announced while the fun was at its height, Smith drove his horse into the open wood hole and closed the door; Pollock, too, enjoying the joke. The master enters, misses P. and inquires for him. The tell-tale face of Smith led Crosby to ask *him* particularly, who promptly replied, "I guess if you look in the wood hole, you'll find my black colt."

On a time when a strict law against whispering was in force, a roll of paper was pushed over the desk by the finger of another lad, which the master seeing, the "General" picked up, put into his mouth, gave a "chaw" and swallowed. "What was on the paper?" asked Crosby. Of course, the "General" knew not, and the other boy said, "An odor," meaning order, "for tobacco." Better in all cases were *only* the order, and not the tobacco swallowed.

In 1824 Mr. Salisbury finished the inside of the "old red." He was Trustee in 1828. He made blackboards as soon as any, "fitted up" the Baptist vestry and assisted in starting the first Sabbath School in the old red school-house, from which time a Sabbath school has been sustained in the village. He was never corrected for misdemeanors in his school days, which may confirm to the initiated that he was even better than "a four-pence between two cents."

District No. 12.

The first district having this number was formerly the "stone school-house" because of the material of which it was constructed. At a later day it was called the "Eagle Peak." "Eagle Pick," according to the "General," for when Henry Clay was a candidate for the presidency a political meeting was held in this district. Some one with chalk drew a picture of an Eagle, picking at the head of Clay, and hence "Eagle Pick," the "Peak" being a corruption. From some equally trivial circumstance sprang the colloquial appellations, "Monkey-town," "Turkey-ville," "Stub-ville," etc. The land was deeded by Mr. Washington Logee to revert in case of a diversion from school purposes. The original cost is set down at $200. Of its history in other particulars we have no record until 1847, when the whole number attending was 50—average 35. One hundred and twenty dollars were expended in repairs in 1848. In 1855, the number had diminished to 27; average 15. School reported "good" in 1857, though there were no visits from the parents. Arrangement of seats in 1861, "bad," otherwise in good repair. In 1864 change of teachers every term. In 1867 had made needed improvements. In 1870, the report says: "The house in Eagle Peak is sadly out of repair. The reason why a renovation of this house has not been urged, is a decided conviction that the educational interests of the people in this district can be secured by another and a better arrangement. A large part of the pupils in this district are within a short distance of the Pascoag school, and the remainder are quite near to the Laurel Hill School. If there are any in the western part of the district who cannot attend either of these schools, they can be accommodated in the Jackson District." In 1871, the report further says: "At the commencement of the year your committee abolished the Eagle Peak District and divided its territory between Nos. 10, 11 and 13. We regarded it as a waste of money and a positive injury to the scholars to continue a school averaging only twelve pupils, located within three-quarters of a mile from two graded schools, which rank among the best in the town." From the committee the district appealed to the commissioner, who, after fully hearing the case, sustained the committee. About this time the "Plainville" district through the action of the committee dropped the No. 17 and took the No. 12, in order to fill the blank in the tables of school statistics. The second No. 12, known as the "Plainville" or "Oakland," (though the present house is nearer the latter than the former village), was formed by a division of No. 4, and a recent alteration of adjacent boundaries. For some time a school was kept in the rear part of a tenement house in Oakland, and taught by Abbie J. Mowry (Reynolds). The place was poor, the teacher good. In 1873, as the school was still continued in the same place, and no ground of hope of a proper schoolhouse, the superintendent recommended the abolition of the district. But it would have been unwise to have abolished it. So the district thought. Steps were therefore taken which resulted in the giving of a lot by Charles Whipple, Esq., and the erection, largely through the liberality of Mr. Whipple and John L. Ross, Esq., of " a neat and attractive school-house, with a pleasant location between the villages of Oakland and Plainville, which, with its modern furniture and fixtures, cost about $2,000." The erection and use of this house puts an end, let us hope, to that period of our school history when private dwellings shall be employed for purposes of public education.

District No. 13.

This district is situated in the south-western part of the town, and was for a time called the "Mathewson." This name is given in a return for the term commencing December 18, 1848, and ending April 6, 1849. The number of families then in the district, was fifteen, all engaged in agriculture. Ten boys and four girls attended school, no one of whom was provided with all the books necessary in the studies pursued by them. Books used, were the Practical Speller, Russell's and Angell's Select, and Angell's No. 2 Readers, Colburn's Mental Arithmetic, Emerson's second part Written Arithmetic, Morse's, Smith's and Mitchell's Geographies and Smith's Grammar. The teacher was Miss Ruth J. Canney, from Dover, N. H., who received $10 a month and board. Ten out of the fourteen scholars engaged in declamation, which must have included all the boys, for whom the way to oratorical distinction was thus prepared. In a return for 1854, the district is called "Jackson," in honor, so far as appears, of Gen. Andrew Jackson. The honor came too late, however, to be of any comfort to the General, who died in June, 1845. Number of families given in this return, twenty, all engaged in agriculture. Sixteen boys, nine girls; teacher, Miss M. L. Joslin, from Thompson, Connecticut, who received $16 a month. By this return we learn the school-house was built in 1835, and repaired in 1854, at a cost of $150. The dimensions were 18x18 and 8 feet feet high.

According to report of 1867, the district made the needed improvements. In 1868, the school is reported as usual in interest, with an average attendance of nine. In 1874 the district had the honor and benefit of a trustee, who did his duty with charming fidelity, and the school-house and school soon began to brighten. For the last year it is to be reported that the school-house has been thoroughly repaired, inside and out. The Winter of 1875-6 saw a larger attendance than usual, and a more satisfactory school in every particular.

DISTRICT No. 14.

This is the most western district in the town, and is bounded by the Connecticut line. It is called "Buck Hill," probably because of the numerous bucks who formerly roamed proudly over the long, well wooded hill, which must be crossed in order to reach this remote district. A return of 1849 tells us the number of families in the district was fifteen, all engaged in agriculture. Extent of territory of district, length 6 miles, breadth 2 miles. School-house built in 1832, cost $200., repaired in 1848 at a cost of $225. Dimensions of school-house, 16 × 18, 8 feet high. Number of pupils registered, 22, 12 boys and 10 girls; average attendance, 11. None of pupils fully provided with books. Teacher's name illegible, age eighteen; wages $8. a month and board. Trustee, Jacob Lewis. 1849.—Teacher, Almira Tourtelotte, wages $1.50 a week and board; average attendance 16. In 1852 the Town Committee were requested to take charge of the school, the request coming from the majority of legal voters to the number of *two*. In 1855 Miss Ann E. Cruff, of Thompson, taught three terms for $10. and $12. a month and board; average attendance, 15. There were three teachers the following year. Total number of pupils each term, 14; average, 8. The parents are said to have interested themselves very much in the education of their children. 1860.—Total number of pupils, 23; average, 16. Mary R. Sheldon, of Thompson, Connecticut, was retained for several terms, and was regarded as a very efficient teacher. 1862.—Total

number pupils, 12; average 8, showing a decrease in numbers. 1863.—
Total number pupils, 17; average, 14. In 1864, total number pupils,
20; average, 17. The school report for this year, after mentioning
teachers' names, says: "We know of no cause of complaint, but from
the remote situation of the district and a failure on part of the Trustee to
notify us of the times of closing the school, it was not visited as many
times as the law requires,—the Trustee having the frankness and honesty
to tell the Committee that both school and teacher could get along about
as well without them as otherwise," which is pretty good for a district
which, in 1852, asked the Town Committee to help them. In 1867,
school-house condemned, small number in attendance. 1868.—Measures
were taken to repair the school-house; average attendance, 9. 1869.—
No school during the Spring or Summer terms. Attendance of Winter
school: total, 12; average, 7. Taught by Miss Mary Lewis, (colored),
to whose "careful and thorough training" the committee call particular attention. In 1872 the school enjoyed eight and one-half months of
schooling under an experienced teacher. Total number pupils for Summer term, 12; average, 8: for Winter term, total, 9; average, 8. 1875.
—For Summer and Fall terms, total, 6 boys; average 4. Winter term,
7 boys; average, 5.

District No. 15.

This district is called "Harris District," probably for the reason that
there were several families of that name residing within its limits. It is
situated about one and one-half miles from Harrisville. Its extent, two
and one-half miles by one and one-half. The inhabitants formerly held
their schools in private dwellings. The present house is their first
school-house; its dimensions being 16 × 16 and 8 feet high. It was
built in 1840 at an expense of $134. The land donated for this building
was only so much as the house might cover; the builders did not seem
to be governed by the idea, more house, more land. The district has no
out-building, no play ground on its own land. Two windows, which may
be lowered at the top, furnish ventilation. In 1847 Job Steere, Esq.,
taught four months, having 27 pupils. In 1857, the total number of
pupils was 19, average 13. The school report for this year speaks
highly of the teachers and says: "Though small, the school is one of the
best in town. We always find a good average for the number registered.
This fact shows an active interest on part of parents, an interest which
renders the school pleasant and easy for the teachers, and profitable for
scholars. In 1858 we learn from the report that the parents are interested and "not *unreasonably fault-finding.*" In 1862 "gratifying suc-

cess, under charge of Miss A. M. Shumway," is recorded. In 1864, the school-house is condemned as unfit for use. 1866.—The house is reported in good order. In 1872 the school report for this year thus speaks of this school: "Though small, it is thoroughly alive and successful, and abundantly proves the wisdom of continuing a good teacher term after term in the same school. Miss Ida E. Steere, who has won a fine reputation as a first-class teacher for schools of this grade, taught the school seven and one-quarter months at an expense of $247.33.

Evening schools for several years have been provided, for those who could not attend the day schools, in three of the larger villages, with good results.

There is at present no free public library in the town.

The care of the schools has employed on the school committees during the successive years of their history, nearly four hundred citizens of the town. To give even the names of so many would occupy more space than can be allowed. Something was done certainly previous to the year 1846, when the work was divided between sixteen persons. More was done, perhaps, when the number was six, and it may be as much has been accomplished since 1857, when the number was lessened to three. The names of the present Committee are James S. Cook, Chairman; Oliver A. Inman, Secretary; and Isaac Steere.

The visiting of schools and the examination of teachers was attended to sometimes by the Committee as a whole, at other times by some one appointed for the purpose. Both of these duties, however, were subsequently assigned to the Superintendent. The first person elected to this position was Rev. Mowry Phillips, July 11, 1871. He was, at the time, the esteemed Pastor of the Baptist church at Pascoag, and continued to discharge the functions of his important offices, until failing health made it needful for him to seek its recovery by change and repose. He resigned the Superintendency in October, 1873. It is gratifying to know that restored health enables him to hold the same office to-day in the mother town of Glocester.

In conclusion, it may be said that what is here presented does not claim to be anything more than "a plain and unvarnished" notice of some persons and some things belonging to the history of the schools of Burrillville. The material for a complete history is scanty and imperfect. This is the result of a limited inquiry and a rapid glance, such as could be made within the narrow circle of twelve days. The writer begs leave to congratulate his fellow citizens on the advance steps which have already been taken in matters of education, and to remind them that we still occupy "that greatest room in the world,"—the room for improvement.

Money Expended.

A *tabular* view of a portion of money expended is appended:

Year.	State Appropriation.	Town Appropriation.
1828	$199 80	$300 00
1839	644 70	300 00
1844	469 06	300 00
1847		400 00
1854	865 86	801 88
1857	1,495 78	600 00
1858	1,481 62	800 00
1859	1,487 62	800 00
1860	1,487 62	800 00
1861	1,478 10	1,000 00
1862	1,478 10	1,000 00
1863	1,459 97	1,000 00
1864	1,459 97	1,000 00
1865	1,459 97	1,500 00
1866	1,459 97	2,000 00
1867	1,459 97	2,000 00
1868	2,032 26	2,500 00
1869	2,576 93	2,500 00
1870	2,571 97	2,500 00
1871	2,592 99	3,000 00
1872	2,526 91	3,500 00
1873	2,529 16	3,500 00
1874	2,515 76	3,500 00
1875	2,513 57	3,500 00

CHARLESTOWN.

By W. F. Tucker,

Superintendent.

At the August session of the General Assembly, held at Newport in 1738, an act was passed dividing the town of Westerly into two towns, the same to be known and distinguished by the names of Westerly and Charlestown. At this period, Charlestown extended from Westerly on the west, to South Kingstown on the east; and from the town of Exeter on the north, to the Atlantic on the south. But on the eighteenth of August, 1747, an act was likewise passed, dividing the town of Charlestown into two divisions, to be distinguished by the names of Charlestown and Richmond; and the Pawcatuck river was selected as a natural and fixed boundary between the two towns. At the first census, taken in 1748, Charlestown had a population of 1,002; and in 1774 a population of 1,821; while the present population, according to the last census, taken in 1875, is 1,054.

Narragansett Indian School.

As early as 1815, the first school building was erected in this town, and named the Narragansett Indian School-house, in honor of the famous tribe of Indians, whose descendants still hold a small portion of the land by reservation. It may seem strange that the Indians owned the first school-house, but it is nevertheless true. This structure stands on a small knoll at the north end of a pond, formerly known to the tribe as Cockumpaug, but more recently named the School-house pond. It is an old wooden building, having the following dimensions:—length, thirty feet; width, twenty four feet; and height, seven feet between floors. There is a rough stone chimney in the building, which gives it an ancient appearance. In this house the few surviving members of the Narragansett Indians hold their annual council, and it is here that they also have their school.

Facilities before Public Schools.

Educational facilities prior to the establishment of public schools were exceedingly feeble in this vicinity. The people supported what were then recognized as private schools, the majority of which being kept in dwelling houses. In selecting a situation for a school it was expedient for them to obtain a central location in the neighborhood, but this was not always done, as there were very many obstacles in the way.

Teachers at this time were hired for stipulated sums ; receiving their wages from the parents and guardians, who paid them in proportion to the number of pupils that each one sent to school. In this community, forty years ago, the practice was as common for a school officer to go into Connecticut to hire a teacher as it is now customary for a person to pay taxes. The school committee often granted certificates to persons whose qualifications and abilities to instruct and govern a school were quite inadequate for the task ; and they seldom visited the schools to ascertain the results. Consequently, the schools were taught, many times, by very incompetent teachers ; by those who could not perform all the examples in the arithmetics, and what is much more discreditable, were unable to give satisfactory explanations of such as they could perform. It frequently happened that persons taught school who had no knowledge of grammar, or in other words, had never studied it. The average length of schools, was between three and four months ; for which reason, educational resources were quite limited.

District System.

In 1828, the General Assembly passed an act to divide the several towns into districts, with which the people readily complied. The District system, in this town was established, June 2d, 1828 ; and a subdivision made November the 19th of the same year, separating the town into six districts.

Next year, on the fifteenth of April, a portion of the district at Cross' Mills, and at Quonocontaug, was set off forming a new district, which was added to the catalogue as No. 7.

The last district subdivision in Charlestown, was made in 1871, when Carolina was taken from Pasquesett, and organized as the eighth school district. In the meantime, perplexities frequently grew out of the imperfect divisions and records of the districts ; and, in 1874, the school committee re-bounded all the districts, giving more definite boundaries to them, and caused the same to be placed on record in the town clerk's office.

Washington.—In 1828, Joshua Card, Joseph Cross, David Clark, Elisha Greenman, William Card, Dan King and others, purchased a piece of land of Henry Greene, containing twenty-two square rods, and erected thereon a building for school purposes. According to date, this was the first school-house built by the white people of Charlestown; and it was named Washington, in honor of the first President of the United States. This district is situated in the north-eastern part of the town.

In 1871, Jason P. Greene, George W. Cross, Amos P. Greene, and Henry S. Greene sold the property to the district; and in the same year, the house was thoroughly repaired, and supplied with modern desks and seats.

Shumuncanuc.—Here in the north-western part of the town, the surface is very hilly, and the people named the district after the most important hill. The citizens of this section met pursuant to notice on the premises of Abram Allen, Esq., and selected a pleasant location for a school. Mr. Allen gave, then and there, the land on which the building was to be erected; and Mrs. Elizabeth Allen, wife of Abram, named it "Union Hill," and paid one dollar for the honor of naming it.

This building was raised on the sixteenth of September, and dedicated by having a meeting in it, on the thirteenth of November, 1831. The first structure, however, was burned down, and on November the 10th, 1845, Arnold and Nancy Hiscox, deeded a parcel of land to the district, nearer the centre, whereon the present school-house stands. Mrs. Elizabeth Allen, who was born June 22d, 1772, is now living and enjoying good health; and possesses a remarkable memory for a person who has lived to see one hundred and three years.

Quonocontaug.—In this section of the State, some of the hills, streams, rivers and ponds, retain, at the present time, the original names given by the Indians. Quonocontaug is situated in the south-western portion of the town, and this name appears first applied to a pond in the neighborhood, from which the district received it. Edward Wilcox, who was Lieutenant Governor from 1817 to 1821, transferred a lot of land to the district, upon which a school-house was built in 1838. Although a respectable number of teachers have gone forth from other schools, still this school is entitled to the honor of educating an unusual number of good and faithful teachers.

Cookstown.—This division joins the town of Westerly, and it is really a rural district. The first school officers elected were the following:— Bowen Briggs, Moderator; Joseph W. Taylor, clerk; Benjamin F. Wilcox, Matthias Crandall, and Rowland Peckham, trustees; Perry Healey, treasurer; and Gardner Crumb, collector. Bowen Briggs and Gilbert

Stanton conveyed a piece of land to the district in 1839; and a school building was erected during the year.

Watchaug.—The people of this district erected a school-house in 1840, but a deed of the land on which the house stands was not granted until August 15, 1864. Watchaug is located in the south part of the town, and derives its name from a large pond on the western boundary, so called by the Indians. There is no other district in Charlestown which has such a grand expanse of water within its limits, or bordering on its territory.

Cross' Mills.—This district is situated in the south-eastern section of the town, and named after the village within its limits. The citizens of the neighborhood built a house for educational purposes in 1843. From 1845 to 1860, perhaps no school in the town excelled this one in literary attainments, and in reference to teachers, without doubt this school has produced nearly as many as all the other schools combined. The school building was repaired and re-seated in 1874.

Pasquesett.—The citizens of this community were in meditation a long time before any conclusion was reached; and, finally, in 1850, they purchased thirty rods of land of Robert Hazard, and built a school-house thereon. The district, which is situated in the northern and central part of the town, takes its name from a small pond, lying on its eastern border. In 1874, the school-house was enlarged and thoroughly renovated, and furnished with desks and seats of the latest pattern. The extent of territory and the advancement of the school, considerably exceeds that of any other in the town. The Indian school-house, heretofore mentioned, is located in the southern part of this division.

Carolina.—In 1845, Rowland G. Hazard, Esq., erected a school-house in Richmond, a little north-west of the village; and, on the 13th of May, 1871, the property, consisting of a house and lot, was sold to the district for $700. Meanwhile, the children from the northern part of the district of Pasquesett, attended school here, as it was more convenient so to do, and paid their proportion of the school fund of Charlestown to the school in Richmond. But on the 27th of January, 1872, district No. 8 of Charlestown, and No. 2 of Richmond, were consolidated and named Carolina joint district. At this period, an addition was made to the school-house at a cost of $2,487.63; making it a very commodious and useful school building. Immediately after the completion of the house, the school was divided into a primary and a grammar department, establishing a graded school.

Improvement and Present Condition.

About forty-eight years ago, the public school system was established in the State of Rhode Island. It was truly the beginning of a new era of educational improvements; and the State, like a living body which is sensitive in every member, was touched by the noble and generous act, in all its sub-divisions. Indeed, literary interests were perceptibly awakened in the minds of the people; and, from that period onward, education has been steadily advancing in the direction of both a higher and a broader culture. The establishment of the permanent school fund and public schools, gave life and vitality to the cause of education, and incited the people to a more united and determined effort, to give better means of instruction to the rising generation. A few soul-inspiring men, faithful servants of a worthy cause, have taken hold of this National work, and have carried it forward to its present condition. The broad foundation of our common schools is favorably fixed, and, with wise legislation and prudent management, improvements will be made as long as time and necessity demand them. The common school is the place where a child should be taught the moral as well as the literary lessons of public life, for morality and learning are indispensable to a nation's success. Charlestown has now resident teachers enough to supply all her schools, and about fifty per cent. of them, have attended State Normal schools. The average length of schools for the year, is little more that eight months, showing quite a contrast in comparison with the school-year of one half century ago. The present advanced condition has been reached mainly through the activity and perseverance of the school committee.

School Supervision.—The school committee which appointed the first town superintendent were elected in April, 1871, and organized soon after by electing Samuel B. Hoxie, chairman; B. F. Greenman, clerk, and Dr. A. A. Saunders, superintendent. The employment of a person to thoroughly inspect the schools, and to direct and assist the teachers in their daily labors, was an important step in educational progress. School supervision is the foundation on which the whole system of popular instruction rests. Unquestionably, what is most needed by our public schools, and what is most essential to their efficiency, is a constant, thorough and impartial supervision. I believe that the more direct and frequent this oversight is, when judiciously exerted, the more satisfactory will be the results.

Evening Schools.—At Carolina Mills, an evening school taught by Messrs. Tanner, Holden, and Collins, has been in successful operation for several weeks, but is now closed. An average of 60 pupils shows the general interest, and under the present administration the cause of education is advancing.

Distinguished Persons. — In connection with the public schools, perhaps, it may be proper to mention some of the persons who have labored faithfully for the advancement of education; and those who have become distinguished for their ability. Dan King was an earnest advocate for popular education, and his sons were educated for various professions. Joshua Card was a notable aid in the cause of public instruction. He was himself a teacher of good repute, and his youngest son, David Card, is now a physician at Willimantic, Connecticut. Dr. Joseph H. Griffin was an earnest laborer for the advancement of schools and the education of his children. Louis P. Griffin, his son, completed a course of studies in medicine, and began his practice in Chicago, Illinois. Samuel J. Cross was an able educator. He moved from Rhode Island to New York, where he became connected with a college during the remainder of his life. Wm. H. Perry, a teacher of large experience, has done much to promote the best interests of our schools. Kate Stanton, daughter of George A. Stanton, and a lecturer of some note, was formerly a teacher in this town.

COVENTRY.

By E. K. Parker,

Superintendent.

The town of Warwick originally included in its territory the town of Coventry. Settlements had been begun, in what is now the latter town, before it was set off from Warwick. Simultaneous with settlement, the work of education began. Probably about one hundred and ten (110) years ago the first school-house was erected in the town of Coventry. Previous to that time the schools were convened in rooms in private houses. As scholars then went two or three miles to school, it is to be presumed that the number of schools was less than at the present time.

The *modus operandi* of establishing and maintaining schools at that period appears to have been as follows: The people of a neighborhood signed a certain agreement, known as articles. By this act they indicated the number of scholars that each would send to school, and also, they were bound (by the act) to meet the expenses in proportion to this number. The wages of the teacher varied from $5 to $10 per month and board. The teacher boarded with the various families which patronized his school. The citizen who furnished the room in his house for the accommodation of the school received, as compensation, the tuition of one scholar. With rare exceptions the qualifications of the teachers were very meagre. But few books were to be obtained. Indeed the spelling-book was nearly the only kind of printed book known to the school-room in the early times. This contained, in addition to the lessons in spelling, lessons in reading. Usually no printed text-book on the science of arithmetic was used. The master had what was called his "ciphering" book. This was in manuscript—a copy of some other master's book. Probably originally it was a copy of a printed textbook on the subject, with the addition of the solutions of the problems. The scholars copied the definitions and rules. Usually the master wrote the problems in the books and then the learners solved them, if able, and copied the solutions into their books. Fractions were omitted as being useless. Much stress was placed upon the "Rule of Three"—especially, what was called the "*Double* Rule of Three." The ability to make a good quill pen was one of the first essentials of a master's qualifications. For writing, the scholars used loose sheets of paper, or a number of sheets stitched together. Copies were written by the masters, some of whom have left proofs, in this form, of wonderful caligraphy. Sixty years ago, the present chairman of the School Committee, Mr. Joseph Tillinghast, and his brothers, Pardon and George, owned in partnership the only copy of Daboll's Arithmetic inside the school-room where they attended, except the teacher's. The length of the school term was about three months in Winter, and from two to three months in Summer. The branches pursued were reading, spelling, writing and arithmetic. The schools were often very crowded and very uncomfortably seated. Stoves were unknown, and as a consequence, the huge chimney with its broad fire-place insured the best of ventilation, thus furnishing the sturdy boys of the olden time an abundance of pure air. In those days, as a general thing, the boys only were sent to school; for the reason, as a venerable yeoman of the period said—"In Winter the distance is too great for them (the girls) to walk, and in Summer they must needs stay at home to help their mothers."

More than a century ago there were built in the town at least three houses which were used exclusively for schools, and it may be, at irregular periods for religious worship. One was located at the foot of the eastern declivity of Waterman's Hill, on the main road; another near what is now known as Spring Lake, probably on the present location of the public school-house; and a third on the same main road leading from Washington over Harkney Hill to the Connecticut line, and about southwest from Summit station. These houses were of rude construction and but poorly adapted to the purposes for which they were designed. Still they marked an educational advance from the crowded room of the private residence. They also served as striking monuments to indicate where the greatest local educational interest prevailed. The men who were especially prominent in the matter of education at this period were the three brothers Bowen—Aaron, Israel and Ichabod,—Richard Waterman, Joseph Matteson and Caleb Vaughn, Jr.

From the revolutionary period up to 1830, the interest in education continued steadily to advance. Two years previous, 1828, the General Assembly had re-established free schools throughout the State. At that time there were as many school-houses in the town as at this writing, wanting two or three. All school-houses built before 1846, were held in shares, and the owners were called proprietors. In regard to the masters, as they were called, of this period tradition has handed down but little. Before 1800, masters Crocker and Knox, natives of Ireland, taught school at Bowen's Hill and vicinity. Some of the oldest citizens of the town now living, who attended school soon after the present century began, tell of Master Lemuel Spaulding, from Plainfield, Conn., who taught in a number of the different school-houses for a period of years. His qualifications were superior to most of his fellow teachers. He not only taught the branches commonly pursued, but carried scholars through surveying and navigation. He is described as a strict disciplinarian of dignified deportment and usually silent. Mr. James Mathewson, now living, a citizen born in West Greenwich, about this time taught a school in what is known as Whaley Hollow, at $5 per month. At a date later there came along a teacher known by the *nomme de plume* of Mr. A. B. It is a mystery to this day unexplained what the true name of this man was. He came like a phantom, proved himself a superior teacher, received no compensation, furnished his scholars with books, won the hearts of old and young, and at the close of his school disappeared as mysteriously as he came. Soon after the re-establishment of free schools, other branches were introduced,—such as English grammar and geography. Among the foremost teachers to encourage these new studies were the Rev. James Burlingame, now living, who taught evening schools, for his older pupils' benefit, two or three nights in the week, and for which he received no extra pay; Charles Horton and his brother Benjamin; Asa Stone, son of Asa, who was for a long time town clerk; all, with the exception of Burlingame, having been pupils of the Rev. Richard Stone, a native of Coventry, and who for a number of years taught a select and Normal School at Bridgewater, Mass. Thus the free schools continued to increase gradually in efficiency and interest.

The next important date in the history of educational affairs is 1846. Radical reform was introduced at that time by the enactment of the new school law. To the credit of the town, it can be said, that but few of its citizens made any effort to obstruct the execution of this law. The people were generously enthusiastic in its support. The schoolhouses were mostly purchased by the school districts, thoroughly repaired and entirely re-seated. In some instances new houses were built, and furnished with a degree of usefulness and elegance before unknown in this part of the State. An efficient School Committee was appointed, which carefully examined candidates for teachers' places, and generally lent its aid in carrying out the various changes that the new law enjoined. Better wages were paid teachers, better talent took the field, and better schools resulted. The citizens of the town who were especially active, indefatigable and self-denying in educational affairs, at this period, were Elisha Harris, Peleg Wilbur, Thomas Whipple, John J. Kilton, James G. Bowen, Stephen Waterman, Caleb Waterman, Isaac G. Bowen, Israel Wilson, Robert N. Potter, in addition to the members of the first School Committee under the new law, whose names were Samuel Arnold, Cromwell Whipple, Oliver G. Waterman, James A. Fenner, Caleb Nicholas.

For the thirty years succeeding 1846, the advanced ground taken at that date has been held, and a general forward movement has been going on. In addition to what is said above in regard to superior school-houses and equipments that had place in 1846–47, we would add that at Washington Village and at Bowen's Hill "District School Libraries" were established. These two districts, with Coventry Centre, were also furnished with a complete set of school apparatus. The Spruce District (now Summit) and the Town House district had nearly a complete set. In the winter term of 1846–47, Israel Wilson, Esq., offered as a prize, a complete set of Mitchell's Outline Maps, to be competed for by three schools, Nos. 5, 7 and 9. The judges were announced to be the School Committee, and their published report the decision. The school that received the most favorable report was to take the prize. No. 7 received it.

From the scholars of the public schools, at different times, have come forth those in whom was instilled so great love of learning that they have been led to successfully pursue a full course of liberal education. This list comprises Hon. Henry B. Anthony, now senator in Congress, Rev. Harris S. Inman, Rev. A. K. Potter, Charles Matteson, now Associate Justice of the State Supreme Court, Samuel H. Albro, Eugene Warner, all graduates of Brown University, and Ezra K. Parker, a graduate of Dartmouth College. Again out of the long list of business and professional men, who in their boyhood attended our public schools and who have been particularly successful in their own chosen walks of life, we deem it neither inappropriate nor invidious to mention Tully D. Bowen, Christopher Whitman, and David Hopkins, manufacturers, William Bowen, the lawyer, John McGregor, the surgeon, and Thomas A. Whitman, the banker.

Having thus traced imperfectly and briefly the progress of education in our town, it will be our purpose to examine its present *status*, and to suggest what may seem necessary to improve it.

Popular Interest.

The people of Coventry appear to be fully sensible of the value of the public school. They seem to understand thoroughly that the boy or girl who is sent into the world unable to read and write, or who has not a common school training, however endowed with superior natural abilities, has not an equal chance in the battle of life. Most of the illiteracy in the town is confined to foreigners.

School Houses.

Many of the school-houses are in good condition, all are planned after good models, a few need slight internal repairs in order to render them more attractive. One district has no house ; maps, charts, globes, etc., are wanting in a few. The two libraries, before referred to, established in 1846, have not been replenished, and in consequence have lost nearly all attraction.

Supervision.

Three gentlemen now constitute the School Committee. All engage in the supervision of the schools. There are eighteen districts in the town ; each member has six schools assigned to him, which he visits twice each term, and oftener if opportunity is presented. A superintendent is appointed who performs all other executive duties of the Committee. It would be a decided improvement in the system of supervision to have appointed a superintendent with a salary sufficient to enable him to devote most of his time to the schools, especially during the winter term.

Evening Schools.

Coventry raises by direct taxation $3,000, for the support of public schools. By a vote of the legal electors one-sixth part of this sum is appropriated to the support of evening schools. These schools do a good work in our manufacturing districts. The principal difficulty in regard to them, appears to be that very often a class of scholars not entitled to be admitted to evening schools get seats. It should be one of the special duties of trustees to remedy this evil.

Teachers should be able to make teaching a business. The great need at the present time is an increase of the public funds so that schools can be continued, at least eight months in the year. To secure this result it is necessary either to increase directly the educational fund, or letting that remain the same, to reduce the number of schools. It might be objected to reducing the number of schools, that the distance would be too far for scholars to attend them. We have before remarked in this narrative that scholars went two or three miles to school before the time of free schools. It is true that the school law provides for a district to vote to tax all its ratable property to sustain its public school, but like many another statute law, on account of the want of public sentiment to sustain it, it is inoperative. Whether or not it is better to reduce the number of schools, or whether or not it is not better to increase in some way the general school fund, we will not attempt to answer, but leave the questions with the few remarks already made.

We will call attention to the great advantages of having our schools continue eight months or more in the year, with a fair compensation for teachers. Now, in most of our schools we have a male teacher in the Winter terms and a female in the Summer. Thus there are usually two teachers called upon to continue the school in a single district for a single year. The male teacher usually works upon a farm or upon odd jobs during the Summer, waiting for a school to instruct through the Winter term of four months. He takes the greater portion of the public money. The district then, to make out two or three months more of school, engages a lady of little experience in teaching, at low wages, to go through with what is called the Summer term. Under such an arrangement it will be impossible to have our teachers keep up to the times in regard to qualifications. They get along by hook or by crook during the time they are not engaged in teaching, and consider it all a pecuniary gain if fortunate enough to secure a term of school to teach. On the other hand, teachers should not be censured too much. The young lady or young gentleman who is well prepared to discharge the responsible duties of a teacher, who has had the advantages of a thorough preparation for the work, should have a field in which to exercise their accomplishments. The situation should be so that such a teacher could make teaching a business and by it live, at least comfortably. Could a teacher be able to find employment for three-fourths of the year at a reasonable compensation, we have no doubt but that young men and young women of the best natural endowments would spend their lives in the honorable service of teaching the public schools.

EAST GREENWICH.

By P. G. Kenyon,

Superintendent.

BEFORE the establishment of public schools, the educational facilities of the town would probably compare very favorably with those of other towns in the State. There were private schools during the winter months, established at convenient places, usually in dwelling houses, throughout the town, which all children could attend by the payment of from two to three dollars for the term of three months; while often during the summer, especially in the more thickly settled portion, there would be opened what would now be called a primary school under the management of a lady. Miss Coggeshall became quite noted as a teacher in schools of this class.

Previous to 1812, Master Franklin was familiarly known as a schoolmaster of considerable reputation, but George Anderson Casey, or Master Casey as he was better known, took the lead for nearly fifty years. The remark is often made by the pupils of half a century ago, "When *I* went to school to Master Casey, he did not allow his scholars to do so and so, or in other words we had to toe the mark every time, and teachers of the present day might profit by his example as regards discipline and thoroughness." He taught only reading, spelling, writing and arithmetic.

In the early part of the present century a school of higher grade was established, where pupils could obtain a classical education, or prepare themselves for college. This school was known as the

KENT ACADEMY.

In 1802 a number of individuals prominent in this community and State, procured a charter from the General Assembly for a school, to be located at East Greenwich and called Kent Academy. In the preamble to their articles of association they assigned as their reason for this enterprise, their anxiety to promote the happiness of posterity, and to continue the blessings of a free and equal government; believing that well conducted seminaries of learning, in which youth may acquire knowledge, with the advantages of places of public worship to incline their minds to morality and religion, are the means most likely to effect this design. This was a worthy motive and that was a noble faith by which it was supported. As the Kent Academy, the institution made an honorable record for itself for thirty-seven years, the students in attendance varying from fifty to one hundred each year.

In 1839 the institution passed into the hands of Rev. Daniel G. Allen, the present efficient Superintendent of Public Schools of North Kingstown. He conducted the school as proprietor and principal with considerable success for about two years, when it became the property of the Methodist Providence Conference, and was called the Providence Conference Academy. In 1848 it was styled the Providence Conference Seminary, and in 1862 the name was extended to Providence Conference Seminary and Musical Institute. In 1873 the management of the school was transferred to the Boston University, and it became known as the Greenwich Academy, under the proprietorship of the Boston University.

ESTABLISHMENT OF PUBLIC SCHOOLS.

At a town meeting holden May 27th, 1828, it was voted and resolved, that a committee of six be appointed in conformity to an Act of the General Assembly relative to public schools. Dr. Charles Eldredge, Thomas Howland, Thomas Tillinghast, Job R. Greene, Joseph P. Briggs, and Daniel G. Harris were elected to be known as the School Committee of the town of East Greenwich.

Their first report was submitted to the freemen of the town at their Town Meeting, August 26th, 1828, as follows:

"Your Committee beg leave to report that they have attended to the duty assigned, so far as to divide the town into five Districts:

"The first to commence at the north-east corner of the town on the Warwick line, and continue on west to the dwelling of Daniel Howland, from thence south in a direct line to the dwelling house of Jonathan Hunt to the Warwick line; all that part of the town east of the said south line to compose one district, and to be called District No. 1.

"District No. 2 to commence on the Warwick line above District No. 1, and run west on said line to the house now owned by the Widow Maplot Rice, thence southerly until it intersects the middle road above the Widow Hannah Spencer's, thence east, including all the inhabitants on the said middle road, until it intersects the west line of District No. 1.

"District No. 3 to commence at the south-west corner of District No. 2, up the middle road, including all the inhabitants on the said road, to the West Greenwich line: and is to include all that part of the town north of the middle road and west of District No. 2.

"District No. 4 commences opposite the house of Joseph P. Briggs, running south by Card's Saw Mill across the French Town road to the Hamilton corner, from thence due south to North Kingstown line, including all the inhabitants on both sides the said road. To include all that part of the town west of the above mentioned line and south of District No. 3.

"District No. 5 to include all that part of the town not included in the above named Districts.

"Your Committee have not attempted to locate any school-houses in the districts, hoping that the inhabitants would relieve them from that duty and agree among themselves upon a location better adapted to their conveniences than the Committee could.

"The town's proportion of the fund appropriated by the State for the support of Free Schools amounts to $181 and some cents. Your Committee think that, with a further appropriation of one hundred dollars by the town, they would be able to procure a teacher in each of the five districts for four months.

"Recorded and compared with the original by

JAMES MILLER, *Town Clerk.*

At a town meeting May 26th, 1829, the School Committee presented their second report, as follows:

"*To the Freemen of the Town of East Greenwich in Town Meeting assembled:*

"Your Committee appointed to superintend public schools within said town, respectfully report: That it has, by virtue of said appointment, after having divided said town into five districts as before reported, opened schools, which have been kept three months in each district. The cost of employing teachers (other expenses attendant on the schools having been paid out of the treasury) amounts to two hundred and nine dollars, leaving a balance in the treasury of seventy-two dollars, which your Committee have appropriated equally in each district for keeping schools during the Summer, agreeable to the original design in establishing public schools.

"Your Committee generally being satisfied that schools of this description promise much public usefulness, provided there can be suitable houses obtained in which they may hereafter be held, and a regular system of arrangements in regard to them established, take the liberty to recommend to the consideration of the town in its corporate capacity, the propriety of erecting, or purchasing, suitable buildings the present season, or as soon as conveniently may be, to be held as the property of the town: or otherwise, to earnestly recommend to the several districts to furnish themselves with such accommodations; trusting that by such means much of that jealously and individual dissatisfaction which has very unhappily been exhibited in some localities during this short experiment would be avoided, and a warmer interest be felt to co-operate with the State Government in their benevolent design to promote and facilitate the education of our youth, and that the location of such houses be under the direction of such committee as the town may appoint to superintend said schools.

All of which is respectfully submitted,

THOMAS HOWLAND,
In behalf of the Committee.

East Greenwich, 5th Mo., 26th, 1829.

It was therefore voted and resolved at this meeting, that whenever the citizens of the several school districts shall build a school-house or houses in either or all of said districts, and complete the same to the satisfaction of the standing committee, they shall or may draw out of the town treasury one hundred dollars towards the expense of each school-house so built. A committee of five citizens of the town was appointed to confer with the School Committee on the best ways and means of building school-houses and the probable expense of the same, and report at the next town meeting.

At a town meeting in November, 1831, it was voted that the representatives of the town in the General Assembly be instructed to procure an Act of said Assembly to empower the town to build school-houses in the several districts, and to pay for the same by a tax on all the ratable property of the town.

In May, 1833, the School Committee were requested to estimate the probable expense of building school houses in the several districts, and report at the next town meeting in August.

The committee reported that, in their opinion, the sum of thirteen hundred dollars would be sufficient to build school-houses necessary in the five districts, consequently it was voted to build school-houses of equal size in the several districts, and the School Committee were appointed to superintend the building of said houses. The town treasurer was authorized to make sale of all the public and school lands belonging to the town, the proceeds of said sale to be used for the purpose of building school-houses.

The school committee report in April, 1834, that schools have been kept in four of the districts during the winter; but for want of a suitable room for the winter season, there has been no school in district No. 2. They likewise report that they have contracted for four school-houses to be completed by October 1st; each house to be twenty-five feet long by twenty feet wide with eight feet posts, for $1,060. The committee did not feel themselves authorized to proceed farther, the balance remaining of the sum voted by the town, being insufficient to pay for another, which is to be located in district No. 1. This district will require a house of larger dimensions, as there are more than double the number of children than are in any other district.

The town treasurer was instructed to sell the school and public lands belonging to the town at public auction on the third Monday of June, apply the proceeds to the erection of the several school-houses. On November 19, 1834, the town voted that $150 be paid out of the town treasury, for the purpose of enlarging the school-house in district No. 1. It was also voted "that no person should have the privilege of sending to the public schools who refuses to furnish his proportion of wood, and board of teacher, and that said proportion of wood be furnished before sending unless such parties be very poor, then the school committee may admit their children into the schools."

The school committee reported to the town May 26th, 1835, that there had been school-houses built in districts Nos. 2, 3, 4 and 5 the past year, and schools of three months each kept in them during the winter. No public school in district No. 1, during the year for want of suitable accommodations. They, however, state that there has been erected in said district, a school-house 30 by 40 feet, with 10 feet posts, with a good cellar underneath, the cost of which, over and above the sum appropriated by the town, has been furnished by donations from individuals.

There is no record of any vote being taken by the town regarding public schools or school property belonging to the town from May 26th, 1835, to May 30th, 1843. A school committee consisting of five members, one from each district, was appointed annually.

At the town meeting, May 30th, 1843, the town treasurer was instructed to pay the registry money to the public school committee, to be used by them according to law. April 3d, 1844, it was voted, that the school committee shall make the necessary repairs for the perservation of the school-houses in the town under the advice of the town council, and shall prosecute for all destruction of the same. Also voted at this meeting, that the temperance society be allowed the use of the several school-houses for holding their meetings, whenever it did not interfere with the schools, or religious meetings previously appointed. The above act was repealed at the next town meeting, May 28th, 1844.

The first public school tax ordered by the town was April 1st, 1846.

Below is a statement showing the amount appropriated by the town for the support of public schools each year from 1846 to 1875:

APPROPRIATIONS.

Year	Amount	Year	Amount
1846	$150 00	1857-8	$275 00
1847	112 50	1859-66	400 00
1848	112 50	1867	520 20
1849	150 00	1868	510 20
1850-3	115 00	1869	500 00
1854	189 60	1870	620 05
1855	181 60	1871-5	1,200 00
1856	181 00		

A town meeting was called August 8th, 1846, by fourteen electors of the town, headed by Dr. James H. Eldridge,—

1st. To determine the manner in which any money, either raised by tax over and above the sum received from the State, or derived from registry tax, funds, grants, or other sources of revenue appropriated to public schools, shall be apportioned among the districts of the town.

2d. To make such orders upon the subject of the school-houses, as may enable the several districts, or any one of them to repair and enlarge the said school-houses, either by conveying the right of the town to the districts, or otherwise as the citizens of the town may determine.

The first vote taken on the proposition to convey the several school-houses to each district was almost unanimous in the negative.

The second proposition to convey the school-house in district No. 1, to said district was lost.

Third. It was voted and resolved, that the school-houses belonging to the town may be used for keeping public schools therein, until further orders of the town, and that the money ordered to be raised by the town by tax at the April town meeting for the support of public schools, and all sums of money now in the treasury received from the registry tax and other sources of revenue appropriated to public schools, and also all sums hereafter raised by the town by tax for the support of public schools, or which may hereafter be received by the town from the registry tax or other sources of revenue appropriated to public schools be divided equally among the districts for the support of public schools therein, and that the same be divided by the school committee.

November 7th, 1848, it being understood in town meeting that the school-house in District No. 2 was very much out of repair, it was voted and resolved, that the school committee be instructed to make such repairs as are only necessary for the comfort of said school, the expense not to exceed from $6 to $10.

At a town meeting holden May 28th, 1850, it was " voted that the town treasurer be authorized and required to execute and deliver a quit-claim deed of the school-house and lot on which it is situated in District No. 1, belonging to the town, to said district." He was also instructed to execute and deliver deeds of the other school-houses belonging to the town to the several districts in which they are situated, whenever said districts shall organize as school districts and become bodies corporate in accordance with law.

MAXWELL SCHOOL FUND.

A notice was given to the electors of the town to meet at the school-house in the village of East Greenwich, on Wednesday the 31st of October, 1849, at 2 o'clock P. M., "To hold a town meeting for the purpose of transacting any business that might be necessary in order to get the legacy bequeathed to the town by Mary Maxwell, late of Philadelphia, deceased, widow of Robert Maxwell. Said bequest will amount to about twenty-four hundred dollars, and is to be invested in bank or other stocks, the interest to be applied to the support of public schools." It was voted and resolved that the principal of said bequest shall always be kept unbroken and entire, according to the intentions of said Mary Maxwell, the donor thereof. That the dividends or interest arising therefrom, shall be drawn by the town treasurer and be applied by the school committee to the support of public schools, to which the children of all the inhabitants, and particularly of the poor, shall be admitted, and instructed in such manner as to make such admission and instruction as nearly equal as possible for all the children of the town.

In January, 1854, Dr. James H. Eldredge was appointed trustee of the above named fund with orders to sell the stock in the Rhode Island Central Bank and invest in some other manner.

His first report was submitted to the town May 30th, 1854, viz. :

Agreeable to the orders of the town, the trustee of the Maxwell School Fund presents the following report :

On the 14th day of February, 1854, one hundred and sixty shares in the Rhode Island Central Bank, belonging to this fund, were sold at public auction at $15 per share, and transferred on the 17th to Christopher Hawkins; on the 21st of the same month the dividends, amounting to $312, were by order of the school committee transferred to the trustee to be invested with the principal. Whole amount of principal and interest $2,712. On the 22d February, 1854 twenty-five shares in the Arcade Bank, Providence, were bought for $55 per share, with interest from the last dividend amounting to $1,360. Also same day, twenty-five shares in the Bank of North America at $53.50 per share, with interest from the last dividend amounting to $1,347; Total $2,707; leaving in the hands of the trustee five dollars. The dividends are payable in July and January.

Respectfully submitted,

J. H. ELDREDGE, *Trustee.*

Dr. Eldredge was the sole trustee of this fund until June 6th, 1874, when he presented his final report to the town and requested permission to transfer the account to the town treasurer, which was granted. The principal has been kept unbroken; amount $2,712. The yearly income, amounting in all to $3,150.58 from July, 1854 to January, 1875, has been appropriated by the school committee yearly to the several districts according to the average daily attendance.

School Supervision.

Previous to 1857, the supervision of the schools in the town devolved upon the school committee, it being customary for each member to have charge of the school in the district in which he resided; he was also trustee of the district, employed the teacher, etc., in those districts which were not organized. In the above year Jeremiah Slocum was appointed by the town to visit the public schools and to receive one dollar for each visit, not to exceed two visits to each school during the year. After 1857, until 1872, the school committee usually appointed some person to visit the schools in the town and report to them. June 1st, 1872, the town elected a superintendent of public schools and voted his salary for the first time, and has continued to do so yearly up to the present time.

The last vote of the town in regard to dividing the money was in June, 1859, which was as follows: "Voted and resolved that the money appropriated from the town treasury, and that from registry tax, be divided equally among the scholars, according to the daily average attendance."

District Organization and Progress.

The first district meeting ordered by the school committee in District No. 1, under the new law passed in 1845, was holden at the school-house, May 30th, 1846. A moderator, clerk, treasurer, collector and three trustees were elected for the year. The trustees were "instructed to ascertain forthwith what school-house and what repairs are necessary on the present school-house; what land can be purchased for a location and what tax will be necessary, and report at the next meeting." At the next meeting, June 8th, 1846, it was voted that each pupil be required to pay the sum of one dollar for every three months' schooling, with the proviso that no child should be excluded whose parents or guardians were unable to pay. The trustees were authorized at this meeting to raise the school-house one story, and make such repairs in and around it, as they might deem advisable. But the school committee did not approve of the alterations and improvements, consequently the proposed repairs were never made.

In 1848, the school-house having become too small to accommodate all the pupils, the trustees were instructed to hire another room and have two public schools. From this time the number of pupils increased, and another school was opened in a short time, but the district could not for a long time agree upon a location, or what size and kind of a school-house was needed. Committee after committee was appointed to select location, plans for building, etc., etc.; their report received and the committee discharged.

At a school meeting, May 24th, 1858, a committee was appointed and they were instructed to purchase the building known as the Old Academy, to have it moved to a suitable location and to put it in good repair. The committee immediately proceeded to act in accordance with their instructions, had the building completed in a short time, and schools were opened in the building in November. The school-house has been enlarged and repaired since. During the past term every room was full, and if the scholars continue to increase there will soon be need of another room.

District No. 2. Organized August 11th, 1855. The school-house belonging to the town was burned a short time before the district was organized, consequently the first business of the district was to furnish themselves with a suitable building for school purposes.

August 20th, 1855, the Trustees were appointed a committee to build a school-house on or near the lot where the old town school-house stood, and the treasurer of the district was instructed to hire such sums of money as might be necessary to pay for building the same. The school-house was completed near the close of the year at a cost of four hundred and twenty-five dollars, above the underpinning.

There being some objections to the location, in 1857 the house was moved to the opposite side of the road. Rev. William P. Place donated to the district a lot 100 × 50 feet, with the privilege of using the whole field of several acres for a play-ground, since which time the buildings have been kept in repair by tax assessed upon the property of the district, and schools have usually been in session eight months in each year.

District No. 3. Organized in 1854. Schools have been kept eight months in every year, with few exceptions. The school-house was never thoroughly repaired until 1875, when over five hundred dollars was expended upon it and the out-buildings.

District No. 4. Organized November 13th, 1854. The school-house was burned in January, 1865. A building committee was appointed February 18th. 1865, and a new school-house was completed in April, at a cost of about one thousand dollars, located thirteen rods east of the old school-house. This district has had at least eight months' school every year. The school-house in this district is now needing paint upon the outside, but aside from that, is in better condition than any other in town, except in No. 1.

District No. 5. Organized March 11th, 1854. April 14th, 1855, a deed was received of the school-house from the town. In 1861 a lot was purchased containing one quarter of an acre, near where the school-house stood, (it then being within the limits of the highway,) and the school-house was removed there. An addition of several feet was put on the front; the outside was thoroughly repaired, and a high board fence was built on three sides of the lot; all of which make it the most pleasing, from the outside, of any school-house in town. The inside has never been thoroughly repaired, but it is in great need of it. Eight months is the usual time schools are in session, four months in the Winter and four in the Summer season.

EAST PROVIDENCE.

BY REV. R. H. PAINE.

SUPERINTENDENT.

The town of East Providence is of so recent birth that her educational history can but be short. On the first of January, 1862, she was received into Rhode Island, being that portion of the town of Seekonk, in Massachusetts, which was at that time set off from Massachusetts, and annexed to Rhode Island. The earlier educational movements belong to the history of the town of Seekonk, which at one time contained a seminary of great reputation, situated within the limits of this present town. Upon the organization of East Providence, a generous policy was adopted in regard to public schools, and the town replaced the oldest school buildings with new and better arranged ones within the first four or five years of her history. All the districts were provided with new school-houses, except District No. 1, where the building was twice enlarged, increasing four-fold its capacity.

There are eight districts. In 1872, the town built a Union Grammar school-house for Districts Nos. 2 and 8, in which a flourishing school has been held up to the present time. In 1875, the school population in District No. 1 had so increased that the building, capable of holding two hundred scholars, was inadequate for the accommodation of the numbers wishing to attend school, caused by the rapid increase of that portion of the town, (Watchemoket,) and a new grammar school-house was ordered, at a cost of $12,500. This was built of wood, and is capable of seating two hundred and fifty pupils.

The old building now intended for primary scholars, is full. About one hundred and forty attend at the new grammar school-house.

Several of the districts are inhabited mainly by a farming population, and are sparsely settled. The schools are liable to great fluctuation in numbers from year to year, as at one time there is but a small school population, and again, in the same districts, in a few years, a large number of scholars. It is the endeavor to have equally good school- in each of the districts, and therefore the cost of education is sometimes more *per capita* in one district than in another, but this, evidently, in a short cycle of years, will equalize itself, and all the youth, at all times, have virtually the same advantages.

At the present time District No. 1 has about three hundred and fifty pupils; No. 2, fifty; No. 3, seventy; No. 4, twenty-five; No. 5, twenty; No. 6, seventy; No. 7, fifteen; No. 8, twenty; Union grammar school, fifty.

Evening schools have been held during the past autumn and winter in the village of Watchemoket and at School-house No. 2. These schools had each one term of ten weeks. That at School-house No. 2 was especially attractive, from the fact that the major part of the scholars were natives of Northern Europe, who gladly availed themselves of this opportunity to acquire the language and modes of expression of our country.

This makes the third year that evening schools have been supported by the town and State appropriations.

In looking back over the fourteen years of our town's existence, we may see that advance has been made. A strong stand in favor of education taken at the first has resulted in a thoroughly good system of schools throughout the town.

But this has not been done without a large expenditure of money. At first the town supplemented the district taxation for the support of the schools, but since 1873 the town has undertaken, without any special district appropriation, the expenses both of school buildings and that of maintaining the schools, meaning to furnish enough for a school year of forty weeks.

The appropriations, including that for evening schools, for the year ending April 30, 1876, are... $8,100 00
To which is added our proportion of the State's money............. 1,443 00
And registry taxes of.. 140 00

In all...$9,683 00

There are about seven hundred children attending school, making the cost not far from $13 per scholar.

GLOCESTER.

By Rev. Mowry Phillips,

Superintendent.

The object of this sketch is to give a brief statement of the origin and growth of our public schools; and also the condition of the town with respect to educational matters, prior to their establishment. This seems especially fitting on this Centennial year of our national life. When the garnered treasures of an hundred years are before us we should not overlook or underestimate the factors which have produced a prosperity which is unparalleled in the history of nations.

Among these, and in the front rank, may be assigned the cause of popular education. This has been, and must continue to be, the glory and strength of the nation. Without this no such prosperity would have been possible. Our natural resources, great as they confessedly are, would have found no such development as the past has witnessed without that general intelligence which popular education has tended to produce. It is mind that lifts the nation, and manhood that constitutes its glory. Our richest mines are not those entered by the "Golden Gate," but those entered by the door of the unpretending school-house. These are mines of thought, where the precious ore is brought out, separated from the dross and coined into qualities which require no governmental endorsement to give them value throughout the civilized world.

More than half the century, however, passed before free schools were established in this town. Prior to 1828, the only schools were private ones, depending for their support on the tuition fees collected from their pupils. These private schools were few in number and generally small in attendance. There being no school-houses, they were kept in private houses and as these were generally no larger than the families needed, the schools were often crowded into garrets or backrooms, some of which were so low that the larger scholars could not stand erect, and so dark that on cloudy days, they would take turns in sitting at the only casement that admitted the light. That such schools, kept in such uninviting places, and taught by persons who were required to pass no examination, and whose work was under no official supervision, could be sustained, is proof of a strong desire for education on the part of the people. In the villages, however, these schools were of a higher grade. The increased patronage called for a higher order of talent on the part of teachers, and ampler and better accommodations for the pupils. Aside from a few who had tastes and means to send their children abroad for a higher culture, a large proportion of the people enjoyed no other educational advantages than those afforded by these private schools, and imperfect as these were, they were closed against all who were unable, or unwilling to pay the required fees.

Free Schools.

In August, 1828, the town voted to raise by tax a sum equal to that furnished by the State according to the provisions of a law passed by the General Assembly for the establishment of free schools in the several towns of the State. The amount raised was small, but it inaugurated a new era, and was an advance step which has never been recalled.

Measures were speedily taken to divide the town into districts, build school-houses and open schools in each neighborhood. From this time, the poorest child, for a brief term in each year, had the priviledge of attending school. For nearly a score of years, the amount raised for free schools was very small. The amounts expended for the three decades ending with the present year, are as follows:

From 1846 to 1856...$12,604 15
From 1856 to 1866... 16,253 05
From 1866 to 1876... 32,727 83

These figures do not include the amounts raised by rate-bills and private contributions to lengthen the schools, nor the amounts raised to build, furnish and repair school-houses.

As the school population has not materially changed, the increased expenditures is a fair index to the improvement made in the public schools in the town.

Larger pay has secured better teachers, and these, working during longer terms and with better appliances in the school-room, such as wall-maps, blackboards, artificial globes, etc., have produced corresponding improvement in the scholarship of the pupils.

The average age of the scholars is less than in former years. A larger proportion of the older and more advanced are sent away to higher institutions in other towns.

SUPERVISION.

Formerly the supervision of the schools was in the hands of the committee and was generally divided among its members. But since the enactment of the law requiring the appointment of a superintendent the care of the schools has been committed to that officer. This gives unity to the work and secures better results.

JAMESTOWN.

By W. H. Gardner,

Superintendent.

The first school-house whose date can be remembered, was erected in December, 1802. Some of the oldest inhabitants can remember the ruins of one, that must have been built from twenty to fifty years earlier, made of stone.

I learn from the oldest inhabitant, that eighty years ago, the schools were kept in private houses, supported by different families, and only kept in winter.

Fifty years ago, there were three school-houses on the island; at present there are but two, which were built about twenty years ago. They are in good repair, arranged with seats fronting the teacher's desk, two scholars at one desk. Blackboards are provided, but no globes or charts.

The schools at present are smaller than they were, owing to there being no foreign population on the island, and the families being smaller than in olden times. Our schools now average about fourteen, registering from twenty to twenty-three. Twenty years ago, the average was twenty, and we registered twenty-eight or thirty; further back, still more. The cost of tuition for scholars, fifty years ago was $2.00, at present it is $8.00.

The first record of any money appropriated by the town, or received from the State, was in 1846. Probably there was some previous to this date, but no record of it can be found.

In the aforesaid year, the appropriations from the State were $66.33; from the town, $24.57. In 1875, received from State, $218.60, from Town, $400.00. Registry taxes, $27.00, besides a small surplus of dog taxes.

We have one district library, established in 1850. At first it was located part of the time in one district and part in the other. For the last few years, it has been used but very little. Having received the grant of $50 this year from the State, that sum has been expended for new books, and it is now in a flourishing condition.

HOPKINTON.

By Rev. S. S. Griswold,
Superintendent.

The cause of education received the early support of the first settlers of Hopkinton, and it may be appropriate to consider briefly the development of this cause, from its beginning up to its culmination in the present system of our common schools.

Educational Facilities before Establishment of Public Schools.

The facilities for education before the establishment of public schools were few. At first, private schools were kept in unoccupied rooms of dwelling-houses, accommodated with rude fixtures, not the most convenient. Within the bare walls of these cold, but well ventilated school-rooms, were gathered the children, the youth, and the full grown young men and women, with their Testaments, Dilworth's Spelling Book and Arithmetic, Murray's Third Part, slate and pencil, and two sheets of foolscap, goose quill and ink blotter.

In the midst of these groups of rustic scholars stood the schoolmaster, ferule in hand, ready to rule their writing paper, or spat the hand of the disobedient.

The three sciences, commencing with an "R," "readin', 'ritin', and 'rethmetic," constituted their curriculum of study. Yet, with all these disadvantages, many obtained a good practical education.

To read the Testament, to write a large, fair hand, to cast "intrust," and to "cipher as *far* as the Rule of Three" in Daboll's Arithmetic, was the *ultima thule* of scholarship in those days.

Such were the facilities, and such was the result, prior to the appropriation by the State for the benefit of public schools. And yet, many still believe that under that system of disadvantage, more practical benefit was gained, than under the present. Most children went to school then to learn, and as they had to pay their tuition, that became a strong incentive to improve their time to the best advantage.

And must it not be confessed, that when the facilities of those days are compared with those of the present, the verdict will be more favorable to the former than to the latter? Then the cost of schooling enhanced its value and forbade the idling of time, while now the very opposite seems to prevail. Then only the substantials of education were taught, while now the substantials often give place to the mere ornamental. Then the stern ruggedness of New England, that required indomitable toil and untiring perseverence, was well calculated to grow men and women, even from such a soil, while the easy circumstances of to-day tend to effeminacy and indolence. Such were the educational opportunities for obtaining knowledge prior to the establishment of the public schools.

ESTABLISHMENT OF THE PUBLIC SCHOOLS.

Public schools were first established in this town in the year 1828. Previous to this time most of the schools were held in private houses, and all were sustained by private contributions. As an evidence of the interest the inhabitants had in the cause of education, five school-houses had been built prior to the appropriation of money by the State for school purposes. Up to this time the town had not been divided into districts.

The following is taken from the records of the School Committee, by which it will be seen that the first school committee was probably appointed at the town meeting in June, 1828. Said Committee held their first meeting July 7th, 1828.

"At a meeting of the School Committee holden within and for the town of Hopkinton, on the 7th day of July, in the year 1828.

"Members present, (viz.), Elder Matthew Stillman, James Wells, Edward Barber, Isaac Collins, Jesse Brown, Nathan Lillibridge, Peleg Maxson, Jonathan N. Hazard, Daniel L. Langworthy, George H. Perry, and Christopher C. Lewis. (Engaged.)

"*Voted*, That Elder Matthew Stillman be and he is hereby appointed President of the Committee for the year ensuing.

Voted, That Christopher C. Lewis be Secretary of the Committee for the year ensuing.

Voted, That this Committee proceed to divide the town into suitable school districts, without reference to the school-houses which are now built.

Voted, That this meeting be and the same is hereby adjourned to the third Monday in September next at this place, (Joseph Spicer's Inn,) at 10 o'clock, A. M.

Witness, CHRIS'R C. LEWIS, Secretary."

At the adjourned meeting September 15th, 1828, the Committee proceeded to divide the town into eleven districts, which number was subsequently increased to thirteen.

From the record of a still further adjourned meeting, we find that Elder Amos R. Wells, Christopher C. Lewis and Jesse Brown were the first committee appointed to examine candidates for teaching in the public schools, and the following named persons were the first who were authorized or certificated by said examining committee to teach in the public schools during the Winter of 1828–29:

Nathan York, Jr., teacher in		....	1st School District.	
Joseph Crandall,	"	....	2d	" "
David Stillman, Jr.,	"	....	3d	" "
John T. Paine,	"	....	4th	" "
Latham Hull, Jr.,	"	....	5th	" "
Amos R. Wells,	"	....	6th	" "
Harriet Wire,	"	....	7th	" "
George Newton,	"	....	8th	" "
Amos W. Collins,	"	....	9th	" "
Thomas R. Holden,	"	....	10th	" "
Christopher Brown,	"	....	11th	" "

From the further records of the School Committee we find that the first apportionment of money from the State for school purposes was in the year 1828, and that the amount appropriated to this town was $329.80, apportioned among the several districts as follows:

Districts.	Statement.	(to wit)	Proportion.
No. 1	9		$28 27
No. 2	9		28 27
No. 3	9		28 27
No. 4	9		28 27
No. 5	9		28 27
No. 6	11		34 56
No. 7	9		28 27
No. 8	9		28 27
No. 9	11		34 55
No. 10	10		31 40
No. 11	10		31 40
	105		$329 80

Here, then, in 1828, was the commencement of that system of public schools, with an appropriation from the State of only $329.80, and with such incipient arrangements as were necessarily subject to great future changes, which has now expanded into such large proportions, that the State now appropriates annually more than $1,500, while the town raises an equal amount for the same purpose, and the districts raise in addition to the above amounts from the State and town, annually from two to three thousand dollars.

Justice demands that a tribute of respect be paid to those honorable and honored names, who composed the first School Committee, and the sub-committee for examining teachers.

The memories of Elder Matthew Stillman and Elder Amos R. Wells are yet fragrant with the rich perfume of the gospel ministry; that of Christopher C. Lewis as the honored town clerk for over forty years; that of Jesse Brown as a worthy citizen, magistrate and postmaster; that of George H. Perry as a skillful physician, and worthy deacon of the Seventh Day Baptist Church in Hopkinton city. The other members of that honorable School Committee, though not as publicly known, expressed the wise selection of the town in their appointment to that important office; while every teacher of the present day will sympathize with those pioneer schoolmasters who first passed the fiery ordeal of examination unscathed and unscorched.

Growth and Improvement.

The development of the school system toward a more perfect system was slow. Like all progress in human arrangements it has required a semi-centennial season to perfect the germ into blossoms and fruit. The distance between the blade, the ear, and the full corn in the ear, is oftener measured by centuries than by years. But though of slow growth our public schools have made progress in the right direction. The rough and rude houses with slab seats, diminutive windows, and yawning fireplaces, have given way to elegant edifices, surrounded with beautiful and ample play grounds, and internally, conveniently and tastefully seated with chairs and desks, and walls decorated with maps, charts, and ornamental pictures, and presiding over all, is the teacher rather than the schoolmaster.

Present Condition.

The present condition of our public schools is most promising.

With some three or four exceptions the school-houses are large, commodious, and well arranged inside, with modern improvements; surrounded without by ample play grounds.

The curriculum of study is enlarged, and the methods and manner of teaching greatly improved. Teachers of more enlarged and thorough education are now employed.

The graded schools are attaining a deserved reputation for good order, mild but firm discipline, thoroughness in class recitations. Corporal punishment is seldom resorted to, and those schools which have entirely dispensed with it rank highest for good order and behavior of the pupils.

The important position our public schools occupy, and their relation to the best interests of the community are being better understood and appreciated. The curriculum of study is becoming more comprehensive, and the examination of teachers now embraces a most thorough series of written questions upon nearly all branches of an academic course; while school officers are made to feel the responsibility of their duties.

It is not too much to say that our schools are taking high rank among the public schools of the State. And, while there is a spirit of conservatism among us, that may retard for a while, yet the public sentiment of a large majority is toward the highest possible attainment, the nearest approximation toward the perfect.

SUPERVISION.

Schools, like every other organization, need to be supervised; and few more responsible duties are devolved upon a town, than in selecting its school supervisors. They should be men or women qualified either by nature or education, for that important position.

School supervision should be parental rather than dictatorial. The entrance to the teacher's position should be carefully guarded by the supervisors of our schools, so that none but those who are competent be permitted to sit at the teacher's desk. For, let it not be forgotten, that every teacher will daguerreotype himself more or less upon his pupils. His manner, habit, demeanor and method of teaching will be reproduced in the scholar. Hence a most strict examination of all candidates for teaching, both as respects their literary attainments, their demeanor, their habits of thought, their method of instruction and their system of discipline, should be instituted.

So, also, each school should be most carefully yet tenderly supervised, and should be made to feel that it is under the ever watchful eye of the Superintendent. Hence the wisdom of that statute that makes it imperative upon School Committees to make rules and regulations for the attendance and classification of the pupils, for the introduction and use of text-books and works of reference, and for the instruction, government and discipline of the public schools, and to prescribe the studies to be pursued therein, under the direction of the School Commissioner.

But a still farther supervision by the State seems to be necessary, in order that our public schools may secure still greater advantages to the children of the State; that is, such a supervision as will require a regular attendance for a certain length of time of all children within certain ages upon the instruction of our public schools.

Thus under the fostering care of the State, and the wise supervision of the town through its school officers may our public schools realize their fullest ideal of an Alma Mater to our children.

SCHOOL LIBRARIES, APPARATUS and OTHER INSTRUMENTALTIES.

There are two libraries in this town. The Manton Union Library of nearly 1000 volumes at Hope Valley, seems not to be appreciated as fully as it might be, owing probably to its lack of the works of modern authors.

The Ashaway Library and Reading Room Association, located at Ashaway, Hopkinton, was organized by the adoption of a constitution, November 5, 1871, for the purpose of furnishing to the inhabitants of Ashaway and vicinity the advantages of such a library. The Association furnishes a reading-room with the current periodicals free to all.

The library contains between 600 and 700 volumes of the latest standard works. The association also provide for an annual course of lectures. Doubtless one reason why libraries are not more patronized at the present day, may be, in part accounted for by the universal flooding of the community with newspaper literature; yet every community should have a library well furnished with the most improved standard works, both ancient and modern.

ACADEMIES.

In 1858 the enterprising citizens of Potter Hill and Ashaway erected the first academical building in the town; in which a school was opened December 1st, under the supervision of the Rev. J. W. Morton as Principal, and Mrs. L. E. Coon, as Preceptress, with other teachers as the school might require.

In 1862, Prof. Morton resigned his position, and was succeeded by Prof. H. C. Coon.

In 1864, Prof. Coon and his accomplished wife resigned their positions, and were succeeded by Prof. A. A. Palmiter, who in 1866 resigned, and was succeeded by Prof. Amos C. Lewis, who in 1869, on account of ill health, tendered his resignation.

Thus closed the school work of Hopkington Academy, after a struggle of ten years against financial embarrassments, and some want of experience in managing such institutions.

With no endowment funds, and no aid from the public treasury, it had to succumb to an inevitable fate. Yet the school has done a noble work and many of its students have taken higher and better stations in life, and become more useful for its having been. Among the names of those who have become somewhat noted, and who perhaps are equally deserving of as honorable mention, is that of Julia Crouch, author and public lecturer.

But the days of academies are ended and graded schools have been born.

In 1873 Districts Nos. 2 and 4 of Hopkinton and 8 of Westerly, resolved themselves into a Joint School District, for the purpose of establishing a graded school, and the stockholders of Hopkinton Academy generously donated their interest in it, to said joint district for the above purpose. And in the fall of 1873 was opened a graded school in this Joint District, under the instruction of Prof. S. S. Scammel as Principal, and Miss Sarah E. Chester, in the Grammar Department, and Miss Emma E. Kenyon, in the Primary Department.

This graded school at present, 1876, under the instructions of Prof. J. A. Estee, his accomplished wife, and Miss Emma E. Kenyon, has attained a high reputation for good order and class recitations. Its future is full of promise.

In this connection it is proper to mention the graded school at Hope Valley. This school also has attained a deservedly high rank. Under its present corps of teachers, Prof. E. F. Lanphear, as Principal, and Mrs. Joanna Dockrey, in the Intermediate, and Miss Hattie E. Frisbee, in the Primary Department, this school is taking a high position. Its future also is full of promise.

At Rockville there is a school of two grades. The Higher Department is under the instruction of Miss Sarah A. Hoxie, and the Primary, under the care of Miss Lillian Gray.

This school has only been graded for the last term, and therefore has not had the opportunity of time as yet, which the other graded schools have had. It however affords sufficient evidence of the utility of the arrangements.

The other schools, though of only one grade, give proof that the cause of education in our public schools, is making progress in the right direction.

In conclusion, the cause of Education, and especially as it stands connected with our public schools, is advancing. And the citizens of Hopkinton may congratulate themselves that their Common Schools will rank not inferior to others of this State, at the Centennial Exhibition.

JOHNSTON.

BY WM. A. PHILLIPS,

SUPERINTENDENT.

CLAIMING no merit as a historian, I simply give such facts, as it is possible to glean from records as found in this office, with such comments as the occasion may demand, to show that public education within our borders has improved during the last half century, and to illustrate the fact that public sentiment in regard to schools has advanced in the same proportion that science has, in the same time.

To begin, it will be hardly fair to compare our present status, as a town, with what it was fifty years ago, from the fact that so many additional advantages are now offered by academy and high school (not to say college) that many of our advanced scholars avail themselves of these privileges at an early age, and keep up a continual drain upon our public schools, thereby lessening our numbers and average; yet we think the comparison, notwithstanding this drawback, will be in our favor.

The first meeting of any school committee, of which any record can be found, was on the second day of June, 1828; and was holden at the inn of Resolved Waterman, at which twelve members were present, and of that twelve, but one remains alive to day. The Hon. James F. Simmons was elected chairman, and Lyndon Knight, secretary.

At this time, it seems no district, or schools supported by the town, existed according to the record, or if such did exist, they were cared for in such a way as to require no committee of the town especially for that purpose.

On the second Saturday in August, the first attempt to divide the town into districts was made, and metes and bounds for ten districts were recorded. For some months following, alterations were made to accommodate any and all parties who might petition the honorable board.

The first Saturday in September, 1828, the school-houses were located and established, and strange to say, with but few exceptions, they remain to-day as then located—one of those particular exceptions, being in District No. 7, at the village of Manton.

The first location was on a bleak hill, with an unbroken country upon every side, and the writer hereof, has many a day sat shivering before an old-fasioned fire-place, while the wintry blast swept around, seeking admission at every corner and crevice; but the old house has passed away, as have many of the occupants; the new house has found a new location, one far more humane as well as economical.

It seems to have been the idea of our forefathers, to locate their institutions of learning upon land that was worthless for any purpose, much more so, for school purposes, as many a school-house to-day will testify. The first advance in public sentiment, is shown in the locations now selected. While formerly the black, rocky, almost precipitons hills received the highest mark of civilization; to-day the most level fertile spot that can be produced is thought almost too poor for the houses in which our children are to receive their first impressions. The eye is first educated, and through the eye the mind. So much for the first step.

At the time of forming the districts and locating the different houses, the question of remuneration for teachers was thoroughly canvased, and wages from twenty to seventy cents per day, were settled upon. We have no doubt that, even at that price, their labor was as fairly remunerated as that of the teachers to-day at the present high rates of everything purchased.

The highest appropriation made at this time to any one district was forty-two dollars, and the lowest thirty-eight dollars, for the use of the schools for the year, and by the records I find that three members of the committee were appointed to visit each school. In this connection we find the following vote recorded in the doings of the school committee:

> "Voted and Resolved: That the several sub-committees heretofore appointed to engage teachers for the several districts, be, and they are hereby appointed the visiting committees for their respective districts, *and that said committees be requested to invite a clergyman to attend to that duty with them.*"

Thus it was evidently intended that the moral and religious culture of the child should not be neglected. We also find a vote recorded repealing the vote of the last meeting, whereby the appropriation was made, and that the appropriation shall now be *fifty cents* less in each district. We also find than appropriation of six dollars and seventy-five cents was "allowed the inhabitants of the northeast part of the eighth district, on and north of the powder mill turnpike, to be by them appropriated to educating their children, at such school as they think proper, and a bill for their education to that amount, being signed by the committee for said district and recorded and countersigned by the secretary, shall be considered as duly certified by this committee."

The custom of appropriating a certain amount to that locality continued for some years, to be expended as above stated.

All bills for teaching were sent to the committee for payment. They had to be signed by the several committees, countersigned by the secretary, and recorded in the book of records, before the amount was allowed.

We find no record of how much money was appropriated for school purposes by the town or State, until March 1, 1833. Although money had been derived from some source, and had been most judiciously expended, yet the amount was left off the record, until this year when we find the following entry:

Money appropriated by the Town for the year 1833................ ..$355 00
Money appropriated by the State for the year 1833................... 241 98

Making a total appropriation of....................................$596 98

This we believe was the first assistance from the State for public schools.

In September, 1831, two schools were established in District No. 4, on account of the long distance the pupils had to walk to attend the one which was situated at the extreme south side of the district; a house being hired for the use of the second school at *twenty-five cents per week*, while in actual use. Surely no fault could be found with the price agreed upon for rent.

June 9, 1832, a new district was formed from parts of Districts Nos. 2, 3 and 5, and was called No. 11.

A school-house was located and the proper machinery put in motion for the accommodation of the inhabitants of that locality. About this time we find the wages had been cut down, as ladies were receiving *one dollar and twenty-five cents*, while male teachers received but two dollars and fifty cents per week; but like the present times the price of service fluctuated as the demand increased or diminished. The appropriations for the next few years varied but little. In the year 1837, the town's appropriation had increased to $350.00 and the State appropriation to $274.84, making quite an addition to the amount for those times, and especially when we consider that the hard times of that year required so rigid economy in all expenditures.

In 1838, the appropriation of the town remains the same while the State gives $666.72 ; which amount seems to have been kept up for some years. On February 8, 1841, Districts No. 12 and No. 13 ; one at Graniteville and the other at Dry Brook, (now Hughesdale,) were formed, the bounds were defined and school-houses were located.

May 1, 1843, the first concise report is given in the records as follows : Number of school districts, thirteen. Number of schools, fourteen. Number of scholars registered, 560 ; average attendance, 400. Number of teachers, 20 ; male, 14 ; female, 6. Average amount per month for instruction, nearly twenty dollars. Time of keeping each school three months.

In January, 1844, District No. 14 was established in the westerly part of the town, and was composed of parts of Districts No. 4 and No. 6. At this time the appropriation was over $1,100.00 from all sources, yet the increase in the number of districts, kept the appropriation for each district small, and not more than three months of schooling could be obtained. One of the reasons is attributable to the fact, that nearly three hundred dollars of the appropriation had to be expended in rents, etc., as so few of the districts were in possession of a suitable house of their own for school purposes.

As yet there were no trustees to look after the wants of each district, but all devolved upon the committee, as a body, or on sub-committees appointed by them for that especial purpose.

Under the new school act of 1846, a new order of arrangements began, the first step being the reduction in the number of the town committee. Under the old order, from twelve to fifteen members composed the board, and according to the records, it was hard to get a quorum together to do business ; as the adjournments testify. At this time but three were elected.

In the year 1846, the State's appropriation was $589.99 ; while the town appropriated $500.00, to which was added $174.46 from registry taxes, making a total of $1,264.45, making quite an increase. This year the first record of trustees appear, and the above appropriation was divided, subject to their draft and order.

Notwithstanding the increase in appropriation some of the districts were anxious to secure more schooling than their proportion gave them, and made a direct tax upon themselves, of one dollar to each scholar, for each three months of school; the Manton District taking the first step in this direction, which was at once approved by the committee, and which gave the inhabitants of this district quite an advantage.

In 1851, the amount of State appropriation had increased to $825.97 while the town's remained about the same, and during this year $1,435.22 were expended for school purposes.

September 3, 1850, at a special meeting of the committee an application from District No. 7 (Manton) was received, and approved for a district tax of $1,200 for the purpose of building a new schoolhouse. The approval was at once acted upon, and soon a new house was ready, accommodating forty-five scholars, and to-day it is an ornament and an honor to those whose good judgment conceived and carried out the idea, that a good, substantial, attractive house is necessary for educating the mind, and who by their acts condemned the old prejudice against innovation upon established rules. It is not my province to write a homily against what is termed old fogy ideas, yet I *know* that there are those to-day who would educate their children in a house they would deem unfit to fatten their pigs in, because of its unworthiness, and general filthiness. The argument so often advanced, that what was good enough forty years ago is good enough now, finds many advocates, and those too, who would scorn to take the slow stage, or await the tedious mails, when the steam car is accessible or the telegraph within fair distance. But, thanks to an intelligent public, the elevating power of the press, and the expanding minds of the rising generation, public sentiment is being educated to new ideas, and the old is fast giving way to the new.

In November, 1852, District No. 3 (Simmons Upper Village), voted to follow the lead of No. 7, and build a house suitable to their wants, which was done, and it stands to day sufficient for all the needs of the district.

In January, 1853, No. 13 expended $900 in enlarging and refitting the school-house of the district.

In 1854, the total amount of school money had reached the sum of nearly $2,000 showing that the liberal sentiment was on the increase, and that educational matters were receiving the attention of the people.

In the year 1867, the appropriation from all sources had reached nearly three thousand dollars, about this time exceeding interest began to be manifest in the different districts and more especially in No. 1. This being the most thickly settled part of the town, and many new dwellings being continually erected, it became necessary to enlarge the school accommodations, and much talk was indulged in in regard to a new brick school-house, with graded schools. Just previous to this time, the village of Merino had established a school, which relieved that of No. 1 materially, yet the need was felt, and the subject was thoroughly discussed. Upon the 14th day of November, 1867, after various attempts to improve school facilities in District No. 1, and failing to agree upon what was needed to meet the wants of the district, or upon what location to decide, the people in the south part of the district, (or more particularly speaking, the Plain Farm) made formal application for a division of said district, which after due consideration was granted, and District No. 15 was formed, with men at the helm who were determined to make a district with accommodations that even our neighbors of the city need not be ashamed of. The work was at once commenced, and on the ninth day of May, a lot 200 feet square had been secured, and plans and specifications for a four-room building were presented to the school committee for approval. This was at once secured, and work began upon the same. It was rapidly pushed to completion, surmounted with a bell, and three rooms furnished with the latest improved furniture.

District No. 13, not to be behind her more ambitious neighbors, at once determined to build a new house; so, after securing a lot, they presented plans and specifications to the committee for a house, 25 by 50 feet of a modern pattern, which were approved October 17, 1868, and the following Spring a new house, with latest improved furniture, was ready for the use of the scholars of the district. The appropriation had at this time reached nearly $4,000.

August 21, 1869, District No. 16 was formed, consisting of the Merino Village and a small territory surrounding the same, which step became necessary from the large number of scholars in attendance at this school, there being an average of forty-four. Although the step thus taken, caused much comment, and some hard feelings, by reducing the territory of No. 1 District, yet when the reason was understood by the more enlightened portion of the inhabitants, the breach was healed and the wisdom admitted.

March 4, 1871, an attempt was made to have district lines abolished, which attempt proved abortive, and the old system prevails. The cause seems to have been the jealous fear of centralization of power, so common to the American public at large. We are no advocate for centralization, yet we honestly believe that the affairs of the public schools can be more judiciously, economically, and faithfully administered in the hands of the few, than by many, and there could be no maladministration of affairs long continued, for the ballot box would soon end the matter.

July 1, 1871 under the new law that each town *must* have a superintendent of schools, whose duty it should be to have personal supervision, and execute the wishes of the committee during the year, a new order of affairs began. Rules and regulations were drawn up and established, and the superintendent was made responsible for their faithful execution. In October of this year the superintendent was ordered to make a thorough examination of the condition of all school-houses in the town, and report the same to the committee, which was accordingly done, and at once in all districts, where needed, repairs were begun, new furniture procured and sanitary measures taken for general improvement, not only adding to the beauty of the different houses, but adding comforts that had long been needed in some districts.

In District No. 5, party spirit ran high, and for months the contest was doubtful, whether there should be a new house or not; but at last the party opposed to improvement prevailed, the old house was condemned, and to-day stands as a blotch upon the otherwise well supplied districts. Suicidal ideas threw the stones under the wheels of progress, and paralyzed the attempt at improvement.

In the Spring of 1872, the Commissioner held the first Teachers' Institute ever held in the town, which proved successful, stimulating the friends of education to renewed exertion, a large hall was filled, and about 700 people attended the evening session, and by act, word and deed, approved the doings of the Institute. This seemed to open a new source of information, and parents began to inquire what they could do to make up for past neglects. But one answer was vouchsafed to them, and that was, visit each school as often as time and home duties would permit, and by their presence encourage both teacher and scholar. I am happy to state, since the advent of institutes in our town, a more decided improvement has been manifest.

On June 21, 1873, Districts Nos. 6 and 14 were consolidated, and were to be known as District No. 6, for the reason that both districts were exceeding small, and the cost to maintain two separate schools, was so much greater than their just proportion as to cause much feeling in other localities. This year the total amount of school money from all sources amounted to the snug sum of $9,118.85, while the direct taxation by a few of the districts would swell the amount to over ten thousand dollars; this includes that appropriated for use of evening schools, four of which it had been decided to establish; which was accordingly done with the very best of success, over three hundred scholars being registered.

During the Summer of 1873, the school-house in District No. 1 was raised and a story put underneath, making a four-room building. It was intended for graded schools, but for some cause, after an expenditure of about two thousand dollars, the house was not filled with furniture, nor occupied, except the old rooms as they were before the alteration.

In the Spring of 1875, it was found to be necessary to alter, and more definitely describe, the boundaries of the several districts. On the 4th day of August that duty began, and after six days' laborious work, it was accomplished, and the new lines were recorded, leaving us at the present time with definite bounds and positive lines for the separation of the districts ; and thus, at this our Centennial year, the town stands well in school matters. We do not claim that no improvement can be made, but admit much ought to be done. Yet we do feel proud, that so many steps have been taken to advance the interests of our children.

Notwithstanding so much has been freely given to that cause, and, with one exception, comfortable houses with a goodly share of comforts with them, there is still an onward tendency, and our most earnest wish is a fruition of our hopes.

MIDDLETOWN.

By John Gould,

Superintendent.

As a preface to the school history of this town I quote from a recently published "Early School History of Newport:"

"As is well known, the first comers divided the Island into two townships, the northerly part called Portsmouth and the southerly part Newport. The inhabitants of Newport who lived in the northward and eastward part of the town were called the wood's company, the wood's people, &c."

From the Proprietors' records I find that

"At a meeting of ye underwritten commity chosen by ye proprics to propose a method dividing of ye Commons and being meet this 11th February, 1702, propose as followeth—We propose that School Land be laid out in the Common called Lintal's plaine, six acres for the benefit of the proprics in that part of the township and that six acres more be laid out for the like use in ye Common beyond Daniel Gould's land for the benefit of proprics in that part of the Town, and if each parsell be not put to the use abovesaid then ye income to goo to ye maintainance of ye poore till put to that use."

These grants were respectively in the above mentioned northward and eastward sections of the township of Newport, and were within a few succeeding years at a survey of the Common laid out in accordance with the Proprietors' act. The first record of building of school-houses in this section is found in the record of the Quarter Meeting, April 24th, 1723,—"Ordered that twenty pounds apiece be paid out of the Town treasury for the building the school-house in the woods in accordance with the plea of petitioners, freemen." The records being in an imperfect state this is thought to refer to the building of two houses, as—

MIDDLETOWN.

"At a Quarter Meeting April 26th, 1732, Ordered, that the two School-masters in the woods part of the town, have ten pounds apiece out of the Treasury for their good service to that part of the town for the time past."

In June, 1743, the northerly and easterly part of Newport was incorporated by the General Assembly by the name of Middletown.

In the record of the first town meeting of the town of Middletown, March 7th, 1743, (O. S.) a motion was made for repairing the school-houses.

April 18th, 1744, "Voted, that the Eastmoss School House be Repaired so much as there is a present necessity, and paid out of the Town Treasury."

August 27th, 1745, "Voted, that a Committee of three be and are hereby appointed to hire or agree with a good School-Master to keep school in the Town by the year or for so many months as they shall think needful, for such a Certain sum. And to keep one half the time in the East School and the other half of the time in the West School House, and to be left to the Judgment of sd Committee when to alter from one house to the other. And said School master to keep school five whole days in each week. And sd committee to have the Care of the School Lands and Rent them out to the best advantage, and the Income thereof to be paid to the School master by sd Committee in part of his wages, and sd Committee to agree with the School master, and set price what the weekly schooling shall be of the Severall sorts, and sd school-master to keep a True Account of all weekly schooling. And if the weekly schooling and the Incomes of the Land do not make up the sum agreed for, Then it shall be paid By the Town in the following manner, Viz.: on application to the Town Council, who shall give an order upon the Town Treasurer. And sd committee be chosen annually."

August 26th, 1746, the Committee report that they have repaired the East School-house, which amounted to £125 13s 11d, which they have drawn out of the town treasury. They likewise presented an account of £6, for their time and trouble, which account was accepted and paid out of the treasury.

May 13, 1747, the act of August 27th 1745, appointing a committee to hire school-masters and rent out the school lands was repealed; and the Town Council empowered to hire school-masters and rent out the school lands as they should think most for the town's advantage.

August 12th, 1747, the act of May, 1747, was repealed, and it was voted in town meeting "that Edward Tew keep school in the East School House Two months, to begin the 17th of this Instant August, and so to continue two months next ensuing, for the weekly schooling, and to have five pounds more out of the rent of the East School Land."

There is no record that this man failed to fulfill the appointment made by the town, but in the record of August 25th of the same year, I find that Elezer Reed was to continue teaching in the east school-house until " He compleat the year from the time he first Entered, at the Rate of five pounds per year. Received of Elezer Reed fifty shillings in part of his year's Rent." Elezer Reed continued teaching in the east school-house until March 25th, 1750, at the same rate of compensation for two years, and an increase of one pound for the last year. Reference is made to another payment of rent by him, and this with other records show that the school-houses were built as dwelling houses and usually or often rented to the person teaching.

January 2d, 1750, " Voted that the Rent of the Westerly School-house and Land in 1750 Be allowed the School-Master for his keeping of school in said House in the said year."

Until the year 1754, there were variations in the management of the schools and school lands, being sometimes superintended by separate committees, at others by a joint committee, and still at other times by acts of the town.

April 17, 1754, " Voted that the Late method of managing the Two Schools in this Town be altered, and that for the future they be managed as followeth, viz. : that the Town be Divided into two Squadrons, one House in Each Squadron, and that Each Squadron shall have the Sole power of managing their own school-houses and Lands by Leasing out the same, and Imploying School-Masters as it shall be most agreeable to them, and the Dividing Line betwene the Squadrons Shall be along the Highway from the South end of Moon's Lane, and so northward along the East Highway to Portsmouth, by James Mitchel's Shop. Passed as an act of the town."

January 3d, 1759, it was motioned to sell the east school-house and land and buy a piece of land and build a house in a more convenient place. This motion was voted out at the next town meeting.

April 15, 1764, " Voted that Joseph Ryder Git a Well-Crotch and Sweep to the well at the East School-House, and Draw the money to pay for the same out of the town treasury."

January 6th, 1768, a proposition to build a new school-house.

June 5th, 1776, the easternmost school-house was repaired to the amount of $48.25, which was paid out of the town treasury. For several years mention is made of the renting of school land and house in the east part of the town ; in 1786 a committee of one was appointed to rent the same " and also to employ a School-master, if any presents agreeable to the Veisenity of the house."

August, 1786, " Voted that the old stuff which is left from the Ruins of the School-House be sold at Publick Vandue, and that the Clerk set up a

Proclamation in the Town offering a reward of £30 to any person or persons who will give information of the principal or accessories in Willfully setting fire to the East School-House."

May 23, 1787, the committee appointed to let out the east school land report that "they have let out sd land to Salisbury Stoddard Esq., until the 25th day of March next, for six Bushels of good Indian Corn." The land was rented in the same way to the same person for the next ensuing year.

April 15th, 1789, "Voted that the eastermost school land be now let out by the Moderator to the hiest bidder for one year, and the said land not to be Ploughed nor to be impovershed by Carring of any hay, stones or any thing that belongs to the premises; which land was Bid of to Salisbury Stoddard, Esq., for thirteen Bushels of Good Merchantable Indian Corn, the corn to be paid and Delivered into the Treasury at or before the Expiration of aforesaid Time.

May 27th, 1789 "Voted that the act made and passed at a Town Meeting in April ye 17th, 1754, for the Town's being divided into two Squadrons and Each Squadron having the sole power of Leasing out the School Land and Imploying schoole Master's, Be repealed, and the same is hereby repealed. And Further voted, that all Persons who send Children to school to the West house shall have the full Power of chuseing a School Master to keep schoole in said house, and all other persons who have no Children to send, shall be Excluded from any vote in chuseing said Schoole Master. Voted that the rents of the School land let out to Salisbury Stoddard, Esq., be applied to use of schooling poor children.

June 17th, 1789, the foregoing act in regard to the management of school lands and selection of teachers was repealed and a return made to the former system of each district—as the term squadron now became—having sole management and benefit of each school land agreeably to act of 1754. Later in the year this act was again repealed and a return made to the act of April, 1789.

Jan. 9, 1790, it was again proposed to sell the eastermost schoolhouse and land and buy other for school purposes.

April 21st, 1790, "Voted to appropriate the rents of the East School land to the use of schooling of poor children for that part of the town."

October 10th, 1790, "Voted that a committee be appointed to inspect into the Rights of Town to the West Schoole House and Land if any they have." At the same town meeting there was sold at "Public Vandue," brick laying on the east school land, at the rate of ten shillings and sixpence per thousand, conditions of pay to be made in silver money or in paper, fifteen for one, or in town orders at the same rate.

Establishment of Free Public Schools. 387

April 10th, 1792, " Voted that the rents due for the Eastermost school land be collected and put on Interest in order to be Imployed toward Building a School House."

April 17th, 1805, " Voted that the Deputies be Instructed to call up the Petition at the next General Assembly, which is now before the House, relating to the free school. and that they use their endeavors to recover what was granted the Town for the purpose of said school."

April 15th, 1807, a committee was appointed to examine the records and " see how the East and West school land stands." They report June 3d, 1807 : " We have sarched the proprietors records and find that the East School Land was Granted for the Benefit of the proprietors in that part of the Town, and the West School Land for the Benefit of the proprietors in that part of the Town but in sarching the Town Meeting book of records we find by the votes of the freemen of the Town in several Town Meetings said school lands have been managed by the Town in many ways. And it is our opinion that they Both stand on one footing as appears by said records."

At a later period this question of the lawful management of the school lands was again brought before the town and the final decision of the Court to which appeal was made, was that in accordance with the tenor, of the original gift by the proprietors, each grant of land was to be used and controlled for school purposes by the proprietors of each section in which said grants of land lay, and each section has since received respectively the benefits thereof.

June 6th, 1810, Peleg Sanford and others made application to the town meeting, for the use and privilege of two rods square of the north-east corner of the " Mill Lot," so called, to erect a school house. " Voted and granted their request."

August 31st, 1819, on application of Alanson Peckham and others for liberty to erect a school-house on the common adjoining the seventh district of highways, the freemen after consideration, "Voted they be allowed a piece of Land in said Common of thirty feet Square for said purpose, in such a part of said common as may sute said purpose, and be least Injurious to said Town, which they and their successors may hold in possession during the time they shall keep a School House thereon for the use of a school, and whenever said School-house cease to be kept as a School, the said Land shall revert back to said Town of Middletown, and they shall not claim the same by Possession."

November 19th, 1828, a request of the school committee for a tax to defray the expense of the free school. "Voted to consider the same."

August 25th, 1829, a tax of $119 was voted to support a public school in this town this year.

August 30th, 1830, report of the public school committee received and accepted by the town. Records of the annual election of public school committee and of their reports being received and accepted, are found up to 1846, when the town was divided into five districts, which is the present number.

April, 1847, "Voted that the school committee consist of three persons, and to receive a compensation for their time and trouble of $4. each per annum; also voted to raise a tax of $125. for the support of the public schools subject to the Public School Committee." In 1848 the amount of the tax was raised to $150. In 1851 the tax assessed was only $100; but the following year it was raised to $200. In 1861 the tax assessed was $500; in 1871 it was $1500. The present appropriation of the town is $1800, which is divided equally among the five districts. Under the present arrangement of the school system, there is annually elected by the town a school committee of five in number, who have a general supervision of the five schools of the town. The committee are elected for one, two, and three years, according to law.

As will be seen attention was early given to the subject of education in this town, and also provision made for educating the poor children, thus showing that our early predecessors realized the value of an educated community. A free school was early established and the increased appropriation of money for school purposes of late years shows the increase of interest in that which is the vital principle of all healthy growth or improvement in our condition as an organized body.

NORTH KINGSTOWN.

By D. G. Allen,

Superintendent.

To record the educational events of one hundred years with but little more to guide the pen than tradition, and the treacherous memory of aged persons, we find no small task. There are but few persons living who can recollect much of the school-room of 1790, but when they contrast the schools of the last decade with those of that date the stretch of improvement is very great. There are many persons, however, who have heard parents and grand-parents relate the many improvements in the mechanic arts, but art as well as science is indebted to the light of knowledge received in the school-room.

At the commencement of the century, the all absorbing topics of the day were: What will the Continental Congress do? Will Washington and his army finally triumph? The first question was settled in Philadelphia, July 4th, 1776. The second at Yorktown, October 19, 1781.

The study of arms and the practice thereof robbed the school-room of its devotees, and the school-master of his patronage. During the war, and for twenty years after, the subject of education received but little attention. The lower classes, comprising the sturdy yeomanry of the country, fancied that learning was ruinous to the young men of the soil; the opulent and the aristocracy were the principal patrons of the few select schools in the more populous places.

Educators, similar to Euclid, Plato, Aristotle and Socrates, did not set forth the philosophy of letters till a later date.

The few designed for the law, divinity or the medical art prepared for college or the university under some divine. Collegiate education was thought to be a useless appendage, save perhaps to a teacher of the classics in the city or large village. Lawyers, ministers, and the higher class of teachers were the guardians of society.

Rooms occupied for school purposes for the common grades were some vacant carpenter's shop, some spare room in an old dwelling house, or, if you will indulge credulity, some unoccupied barn with a stove pipe chimney.

School-rooms in those days were unique and curious to the refined taste. The old stone chimney with a fire-place six or eight feet wide, and stone andirons, with a glowing fire made of oak or walnut wood, the cross-legged table and the long writing desks on two or three sides of the room, the benches of saw mill slabs, and round legs with the bark on, are true emblems of " ye olden times."

Fancy yourselves in that antiquated school-room before a clownish pedagogue surrounded by a score or more of rude, uncouth boys and girls from three to five years in their " teens," all dressed in red or moss-colored flannel, or sheep's-gray kersey just from the spinning wheel and the loom.

Behold the school-master clad in the old English costume, the standup collar, the large broad skirts and lapels, the velvet knee-breeches buckled tight below the knees, the long gray stockings and the shoes with broad buckles; to crown all, the powdered hair and braided cue tied with a black ribbon down the back.

The word is given for order, and all are seated on the benches. The morning devotions, consisting of a lesson from the New Testament, read by each scholar in turn that can read, being over, the usual routine of studies is commenced,—ciphering and writing in the forenoon, reading, ciphering, writing and spelling in the afternoon. The small scholars in the alphabet, in reading and spelling fill up the measure of the day. The room, the teacher and scholars were all well adapted to each other.

Reading, writing, ciphering, and spelling were the only branches usually taught in the common or lower schools, and but two classes were ever called upon the floor to recite, the reading class and the spelling class.

In arithmetic the scholar was often required to write in a manuscript all the sums and principal rules, except in fractions, which but few teachers were acquainted with. A teacher generally had a manuscript of his own, and if he could not readily work out the sum for a pupil, he would resort to it for aid.

It was not often that he could explain or demonstrate a problem. He would work it out on the slate or copy it from his manuscript; the scholar would then take it to his seat; if he could solve it, well, if not, it was all the same. I have seen manuscripts an inch and a half thick, large sheets, containing all the sums in Pike's Arithmetic and some in Daboll's.

The books used in the schools were Pike's and Daboll's Arithmetics, and Thomas Dilworth's, with a few others of British origin. In 1783, Noah Webster published his spelling-book, English grammar, and a compilation for reading. These were the first books of the kind published in this country. Their popularity soon won general patronage and those of British make went out of date.

Writing-books were made of coarse, plain, English paper, covered with a coarser article, ruled with a flat piece of lead. Goose-quill pens were the only ones in use. Stone slates and pencils had not been intruded upon by patent rights.

Rules for governing schools were few, arbitrary, and often led to severity. One punishment inflicted upon disobedient scholars, was to cause them to hold up a block of wood of three or four pounds weight by the left hand at full arm's length for five, ten or fifteen minutes, according to the nature of the offence. Another was to whip the hand with a ferule or a leather strap. Another was to yoke two scholars together by the neck with a yoke made with two bows like an ox-yoke. To make the punishment more humiliating a boy and girl were yoked together; sometimes a colored girl was yoked with a white boy or girl. Sometimes they were as wild and frantic as a pair of half-tamed steers. An instance was related to me of two scholars who were required to whip each other with birch whips. William Hall drew a picture of a noted corpulent dignitary of the trustees of Washington Academy the fifth or sixth year of its age, with a pipe in his mouth, and passed it to Gideon Freeborn. The teacher's keen eye fell upon its transit. Gideon was called up and was compelled to expose its author, whips were sent for, and each was to whip the other till he cried. Gideon being the younger was the first to shed tears, but he failed to produce them from William. The teacher therefore said it was his rule to whip till the tears come, and so whipped William till he cried.

The quarter of twelve weeks having ended, and the teacher's bills being made up, they are distributed:

Mr. Jones, Dr. to Tuition of son Stukely or Sally Ann (as the case may be) 12 weeks at 8 1-3 cents per week $1.00

A ninepence was thought to be too much. The bill is paid in barter; a bushel of corn, a few lbs. of meat, flax, wool, or a Spanish milled dollar, according to circumstances. Continental money had depreciated in value, or had ceased to be currency. Thus ends the first twenty-five years of our school record.

At the close of 1779, there was but one meeting-house in our town, that belonging to St. Paul's Episcopal Church in the village of Wickford.

The several orders of Baptists worshipped in dwelling-houses in different localities in the town.

The Quakers, not numerous, worshipped in some rented room in Wickford. At this date, they are nearly extinct. There are at present one Episcopal Church, five Baptists and one Catholic.

In 1800, there was not a school-house in the town, and but one literary institution beside Brown University in the state. At this period a new era dawns upon the people. Statesmen, merchants and divines consult the interests of the country, and the interests of the people. How can they be made wiser, more virtuous and better citizens?

The diffusion of knowledge among the masses was the only hope of the perpetuity of the new democratic government. School-houses must be built, and the common people must be educated. The subject had scarcely been thought of, and there was a large per cent. of the common people that could neither read nor write. There was an increasing demand for knowledge, for teachers, and for places of education.

With these things in view some of the first citizens of Newport, Providence, and North Kingstown united in the establishment of an Academy, and Wickford was the place decided upon for its location.

Washington Academy.

The records of this institution, mainly, have been kept on sheets of paper, except two small manuscripts, one copied from the papers of the first two years, and the other at the renewal of the charter in 1833.

The subscription-paper with the names of the donors and the sum each one gave, together with the amount realized from a lottery, are not to be found, but it appears evident that the expenses were defrayed partly by shares of $20 each and partly by a lottery.

The custom of building meeting-houses, academies and bridges by such means had not quite gone by in those days. Strange philosophy: —doing evil that good might come.

At the first regular meeting of stockholders sixty-seven shares were represented. At another seventy-two; probably there were one hundred which would make $2,000 realized by subscription, and about as much by the lottery.

The first meeting under the Articles of Association was held March

10, 1800, at the house of Oliver Spink in Wickford. The meeting was organized by the election of Peter Phillips, chairman ; Benjamin Fowler, treasurer, and William G. Shaw, clerk.

A committee was appointed to draft a charter and draw a petition to be presented to the General Assembly to be holden in June. At a subsequent meeting the following named persons were elected trustees :

Lodowick Updike,	Benjamin Fowler,
George Thomas,	Daniel E. Updike,
Thomas Rumereil,	William G. Shaw,
Benjamin Reynolds,	Ray Greene,
John Allen,	Walter Channing,
William Ellery.	Christopher G. Champlin,
Robert N. Auchmuty,	Asher Robbins,
Daniel Lyman,	John G. Clark,
Samuel Elam,	William Hunter,
John Brown,	Phillip Tillinghast,
Joseph Reynolds,	Robert Eldred,
Peter Phillips,	Thomas P. Ives,
Nicholas Brown.	

The first meeting of trustees under the charter was held the 27th day of August, A. D., 1800, the time set for the annual meetings.

Samuel Elam, was elected	President.
Peter Phillips, "	Vice President.
Benjamin Fowler, "	Treasurer.
Daniel E. Updike, "	Secretary.

At this meeting an offer of four acres of land was presented to the trustees of the institution as a suitable place for the edifice by " Mr. Nicholas Spink and Ann his wife, and Mr. John Franklin and Hannah, his wife," which was graciously accepted. A vote of thanks was passed and the president was requested to communicate them to the parties.

Besides the shares actually paid in, Mr. Samuel Elam of Portsmouth, gave $100 as a present, and as tradition has it, wanted the institution named after himself—Elam Academy. Mr. Elam was an English gentleman of wealth, a bachelor, and owned a valuable farm in the vicinity of its location, and it was thought he would have endowed it with the gift of that farm had his wishes been gratified, but the indomitable Daniel E. Updike persisted in calling it Washington Academy, and so the matter rested.

Meetings were notified and adjourned often for want of a quorum, and much time was wasted, causing great delay in the progress of the buildings. November 4, 1801, the building committee reported the work nearly completed, but there was a deficiency in the treasury. New subscription papers were sent out to raise a further sum to finish the contract. And here we regret to find the record of the secretary at an end.

A committee of eleven persons was appointed to nominate a suitable person for principal or head instructor. By tradition, we find that Alpheus Baker of Newport was elected principal, and Remington Southwick, assistant teacher. These men were said to be liberally educated.

The school commenced early in 1802 with but seven scholars, but the number was soon increased to about one hundred. Students resorted to this place from Providence, and Newport and from other States of the Union. There are several citizens in this State who received instruction in the old Academy in its earliest days, and many from that time down to the present.

Alpheus Baker continued as principal for five or six years and resigned in November, 1806. Remington Southwick went up the ten-rod road to survey for a contemplated turnpike, and on his return home was thrown from his horse and instantly killed.

Several teachers succeeded these gentlemen, but we fail to find the time and order of their teaching, but we should judge the periods to be from six months to seven or eight years. We give their names as we have gathered them. Wilbur Tillinghast, Linden Fuller, Amanuel Northup, and his brother, Carr Northup, Barton Ballou, Mr. Wood, and Francis Chappell, Esq., so well-known to the citizens of Wickford. He was first a teacher of select schools in the village, and the latter part of his teaching, in the academy. He commenced the profession in 1815, and followed it for about forty years. For many years he had charge of the free schools in connection with the select. But few men could boast of having been in the service so long.

Washington Academy Revived.

The interest in the Washington Academy having subsided very much after twenty-five or thirty years of life, the buildings, by neglect, became much impaired, and it was evident that the edifice must be repaired or fall to ruin. Happily at this crisis, April 13th, 1833, the citizens of Wickford rallied once again. Calling some of the liberal men of wealth in Providence and Newport to their aid, they held meetings, discussed the benefits of education, the good the old academy had done in its better days; and resolved to resuscitate it for the benefit of the youth in the town and state.

The charter granted in June 1800, in consequence of neglect and non-conformity to its requirements, became annulled, and in October, 1833, a petition was sent to the General Assembly praying that the old charter might be revived, with an amendment to the effect that it should not become forfeited by neglect to hold the annual meetings.

The Trustees under the charter as amended, were:

Nicholas Brown,	Thomas P. Ives,
Daniel E. Updike,	Robert Eldred,
William G. Shaw,	William Hunter,
Asher Robbins,	Chris. G. Champlin,
John Brown Francis,	William Sprague, Jr.
James Allen,	Jonathan Reynolds,
Peleg Weeden,	Joseph Sanford,
Pardon T. Hammond,	George Hammond,
Euclid Chadsey,	Jeremiah G. Chadsey,
Christopher Allen,	Benoni P. Bates,

At the regular meeting, November, 1833, His Excellency

John Brown Francis was elected......................President.
Jonathan Reynolds   "   ....Vice President.
Pardon T. Hammond   "   ....Secretary.
Joseph C. Sanford   "   ....Treasurer.

John Brown Francis, Jona. Reynolds and Pardon T. Hammond were elected year after year, until the institution became the property of School Districts 3 and 4. A subscription of $457. was obtained early in the year, and the buildings were put in good repair.

The first Monday in June, 1833, William D. Upham, assisted by Miss Caroline Whiting, commenced school. Mr. Upham's salary was $100. per quarter of 12 weeks, and one-half of the proceeds from tuition that might occur above the regular salaries. The Principal's pay amounted, for the year, by this method, to $427. Miss Whiting's amounted to a little more than $200. Miss Harriet Hall and Miss Margaret Grafton, were assistants part of the time.

A respectable number of students from abroad attended the school, and it flourished about two and a half years. On November 21, 1836, Mr. Upham sent in his resignation as principal, and was succeeded by William H. Taylor, in March, 1837. He was hired for six months for $225.

Subsequent teachers remained but short periods each, and the interest soon waned.

Francis Chappell occupied a room in the building for free schools several years, in connection with his select schools.

The general interest in education was not sufficiently great nor the place sufficiently attractive to draw pupils, and consequently teachers liberally qualified were not called to fill the Preceptor's chair. After Mr. Upham retired not much was heard of the Washington Academy till 1848, when the school committee required the several districts to build school-houses or lease buildings for a term of years.

Lease of Washington Academy.

May 27, 1848 several of the trustees of the academy requested Pardon T. Hammond, Esq., Secretary, to notify a special meeting of the trustees to be holden on Tuesday, the 30th, inst., to take into consideration the expediency of leasing the academy for a term of years.

This meeting was adjourned to the 10th of June, when it was voted to lease the academy and lot to School Districts Nos. 3 and 4, for the term of ninty-nine years, at the price of one cent per annum; the District keeping in good condition the buildings and fences. Thus it continued till September 8th, 1874, when, by the incendiary's torch, it was burned to the ground.

The building at the outset was large and conveniently arranged; sixty by thirty feet, high posted and airy. There was on the first floor one room thirty by twenty-four feet, and two recitation-rooms, one on either side; and the second floor was precisely the same, except not quite so high studded.

This building stood on the hill, overlooking a small cove, or sheet of tide water, on the north, and facing the ever memorable Ten Rod Road on the south. The surrounding view was picturesque and somewhat extensive. It being on the southern outskirt of the village, it was quite convenient for all the people of the place.

With the insurance of $2,000. realized from the old building, and $9,500. raised by a tax on the ratable property of the districts, the present beautiful edifice was constructed in 1875. It is an honor to the place, the cause of education, and the committee who planned it, and superintended its construction. It is to be regretted that the worthy committee was not honored with a vote of thanks for their assiduous labors, and the building with dedicatory services.

The new building is on the foundation of the old, eight feet longer and five wider. There are two school rooms, one on either side of a ten feet hall, twenty-three by thirty-three feet, with dressing-rooms on the outer side of each, and closets for washing hands. The rooms are hard finished, and furnished with patent desks and chairs, one for each scholar. The teacher's platform is raised one foot, and faces the scholars.

The school is graded. The Grammar department is in charge of Mr. F. E. McFee. The Intermediate is in charge of Miss Carrie A. Barton, and the Primary is in charge of Miss Jennie F. Johnston. The number of scholars during the year has been from 130 to 140.

We take pleasure in recording the staid and quiet order of the school-rooms of this place, as well as other school-rooms of the town.

Corporal punishment has become very nearly an obsolete thing in our schools. We can remember well, when the school was governed by the ferule and the whip. It is better, far, when a scholar is persistent in disorder, to dismiss him at once, than to demoralize a whole school by flagellation. Semi-barbarism has yielded to moral suasion.

For seventy-five years has this hill been adorned with an institution of learning—the second of the kind in the State. Its first patrons and benefactors, the first and most distinguished men of Rhode Island, have had their day and have passed away. Of the trustees of 1833 but one survives, Mr. George Hammond, of Wickford.

The Institution has just entered upon the last quarter of the century. Its prospects for usefulness were never better than to-day. Its compeers are numerous. The Friends' Boarding School, the Lapham Institute, the Greenwich Academy, and the High Schools in the cities and large villages are doing a work that tells in the history of the State, and especially in the cause of education.

If education advances in the ratio it has for the hundred years past, who can compass its magnitude, or estimate the moral good it will do to our country and the world.

LIBRARIES.

Soon after the establishment of the academy the nucleus of a library was commenced by subscription and near 300 volumes of valuable books were placed in the institution for the benefit of the teachers, scholars, and people of the village. This library was selected from the most approved standard authors then extant, and it is a wonder that an intelligent reading public would allow so valuable a treasure to become scattered and lost as it was.

A library gotten up in 1821, at a cost of $176.79, by the citizens of the village, called "The Library Society," and numbering 223 volumes, was sold at public auction, January 24th, 1829, each shareholder receiving his portion of the sale.

Since that time there has been no library in the town, save one small circulating library, where a fee of six or eight cents a week was charged; and the libraries connected with the Sunday schools of the several churches.

The Catalogue of this library and the cost of the books may be found on file with the papers of the Washington Academy, in a good state of preservation, at the residence of the late Pardon T. Hammond, Esq., who was the careful Secretary of that institution so many years.

From the number of young and middle-aged men to be seen in the village of Wickford, we are led to inquire whether there is a literary society in the place or not. Some twenty years since, there was an organization for the mutual improvement of its members in reading, writing essays, and public speaking.

This society had its origin, lived a few brief years, was useful and interesting, but died from the feebleness of the will, as such institutions are sure to, when left to the natural inclination of the public.

School Houses.

Soon after the establishment of the academy in Wickford, school-houses were built. The first in the town was built by Thomas Allen, John Wightman and Thomas G. Allen, about the year 1806. Soon after, the last named gentleman bought the rights of the other two, and it was used for meeting and school purposes till 1837, when it was moved and became a part of the dwelling house on the Gould's Mount farm.

This school-house stood in the northern part of Quidnesette, now District No. 1, a little in front of the present new one. It was about 24 feet by 26, with an entry across the east end, nine feet posts and arched overhead. There was an elevated pulpit and desk, with *balusters* on three sides, but the old fashioned writing desks and benches without backs were the only conceivable furniture for a school-house in those days; and these must be fastened to the walls of the house on two sides firmly, or they would not long endure the wear and tear of a school-room.

The second house was built by William Reynolds in 1808. It stood on the hill, one-fourth of a mile south of Potowomut Mill, and near the residence of the owner. After having been occupied for school and meeting purposes a few years it was moved and converted into a dwelling house. About this time a school-house was built near the Davisville Depot, by Ezra and Jeffrey Davis, that has been supplanted by another of much larger dimensions in a more central locality.

Several school-houses were built in different parts of the town a little previous to the introduction of free schools. New school-houses, with modern improvements, and furnished with the best and most convenient common school appliances, have been built in half of the districts. The northern part of the town was first to build school-houses, though indebted to Wickford for the first impulse.

The modern improvements in school-houses commenced in our town about 1855. Patent desks and seats, chairs and settees are the necessary appendages of all newly-modeled school-houses. When these are contrasted with those of 1810, 1820 and 1830, the improvement is very apparent—especially when we take those furnished with the long writing desks on either side of the house, and the seats without backs, made of slabs. Comfort, convenience and ease in the school-room were not thought of in those days, by parents or teachers. Taste and refinement follow in the path of knowledge, light and civilization.

The establishment of the Academy at Wickford in a few years created a marked difference in the construction of houses, as well as in the class of teachers and in the character of the schools. At first the buildings were not painted. The farm houses were small, half finished and low studded. The taste of half a century has remodeled every building. School-houses, dwelling-houses and even barns are painted, and show the march of improvement.

Half a century since, grammar and geography were not known in the common schools. These important branches were long neglected. We can recollect the time when the teachers of the country schools were entirely ignorant of them.

The progress of teachers and scholars toward a higher standard, though slow, was visible from year to year till 1828, when money was appropriated by the State, and the District system commenced.

Teachers.

Among the earliest country teachers of the nineteenth century made known to me is Daniel Havens, late of Wickford. His school-room was in the north chamber of Royal Vaughan's house, now owned by Nathan Carpenter, a little north of the Devil's foot rock, on the post road from Wickford to Greenwich.

The description of the room and school was given me by Mr. Henry R. Reynolds, a pupil. It was about the year 1807. The room was about fifteen feet square, lighted by one window on the east side and one on the north. The fire-place was on the west side. In the middle of the room was a table three and a half feet by six or seven, made of two boards battened together, and mounted on two cross legs made of small joists. On either side was a slab bench for seats.

Two sides of the room were occupied with desks and slab seats for writing and ciphering.

The walls of the room were plastered, but overhead it was neglected, as it was evidently too hard work for the mason. Smoke and cobwebs had colored brown the timbers and boards.

The number of scholars in this school was about twenty-five. Usually it varied according to the season and the popularity of the teacher.

The usual books, Dilworth's, Webster's and Daboll's, furnished drilling matter for the common elementary schools.

The size and age of scholars varied from five to twenty-five years. Advantages and disadvantages accelerated or retarded the progress of education in those days, as now. Some were apt scholars, and by industry and perseverance learned, and others wasted their time, and made but little progress. Probably this school was a fair sample of the schools of this time, and even of an earlier date.

Among other antiquated teachers of a later date may be mentioned Susan Greene, Orner Chadsey, Stephen Branch, Nathan A. Arnold, Ashael Otis, Joseph W. Allen and Samuel R. Ailsworth.

Hon. Jeremiah G. Chadsey, late of Wickford, was a teacher in the Kent Academy two and a half years, under the Rev. Abner Alden, first Preceptor of that institution. Afterward he taught five years in Apponaug in Warwick. As he was a known scholar, and had acquired the reputation of a good teacher, some of the most eminent officers and statesmen of Rhode Island were his pupils.

Benjamin Allen, LL. D., some ten years the senior of Chadsey, and near his birth place, was born in 1772, in Quidnesette, North Kingstown. When fifteen years of age he ran away from home to seek an education. His cousin, Hon. John Allen, happening to meet him very early in the morning, persuaded him to return with him to his father, and he would intercede for the father's assistance. He was found lenient, and the aid so much coveted was immediately proffered. By the father's help and his own untiring industry as a teacher, he graduated with high honors in 1797 at Brown University, and was a tutor in that institution for one year, after which he was elected principal of the Plainfield Academy, in Connecticut. A few years later he was a professor in a college in Pennsylvania, and later, in a college in New York State.

For several years he had a select school for boys and young men at Hyde Park, on the banks of the Hudson. He died in 1836, aged nearly 64 years.

COMMON SCHOOLS.

Early in the present century the subject of supporting schools by taxation began to attract the attention of the pulpit, the press and the legislative men. In 1825 the Rev. Thos. H. Gallaudet, of Hartford, commenced his essays on popular education, at the same time Jas, G. Carter, Horace Mann and Emerson Davis, of Massachusetts, with a Wayland, of Rhode Island were sending forth bright sparks from their ever fertile minds. In 1828 the Legislature of this State appropriated money for the support of public schools. This act of the Rhode Island Assembly is easily traceable to the great light emanating from these distinguished men.

The record does not show what was North Kingstown's proportion of the money the first year, but judging from the amount of several succeeding years, it must have been about $331 from the State, and rate bills collected from the parents of those children in attendance, by the teacher, made up the balance. The teachers boarded around among the scholars. Teachers' wages were usually $10 to $12 per month. They were required to be examined in all the branches usually taught in the common schools.

When the examination of teachers for the District Schools commenced, a class of teachers that had the monopoly of the lower schools soon went out of vogue, and teachers from the Friends' Boarding School, of Providence, and from the Academies of Greenwich and Wickford, took their places.

New books began to take the place of Webster's, and literature opened a new field to the lovers of learning.

At the June town meeting, 1828, a School Committee of fifteen persons was elected, comprising the most substantial citizens of the town. They were Rev. Lemuel Burge, Francis Chappell, Joseph W. Allen, William P. Maxwell, Willet Carpenter, Ezbon Sanford, Silas Richmond, Beriah Brown, Samuel Browning, Jeffrey Davis, William Reynolds, Philip N. Tillinghast, Perry Greene, James Allen and Daniel Congdon. Well would it be if such a class of men could be found in these days to look after the affairs of education. At the first meeting of this Committee, held June 21, 1828, Lemuel Burge was chosen chairman, and Silas Richmond secretary.

The town was divided into ten districts; soon after another was added. The record does not show the amount divided the first year.

October 28, 1828: "Voted, That schools be opened in each district on the first Monday in December, and be continued twelve weeks."

"Voted, That each teacher keep an exact account of the actual attendance of each scholar, and lay the same before this Committee at the end of the quarter."

"Voted, That the money received from the State be divided among the districts, in proportion to the number of children that shall have actually attended school."

"Voted, That Lemuel Burge be a Committee to examine such teachers as shall be directed to him."

"Voted, That the Committee of each District shall hire the teachers, pay their portion of the money, and the balance they must receive from the parents of the scholars, and each committee is to locate the school."

We should judge from the Report of the Committee to the "Freemen of the town" in June, 1829, that the town appropriated money equal to the sum received from the State. There was divided $378.84 among the schools in March and April, 1830. A like sum was probably divided the year before. The number of scholars was 1,184 under the age of 16 years. The above sum we find larger than an average for several years. School-houses were then joint stock enterprises, or owned by private individuals. On April 27, 1833, $331.05 was divided among thirteen districts, the census remaining the same.

At a meeting of the School Committee, held November 9, 1835, it was voted to take a new census of all the white children under the age of 15 years, and of the colored children under 10 years of age. In October, 1838, the Committee reported fourteen districts and $916.22 from the general treasury, and 1,044 children under 16 years of age, no distinction being made as to color. In 1846 the districts were organized as incorporated bodies, and trustees, clerks, collectors and treasurers were elected. A census of all the children between 4 and 16 years was taken, and the number was 449. The sum divided among the districts was $1,078.64. Number of districts fifteen. In this connection we would say, that the discrepancy in the census is caused by the number of children under 4 years of age, the Irish children, and the great number that did not go to school, who were more numerous then, than in these days.

In 1848 the School Committee voted that districts having no schoolhouses should build, or the public money should be withheld. During this year and the next, the school-houses became the property of the districts, being either built or purchased for that purpose.

In 1850 the number of scholars was 457, and the amount of money divided was $1,340.29.

In 1860 Hamilton District was made from the three contiguous districts. The number of scholars was increased to 578, and the average attendance was 421. Money divided was $2,033.29. In 1865 the average attendance was 366. The diminution in attendance was evidently caused by the severity of the weather. The schools are affected by the weather from 50 to 75, as appears from the annual reports. This year there was expended $1,881.83, and the sum of $391 remained undrawn at the end of the year. In 1868 the average attendance was 397. Money divided $3,042.26, and $164.76 undrawn.

In 1870 the State appropriated $2,083 16 and the town $1,500. Hitherto there has been no distinction made in the source of the school revenue. This year $288 were added from the registry taxes. The average attendance was 381. In 1872 the average attendance was 404. Money from the town and State $4,583.12.

In 1875 the average attendance was about 440, and the total number was 509. Revenue divided was, from the

State	$1,902 39
Town	2,500 00
Registry Taxes	277 70
Dog Fund	147 25
Total	$4,827 34

With the increase in the expenditures for schools the number of scholars has been increased, and there are less truancies. Moreover, a general increase of interest in the schools has been produced. The great improvement in school-houses, in the furniture, in the class of teachers, and in the order of the school-room, have made the subject of education both a pleasant and an agreeable one to consider.

As the sciences and arts, together with general education, advanced, the necessity of a change in school books became apparent. Webster's, Alden's and Daboll's books were the principal ones used in the schools at the beginning of the Public School system in 1828. Since that date we need only say, that the text books have undergone many changes, till at the present time it is believed the schools are supplied with as good books as are published.

In 1853 George H. Church, M. D., was allowed $22 for visiting the schools of the town during the winter. Formerly the School Committee visited them in turn, but it was a tax upon the time of business men to leave their work to visit schools, and they were often neglected.

In 1868 it was voted to pay Alfred B. Chadsey $50 for visiting the schools, and $20 for printing his report. J. H. Rockwell was paid $60 in the year 1870 for supervision. In 1872 the Superintendent was paid $80 for his services, and $20 for printing his report. In 1875 A. B. Chadsey was paid for superintending schools $100, and $40 for printing his report.

RICHMOND.

By N. K. Church,
Superintendent.

The towns of Charlestown, Richmond and Hopkinton were originally included in the township of Westerly, which was incorporated in 1669, and was then the fifth town in the Colony of Rhode Island. In 1738 the town of Westerly was divided into two towns, known by the names of Westerly and Charlestown. In 1747 the town of Charlestown was divided into two towns, and all the land north of Pawcatuck River was incorporated into a township by the name of Richmond.

Of the early educational history of the town of Richmond but little is known. There were no school-houses, and tradition informs us that there were but few schools, and those rarely continued more than two or three months in a year. The children were mainly instructed by their parents, at home, in whatever they were capable of teaching. Sometimes several families in a neighborhood would unite and establish a school. In that case the best qualified person that could be had for a stipulated sum was usually employed to teach the school. The wages varied from four to ten dollars per month, rarely exceeding the latter amount.

The schools were usually kept in some large room, having a fire-place from six to ten feet in length, and from four to six feet in height. In this fire-place during the cold weather a large fire was kept. Round the walls of the room on three sides, wide boards were fastened at a suitable height and inclination, for writing-desks; in front of which, seats, usually made of slabs or plank, were placed. The rooms were sometimes ceiled, but rarely if ever plastered. The huge fire-place, and numerous cracks, served for ventilation.

The studies usually pursued in the schools were reading, writing and arithmetic. Some teachers could cipher no farther than fractions; others as far as the " Rule of Three ; " occasionally a teacher could perform all the examples in the text-book then in use. Sometimes a teacher would have some knowledge of either Surveying, Navigation, Geography or English Grammar. The possession of a knowledge of any one of these branches was considered a very high attainment and readily commanded the highest wages.

Methods of Teaching.

The letters of the alphabet were taught by pointing them out in succession until they were learned. This usually occupied several months. Having learned the letters, the next thing was their combinations called "a-b-abs." These consisted of vowel and consonant combinations, thus: ba be bi bo bu by, ab eb ib ob ub, bla ble bli blo blu bly, sla sle sli slo slu sly, &c. Having mastered these combinations and having got as far as " baker " in the old fashioned speller, they were considered as being on the high road to learning, and were soon put to read in the Testament. In reading, but little attention was paid to inflection, emphasis, or the qualities of the voice, but the scholars were carefully instructed to mind the pauses, and always let the voice fall at a period.

In the study of arithmetic, the scholar was directed after having performed a question, to write it down and record the operation in a book made for the purpose, called a ciphering-book. In this book every rule and example in the arithmetic were written down and the operation recorded. A number of these old ciphering-books, which must have required months of labor to complete, are now in existence, and some of them are models of skill and neatness in penmanship.

Black-boards were not in use. Wide, smooth boards were sometimes used as a substitute for slates, on which the scholars marked with chalk or charcoal.

Books Used.

Among the oldest text-books used in the schools that we have an account of, were Alden's, Dillworth's and Webster's Spellers, Alden's Readers, Columbian Orator, National Preceptor, Dwight's and Daboll's Arithmetics, and Dwight's Geography.

Discipline.

The discipline of the schools was of the strictest kind. The authority of the teacher was absolute. A strict obedience and an unquestioning submission to his authority both in word and manner, were required; and from what we gather from tradition, it appears that not unfrequently, severe chastisements were inflicted for trivial offences, and that the teacher by a vigorous use of the ferule and hickory labored to secure the necessary penitence for past offences and at the same time to convince the scholar of the great necessity of respect for authority and obedience to government.

School Houses erected before 1828.

The first school-house in this town was erected about 1806, in District No. 7, on the highway near the burying ground a little west of H. P. Clark's. This house was built by Amos Lillibridge, George Perry, David Kenyon, and Sprague Kenyon. In this house schools of more or less note were kept until about 1825, when it was burned down. The the same year, in District No. 8, a building partly of stone was erected by Caleb Barber, near his house. It was called Barber's Academy. In this building schools were kept for several years.

A few years after these houses were built, Judge William James built a house near where Silas James lives in District No. 8. This house was afterwards moved up on Tefft's Hill, and used for a school-house for a number of years, until 1838, when the new district school-house was erected.

About 1812, two houses were erected; one called Clark's school-house, erected near Stanton's corners, in District No. 15, built by Judge Samuel Clark; the other, called the Kenyon school-house, erected near the residence of the Rev. Gilbert Tillinghast, in District No. 13. This house was built by the Kenyons, five brothers, namely: Samuel, John, Silas, Benedict and Cory. In these houses schools were kept for a number of years.

In 1826 a school-house was erected in District No. 9. This house was called the Bell school-house, and was built by Jesse Reynolds, Robert Reynolds, Wells Reynolds, Reynolds Hoxsie, Clark Sisson, Job Hoxsie, Rouse Hoxsie, Varnum Hoxsie and others. It was considered at the time to be a very nice house and readily shows their enterprise and interest in the cause of education. A few years after the passage of the free school act, in 1828, this house was received as a district school-house. It has since been repaired and furnished with new seats, and is now far from being the poorest school-house in the town. The schools in this district have uniformly been in good hands.

Free Schools.

Some years before the establishment of free schools by the State, an eccentric individual, giving his name as A. B., came into what is now District No. 9 and established a free school. Having taught the school during the winter term, he hired a lady to teach in the same school during the summer term. He paid his own board and all the expenses of the schools.

The history of his life he never told to any of the people, nor was it, so far as I know, ever known. He was considered to be a man of fine education and good moral character. He gave as his reason for teaching that he thought the children ought to have a chance to obtain an education. His discipline was mild but efficient. The conditions upon which children could attend his school seemed to be that they should behave well and mind their studies. Great benefit was derived from the school and much interest awakened in the cause of education.

Soon after the passage of the act of 1828 establishing free schools, the town was divided into twelve districts. From the subdivision of these, three more have since been formed, making fifteen school districts.

District No. 1.

The school-house in this district, built in 1839, was a small, cheap affair, located in a field near pine woods, and at a considerable distance from the public highway. It was abandoned in 1859, and a neat, substantial house with modern improvements was erected on the highway. There has been in this district at various times considerable zeal exhibited in contending for individual rights in relation to the location of school-houses and the management of the schools. In 1865 the village of Plainville having been recently built up in the south-west corner of the district, it was thought best to divide the district, which was done, and a new district was formed. In this new district, in a short time, a very pretty house of suitable size was erected, in which schools have since been kept with uniform success. Soon after the new district had been set off, the school-house in District No. 1 was moved farther north to its present location.

District No. 2.

A school-house was built in this district in 1836, on the north side of the highway, north of the village. The house was of rather meagre proportions, but owing to the conflicting interests and difference of opinions it was the occasion of no inconsiderable amount of contention among the tax payers of the district.

Schools were kept in this house for about nine years, until, in 1845, Rowland G. Hazard, after having built up the village of Carolina, erected on an eminence in a grove, a little back of this village, a nice stone building in which the district school has since been kept. In 1871 the district purchased this house and lot and built on an addition to the south end of the house, making two large rooms, one for a primary and the other for an intermediate department, re-seating the old room, and furnishing the house throughout.

In 1850 this district became joint with a portion of No. 5, of Charlestown. In 1871 the Charlestown portion was withdrawn and formed into a separate and independent district, but afterwards became the second time joint with this district.

This school is the largest in the town, and at present is in a very prosperous condition.

District No. 3.

The school-house in this district was not erected till 1844. But when the villages of Shannock Mills, Clark's Mills and Kenyon's Mills were built up, it was found that the house was inadequate for the wants of the district, and in the year 1867 the district was divided, and a new district, No. 15, was formed. In this new district was erected soon after, at a little distance from Kenyon's Mills, a neat, substantial house, in which schools of more or less interest have since been kept. In 1868 the old school-house in District No. 3 was abandoned, and a new one, similar to the one in No. 15, was erected. Difficulties have rarely occurred in this district, and the schools have generally been successful.

District No. 4.

This district became joint with No. 17, of South Kingstown, in 1838. The school-house is located in that town.

Districts Nos. 5 and 6.

School-houses were erected in Nos. 5 and 6 in 1836. The house in No. 5 was pretty thoroughly repaired and furnished with new seats in 1866. Both houses are small, but are sufficient to supply the wants of the districts at present.

DISTRICT No. 7.

A school-house was erected in District No. 7 in 1837. The house was too small to supply the wants of the district, and in 1862 very kindly withdrew from public service by burning down. A fine, new house was erected in 1864, with accommodations for two departments. A portion of District No. 9, of Hopkinton, became joint with this district in 1838. In 1870 a new and independent district was formed in Hopkinton, and became joint with this district.

DISTRICT No. 8.

In 1837 a house was erected in District No. 8. The conflicting interests in this district occasioned at the time rather more than the ordinary amount of controversy. Competent teachers have mainly been secured to teach the school, and have been rewarded with fair success.

DISTRICTS Nos. 9, 10 AND 11.

No. 9 has already been alluded to. Houses were erected in Nos. 10 and 11 in 1836. These houses are both small, but the schools at the present time are correspondingly small. Schools of more or less note have been kept from time to time in both of these districts.

DISTRICT No. 12.

A school-house was erected in No. 12 in 1837. This was a small, badly arranged house, and in 1869 it was abandoned, and a new and commodious house of suitable size was erected on the same site. The schools in this district have been uniformly successful.

DISTRICT No. 13.

A house was erected in this district in 1842. In 1851 it was moved to its present location and enlarged. At the same time the district was made joint with portions of Nos. 3 and 4, of Exeter. Recently portions of Nos. 3 and 4, of Exeter, have been formed into a separate and independent district, and made joint with this district. The school-house is poor and unsuitable for the wants of the district. The indications are that a new house will soon be erected in its place. Nos. 14 and 15 have already been alluded to.

It appears that there has always been a commendable interest on the part of the inhabitants of the town in the cause of public schools, and, although they have not improved as rapidly as might have been desired, yet there appears to have been a healthy growth and a steady advancement.

That which has, perhaps, contributed as much as any one thing to the improvement of our schools, has been the examination of teachers, and the refusal to grant certificates to any but those who were competent to teach. The era of this much needed reform seems to have begun in 1845, when Dr. L. A. Palmer, Elisha L. Baggs and Nathan L. Richmond were appointed a committee to examine the qualifications of teachers. The sifting and purging which this committee gave to the material offered as teachers, at once gave new energy to the cause, and operated most gloriously in the advancement of our schools, and from that time to the present the growth and advance of our schools have depended largely on the faithfulness and efficiency of our school officers in this respect.

Present Condition of the Schools.

It should be understood that the town of Richmond contains an area of nearly thirty-nine square miles, and is at present divided into fifteen school districts; that the number of children under the age of fifteen years, as appears by the census of 1875, is 536. It should also be understood that while the State appropriates $90,000 for the public day schools, by far the greater portion, $63,000, is divided according to the number of children in the towns under the age of fifteen years, the town of Richmond receiving only $143.57 from this division; that the remaining $27,000 is divided equally among the districts in the State, this town receiving $941.86, making from both divisions $1,385.43.

Dividing this equally among the districts gives $92.36 for each district, which is the whole amount received from the State. An equal amount being raised by the town, gives $184.72 for each district from these sources. Now, as the law requires that the schools in each district shall be kept for at least six months during the year, using all the money derived from these two sources and dividing it equally among the districts, we can pay for teachers' wages only $30.79 per month. To this, however, may be added the registry tax, which varies, and is more or less, according to the interest taken in politics, and a small amount which is sometimes received from the dog fund, but as a portion of the fund is divided by the school committee of the town, according to the average daily attendance of the schools, it will readily be seen that under these circumstances it is impossible in some of the districts to pay a really competent teacher a fair compensation and continue the school six months, without a considerable tax on the property of the district. And yet it appears, that the tax-payers of this town are paying more than twice as much tax on the hundred dollars for school purposes, as many of the other towns in the State.

It is to be hoped that a larger portion of the $90,000 appropriated by the State may be divided by districts, thus giving the schools of this town and those of other sparsely populated towns, more equal school facilities. It is also hoped that a more equal basis of local town tax rate for schools may be established.

Some of our schools have been good, and the scholars have made excellent improvement during each term; others have done fairly, a few only have been poor.

The chief points of failure have been: First, Discipline. Some of our teachers, otherwise unexceptionable, have failed to keep the good order which is so necessary for the advancement of their schools. This is much to be regretted, not only on account of its injury to the schools, but on account of its consequent effect on society; for if children are not held in proper restraint, and taught respect for authority and obedience to government in the schools—the schools being in this respect models of government—it can hardly be expected that they will become the peaceable, law-abiding citizens so essential to the welfare of the State. Second, some of our teachers have not the necessary literary qualifications, and consequently must always expect to fail. If more care was exercised in the selection of teachers, and all interests, except the interest of the schools, laid aside, and none but competent teachers employed to teach, it would undoubtedly result in a very great improvement in many of our schools.

EVENING SCHOOLS.

Evening schools have been established at Carolina and at Wyoming. Considerable effort was required at first to get them started, but they have been decidedly successful, and we see no reason why they should not be continued from year to year.

LAPHAM INSTITUTE.

NORTH SCITUATE.

This Institution, formerly known as Smithville Seminary, is located on a slight eminence overlooking the village of North Scituate, ten miles west of Providence.

It was founded in 1839 by the Rhode Island Association of Free Baptists, for the purpose of furnishing facilities for a liberal education to the youth of both sexes. Fine, commodious buildings were erected at a cost of nearly $30.000. and the Association, or Trustees on its behalf, were so fortunate as to secure the Rev. Hosea Quimby as Principal.

The school opened prosperously in the autumn of 1839, and continued to prosper without change of management for fifteen years. Mr. Quimby united rare skill in the management of the young, with fine executive ability and facility in teaching. In short, he kept a most excellent school, and the people were not slow to appreciate it.

Three courses of study were provided: one for young men fitting for college; one for young ladies, embracing four years, including the studies of Latin, French, German, Natural Science, History, Philosophy, English Language and Literature; and third, an adjustable course to meet the wants of those pupils who only attended for one or more terms.

The great want of the institution has ever been an endowment fund. The entire amount of money raised at the start was absorbed in buildings, grounds, and furnishings, and as the denomination controlling the school was neither large nor wealthy, no endowment was ever raised.

Of course so high a standard could not be maintained by the natural income of the school, and the Association finding itself heavily taxed for its support, sold the property about the year 1850, to Mr. Quimby, the

Principal. He hoped by careful management, and retrenchment in some departments, to make the school pay its way, but after four years he succumbed to overwork and anxiety.

The next principal was Samuel P. Coburn, who hired the property of Mr. Quimby. He remained three years and the school continued to prosper under his management. In 1857, Rev. W. Colegrove purchased the property and conducted the school two years, after which it was closed for considerable time.

In 1863, the Free Baptists again took charge of the Institution. The Hon. Benedict Lapham and others became sureties for any deficiencies which might accrue. For this act of generosity on the part of Mr. Lapham, the name of the school was changed from Smithville Seminary to Lapham Institute.

Rev. B. F. Hayes was chosen Principal under the new arrangament, and conducted the school very successfully, until the close of the school year in 1865, when he was elected to the chair of Mental and Moral Philosophy, in Bates College. His assistant, Prof. Thomas. L. Angell, succeeded him, and remained until two years later, when he was elected to the chair of Modern Languages in Bates College.

Then came Prof. George H. Ricker, widely known throughout New England, as a thorough Classical scholar and efficient instructor. Prof. Ricker continued his successful management of the Institution for seven years, and gave it a character for thoroughness in all its departments, such as few schools of the grade enjoy. In 1874, Hillsdale College, Michigan, invited Prof. Ricker to the chair of Latin and Greek in that institution, which he accepted, again leaving Lapham Institute to be provided for.

This was done by choosing A. G. Moulton as principal of the school. He died soon after the close of his first year, having endeared himself by his genial ways and fine culture, to all who came in contact with him. The present incumbent, W. S. Stockbridge, succeeded him in the autumn of 1875.

This completes the thirty-seventh year of the school's existence, or deducting the three years during which it was closed, the thirty-fourth of its active life. In that time nearly fifteen hundred pupils have been instructed in its halls, most of them going directly from it to the active duties of life. Thus its influence has been wide, and we are glad to believe, widely useful. It has always granted its privileges on moderate terms, and in this way many have obtained a liberal education, who otherwise would not have been able.

Among the distinguished graduates of the Institution, are President

James B. Angell, of Michigan University, the late George T. Day, D. D., Editor of the *Morning Star* newspaper, ex-Gov. Howard, of R. I. Prof. Thomas L. Angell, of Bates College, and Mary Latham Clarke, author of several popular works.

The school is supported at the present time by the munificence of William Winsor, of Greenville, R. I., who stands instead of an endowment. Its facilities for thorough work, and for doing good, were never better than now. It has a full corps of teachers, a good library, chemical and physical apparatus, &c. The buildings are in excellent repair and its location is as healthy as can be found in New England.

SMITHFIELD.

By S. W. Farnum,

Superintendent.

At a meeting of Superintendents of Public Schools of Rhode Island it was unanimously voted that the Superintendent of each town should collect and write a brief historical sketch of said town. And that what meagre facts are here presented will be received in the same spirit in which they are given, is the wish of the author.

Rhode Island being settled by such a whole-souled and purely Democratic man as Roger Williams, nothing could be expected but that education would be promoted in a liberal sense. It is well known that Roger Williams was driven from Massachusetts for difference in religious opinions, and in the dead of the Winter of 1635–36, he came to Providence, the Indians meeting him with the words "What Cheer," the same as our "how do you do;" and in this little State of Rhode Island was man given the right to worship God as his heart dictated. The following extract from Arnold's History of Rhode Island will show that Rhode Island was not behind the times in public education:

"It has been said that Rhode Island at one time was behind all other States in providing for the education of her people. However true this may be as to some portions of the State, it was not so on the island of Rhode Island. At this Court Robert Lenthrall was admitted a freeman. He had been invited to come and conduct public worship (which had previously been done by Mr. Clarke), and to take charge of a school. By a vote of the town of Newport he was called to teach a public school, and, for his encouragement there was granted him and his heirs one hundred acres of land, and four for a house lot; it was also voted that one hundred acres should be laid forth and appropriated for a school, for encouragement to the poorer class to give their young an education, and Mr. Robert Lenthrall to have the benefit thereof while he continues to teach. This was in 1640, two years after the settlement of the Island."

1704 they had one meeting-house, and 1719 they built another, near Woonsocket.

In 1730 Providence was divided into four towns, Smithfield, Scituate and Glocester being set apart as separate towns. These towns have since been again divided—Smithfield into Lincoln, North Smithfield and Smithfield; Scituate into Foster and Scituate; and Glocester into Burrillville and Glocester.

The first census taken in Smithfield was in 1748, when it contained 450 inhabitants. At its last census it contained 2,857.

In 1800 an act was passed by the Assembly establishing free schools throughout the State, making it the duty of the Town Councils to divide their towns into school districts. "Smithfield shall cause to be established, and kept every year, so many free schools as shall be equivalent to three such schools six months in the year."

There were at that time, in what now constitutes Smithfield, five public school-houses in use, some of them free schools. This law met with great opposition, and was repealed in 1803, Providence being the only town that carried the act into effect.

At the January session of the General Assembly in 1828 an act was passed to again establish public schools, and in 1830 the town had free schools.

In 1838 an act was passed authorizing Smithfield school districts to build school-houses, and giving the districts special powers to elect their own school committee. Again, in 1839, an act was passed to further the interests in public schools.

In 1840 the school population of Smithfield was 3,311. In 1844 the appropriations for schools were: From State, $2,175; from town, $1,000; and registry tax, $788.

In 1844 the General Assembly passed the act establishing the present school system, and in 1845 the most of the present districts organized under it. In 1845 an act was passed appropriating annually $2,500 of State money for public schools.

In 1845 there was held in the town of Smithfield ten Teachers' Institutes, creating great enthusiasm among friends of education. Among the officers and members were some of the most ardent and intelligent friends of education.

In June, 1847, the School Committee of the town of Smithfield made their first report upon the condition and standing of the schools. This was the second report that was ever made in any form upon the subject of free schools. This year the appropriations from the State were $2,175; town, $2,500; registry tax, $616.83; the expenditures from town and State, $5,292.16; raised by districts and individuals, $1,435.75; donations for libraries and appurtenances, $1,175; aggregate for building and repairing school-houses, $6,005. This year Woonasquatucket district was dissolved, leaving thirty-four districts in the town. There were five new school-houses built this year, at an average cost of $1,200 each. There were fifty-four different schools taught, the average length of the schools being six and a quarter months. The whole number of pupils registered, 2,012; average daily attendance, 1,575. The School Committee was composed of the following gentlemen: Charles Hyde, James Bushee and Ahaz Mowry, all being practical school teachers. Mr. Bushee was Principal of the Smithfield Academy, an institution of great reputation in those days.

In 1846 Rhode Island, for the first time in two hundred years, voted and collected into the treasury a school tax in every town in the State.

In 1856 Smithfield expended $600 for building or repairing school-houses. The State appropriation for schools in Smithfield was $4,126.19; town, $4,500. It had thirty-five districts, Woonasquatucket being in existence again. It had forty-four schools, thirty-one male teachers, twenty-three female teachers, and 2,419 pupils enrolled. Average attendance, 1,751; length of school, 29 3-4 weeks; the number of school children, 2,726. The town paid $1.99, State $1.82 for each pupil attending. Total cost per pupil, $3.81.

In 1857 the schools were reported to be in an excellent condition. The same amount was appropriated as in 1855 and 1856. Average daily attendance, 1,705.

The committee this year report a general prosperity in the schools, and have met with but very few difficulties. They recommended the school system of the town very highly. The committee were, Howard W. King, M. D., J. G. Richardson and William H. Seagraves.

The same appropriation was made in 1858 as in years before, there being seventeen male teachers and thirty-two female teachers, and 2,524 pupils enrolled. Average daily attendance, 1,803.

In 1859 there were the same appropriations, fifteen male teachers, thirty-two female teachers and 2,445 pupils enrolled. Average daily attendance, 1,902. The teachers during this year were very highly spoken of.

The same appropriation was made in 1860 as in former years, there being employed thirteen male teachers and thirty-three female teachers, and 2,576 pupils enrolled. Average daily attendance, 1,959, being a gain of 564 in the number enrolled, and 385 in average daily attendance since the first report was made in 1847. The schools bore a very good reputation during this year.

In 1861 the State appropriation was $3,922, a decrease of over $200. The town appropriation was $4,500, the same as it had been for a number of years; and there were employed fifteen male teachers and thirty-one female teachers, and 2,263 pupils enrolled. Average daily attendance, 1,971. The committee this year were Rev. Mowry Phillips, S. O. Tabor and Thomas L. Angell, a very able committee; Rev. M. Phillips being among the most eminent of the Free Will Baptists, and now Superintendent of the Public Schools in Glocester. Mr. Tabor was more or less connected with the public schools of this town for a number of years, and Mr. Angell, a native of the present town, has been Principal of Lapham Institute, and at present is Professor of Modern Languages in Bates College, Lewiston, Me.

In 1866 the town appropriated $6,000, which was $1,500 more than in 1861; there were six male and forty-four female teachers; 2,272 pupils enrolled; average daily attendance, 1,592. The schools were more prosperous than usual during this year. The committee for this year were G. W. Miner, G. A. Kent, G. A. Buck and R. Woodworth.

In 1867 the State made the same appropriations as formerly, the town advancing to $8,000. There were employed thirteen male teachers and thirty-eight female; 2,773 pupils enrolled; average daily attendance, 2,496, a gain of 761 in enrolled pupils, and 919 in average daily attendance in twenty years. The committee were Edwin A. Buck, Rev. R. Woodworth, George W. Gile, James E. Dockray, A. D. Nickerson and George A. Kent.

The State appropriation for 1868 was $5,459.70, a gain of $1,537.18; the town appropriations, $14,000; there were nine male teachers employed and twenty-seven female; 2,493 pupils registered; average daily attendance, 1,831. The committee this year were James E. Dockray, Marshall I. Mowry, George A. Kent, Ansel D. Nickerson, Robert Murray, Jr. The schools were doing nicely this year, but there was not as much attention paid to reading as should have been. The committee recommended the consolidation of Greenville and Woonasquatucket districts.

In 1869 the State appropriation was $6,944.04; town, $18,000; there were employed this year ten male teachers and fifty female; number of pupils registered, 2,317; average, 1,745, divided into thirty-five different schools.

A report in a Providence paper, stating that the country schools are on the retrograde, is utterly refuted by the School Committee of the town. They affirm that the schools are as good as like grades anywhere in the State. The School Committee recommended Evans, Stillwater and Spragueville districts to build new school-houses. Stillwater and Evans have since done so. Allenville and Angell districts have made some needed repairs upon their school-houses. The committee this year were George A. Kent, Robert Murray, Jr., Marshall I. Mowry, Ansel D. Nickerson, S. O. Tabor and Charles E. Handy. They reported the schools to be in fair condition.

In 1870 the State appropriation was the same as in 1869; town appropriation, $19,000, $1,000 more than the year before, and reaching the highest sum appropriated by the town of Smithfield. During this year Smithfield was divided into three towns—Smithfield, North Smithfield and Lincoln. This division left Smithfield only ten districts, Allenville, Stillwater, Wionkhiege, Evans, Spragueville, Georgiaville, Angell, Dexter, Greenville and Woonasquatucket, and a school population of only 760. A special meeting was held by the committee May 20th, 1871, and a sub-committee appointed to take a school census. At the taking of the census Lincoln had 2,715, from five to fifteen years of age; North Smithfield had 826; Woonsocket set-off, 985; Smithfield, 760.

In 1869 and 1870 Smithfield held the post of honor in the school system in this State, having appropriated the highest per cent. on its valuation, having employed successful teachers, and attained to a high degree of proficiency in the studies pursued.

The committee, at the breaking up of the old town, was composed of George A. Kent, Robert Murray, Jr., Maxcy W. Burlingame, Lysander Flagg, Marshall I. Mowry and Samuel O. Tabor. The average daily attendance of what remained of Smithfield was: Allenville, 35; Georgiaville, 63; Angell, 9; Dexter, 17; Stillwater, 31; Wionkhiege, 7; Evans, 15; Spragueville, 30; Greenville, 62; Woonasquatucket, 18.

In 1871 the State appropriation was $1,374.74. Town, $2,600. Average daily attendance, 249. There were ten districts, and eleven schools were taught during the year. There was an average of thirty-seven weeks taught during the year. No school but what registered over ten pupils. There were registered 784 pupils, being twenty-four more than the school population between five and fifteen years of age. This year the School Committee re-numbered the school districts, as follows: Allenville, No. 1; old number, 17; Georgiaville, No. 2; old number, 16; Angell, No. 3; old number, 29; Dexter, No. 4; old number, 18; Stillwater, No. 5; old number, 15; Wionkhiege, No. 6; old number, 12; Evans, No. 7; old number, 13; Spragueville, No. 8;

old number, 28; Greenville, No. 9; old number, 14; Woonasquatucket, No. 10; old number, 20. The lines were somewhat changed at this time, but have been set back in nearly all cases except Spragueville District, which was enlarged, and remains nearly the same as arranged at that time. The School Committee this year, being the first elected since the division of the town, were Marshall I. Mowry, Maxcy W. Burlingame and Burrill R. Mowry; the latter being the only new member added.

The State and town appropriations of 1872 were the same as the year before, with an average of thirty-two weeks during the year, and twelve schools in operation, one school in the town having less than ten pupils registered. There were 562 pupils registered. The School Committee were the same, except Daniel W. Latham being added in place of Burrill R. Mowry, who retired.

The State appropriation in 1873 was the same as the year before, and that of the town the same for day schools, with $200 more for evening schools. There were twelve day schools and four evening schools this year, an average of thirty weeks, and 562 pupils registered. Rev. Maxcy W. Burlingame was appointed Superintendent of Public Schools. Until 1872 the supervision had been assigned to the committee that had jurisdiction in their respective districts, but this year Mr. Burlingame was appointed, and had supervision over the whole town, a system that is now adopted in every town in the State. The appropriations for this year were the same as the previous year. There were twelve day and four evening schools, an average of thirty-eight weeks in the day schools. Number of pupils enrolled, 593. Average daily attendance, 272. There were four male and fourteen female teachers employed. These schools were reported to compare favorably with the schools in adjoining towns; also, teachers that are educated for teaching are recommended. A Teachers' Institute was held in Georgiaville, December 22d, conducted by Thomas W. Bicknell, Commissioner of Public Schools in Rhode Island, and Prof. J. C. Greenough, Principal of Rhode Island State Normal School. All the teachers in the town were present but one, as well as many friends of public education.

The following set of rules were adopted this year by the School Committee, to govern the schools in the town:

PREAMBLE:—Teachers and candidates for teaching in the Public Schools, previous to entering upon their engagement, should consider it of great importance to become familiar with some of the most approved plans of teaching and governing a school, and should endeavor, as far as possible, to possess themselves of definite ideas in regard to the solemn duties and responsibilities of their profession, and in order to aid and assist them in establishing a uniform and systematic course of instruction and discipline, the committee would respectfully submit the following rules:

1. All the teachers of the public schools are required to be at their respective school-rooms, and to ring the bell from ten to fifteen minutes before the time of commencing school in the morning and in the afternoon. They shall require the pupils, as they enter the room, to be seated in an orderly manner and prepare for study.

2. The bell shall again be struck, or the hand-bell rung, precisely at the specified time for beginning the school, as a signal for commencing the exercises; previous to which all the scholars are expected to be present and to have made all needful preparations for carrying on the business of the school, in order to prevent all unnecessary movement after the exercises commence.

3. All the public schools shall be opened in the morning by reading a portion of the Scriptures, which may be done by the teacher alone, or in connection with the older pupils, the whole school being required at the same time to suspend all other subjects, and to give proper and respectful attention, and this exercise may be followed by prayer or not, at the discretion of the teacher.

4. Every scholar who comes in after the school bell rings must present a satisfactory excuse, and all who cannot do so shall be considered delinquent and marked tardy on the teacher's register, subject to examination by parents, trustees and school committee.

5. No teacher shall permit whispering or talking in school, or allow the scholars to leave or change their seats, or to communicate with each other during school hours without permission; but shall strive to maintain that good order and thorough discipline which are absolutely essential to the welfare of the school.

6. It shall be the duty of teachers to guard the conduct of the pupils, not only during the hours of school, but at recess, and on their way to and from school, and to extend at all times a watchful care over their morals and manners, endeavoring to inculcate those virtues which are a sure foundation for future usefulness and happiness.

7. The government and discipline of the school should be of a mild and parental character. The teacher should use his best exertions to bring scholars to obedience and a sense of duty by mild measures and kind influences, and in cases where corporal punishment seems absolutely necessary, it should be inflicted with judgment and discretion, and in general not in presence of the school.

8. Teachers should ever avoid those low and degrading forms of punishment, such as tying scholars' hands and compelling them to hold a weight in their hands with their arms extended, pinching, pulling and wringing their ears, cheeks and arms, and other similar modes, which are sometimes used, as the committee are decidedly of the opinion that a judicious teacher will find other methods of governing more consistent and more effectual.

9. In cases of obstinate disobedience or wilful violation of order, a teacher may suspend a pupil from school for the time being, by informing the parents or guardians and school committee thereof, and re-admit him on satisfactory evidence of amendment, or such pupil may, at the discretion of the teacher, be re-

ferred directly to the committee, to be dealt with as their judgment and legal authority shall dictate.

10. The teachers shall classify the pupils of their respective schools according to their age and attainments, irrespective of rank or wealth, and shall assign them such lessons as seem best adapted to their capacities, and render them all possible aid and assistance, without distinction or partiality.

11. For the purpose of preserving that system and order so essential to a well-regulated school, and securing to the pupils a thorough knowledge of the subjects pursued, there should be a specified time for every exercise and a certain portion of time devoted to it, and in no case should any one recitation interfere with the time appropriated to another, and whatever the exercise may be, it should receive for the time the immediate, and, as far as practical, the exclusive attention of the teacher.

12. Exercises in declamation and composition shall be practiced by the older and more advanced pupils, at the judgment of the teacher, under the advice of the committee.

13. Singing may be encouraged, and, as far as practical, taught in all the schools, not only for its direct intellectual and moral uses, but as a healthy exercise of the lungs and agreeable recreation to the pupils and an auxiliary in good government.

14. There shall be a recess of at least fifteen minutes in the middle of every half day.

15. It shall be the duty of teachers to see that fires are made in cool weather, in their respective school-rooms, at a seasonable hour, to render them warm and comfortable by school-time; to take care that their rooms are properly swept and dusted, and that a due regard to neatness and order is observed, both in and around the school-house

16. As pure air of a proper temperature is indispensable to health and comfort, teachers cannot be too careful in giving attention to these things. If the room has no ventilator, the doors and windows should be opened before and after school, to permit a free and healthy circulation of air; and the temperature should be regulated by a thermometer, suspended five or six feet from the floor, in such a position as to indicate, as near as possible, the average temperature, and should be kept at about sixty-five degrees Fahrenheit.

17. The teachers shall take care that the school-house, table, desk and apparatus in the same, and all the public property intrusted to their charge, be not cut, scratched, marked or injured, or defaced in any manner whatever. And it shall be the duty of the teachers to give prompt notice to one or more of the trustees of any repairs that may be needed.

18. Every teacher shall keep a record of all the recitations of every class, and of the manner in which every member of the class shall acquit himself in his recitation, using figures or otherwise, to mark degrees of merit; also every act of disobedience or violation of order shall be noted, and registers shall be at all times subject to the inspection of parents, trustees and committee.

19. The following shall be the construction of teachers' engagements, unless otherwise specified in the written contract: They shall teach six hours every day, including a recess, and shall divide the day into two sessions, with at least one hour intermission. They shall teach every day in the week except Satur-

day and Sunday, and four weeks for a month, and they may dismiss the school on the 4th of July, on Christmas and on days of public fast, and Thanksgiving, and one day out of every month for the purpose of attending Teachers' Institutes, or of visiting schools.

20. Good morals being of first importance and essential to their progress in useful knowledge, the pupils are strictly enjoined to avoid all vulgarity and profanity; to conduct themselves in a sober, orderly and decent manner, both in and out of school; to be diligent and attentive to their studies; to treat each other politely and kindly in all their intercourse; to respect and obey all orders of their teachers in relation to their conduct and studies, and to be punctual and constant in their daily attendance.

21. Every pupil who shall accidentally, or otherwise, injure any school property, whether fences, gates, trees or shrubs, or any building, or any part thereof, or break any window glass, or destroy any instrument, apparatus or furniture belonging to the school, shall be liable to pay all damages.

22. Every pupil who shall, anywhere on or around the school premises, use or write any profane or unchaste language, or shall draw any obscene pictures or representations, or cut, or mark, or otherwise intentionally deface any school furniture belonging to the school estate, shall be punished in proportion to the nature and extent of the offence, and shall be liable to the action of the civil law.

23. No scholars of either sex shall be permitted to enter any part of the yard or building appropriated to the other, without the teachers' permission.

24. The scholars shall pass through the streets, on their way to and from school, in an orderly and becoming manner; shall clean their feet on entering the school-room, and take their seats in a quiet and respectful manner as soon as convenient after the first bell rings, and shall take proper care that their books, desks and floor around them are kept clean and in good order.

25. No scholar should try to hide misconduct or screen them from justice, but it shall be the duty of every pupil who knows of any bad conduct or violation of order, committed without the knowledge of the instructor, to the disgrace and injury of the school, to inform the teacher thereof and to do all in his power to discourage and discountenance improper behavior in others, and to assist the teacher in restoring good order and sustaining the reputation of the school.

SPECIAL RULES AND REGULATIONS IN REGARD TO SCHOLARS.

1. No child under five years of age shall be admitted as a scholar into any of the schools of this town, unless by special permission of the member of the committee having that district in charge.

2. No scholar who comes to school without attention having been given to the cleanliness of his person, or of his dress, or whose clothes are not properly repaired, shall be permitted to remain in the school.

3. Scholars who fail to attend school regularly (except such scholars as present to their teacher a written excuse from one or both of their parents or guardians) shall not be entitled to the privileges of our schools.

4. Any scholars who tyrannize over the younger and smaller ones of the

school, thus constantly annoying their teacher by complaints of their conduct, shall be excluded from our schools.

5. Any scholar who persists in using profane or obscene language, or has in his or her possession any obscene literature, or circulates the same among the other scholars, shall be excluded immediately from our schools.

6. Smoking or chewing tobacco in the school-house or upon the school premises are forbidden.

SPECIAL RULES AND REGULATIONS IN REGARD TO TEACHERS.

1. Teachers must, in all cases, be examined by proper authority, and receive a ticket from such that they are qualified to instruct the schools in this town, before they commence to teach. Any departure from this law, however slight will be sufficient reason, in the minds of the committee, for withholding a certificate.

2. No teachers shall use, or encourage the use of any other books than those recommended by the committee.

3. Teachers shall take care that their rooms and entries are kept neat and clean, and are at all times ventilated properly.

4. Teachers must give notice to the committee of the time when term will begin and close, so that the school may be visited as the law requires.

5. Teachers will be held responsible by the committee for the prompt and efficient enforcement of the above rules.

6. Every teacher shall keep a copy of these rules and regulations posted up in the school-room and shall cause them to be read aloud at least once in every month; and in case of any difficulty in carrying out these regulations, or in the government or discipline of the school, it shall be the duty of the teacher to apply immediately to the committee for advice and direction.

This year Mr. Burlingame withdrew from the Committee, and Samuel W. Farnum was elected in his place, and was also appointed Superintendent.

The State appropriation for 1875 was the same as the year before; the town appropriation was $3,500 for day schools, and nothing allowed for evening schools. There has been an average of thirty-two weeks of school during the year, having twelve schools, with five male teachers and fourteen female. Total number of pupils registered, 539; average number belonging to schools, 347, and an average daily attendance of 283.

In 1874 there was a joint district formed between North Smithfield and Smithfield, placing the old Andrews district together, as it was before the division of the town.

At the October session of the General Assembly, in 1808, an act was passed incorporating the Smithfield School Society, also the Smithfield

School Districts.

Academy Society. Among the incorporators of the Smithfield School Society, are the names of Samuel Clark, Jeremiah Whipple, Simon Aldrich, Simon Whipple, John Jenks, Abab Mowry, Nathaniel Mowry, Winsor Aldrich, James Aldrich and Susannah Jenks, being citizens of different parts of the town. They were made a body politic and corporate for school purposes, with powers to sue and be sued, and to assess taxes. They were to meet annually, on the first Monday in January, for the election of officers and such other business as might come before them for school purposes.

In giving the local history of the districts, I am indebted to some of the older inhabitants of the town, who have always been connected or interested in public education. Allenville district, No. 1, is the oldest district in the town that has had a house set aside for school purposes. One hundred years ago there was a school-house in the district and a school taught there. The next new school-house is now a dwelling house occupied by Benjamin Britton. It was known as the Barnes school, and school was taught there about seventy years ago. The next school was taught in Captain Elisha Smith's house, now occupied by his son, Henry E. Smith. In 1816 Jesse B. Smith was teacher, a native of Smithfield, and afterwards a merchant in Providence.

The Hon. Philip Allen, once Governor of Rhode Island, built a cotton mill in this place in 1812 or 1813, from whence it received its name, and in 1820 he built a school-house and gave the use of it for public schools, the district using it until they built the present house.

In 1849 the citizens of this district voted for, and built, the present school-house, upon land owned by Capt. Elisha Smith, he giving the land for that purpose. The house and furniture cost $1,000. There was a free school in part in 1830. Capt. Smith was the Trustee, being the first Trustee of whom there is any record. There was a rate-bill assessed to help defray the expenses of the year. The school kept at this time averaged six months. The present school system was adopted in this district September 12th, 1846, and the district was organized under the same, or nearly the same, boundaries as at present. The first Trustees were Capt. Elisha Smith, Jeremiah J. Young and Edwin W. Mowry; and, with Mr. John Fenner, they have been more or less connected with the schools in the district until 1870. There never had been an entire free school here, a rate-bill having to be collected to help out the school of forty weeks. Since then the town and State appropriations have amounted to enough to carry on the schools for that length of time. Among the instructors who have taught in this district, are

Caleb Farnum, who afterwards was Principal of the Elm Street Grammar School, Providence, and an author of a Grammar; Mr. Scott Mowry, a successful merchant in Providence, and George L. Sayles, a lawyer, also of Providence. The school is now in a flourishing condition, having as many pupils as the house will seat, who are progressing finely in their studies. In the years 1874-75 it had an average daily attendance of forty-two pupils.

Georgiaville District, No. 2, was a part of No. 1 until about 1815, when a school was started in Caleb Farnum's shop. In 1820 a school was opened in what was called the Dye House, a stone building situated near the river, and owned by Samuel A. Nightingale. This school was taught by Horace Hawes, a successful teacher in those times. He came from Foster to this place, and taught here two years. In 1827 Samuel A. Nightingale built a large building for public schools through the week, and religious services on the Sabbath. This building cost at that time $300. There was a district system established, and officers elected here, for the first time, in 1830. The school was kept six months as free, and after that time a rate-bill was collected for three months more. On April 21st, 1846, this district organized under the present law, and the first Trustees were Ephraim Whipple, John C. Westcott and Waterman F. Brown, all of whom have passed away except Mr. Brown.

A special meeting was called January, 1850, to take measures to build a school-house. Junia S. Mowry, Ephraim Whipple, Waterman F. Brown, James H. Arnington, Waterman Smith, Austin Sawyer and Edwin Farnum were appointed a committee to propose a plan, to procure a site, and to report the same at an adjourned meeting. They reported the site where the school-house now stands, and a building twenty-five feet wide and fifty feet long, which was accepted, and a house built upon the plan, at a cost of $1,400. This year there was a free school for nine months, also a graded school established.

In 1854 male teachers received $10 per week, and females but $4. In 1857 the amount received for schools from the town was $296.90; rate-bill, $216.13. Again in 1863 the amount raised for teachers' wages was $333.70. The rate-bill was abolished in 1869. Until that time there was generally a rate-tax collected.

In 1873 the present house was raised and a story given to each department. The single desk was put into the house in this year. The committee to do the repairs were Samuel W. Farnum, Henry C. Bowen and Orrin B. Brayton, which cost $2,139.63. At present there are two departments, and free schools of forty weeks during the year. No tax was assessed for school purposes during the past year. There has been an average daily attendance during the years of 1874 and 1875 of sixty-five pupils. At present the school is in a flourishing condition, as regards attendance, studies and number of pupils belonging to the school. Among the instructors who have formerly taught here, are Samuel W. Crawford, a Surgeon at Fort Sumter at the time of its fall in 1861, who afterwards rose to the rank of Major General in the late Rebellion. He was a very successful teacher. Miss Carrie F. Peirce, who had a Young Ladies' High School in Providence, was also a successful teacher here.

Angell District, No. 3, was, one hundred and ten years ago, in 1766, an original district, and had a public school house. The building is now destroyed. It stood near the corner where Mrs. A. Angell's house now stands. The next place where there is any account of a school being taught, was in what was Peter Ballou's cooper-shop. About 1816 the schools were taught in three private houses in the district.

In 1832 Jonathan Harris, Asahel Angell, Daniel Angell, Robert Harris, David Harris, Colonel John Angell and Arnold Smith built the present school-house and gave it to the district. It cost about $300. Miss Huldah Farnum was the first teacher who taught in this house. She was a successful teacher, among the oldest teachers of this town. Mr. Timothy Mahoney taught in this district. This school is at present (as in all rural districts throughout the State) small in numbers. The pupils here are quite young, not placing them on so high a grade as some rural schools are. During the years of 1874 and 1875 there was an average daily attendance of only thirteen pupils.

Dexter District, No. 4, has one of the original district schools, a school being kept here as soon, or nearly so, as anywhere in the town. In 1816 the present school-house was erected. This was the first house devoted to school purposes in the district of which there is any record. About twenty-five years since there was an addition put on the house. Before the erection of this house schools were taught around in private houses, but since then there has been in part a free school, the remainder being raised by a rate tax. This, like the Angell school, is small, being affected by the division of the old town of Smithfield, about half of the district belonging to Lincoln. Among the teachers are Timothy Mahoney, and also George Newell, who is now one of the firm of Smith, Grant & Co., merchants, of Pawtucket. In 1874 and 1875 there was an average daily attendance of seven.

Stillwater District, No. 5, was an original district. In 1776 there was a house for the use of public schools, on land now owned by John A. Mowry. A school was taught here, and children from a large territory attended. In 1830 the district built another school-house, nearly opposite the other, using it for that purpose until 1874, when the district built another house. The old school-house is made into a dwelling-house. The new one is in the village of Stillwater. It is two stories high, each floor capable of seating sixty-four pupils. At present there is but one floor occupied, having fifty-six single desks, having the modern improvements attached. Among the teachers who have taught in this district are Jencks Mowry, a very popular teacher, and at present the senior Principal of Mount Pleasant Academy, of Providence; also, the Rev. Martin J. Steere, a popular Universalist minister in Connecticut. He is a native of this district, and here first learned the rudiments of his education. The school at present is doing finely; the average daily attendance was thirty-one pupils for 1874 and 1875. The first strictly free school in this district was in 1830, keeping three months in the year, and from that time to the present there has been a free school from three to ten months in each year. They have now forty weeks of school this year. The school under the present law was commenced in 1845.

Wionkhiege District, No. 6, was organized as early as 1816, but did not have any public house for school purposes until 1856, when the present school-house was erected. Mr. Daniel Aldrich was appointed a committee this year to procure a site and build a house upon it, subject to the approval of the School Committee of the town. Its present site was approved, and the house was erected at a cost of $800. The building is capable of seating fifty-six pupils, and is a neat and nicely contrived house for an ungraded country school. Before the erection of this house schools were taught around in different dwellings, rooms being fitted up as well as could be for this purpose. Among the teachers of this district were Jencks Mowry, a native of this district, where he first began his early education; Benjamin Franklin Latham, a rising young lawyer of this State, who died before his talents were fully developed; also, L. L. Swan, M. D., a native of the town, who was a talented physician, but death came upon him ere he was aware. This being strictly a rural district, has been reduced to a very small school, the average daily attendance for 1874 and 1875 being only seven pupils. The schools in this district have in part been free since 1830. For the last few years they have only kept from twenty to thirty weeks. The present year they have forty weeks of school. Although the school is small, the studies pursued here are of as high a scale as anywhere in the town.

In 1874 a portion of this district was made joint district with the Andrews district of North Smithfield, it being that portion that formerly belonged to this district before the division of the town. School was also taught here in the Jemima Wilkinson Meeting House. This house was built for Jemima Wilkinson, a founder of peculiar religious principles. She was born in Cumberland, R. I., in 1753, and educated among the Quakers. When about twenty-three she was taken suddenly ill and apparently seemed to die. On recovering she proclaimed she had risen from the dead, claiming to be invested with Divine attributes, could instruct mankind in religion, foretell future events, discern secrets of the heart, and heal diseases of persons who had faith in her skill, and offered to prove her ability for these things by walking on the water. A frame was erected at Seneca Lake, N. Y., for that purpose. At the appointed time she appeared and approached within a few hundred yards of the water, and alighted from an elegant carriage and walked to the platform; asked the crowd if they had faith in her ability, and being answered in the affirmative, she turned and went back to her carriage, saying it was useless to walk on the water, as they all believed she could do so. She was called the Universal Friend. She was illiterate, of respectable appearance, and possessed of a retentive mind. She died at Penn Yan, N. Y., in 1819.

Evans District, No. 7, is an original district, having been formed as early as 1806. The first school of which we have a record, was in this year taught in Augustus Winsor's house, a gentleman very much interested in schools at that time. Schools were also taught in Daniel Mann's shop and at the Tucker place, the house where John Tucker was born, a gentleman who was deputy sheriff of Providence county several years since; and in other dwellings in the district, they being fitted up for these purposes. The school was first taught in the present house in 1830, remaining as a private building until 1872, when the district purchased it and converted it into a public school building.

The first free school in this district was in 1835, and has since been carried on as such, in full or in part. Among the teachers who have taught here, are John Tucker and George M. Appleby, a gentleman to whom I am under obligations for information received of the schools in this district. He is, and has always been, a firm friend of public schools. This being a rural district, it is necessarily a small school, the average daily attendance for 1874 and 1875 being only nine pupils.

Spragueville District, No. 8, was formerly a part of the Evans District. They were divided in 1840; however, in 1808, there was a school taught here before the division. It was taught in a Mr. Burgess's house, which is now an L of Henry W. Smith's house, near Spragueville. This L at the time furnished room for the school and the residence of the teacher. It is remarked that Mr. Burgess smoked his pipe during school hours. Schools were taught in different dwelling houses in this district until Daniel Mann and Gideon Evans erected the present school-house in the Evans District. Captain Sprague, the founder of Spragueville, in 1844, or thereabouts, erected the present school-house in Spragueville, and the School Committee made the present district. In 1845 the schools went into operation under the present system. Among the teachers employed here, mention is made of Israel Tucker, an excellent land surveyor, and a native of Evans District. I am under obligations to George W. Appleby, also, for valuable information of this district. The average daily attendance for 1874 and 1875 was twenty-four pupils. The school is doing well at present.

Greenville District, No. 9, has the first record of any school in this town. The division of the town was in 1730, and twenty years afterward there was a public school-house standing where the present house now stands.

In 1812 a petition was sent to the General Assembly for a charter of Greene Academy. This Assembly being willing to encourage and promote the cause of education, " do enact, and by authority thereof, it is enacted, that Duty Winsor, Daniel Winsor, Aaron Mowry, Elijah Day, Emor Olney, Nathan B. Sprague, Augustus Winsor, Ziba Smith, Abraham Smith and Asa Winsor, and all others that may be hereafter admitted, shall be members of said corporation, by style and name of the Trustees of Greene Academy, and by name be perpetual, capable in law to hold any personal or real estate, not to exceed $5,000." Duty Winsor was President; Samuel Winsor, Vice President; Aaron Mowry, Treasurer; and Asa Winsor, Secretary. A lottery was granted by the General Assembly, the proceeds to go towards erecting the building. Asa Winsor and Nathan B. Sprague were managers of said lottery. The house was built in 1813, where the present house now stands. In 1819 the charter was re-enacted, on account of failure to elect officers. In 1836 the charter was revised and amended : " Provided said corporation fails to elect officers, the old ones to hold over until an election of officers are held." About 1840 the building and lot were given to the district.

One hundred years ago there were schools taught around in the dwelling houses, the tuition being $12\frac{1}{2}$ cents per week for each pupil, which continued in session four months, and after awhile six months, and at present school is taught forty weeks each year. They employed lady teachers in Summer, and male teachers in Winter, until the past year, when ladies have taught the entire year. The district was formed under the present system May 29, 1848, when Emory Fisk, William F. Brown and John Foster, the first Trustees, voted that all scholars should be accommodated with school room. A school meeting was called by the Town Committee, George C. Wilson, Chairman, for the district to organize March 24th, 1849. This year the district had to raise a tax to continue the school for four months. In 1858 the school was kept thirty-eight weeks, and has been continued that number of weeks up to 1875. In 1875 the present beautiful house was erected and dedicated to public schools, it being a model house for this purpose. It cost about $9,000 to complete it. It is of two stories, each floor having a separate school, the single desk and other modern improvements being placed in the rooms. Each room will seat seventy-two pupils comfortably.

In 1848 the schools were graded into Grammar and Primary departments. Among the teachers here employed may be found Henry Hartwell Jenks, a teacher of note, and for a number of years one of the School Committee of Smithfield. This school is doing finely, and has an average daily attendance of sixty pupils for 1874 and 1875.

In 1840 there were nineteen districts in Smithfield; and Woonasquatucket district, No. 10, was a part of Greenville, but soon after it was made a separate district. In 1847 this district was dissolved, and re-established in 1856. In 1872 it was consolidated with the Greenville district, but in 1873 was made a separate district again. This district has never owned a house, but occupies a building belonging to the Winsor Mills Company, they giving the use of the building to the district. This district has had many disadvantages; at one time having an average daily attendance of only two pupils per year. In 1874-5 it had an average daily attendance of twenty-three. The school is now prospering.

Evening Schools.

The first evening school in what now constitutes the town of Smithfield was, in 1853, at Georgiaville, taught by Carrie F. Pierce. Again, in 1870, the town started schools in different parts of the town, one being at Georgiaville.

In 1873 there were schools taught, one at Allenville, one at Georgiaville, one at Spragueville, and one at Woonasquatucket. In 1874 evening schools were taught in the same districts, and in 1875 there was only one, and that at Georgiaville. The town failed to appropriate anything for that purpose, and the Bernon Manufacturing Company carried on the school.

LIBRARIES.

In this town there is but one public library, that of the Bernon Manufacturing Company at Georgiaville. This was founded in 1872 by the said Company. The revenue is derived by rent of Bernon Hall, and the amount received by loan of books, the price per week being five cents, the amount annually received being about $100, which is expended for books, adding about fifty volumes each year. It contained about 500 bound volumes in 1875. Herbert R. Farnum, Librarian.

Of Sunday School Libraries the Baptists have three and the Episcopalians one.

The Allenville Sunday School Library was founded by Hon. Philip Allen in 1830. It is free to scholars attending Sabbath School. The annual receipts are $50, and that amount is expended for books. In 1875 it contained 300 bound volumes; there are added twenty-five volumes each year; the annual circulation is 1,560 volumes; the population represents 200, and the denomination is Baptist; the Librarians are Henry Collins and Allie A. Staples.

The Georgiaville Sunday School Library was founded by Samuel A. Nightingale in 1827; it is free to all attending Sabbath School; the annual receipts are $50, collected by contributions; there are $50 annually expended for books; there are about fifty bound volumes added each year; in 1875 there were about 300 bound volumes in the Library; the annual circulation is 5,200 volumes; the population represents 1,000 inhabitants, and the denomination is Baptist. Henry F. Tyler, Librarian.

The Greenville Sunday School Library was founded by the First Freewill Baptist Society, of Greenville, in 1820, and was free to all attending Sabbath School. It collects about $50 per year, and expends the same for books; it adds seventy-five volumes to its Library every year; there are 500 bound volumes in the Library; it circulates annually 5,200 volumes; the population represents 1,000 inhabitants. Lewis Winsor, Librarian.

St. Thomas Episcopal Sunday School Library was founded by Rev. Dr. Eames in 1850; free to scholars attending; it raises, by voluntary tax, $75 per year, and expends the same for books; there are fifty bound volumes added each year, and it contains 450 bound volumes; it circulates 2500 volumes annually; the population represents 1,000. George Smith, Librarian.

WARWICK.

By John F. Brown,

SUPERINTENDENT.

It appears that the first school-house erected in Warwick was built in what is now known as Old Warwick, about the year 1716, and was used both as a school-house and for town meetings. The date of its demolition is unknown, but it appears that before the close of the century another was built in the same district. Among the earlier teachers were Joseph Carder, Charles Morris, Thomas Lippitt and Ephraim Arnold.

It is evident that the subject of education was agitated to a considerable extent, and with a marked effect, just prior and subsequent to the commencement of the present century, from the fact that several educational societies were incorporated between 1793 and 1808.

In 1798 a school-house was built about a mile east of the present village of Crompton, at an estimated cost of $200.

The school was supported by a tuition tax, and at that time furnished educational facilities for all the families living in that part of the town. The house was used for school purposes until about 1830. Among the early teachers were James Pollard, Bennet Holden, Miss Lucy Glover, Miss Pond and Oliver Johnson.

In 1803 a building was erected in the present village of Centreville, and used for both school and religious purposes. The first school taught in it was commenced September 10, 1803, with Mr. Joseph B. Pettis as teacher, who was followed by Samuel Greene, Sabin Lewis and Oliver Johnson. In May, the same year, the Warwick Educational Society was incorporated with nineteen charter members.

Prior to 1818 we find no mention of schools in Phenix. At that time, and subsequently schools were taught in private houses and rooms rented for the purpose, as opportunity presented. Miss Amy Gorton,

Mr. Elisha W. Baker and a Mr. Austin are mentioned as teachers. The first building erected for school purposes was built by the "Lippitt and Phenix Sabbath School Society," in 1827, at a cost, including the lot, of a little less than $900. Samuel Briggs and Peter D. Healy are mentioned as early teachers. By a vote of the Society, in 1847, the house was sold to the school district for $800.

In River Point, it is probable that the school-house now standing is the only building ever erected for that purpose; while Natick has boasted of two, both of which are now standing, though the older was changed into a dwelling house many years ago.

The building now used was erected in 1850, at a cost of $2,355. Among the early teachers were William B. Spencer, Rev. Arthur A. Ross, Rev. Jonathan Brayton, Alanson Holley, E. M. Tappan and E. M. Hopkins.

The school buildings in the Plains District, the Potowomut District, and in the Arctic District, have been built but a few years. That at Arctic was completed in September, 1875.

The first School Committee, elected after the inauguration of the public school system, was composed of the following gentlemen: John Brown Francis, Thomas Remington, Joseph W. Greene, George A. Brayton, Augustus G. Millard, Elisha Brown, Franklin Greene, Henry Tatem, Daniel Rhodes, Thomas Holden, Jeremiah Greene, Sion A. Rhodes, Rice A. Brown and Waterman Clapp. In 1828 the town was divided into eleven school districts, while Crompton District was set off from Centreville and Coweset in 1830. Since 1830 Pontiac, River Point, Central, Hill's Grove and Arctic Districts have been set off from districts previously existing.

In 1845 the Crompton District built a school-house at a cost of about $3,000, including cost of the lot, which was destroyed by fire in 1867. In February, 1868, another having been built, was dedicated. The present building is of brick, 34 by 36 feet, and arranged for three departments. Its cost was about $6,000. The names of William Baker, Samuel Sandford, Rev. Henry A. Cook, Rev. L. W. Wheeler, Misses Annie B. Holden, Emily Bennett and Myrtilla M. Anthony, Messrs. James B. Spencer and D. R. Adams appear as teachers in the old school-house, while Mr. John M. Nye and Miss Ella J. Hathaway are the present teachers.

The report of the School Committee for 1829-30 informs us that there were 763 scholars in attendance, and that the amount of money expended was $908.50. By a report for 1851-2, it appears there were 1,244 scholars registered, with an average attendance of 812, and an expenditure of $3,463.90. In 1868 there were 1,969 registered, with an average attendance of 1,244, and an expenditure of $5,301.45. Since that time the number registered has decreased somewhat, though the average attendance remains nearly the same, showing a better percentage of attendance. The expense per average scholar has increased from $4.26 in 1851 to $6.75 in 1874.

In 1848 Rev. Zalmon Tobey was elected Superintendent of Public Schools, since which time Rev. George A. Willard, Rev. Benjamin Phelon, Rev. O. P. Fuller, Ira O. Seamans, Esq , Wm. V. Slocum, Esq., and John F. Brown have served in that capacity. A salary of $50 per year was at first paid, which has gradually increased to $200.

For the year ending May 1, 1875, schools were taught in sixteen districts for an average of eight and one-half months, registering 1,644 scholars, with an average attendance of 1,197, at a total expense of $10,856.50.

The writer desires to express his indebtedness to the "History of Warwick," by Rev. O. P. Fuller, for a large portion of the above facts.

WOONSOCKET.

By Erastus Richardson.

THE spirit of civil and religious liberty for which Rhode Island has been so distinguished, is due in no small degree to the influence which the Quakers exerted in shaping the politics as well as the religion of the colony in which they had sought refuge, and where, for many years, they were its lawgivers.

In the year 1656, while the population and the anarchy of our little colony were rapidly increasing, this despised and persecuted sect appeared in New England. After a few trifling incidents, in which the persons of many bore striking evidences to the pious zeal of the Massachusetts saints, they arrived within the limits of Rhode Island.

They were not received with open arms. They were simply tolerated. But in the short space of sixteen years, a majority of the freemen of the colony had become impressed with the simple and beautiful truths which they enunciated.

In the year 1718 the "Providence Monthly Meeting" was set off from the "Greenwhich Monthly Meeting," and the records began at this place. Thus Woonsocket became, first a religious, and afterwards an educational, centre of the large territory now comprised within the counties of Worcester, Mass., and Providence, R. I.

A patient perusal of these records will reward one with much valuable material. The historian will find therein when and where their meeting houses were erected at Providence, Woonsocket, Mendon, Uxbridge, Leicester and other places within the "diocese," and obtain a deeper insight into the manners and customs of a rapidly declining sect; the genealogist will discover many wanting links, and perhaps a few "black sheep" in ancient families; the philosopher will ascertain that the broad-brim was not always a symbol of virtue, and that even a Friend occasionally " got drunk and kicked his wife out of doors;" the patriot will learn that, although the Quakers objected to take an active part in the War of the Revolution, they "turned out of meeting" one of the Rhode Island signers of the Declaration of Independence for *refusing to manumit his slaves;* and all will be vexed that the clerks of the meetings were such abominable penmen.

From these Records, which have been kept at Woonsocket for upwards of one hundred and fifty years, I extract the following in relation to educational matters:

"6th Month, 1771.
"It is thought necessary yt poor children be schooled."

4th Month, 1777.
"Moses Farnum, Moses Brown, Thomas Lapham, Job Scott, Elisha Thornton, Samuel Aldrich, George Arnold, Antepast Earle and David Steere, are appointed to draw up a plan for establishing a FREE school among Friends.

The following 6th Month the committee presented their report to the meeting, recomending,

"1st. That the donation of Rachel Thayer be appropriated towards the support of a school.

"2d. That subscriptions be received at each preparative meeting.

"3d. That a teacher be procured at once.

"4th. That a committee of ten judicious Friends be appointed, any seven of which shall be empowered to act. The duties of this committee to be—1st, to select a place or places for the school from time to time; 2d, to agree with teachers; 3d, to inspect the poorer sort of Friends' families, to determine who shall be schooled from the fund; 4th, to raise and forward subscriptions; 5th, to make rules and regulations; 6th, to receive the income of the Rachel Thayer donation; 7th, to act and transact all other matters and things belonging to the school."

The meeting accepted the report and appointed the following persons as probably the first school committee in Northern Rhode Island: Thomas Steere, Moses Farnum, David Steere, Moses Brown, Ezekiel Comstock, Benjamin Arnold, Rufus Smith, Daniel Cass, George Smith, Samuel Aldrich, Gardner Earle, David Buffum and Thomas Lapham, jr.

The efforts of the Quakers awoke such an interest in educational matters, that measures were taken at the beginning of the present century to establish a school which should be *free to all.* This was partially accomplished, but was finally defeated by those for whom it was designed. By a vote of the ignorant backwoodsmen of Smithfield, many of whom were unable to write their names, the first Free School in these regions was brought to an end. In the years 1800 and 1801 the town of Smithfield appropriated $2,200 for Free Schools. This sum was distributed among 24 schools. At the August Town Meeting of 1802, a similar sum was voted, but at a special Town Meeting in the following month the vote was " repealed."

Is it strange that the same intelligent freemen should have " vandued " the poor of the town to the lowest bidder, and have rejected the Constitution of the United States by a vote of 159 to 2?*

But by the efforts of the women in these parts a *Free School* was finally successfully inaugurated, and the enterprise continued for several years. A public Library was also in existence at Woonsocket during the first thirty years of the present century. About the same time a Library, known as the " Social Library," was in Northern Cumberland, and continued for many years. But the Private Schools in these parts in the last generation, are all that it is worth while to say much about.

A short time previous to the Revolution, a young man of studious habits and amiable disposition became a citizen of these regions. From a natural impulse to benefit his fellow man, and for the purpose of earning a living, he devoted a large portion of his time and of his dwelling house to the cause of education. He had an ample field before him, for the ignorance of the inhabitants of Smithfield at that time was only equalled by their niggardliness. The grammar and the penmanship which recorded their highways, as well as the highways themselves, were an abomination in the sight of the Lord. The poor immigrant was treated as a criminal, and invariably ordered out of the town. Sometimes he would return. It would then be voted that the " transhunt person" either be *whipped* or " suffer *corporal punishment by being fined*," or allowed to " remane," provided he behave " hisself."

I find the following " prescriptions " among the papers of a celebrated " doctor " of those days, whose learning and skill are spoken of by his descendants with much euthusiasm :

"Jonathan should wash and hold his feet some time in warm water; then bleed; then Put on the Plaster on his feet, go to bed with the bed warmed; also with a Blister Plaster on the back side of his Neck, and when the blister is near don running, then take the pills, two of them just before bed, about as big as a " middling Pee," if they work five times once in three nights; and if it doth not work much, every other Night. Also steep Burdock rotes, biter sweet rotes and Lovage. Steep them for a drink. So when gone threw with, then gow a short voiage to See."

*R. I. Col. Rec., Vol. X, Page 275, say 158 to 2; but the Records of Smithfield Town Meetings say as above.

I have been unable to ascertain whether or not Jonathan went to "See."

Next comes a "Surrop" for the Rickets:

"One gill of Easworms, Petemorel Rotes, one handful of Rock leather, Low Polepode Rotes—Solomon's Seal Rotes,—Learge Polepode Rotes—Cunefry Rotes—Hemlock Bark from the rote on the North side of the tree,"—and so on.

But they who are most in need of education, appreciate it least. Elisha Thornton, who was the young teacher to whom I have referred, would have starved had he depended solely upon the patronage of his neighbors. Nay, his very mental attainments caused him to be regarded with suspicion and dread. His telescope and his globe, by which he illustrated the grand harmony of the universe, aroused the superstitious fears of the ignorant boors in the vicinity to such an extent that they expostulated with him for teaching the "Black art."

The Thornton Academy was located near the present village of Slatersville. The fame of this school was as extensive as it was well deserved, and pupils came from distant regions to be mentally and morally enlightened by the great and good man who was its principal. Elisha Thornton was at the head of this school for thirty years, the existence of which was terminated about the beginning of the present century.

Elisha Thornton was born, according to his own account, the 30th of 6th Month (O. S. August), 1747; according to the Quaker Memorial, the 30th of 4th Month, (O. S. June), 1747; and according to the Records of the Town of Smithfield, June 30th, 1748. His father, Ebenezer Thornton, and his mother, Ruth Smith, were joined in marriage by "William Arnold, of Smithfield, Esq.," October 7th and 8th, 1735. Whether the lovers arrived at the house of the Hon. Justice of the Peace on the midnight of October 7th, or whether it took two days to perform the ceremony, I have been unable to ascertain. But I am sure that it was imperatively necessary that the knot should have been effectually tied, for previous to the technical formalities of their union, they had been blessed with two children. Of his parents too little cannot be said. They were careless and improvident in their manner of living, and were spared the disgrace of dying in the poor house through the love of their son.

At ten years of age Elisha had received two months schooling, and was "placed abroad" to live. At twenty-three he joined the Quakers, and three years afterwards became an Elder in the Society. In the meantime (4th Month, 1st, 1773), he had married Anna, the daughter of John Read, and commenced his Academy. The temperament, tastes and early education of this man all seemed to be in opposition to the life of self-denial which he marked out for himself. Nervous, sensitive and timid, with a slender frame of body and a large heart, he had been thrown upon his own resources almost from infancy. The material wants of his nature, and the formation of his character through childhood and youth, had been left entirely to himself. His love of Nature amounted to a passion. His attachment to his friends was only equalled by their attachment to him. The cheerful voices of Spring, and the sad strains of Autumn were his delight; and the vibrations of his fiddle-strings were the delight of his youthful companions. Fully alive to mirth and pleasure, and keenly sensitive to ridicule and contempt, he cut himself aloof from his youthful associates, and devoted the remainder of his life to piety and self-denial. His zeal in educational, as in religious matters, was not confined to these parts. Through his influence with Moses Brown, the Friends' School at Providence was inaugurated. At last, having spent thirty years of his life in doing good, and receiving nothing therefor save a scanty subsistence, and a consciousness of having done his duty, he removed to New Bedford, where he passed the remainder of his days.

About this time, schools were started in various places hereabouts. The inhabitants of "neighborhoods" united themselves, built school houses, and employed teachers from time to time. The L of Deacon Stephen Hendrick's house in Union village, what is now a barn on the Brownell estate, and what is now the wood house of Elisha T. Read, were once temples of knowledge. A school-house was once where now stands the blacksmith shop of Proctor Bros., at the Globe, and another was located at the "Daily Hole." Nor must I omit the good work of Aunt Delphi Warren, on what is now Arnold street. In addition to these the father of Otis Bartlett procured students from Brown University to teach at his house. Although some of the teachers in these institutions were, to use the language of a pupil in one of them, too stupid to get their living by any other means, still they kept the people from lapsing into barbarism.

This brings me to a point where I am permitted to speak of an institution of learning which had its seat among the inhabitants of these regions, and which the citizens of Woonsocket have reason to remember with peculiar pride and satisfaction—in which the facilities for teaching and illustrating the various branches of science were at one time beyond that of any academy in New England—whose cabinet of minerals, and chemical and philosophical apparatus, were equal to those of Brown University, among whose teachers have been men well known in after life to fame and honor, and among whose pupils were many who have become justly ce'ebrated in science, art and literature. I refer to the *Smithfield Academy*.

The movement to erect the building was started about the year 1810. The method for raising funds for the enterprise was by a *lottery*. The first class resulted in failure. The second class, started by George Aldrich and others, was more successful. But the money thus raised was insufficient to complete the work, and the balance was finally adjusted by Joel Aldrich. The building eventually became his private property, but he leased the same at a nominal figure. The building was erected in 1811, and in the Autumn of that year, David, the son of Joel Aldrich, became the first teacher therein. This man is spoken of as a deep student and a successful teacher. He died in 1814. From then until 1830 there was no settled teacher therein. Spindle-shanked pedagogues and soft-haired students, pedants and coxcombs, tried their hands from time to time, sometimes successfully and sometimes not. Among the successful teachers were John Thornton, son of Elisha; George D Prentice, afterwards of the *Louisville Journal*; and Christopher Robinson, since Representative in Congress, and Minister to Peru

In the Autumn of 1830 James Bushee commenced his labors therein, which continued until 1853, when the career of the Academy was brought to an end. A beautiful grove of linden trees, planted by the last teacher within its honored walls, is all that now remains to mark its ancient site.

In the meantime the people had begun to awaken to the fact that a free school is one of the necessities of a free government, and to take measures to place the advantages of education within the reach of all.

The town of Woonsocket was made up of two school districts of Old Smithfield, and six school districts of Old Cumberland. When, about half a century ago, these districts were formed, the inhabitants were but a step above barbarism. Many of the School Committee were rude in manner and in speech, and many of the pupils were vulgar and uncouth to a degree. So much so, indeed, that the capacious spitboxes which polluted the school-houses, were inadequate to contain the floods of tobacco juice, which would run down and stand in pools in the centre of the rooms.

The Smithfield districts were the Globe and the Bernon. The first public school-house in the Globe District was built about the year 1841. Up to 1858 the school was maintained in this building chiefly from the fund distributed by the State. It was therefore limited to a short Summer, and a somewhat longer Winter term. At this time the progressive men in the district succeeded in awakening the public mind to such an extent that an appropriation was made, and a teacher engaged at a salary of $500 per annum. The old house has recently been abandoned. The new and beautiful edifice on Providence street was dedicated April 22, 1875, with appropriate ceremonies.

The Bernon District is not as yet the proprietor of a school-house. But a movement is now being made to that end, and in a few months a beautiful building will crown one of its hills. Although the district has not owned a house, the factory owners, since 1832, have leased a building for school purposes, and schools have been kept therein which have been an honor to the town.

The Cumberland portion of Woonsocket comprises what is now the educational as well as the business centre of the town, and deserves a more extended notice.

In the year 1828 the town of Cumberland was divided into sixteen school districts. District No. 1 comprised what was then called the "Village of Woonsocket," which was the region extending from the "Falls" to the "Social Village." District No. 2 was the Social and Jenckesville villages, and District No. 3 was what is now known as the "Union District."

At the first meeting of the School Committee, the Jenckesville District was set off from District No. 2, and designated as No. 17.

There were no "Trustees" in those days. The School Committee was composed of a man from each district, who performed the duties that were afterwards assigned to Trustees. The money received from the State was apportioned by the School Committee in 1829, as follows: One-half equally among the several districts, and the remainder according to the number of pupils. The following table shows the names of committee, number of pupils and money received for school purposes in 1829 at Woonsocket:

DISTRICTS.	COMMITTEE.	NO. PUPILS.	MONEY RECEIVED.
1	Dexter Ballou.	198	$79 83
2	Smith Arnold.	70	43 74
3	Reuben Darling.	81	46 84
17	Nelson Jenckes.	74	44 86

In August, 1838, a new district was formed from No. 1, and designated No. 19. Committee, pupils, etc., were then as follows:

WOONSOCKET.

DISTRICTS.	COMMITTEE.	NO. PUPILS.	MONEY RECEIVED.
1	Eli Pond.	194	$116 79
19	Ariel Ballou.	145	100 37
2	Melville Knapp.	304	153 64
8	Welcome Cook.	82	79 27
17	Albert Jenckes.	75	76 92

January 13, 1840, a new district was formed from No. 2 (making the second time that No. 2 had been divided), and designated No. 20. The committee, pupils, etc., were as follows:

DISTRICTS.	COMMITTEE.	NO. PUPILS.	MONEY RECEIVED.
1	Abner Rawson.	183	$121 09
20	Ariel Ballou.	160	113 28
2	James M. Cook.	152	110 56
10	Joseph Smith.	184	121 44
3	Olney Burlingame.	67	81 60
17	George Jenckes.	81	86 42

In 1845 the act was passed authorizing the several districts to elect a Clerk, Treasurer and three Trustees.

Friday, November 30, 1849, the voters of districts 1, 19, 2 and 20 met for the purpose of organizing these four districts into one, which has since been known as the *Consolidated District*. The movement to this end was begun in 1846. The school officers in 1849 were: John Boyden, Moderator; Olney Arnold, Clerk; Elijah B. Newell, Treasurer; Christopher Robinson, Bethuel A. Slocomb, Robert Blake, Trustees. The pupils, etc., were as follows:

DISTRICTS.	AVERAGE ATTENDANCE.	MONEY.
1	81¾	$244 48
19	78½	238 04
2	101	282 62
20	98	276 67
17 (Jenckesville)	24	130 09
3 (Union)	35½	152 88

This consolidation was a great victory for the friends of education, for thereby the schools could be graded, and a High School established.

The High School building was in process of erection during the years 1848-9. It was built on land kindly given to the district by the late Hon. Edward Harris, and cost about $8,000.

On July 17, 1849, passed away one of the pioneers of modern Woonsocket, and an earnest worker in the cause of education. I refer to Dexter Ballou. He was an active member of the School Committee for many years, and at the time of his death bequeathed fifteen shares of Providence and Worcester Railroad stock to the "Secondary or Grammar School of Woonsocket."

The district also received a legacy from Mrs. Rachel F. Harris of thirty shares of Providence and Worcester Railroad stock.

The history of educational progress in Woonsocket would be incomplete that should omit an allusion to the labors of Rev. John Boyden in that direction. His name first appears in 1841, and for a quarter of a century it continued to adorn the school records. The veneration and respect with which his memory is held at the present day, is a sufficient evidence of his zeal and philanthropy.

A movement is now on foot to consolidate all of the districts of the town. That it may eventually be consummated is the earnest wish of every true friend of educational progress.

Aside from its public schools, the town enjoys the free use of a magnificent building through the munificence of the late Edward Harris. Here the Woonsocket Lyceum holds its weekly session, a public Reading Room is daily visited, and a large and well selected Library is opened to all A portion of this library was originally the property of a distinct organization, named in honor of its most liberal benefactor—the late Edward Carrington. This afterwards was annexed to a library founded and endowed by Edward Harris, and the whole now bears the name of the "Harris Institute Library."

In conclusion, it remains to be said that Woonsocket has reason to congratulate herself for the mite which she has contributed during the last century for the cause of Education, and to feel that she has fairly earned the applause of the Christian, the philanthropist and the patriot.

INDEX.

Absences from school..84, 98, 200, 255, 257
Academies..30, 353, 373, 392, 442, 444
Addeman, J. M...90
Aldrich, Joel..444
Allen, Benjamin, LL. D..400
Allen, Daniel G..353, 389
Allen, Elizabeth..342
Allen, Gov..427
Allen, Paul..15, 16, 153, 159
Allyn, Rev. Robert...84
Allen, Zachariah..244
Angell, Oliver..170
Anthony, Richard...18
Appropriations, 154, 253, 258, 312, 339, 357, 363, 365, 370, 376, 377, 378, 381, 388, 402, 410, 418, 426
Arnold, General..12
Atwell, A. M...16
Atwell, Amos...234, 238

Baker, Alpheus..394
Baker, George..177, 242
Baker, Wm. S..125
Ballou, Dexter..447
Barker, Peleg, Jr..10
Barnard, Henry.....................................21, 81, 85, 87, 98, 118, 120, 123, 124, 283
Barnes, D. L...13, 16
Barrington..9, 19, 49, 50, 94, 96, 281
Barton, Col. Wm..234
Bible in Schools...81
Bicknell, T. W...88, 90, 91, 92, 300, 422

450 INDEX.

Bingham, Caleb......22
Bishop, Nathan......123, 195
Blind, Education of......73
Board of Education......127
Boss, John L......35
Bowen, Gov. Jabez......8, 13, 16, 135, 154
Boyden, Rev. John......447
Brett, Mary......10
Bridgham, S. W......14, 152, 175, 188
Bristol......4, 9, 19, 49, 50, 81, 94, 96, 120, 285
Brown, Betsey......328
Brown, John Carter......222
Brown, J. F......436
Brown, Moses......8, 15, 136, 153, 443
Brown, Nicholas......220
Brown University......11, 81, 119, 211, 217, 243, 416
Browne, Geo. H......327
Burges, Tristam......22
Burrill, G. R......14
Burrill, James, Jr......14, 16, 152, 310
Burrillville......94, 96, 310, 418
Butler Asylum......242
Byfield, Nathaniel......287
Byfield School-house......307

Cady, Isaac F......281
Callender, John......5, 6, 7
Carlile, John......15, 16
Casey, Geo. Anderson......352
Chadsey, Jeremiah G......400
Champlin, George......14, 33, 34, 152
Champlins, Misses......10
Channing, G. G......36
Chapin, Dr. J. B......87, 88
Charlestown......19, 48, 50, 94, 96, 340, 404
Church, N. K......404
Clarke, J. I......15
Clarke, Rev. Dr......5
Clarke, Thos. H......261
Classification......197
Clergyman......376
Cobbit, Samuel......286
Colburn, D. P......81, 119, 120, 302
Collins, Lieut. Gov......43
Colonial Schools......1
Colored Schools......10, 30, 51, 98, 169, 189
Comparison of Statistics......94, 283
Compulsory Education......90, 99, 373
Cooke, Dr. Nathan B......299

INDEX. 451

Cook, Theodore.... 119
Corliss, John..16
Course of Study..260
Coventry...19, 94, 96, 346
Cozzens, W. C...36
Cranston...19, 48, 50, 94, 96
Cranston, Samuel..6
Crawford, S. W...429
Cumberland..19, 49, 50, 94, 96

David, Rev. Ebenezer...212
Davis, J..21
Deaf Mutes, Instruction of...73
Dennis, Thomas...35
Deux-Ponts, Chevalier de..10
Devotion, John...282
DeWolf, Capt. James..296
Dexter, Col. John S...239
Dexter, Marshal E. K..41
Discipline..322, 324, 391, 397, 406
Districts, 282, 292, 297, 309, 312, 341, 353, 359, 370, 375, 378, 382, 388, 401, 407,
427, 437, 444, 445
Donally, Terrence..7
Doyle, Thomas A...207
Drawing in Schools..91, 92, 93, 199
Dr. Stockbridge's School for Young Ladies...............225

East Greenwich...................................19, 48, 50, 94, 96, 352
East Providence...94, 96, 362
Educational Suffrage..90
Edwards, Rev. Morgan..212, 218
Elam, Samuel...393
Eldridge, Dr. J. H...357, 358
Evening Schools..........29, 88, 127, 201, 304, 338, 344, 350, 363, 381, 411, 433
Exeter...4, 19, 48, 50, 94, 96, 417
Examinations of Teachers...410
Expenditures..201

Farnum, S. W...415, 426
Female Benevolent Society...80
Female Teachers...78, 81, 284
Fenner, Gov..42
Finch, Elizabeth..36
Finch, Joseph...35, 36
First Graduates of Brown University.........................218
Fisher, Nathan...18

Fisk, Rev. John...5
Fitz, Rev. William... 310
Foster...19, 48, 50, 94, 96
Foster, John...11
Fox, Thomas... 6
Franklin Lyceum..247
Freeborn, Gideon...391
Free Schools, 136, 144, 145, 149, 150, 162, 163, 291, 310, 311, 353, 365, 369, 400,
407, 418, 440
Friends' Seminary.. ....49, 417, 443
Fuller, Rev. O. P.. 438
Funds.............................144, 254, 288, 309, 321, 332, 344, 356, 381, 412

Gallaway, Mr... 6
Gammell, William...119
Gano, Dr...16, 154, 155
Gardner, Peregrine..8
Gardner, W. H..367
Gates, General..12
Geography..155, 199, 324
Gibbs, George...33, 34
Gibbs, Job..35
Gilbert, William...6
Girls, Education of..11, 25, 28, 29, 40, 42, 47, 347
Glocester...19, 49, 50, 94, 96, 310, 364, 418
Gould, John...383
Goddard, Prof. William..193, 208
Graded Schools...197, 295, 301, 374, 428, 433
Grammar...155, 324
Greene Academy...432
Greene, Simon H..183
Greene, S. S..81, 119, 120, 195
Greenough, J. C...81, 121, 422
Griffin, Dr. S. O...319
Grinnell, Peter..18
Grinnell, Wm. T..246
Griswold, Rev. S. S...368
Guyot, A..81, 119

Hallett, B. F...43
Halsey, T. L..13
Hamilton, Alexander..238
Hammett, John..416
Hammond, Geo..397
Harris Institute..447
Harris, Rachel..447
Havens, Daniel...399
Hawkins, Lydia..8

Hawkins, William. ...8
Hays and Pollock. ...34
Hazard, Rowland G. ...343, 408
High School. ...176, 191, 260, 299, 446
Hitchcock, Dr. ...16, 17, 22, 23, 141, 160
Holden, Levi. ...247
Hopkinton. ...19, 48, 50, 94, 96, 368, 404
Hoppin, Gov. ...120
Howell, David. ...235
Howland, Benj. B. ...7
Howland, Capt. George. ...46
Howland, John. ...12, 21, 23, 35, 39, 46, 47, 97, 149, 238, 240, 241, 310
Hughes, John L. ...183
Hunter, Misses. ...10
Hutchinson, Mrs. Anne. ...2

Illiteracy in Rhode Island. ...89
Indians, Narragansett. ...4, 54, 73, 416
Institute, Rhode Island. ...79, 118, 123
Institutes, Teachers'. ...381, 418
Indian School. ...340
Ives, T. P. ...13

Jackson, Daniel. ...247
Jackson, Richard. ...14, 15, 16, 152, 153, 154
Jackson, Sally. ...138
Jamestown. ...4, 19, 49, 50, 94, 96, 367
Jencks, Joseph. ...23
Jethro, John. ...6
Jillson, Wm. E. ...299
Johnston. ...19, 48, 50, 94, 96, 375
Johnston, Judge. ...10

Kay School. ...31
Keach, H. A. ...312
Keach, S. B. ...320
Keene, Charles. ...234
Keep, Calvin S. ...324
Kendall, Joshua. ...81, 120, 302
Kent Academy. ...353
Kenyon, P. G. ...352
King, David. ...267, 271
King, Geo. G. ...272
Kingsbury, John. ...85, 123, 225

Lancasterian System. ...254, 256, 294
Lapham, Benedict. ...413

Lapham Institute...................412
Larned, William...................14
Lauzun, Chevalier de...................10
Laws, *see School-laws.*
Lawton, Isaac...................417
Leach, Rev. Daniel...................196, 204
Lectures...................239, 242, 244, 248, 270, 271, 272
Lenthal, Robert...................5, 6, 413
Libraries, 55, 80, 97, 127, 241, 248, 267, 277, 338, 349, 367, 373, 397, 434, 441, 447
Lincoln...................94, 96, 418
Lincoln, J. L...................226
Little Compton...................19, 21, 49, 50, 94, 96
Locke, John...................83
Lockwood, Miss Avis...................177
Lotteries...................32, 42, 269, 432, 444
Luther, Eleanor R...................121, 283
Lyon, Emory...................215
Lyon, Merrick...................215

Magazines...................125, 126
Mann, Ebenezer...................5
Mann, Horace...................59, 79, 98
Manning, Rev. James...................11, 144, 145, 211, 212, 217
Manufacturing Establishments...................90, 98
Massasoit...................281
Maxcy, Rev. Jonathan...................16, 17, 23
Maxwell School Fund...................358
Mechanics' Association, Providence...................13, 149, 150, 151, 177, 234
Meeting Street School-house...................139, 144, 211
Memorials...................240, 243
Metcalf, Joel...................15, 16, 18
Methods of Education...................169
Methods of Teaching...................405
Middletown...................5, 6, 19, 48, 50, 94, 96, 383
Milton, John...................1, 83
Moravian Society...................416
Morley, Frank G...................300
Morse, Dr...................17
Mowry & Goffs' English and Classical School...................228
Mowry, Wm. A...................314
Mount Pleasant Academy...................232, 430
Mr. A. B...................348, 407
Music in Schools...................29, 203
Myles, Rev. John...................9, 282

Newport...................3, 4, 5, 6, 9, 14, 19, 47, 50, 92, 93, 94, 96, 152, 220, 253, 384, 416
New Shoreham...................19, 49, 50, 94, 96
Newtown...................5

Normal School...81, 98, 118, 127, 284, 302, 344
North Kingstown 4, 19, 48, 50, 94, 96, 389
North Providence...19, 48, 50, 94, 96
North Smithfield...94, 96, 418, 426
Noyes, Wm. R. 293
Nutting, John..287

Officers, Rhode Island Institute 124, 126, 127
Officers, School, 145, 148, 176, 183, 187, 195, 204, 258, 259, 261, 291, 298, 309, 311,
353, 401, 419, 437, 445

Paine, Rev. R. H..362
Parker, E. K..346
Pastors' and Teachers' Lands..281
Pawcatuck,...49
Pawtucket..48, 94, 96
Padelford, Gov...121, 183
Pearce, Dutee J 39
Phillips, Rev. Mowry..338, 364
Phillips, W. A..375
Portsmouth..4, 19, 48, 50, 94, 96, 416
Potter, E. R...1, 4, 80, 84, 90, 120
Potter, Simeon..34, 35
Prescott, General..12
Presidents of Redwood Library 276
Private Schools...........11, 25, 57, 93, 258, 320, 352, 364, 368, 369, 373, 417, 441
Promotions...197
Proprietors' Schools 145, 311, 383
Providence, 7, 8, 9, 11, 12, 14, 15, 19, 22, 23, 24, 49, 50, 81, 87, 88, 93, 94, 96, 120,
121, 131, 416, 417, 418
Providence Association of Mechanics and Manufacturers, 13, 149, 150, 151, 177,
234
Providence Franklin Society..239, 246
Providence Institution for Savings...241
Providence Monthly Meeting 439

Quimby, Rev. Hosea...412

Rate-bill System..81, 428
Reconstruction of the Schools..163
Records...384, 440
Redwood Library..267
Reed, Elezer..385
Religion in Schools..81, 376
Remington, Southwick..394
Reynolds, Grindall..13, 18, 151

Richardson, Erastus..439
Richmond......................................19, 48, 50, 94, 96, 404
Richmond, Barzillai..234
Richmond, William.......................................13, 14, 16, 18, 19
Ricker, Geo. H..413
Rousmaniere, Henry..87
Rules and Regulations...138, 140, 153, 154, 156, 158, 161, 168, 184, 254, 401, 423
Russell, Mr...81, 119

Salisbury, Moses..332
Scholfield's Commercial College..................................227
School-books, 11, 17, 22, 24, 27, 93, 98, 157, 161, 169, 177, 288, 289, 294, 335, 346, 368, 391, 403, 405
School-houses, 5, 6, 7, 15, 20, 26, 34, 35, 39, 56, 77, 85, 87, 133, 135, 136, 137, 139, 144, 147, 148, 200, 204, 253, 259, 260, 283, 284, 287, 289, 291, 296, 312, 318, 320, 321, 322, 324, 329, 332, 333, 342, 346, 347, 350, 362, 367, 369, 376, 379, 383, 390, 392, 398, 399, 406, 436, 443
School Lands.................................132, 287, 292, 384, 386, 387
School Law of 1800, 19; of 1828, 43; of 1839, 51; of 1843, 60; of 1845, 64; of 1876, 101
School Reports............................187, 188, 255, 257, 418
School System..371, 378, 380
Schools under a City Charter.....................................175
Scituate...19, 49, 50, 94, 96, 412, 418
Scott, Edward...416
Sewall, Judge..10
Sewing in Schools..93
Sewall, Samuel..417
Shepard, Thos., D. D..303, 309
Shove, Wm. B..247
Society to Propagate the Gospel..................................416
Slater, Samuel..241
Slavery in Rhode Island 4, 10
Small, A. D...261
Smith, Amos D..119
Smith, Capt. Elisha..427
Smith, Elbridge..215
Smithfield...19, 48, 50, 94, 96, 415, 440, 444
Smithfield Academy...444
Smithfield Academy Society.......................................427
Smithfield School Society..426
Society of Friends...147, 148, 440
South Kingstown..4, 19, 49, 50, 94, 96
Spelling..199
Staples, Judge...7, 8, 11, 33
Steere, Chas. L..324
Stiles, Rev. Dr. Ezra..268
Stockwell, T. B..92, 97

INDEX. 457

Stone, E. M...119, 129
Studies...257, 267, 301, 390
Studies now pursued in Schools...92
Suffrage, Educational...90
Supervision, 135, 139, 140, 146, 162, 176, 195, 201, 344, 350, 359, 366, 372, 381, 422

Talbot, Rev. M. J...261
Taylor, A..21
Taylor, George...7, 11, 137
Taylor, Jeremy..83
Teachers...405, 411
Teachers' Wages, 132, 134, 137, 140, 147, 169, 177, 282, 286, 319, 329, 341, 346,
376, 377, 428
Tew, Edward...384
Text-books, *see School-books.*
Thacher, Judge..12
The Association of Aid for the Aged.......................................277
The Peoples' Library..277
Thornton Academy...442
Thornton, Elisha..442
Throope, Amos..289
Thurber, Isaac..243
Thurber, Samuel..11, 18
Tillinghast, Joseph L..43
Tilton, F. W..261
Tiverton...19, 49, 50, 94, 96
Townsend, Christopher...277
Transit Street School...154, 158, 159
Trenton, N. J..19
Truancy..90
Tucker, W. F...340
Turpin, William..8, 9, 132, 416

University, Brown.......................................11, 81, 119, 211, 217, 243, 416
University Grammar School...211
Updike, Daniel...393
Updike, Hon. Wilkins..283
Upham, Wm. D...395
Ushers..160

Vacation Schools...202
Vandeleur, Francis..10
Ventilation...204

Walker, John..24
Warren...19, 49, 50, 94, 96, 211, 218
Warwick......................................3, 4, 19, 48, 50, 94, 96, 346, 436

Warwick Educational Society..436
Washington Academy............ 392
Washington, George................. ....12, 238
Wayland, Francis..163, 169
West, Dr. Benjamin...11
Westerly................................ .....3, 19, 49, 50, 94, 96, 340, 404
West Greenwich..19, 48, 50, 94, 96
Wheeler, Bennett..234
Whipple Hall..136, 144, 147, 153, 158
Whipple, Capt. Joseph..137, 210
Whipple, John, Jr............. 7
Wickford... ....2, 48
Wight, John..289
Williams, Roger.......................................1, 2, 3, 131, 244, 415
Wilkinson, William...... 212
Wilkinson, Jemima..431
Winsor, William..414
Women on School Committees...88
Woonsocket.. ....48, 98, 439

www.ingramcontent.com/pod-product-compliance
Lightning Source LLC
Chambersburg PA
CBHW022116300426
44117CB00007B/738